D0881370

INDUSTRIALIZATION IN TWO SYSTEMS:
ESSAYS IN HONOR OF ALEXANDER GERSCHENKRON
By a Group of His Students

The day is short, and the work is great, and the labourers are sluggish, and the reward is much, and the Master is urgent.

Sayings of the Fathers

ALEXANDER GERSCHENKRON

Walter S. Barker Professor of Economics
Harvard University

INDUSTRIALIZATION IN TWO SYSTEMS:

ESSAYS IN HONOR OF ALEXANDER GERSCHENKRON
By a Group of His Students

HENRY ROSOVSKY

EDITOR

JOHN WILEY & SONS, INC.
NEW YORK · LONDON · SYDNEY

The Editor wishes to express his gratitude to Prof. David S. Landes of Harvard University for suggesting the title of this volume.

Library of Congress Catalog Card Number: 66-13514
Printed in the United States of America

CONTRIBUTORS

Joseph S. Berliner, *Professor of Economics, Brandeis University, Waltham, Massachusetts*

Robert W. Campbell, *Professor of Economics, Indiana University, Bloomington, Indiana*

Paul A. David, *Assistant Professor of Economics, Stanford University, Stanford, California*

Albert Fishlow, *Associate Professor of Economics, University of California, Berkeley, California*

Gregory Grossman, *Professor of Economics, University of California, Berkeley, California*

Franklyn D. Holzman, *Professor of Economics, Tufts University, Medford, Massachusetts*

Herbert S. Levine, *Associate Professor of Economics, University of Pennsylvania, Philadelphia, Pennsylvania*

Goran Ohlin, *Development Center, OECD, Paris*

Henry Rosovsky, *Professor of Economics, Harvard University, Cambridge, Massachusetts*

Peter Temin, *Assistant Professor of Economics, Massachusetts Institute of Technology, Cambridge, Massachusetts*

vii

CONTENTS

PART ONE

INDUSTRIALIZATION IN MARKET ECONOMIES

Historical research consists essentially in application to empirical material of various sets of empirically derived hypothetical generalizations and in testing the closeness of the resulting fit, in the hope that in this way certain uniformities, certain typical situations, and certain typical relationships among individual factors in these situations can be ascertained. None of these lends itself to easy extrapolations. All that can be achieved is an extraction from the vast storehouse of the past of sets of intelligent questions that may be addressed to current materials. The importance of this contribution should not be exaggerated. But it should not be underrated either. For the quality of our understanding of current problems depends largely on the broadness of our frame of reference. Insularity is a limitation on comprehension. But insularity in thinking is not peculiar to any special geographic area. Furthermore, it is not only a spatial but also a temporal problem. All decisions in the field of economic policies are essentially decisions with regard to combinations of a number of relevant factors. And the historian's contribution consists in pointing at potentially relevant factors and at potentially significant combinations among them which could not be easily perceived within a more limited sphere of experience. These are the questions. The answers themselves, however, are a different matter. No past experience, however rich, and no historical research, however thorough, can save the living generation the creative task of finding their own answers and shaping their own future.

Alexander Gerschenkron
Economic Backwardness in Historical Perspective.

THE MECHANIZATION OF REAPING
IN THE ANTE-BELLUM MIDWEST

Paul A. David
Stanford University

I

The widespread adoption of reaping machines by Midwestern farmers during the years immediately preceding the Civil War provides a striking instance of the way that the United States' nineteenth-century industrial development was bound up with *concurrent* transformations occurring in the country's agricultural sector. On the record of historical experience, as Alexander Gerschenkron has cogently observed, "the hope that industry in a very backward country can unfold from its agriculture is hardly realistic."[1] Indeed, even when one considers countries that are not very backward it is unusual for agricultural activities to escape an uncomplimentary evaluation of their efficacy in creating inducements for the growth and continuing proliferation of industrial pursuits. As Albert Hirschman puts it, "agriculture certainly stands convicted on the count of its lack of direct stimulus to the setting up of new activities through linkage effects: the

● I wish to acknowledge my gratitude to Peter Temin for stimulating criticism and helpful suggestions offered when this paper was first being drafted. The present version has benefited from the comments of my colleagues in the Economics Department, the members of the Graduate Seminar in Economic History at Stanford University, 1964–1965, and many participants in the Purdue Conference on Quantitative and Theoretical Research Methods in Economic History (February 4–6, 1965). My debts on this account are so numerous that those who hold them must perforce remain anonymous. Errors or deficiencies that have survived all this counsel are assuredly mine alone.

[1] A. Gerschenkron, *Economic Backwardness in Historical Perspective*, Harvard University Press, Cambridge, Mass., 1962, p. 215.

superiority of manufacturing in this respect is crushing."[2] But having conceded that much regarding the general state of the world, the student of economic development in nineteenth century America is compelled to stress the anomalous character of his subject, to insist that in a resource-abundant setting, highly market-oriented, vigorously expanding, and technologically innovative agriculture did provide crucial support for the process of industrialization.

Such support in the form of sufficiently large demands for manufactures and supplies of raw material suitable for industrial processing would, undoubtedly, have been less readily forthcoming from a small, or economically backward agrarian community. It is precisely in this regard that United States industrialization may be seen as having diverged most markedly from the historical experience of continental European countries, where backward agriculture militated against gradual industrial growth, and the successful pattern of modernization of the economy tended to be characterized by an initial disengagement of manufacturing from the agrarian environment.[3]

However, to treat the generation of demand for manufactures during the process of industrialization as taking place within a framework of static, pre-existing intersectoral relations, summarized by a set of input-output coefficients, does not prove to be an entirely satisfactory way of looking at the connections between the character of agriculture and the growth of industrial activities in the United States. Adherence to such an approach leads one, *inter alia,* to gloss over the problems of accounting for alterations in the structure of intersectoral dependences, although those alterations often constitute a vital aspect of the process of industrialization. It is not wholly surprising that pursuit of a static "linkage" approach has tended to promote the misleading notion that the expansion and modernization of the agrarian sector constituted a temporal pre-condition for rapid industrial development in the United States,[4] whereas in many crucial respects it is far more useful to regard the two processes as having gone hand in hand. As a small contribution to the study of the interrelationship between agricultural development and industrialization in the American setting, this essay ventures to inquire into the way that—with the adoption of mechanized reaping—an important element was added to the set of linkages joining these two sectors of the mid-nineteenth century economy.

[2] A. O. Hirschman, *The Strategy of Economic Development,* Yale University Press, New Haven, 1959, pp. 109–110. On the now familiar concepts of "forward" and "backward" linkages between a sector of the economy (or an industry) and other sectors (or industries) that buy its output and supply it with inputs, respectively, see, *ibid.,* Ch. 6, *passim.*

[3] See Gerschenkron, *op. cit.,* pp. 215, 354, 107–108, 125–126.

[4] See, e.g., W. W. Rostow, *The Stages of Economic Growth,* Cambridge University Press, Cambridge, 1960, pp. 17–18, 25–26.

II

The spread of manufacturing from the eastern seaboard into the transmontane region of the United States during the 1850's derived significant impetus from the rise of a new demand for farm equipment in the states of the Old Northwest Territory. That impetus was at least partially reflected by the important position which activities supplying agricultural investment goods came to occupy in the early structure of Midwestern industry. In the still predominantly agrarian American economy of the time it is not unexpected that a substantial segment of the total income generated by industrial activities was directly attributable to the manufacture of durable producers' goods specifically identified with the farmer's needs—leaving aside the lumber and related building materials flowing into construction of farm dwellings, barns, sheds and fences. If, in addition to value added in the production of agricultural implements and machinery in 1859/60, one were also to include half the value added by the manufacture of wagons and carts, saddles and harnesses, and the variety of items turned out by blacksmiths' shops, the resulting aggregate would represent over 4 per cent of the value added by the nation's entire industrial sector. That is, rather more than the proportion contributed by the manufacture of machine shop and foundry products, which at the date in question ranked as the country's seventh largest industry in terms of current value added.[5] However, on the eve of the Civil War the production of agricultural implements and machinery *alone* generated just as large a proportion of total industrial value added in the preponderantly agrarian Western states; in Illinois, this single branch of manufacturing accounted for fully 8 per cent of the total value added by the state's industries in 1859/60.[6]

To appreciate the importance of the position that the agricultural implements and machinery industry assumed in the structure of Illinois' early manufacturing sector, it must be realized that at the time there was no single branch of industry which in the nation as a whole contributed so large a portion of aggregate value added in manufacturing. Cotton goods production, America's largest industry in 1859/60, accounted for only 6.6 per cent of the national aggregate.

When one looks at a rapidly developing center of industrial activity in the Midwest such as was Chicago during the 1850's, the manufacture of agricultural implements and machinery is found to have had still greater relative importance as a generator of income. The growth of agricultural

[5] See *U.S. Eighth Census* (1860), "Manufactures," pp. 733–742.

[6] See *ibid.*, pp. ccxcii, 725, 729. The "Western" states here are: Ohio, Indiana, Michigan, Illinois, Wisconsin, Minnesota, Iowa, Missouri and Kansas. The share of the agricultural implements industry in aggregate value added by U.S. manufacturing was 1.4 per cent, according to the Census of 1860.

commodity-processing industries, especially meat-packing in Chicago during the latter half of the century suggests that the Garden City's meteoric rise to the status of second manufacturing center in the nation by 1890 might be taken as a demonstration of the strength of *forward* linkages from commercial agriculture. It is not an object of the present essay to assess the validity of that impression. Nevertheless, it should be remarked that during Chicago's first major spurt of industrial development, a movement which saw manufacturing employment in the city rise from less than 2000 in 1850 to approximately 10,600 by 1856, the forward-linked processing industries were less significant to the industrial life of the city than was an activity based on *backward* linkage from agriculture. The branch of manufacturing in question was the farm implements and machinery industry: in 1856 it accounted for 10.8 per cent of total value added by Chicago's industrial sector, compared with 6.3 per cent contributed by the principal processing industries, meat-packing, flour- and grist-milling, and distilling, combined.[7]

Among the salient characteristics of the agricultural scene in the ante-bellum Midwest, two appear as having been crucial to the emergence during the 1850's of a substantial regional manufacturing sector bound by demand-links reaching backward from commercial agriculture. First, the settlement of the region and the extension of its agricultural capacity during that decade proceeded with great rapidity, encouraged by favorable terms of trade and improvements in transportation facilities providing interior farmers with access to distant markets in the deficit foodstuff areas to the east. Between the Seventh and the Eighth Censuses of Agriculture over a quarter of a million farming units came into existence, and about 19 million acres of improved farm land were added in Illinois, Indiana, Michigan, Iowa and Wisconsin. This represented a rate of increase in the number of farms of 7 per cent per annum, and a 9 per cent annual rate of expansion in improved acreage.[8]

Secondly, agricultural practise in this region of recent settlement was not the static crystallization of long experience typical of stable agrarian societies. Far from being a closed issue, choices among alternative produc-

[7] See P. A. David, *Factories At the Prairies' Edge: A Study of Industrialization in Chicago 1848–1893* (Manuscript), Appendix C, Table C-2, for annual estimates of manufacturing employment in Chicago; Appendix A-III and Ch. 3 for industrial value added estimates cited. Estimates of value added in Chicago industries are based on local census statistics for gross value of product (in 1856) and the ratios of value added to gross product in the corresponding industries reported by the U.S. Eighth Census (1860) for Cook County, Illinois. In 1859/60, according to the latter source, meat-packing, milling, and distilling together accounted for 8.7 per cent of manufacturing value added in Cook Co., compared with 7.9 per cent contributed by the agricultural implements and machinery industry.

[8] See *U.S. Eighth Census* (1860), "Agriculture," p. 222.

tion techniques were rapidly being altered and Western farming was thereby being carried in the direction of greater capital-intensity and higher labor productivity. On the eve of the Civil War this burgeoning farm community was in the midst of a hectic process of transition from hand methods to machine methods of production, from the use of rudimentary implements to reliance on increasingly sophisticated machinery. Among the items of farm equipment being introduced on a large scale in the Midwest during the 1850's were steel breakers and plows, seed drills and seed boxes, reapers and mowers, threshers and grain separators.[9] An editorial pronouncement appearing in the *Scientific American* during 1857 suggests the extremes to which the mechanization of farming had proceeded:

> every farmer who has a hundred acres of land should have at least the following: a combined reaper and mower, a horse rake, a seed planter, and mower; a thresher and grain cleaner, a portable grist mill, a corn-sheller, a horse power, three harrows, a roller, two cultivators and three plows.[10]

The importance that the newly introduced reaping and mowing machines (especially the former) had assumed among the products of the agricultural implements and machinery industry of the Midwest by the end of the 1850's provides some indication of the direct impact of the shift to more capital-intensive farming techniques upon the expansion of an agrarian market for industrial products.[11] According to the Census of 1860, reapers and mowers accounted for 42 per cent of the gross value of output of all agricultural implements and machinery in Illinois and for 78 per cent of the gross value of output of the corresponding industrial group in Chicago. A few years earlier, in 1856, when the Midwestern boom was still in full swing, reaper and mower production in Chicago

[9] See Leo Rogin, *The Introduction of Farm Machinery in Its Relation to the Productivity of Labor in the Agriculture of the United States during the Nineteenth Century,* University of California Press, Berkeley, (Publications in Economics, Vol. IX) 1931, esp. pp. 33–34, 47, 72–80, 165–166, 196, 201.

[10] Quoted in C. Danhof, "Agriculture," in H. F. Williamson (ed.), *The Growth of the American Economy,* (Second Edition), Prentice-Hall, Inc., New York, 1951, p. 150.

[11] The term "direct impact" is used here with two considerations in mind. First, this neglects the indirect (input-output) effects of expanded reaper and mower production on the production of intermediate inputs used by the industry, e.g., pig iron, bar iron, malleable castings, cast steel, brass castings, sheet zinc, leather, oils, paint, turpentine, physical input coefficients for each of which are available. (See, David, *op. cit.,* Ch. 3.) Secondly, we here neglect the favorable indirect impact on the growth of agricultural demand in general, arising from the fact that substitution of machinery for labor on the farms raised labor productivity and facilitated faster expansion of agriculture during this, and subsequent periods. The latter point is discussed further below.

had dominated that center's farm equipment output-mix to an even greater degree.[12]

Despite the fact that the history of commercial production of mechanical reaping machines in the United States stretched back without interruption to the early 1830's, this industry was one that only began to flourish in the 1850's. From 1833, the date of the first sale of Obed Hussey's reaping machine, to the closing year of that decade, a total of 45 such machines had been purchased by American farmers. At the end of the 1846 harvest season Cyrus H. McCormick determined to abandon his efforts of the previous six years at manufacturing his reaping machine on the family farm in Rockbridge County, Virginia, and set about transferring the center of his activities to a more promising location, Chicago. The known previous sales of all reaping machines at that time aggregated to a mere 793, but by 1850 some 3,373 reapers in all had been produced and marketed in the United States since 1833. A scant eight years later it was reckoned that roughly 73,200 reapers had been sold since 1845, fully 69,700 of them since 1850. And most of that increase had resulted from the burst of production enjoyed by the industry during the five years following 1853![13]

The major portion of this production had taken place in the interior of the country, and it is apparent that in the absence of farmers' readiness to substitute machinery for labor during the 1850's, an equally rapid pace of agricultural expansion—had such in fact been feasible—would have

[12] See, *U.S. Eighth Census* (1860), "Manufacturers," Table 3, pp. 11, 86. The enumeration of establishment output given in the (Chicago) *Daily Democratic Press,* "Review of 1856," shows that 5860 reapers and mowers contributed 87 per cent of the gross value of all agricultural implements and machinery produced in Chicago in that year. (Separate mowers, in contrast to reapers and combined reaper-mowers, accounted for less than 32 per cent of the value of reaper and mower production in Chicago in 1856.) The balance of Chicago's production for 1856 consisted of a miscellany of 541 threshers, 200 separators and horse powers, 1000 plows, and an unknown number of corn-shellers and cob-crushers.

[13] See Rogin, *op. cit.,* pp. 72–78, for the record of reaper production before 1860. The figures given above are cumulated from yearly sales data, save for the estimate of 73,200 reapers sold between 1845 and 1858. The latter figure can be traced to pro testimony in the litigation over extension of the McCormick Patent of 1845, not the original 1834 Patent. At that time it was asserted to represent the number of machines sold that had made use of principles patented by McCormick; the claim was sweepingly inclusive, as it covered the 23,000 machines sold by McCormick (directly and under license) and all other machines sold since 1845. See William T. Hutchinson, *Cyrus Hall McCormick,* Vol. 1:*Seed-Time, 1809–1856,* The Century Company, New York, 1930, p. 470. Leo Rogin (*op. cit.,* pp. 78–79) erroneously accepts this figure as an estimate of the stock of reaping machines in operation on farms west of the Alleghenies in 1858, evidently following a misinterpretation perpetrated by *Country Gentleman,* Vol. 13 (1859), pp. 259–260, the proximate source cited by Rogin for the number in question.

provided a considerably weaker set of demand stimuli for concurrent industrial development in the region. The latter facet of the late ante-bellum agrarian scene must, therefore, be the prime focus of our interest; it cannot be taken as a given, but must be explained. That should not, however, be regarded as a dismissal of the first-mentioned aspect of Midwestern agricultural development in this period. As shall be seen when we come to grips with the problem of explaining the movement of mechanization, the speed of agricultural expansion and the substitution of machines for farm labor were intimately connected developments between which causal influences flowed in both directions.

III

In view of the consequences for agricultural and industrial development that followed from the mechanization of reaping during the 1850's, it might be supposed that this episode in the modernization of American farming and the formation of backward linkages between the enterprises of field and factory would have been thoroughly explored by economic historians. To be sure, virtually all the standard accounts of the development of agriculture in the United States up to 1860 mention the introduction of the machines that Obed Hussey and Cyrus H. McCormick had invented in the 1830's. Yet, the literature remains surprisingly vague about the specific technical and economic considerations touching the adoption of these devices by American farmers. We have called attention to the fact that although the twenty years prior to 1853 had witnessed a slow, limited diffusion of the new technique, the first major wave of popular acceptance of the reaper was concentrated in the mid-1850's. Thus, the intriguing question to which an answer must be given is: why only at that time were large numbers of farmers suddenly led to abandon an old, labor-intensive method of cutting their grain, and to switch to the use of a machine that had been available since its invention two decades earlier?

In this inquiry, the impact of the mechanization of small grain harvesting upon U.S. agriculture is not the prime subject of concern.[14] Nevertheless, it would hardly be possible to account for the upsurge of demand for reaping machinery without considering the economic implications of the new harvesting technology and the specific circumstances surrounding

[14] See William N. Parker, "Productivity Change in the Small Grains," National Bureau of Economic Research Conference on Research in Income and Wealth, September 4–5, 1963 (mimeographed), for a recent quantitative study which attributes to mechanization the major part of the increase of labor productivity in U.S. small grain production during the nineteenth century. Wheat, oats, and rye are the small grain crops considered in the present paper.

its introduction. The traditional story of the ante-bellum adoption of mechanical reaping, a version to be found in any number of places,[15] is set out along the following lines. During the first half of the nineteenth century arable land was abundant in the United States, but the amount of small grains (especially the amount of wheat) that an individual farmer could raise was limited by the acreage that could be harvested soon after the ripening of the crop. Labor was scarce, and harvest labor notably dear as well as unreliable in supply. Compared with the method of harvesting using the grain cradle—an improvement on the sickle that had come into quite general use even in the transmontane wheat regions by the middle of the century—the new mechanical reapers effected a saving in labor. When Midwestern farmers were led to increase production as a result of the rise in wheat prices during the 1850's (a rise augmented by the impact of the Crimean War upon world grain markets), the demand for reaping machines rose, and their adoption went forward at an accelerated pace. The movement thus initiated received renewed impetus from the extreme shortage of agricultural manpower occasioned by the Civil War. By saving labor, and therein relaxing the constraint on cultivated acreage imposed by hand methods of harvesting, the introduction of the reaper made possible the rapid expansion of small grain production that occurred during the latter half of the nineteenth century.

This account may vary in some details from any particular historian's version of the events in question, but it contains all the generally accepted elements of the story. It specifically follows the historiographic tradition of ascribing to the rise in wheat prices during the 1850's a causal role in bringing about the transition from cradling to mechanical reaping prior to the outbreak of the Civil War.[16] Upon a moment's reflection, the latter is

---

[15] Monographic and textbook treatments of the subject include, e.g., Percy W. Bidwell and John I. Falconer, *History of Agriculture in the Northern United States* (Publication No. 358), Carnegie Institution of Washington, Washington, D.C., 1925, pp. 281–294; Clarence Danhof's essay, "Agriculture," Ch. 8, in Harold F. Williamson, (ed.), *op. cit.,* pp. 144–146; Paul W. Gates, *The Farmer's Age: Agriculture 1815–1860,* (The Economic History of the United States, Vol. III), Holt, Rinehart, Winston, 1960, pp. 258–288; Ross M. Robertson, *History of the American Economy,* Second Edition, Harcourt, Brace, and World, Inc., New York, 1964, pp. 257–258.

[16] Although it is generally accepted that the Civil War provided an important stimulus to the widespread use of agricultural machinery in Northern agriculture, the extensive use made of reapers and mowers in the West during the 1850's is now regarded as a well established point. See Leo Rogin, *op. cit.,* p. 79; and Emerson D. Fite, *Social and Industrial Conditions in the North during the Civil War,* Macmillan Company, New York, 1910, p. 7. Rogin estimates that about 70 per cent of the wheat harvested west of the Alleghenies was cut by mechanical reapers on the eve of the War. There are grounds for questioning the validity of that figure, although they are not such as to lead us to doubt that the reaper had won general acceptance,

seen to be the analytically unexpected aspect of this tale of a change in technology; it is far more usual for discussions of the choice of technique to be couched, implicitly or explicitly, in terms of the relative prices of the substitutable factors of production (grain cradlers and reaping machines in this instance) and to say nothing about the price of the commodity being produced.

Yet, precisely why this departure from the classical (or, properly speaking, neoclassical) treatment of the choice between labor-intensive and capital-intensive factor proportions is called for in the case of the adoption of the mechanical reaper, is not revealed by the statement. That it remains

---

if not universal adoption, in Midwestern agriculture by 1860.

Rogin's estimate is based on his acceptance of a figure, (73,200), giving the number of reaping machines sold in the U.S. between 1845 and 1858 as an estimate of *the stock of reapers in operation on western farms* in 1859. Since the average life of a reaper was roughly 10 years (see Appendix A, section 2b), a calculation of the stock of machines net of replacements (but gross of depreciation, i.e., the gross stock, assuming reapers simply fell apart after 10 years in the manner of the "one horse shay") would require disregarding at least the sales of machines prior to 1848. This would merely lower the stock estimate from 73,200 to approximately 72,300. (See annual sales data given by Rogin, *op. cit.,* pp. 72–78.) However, if one allows for continuous straight-line decay of the machine at the rate of 0.1 per annum, and takes the time pattern of known sales of machines by the McCormick Company during 1848–1858 (from data in William T. Hutchinson, *op. cit.,* p. 369, n. 60.) as a representation of the time distribution of all reaper sales, it is found that the net stock figure for 1858 should be only 56 per cent of the cumulated number of machines sold during 1848–1858, or the equivalent of 43,400 full-capacity machines. This probably understates the true net stock, since the time distribution of McCormick's production was less skewed towards the latter half of the period of 1848–1858 than was the time distribution of aggregate reaper production in the country; 50,000 full-capacity machines might be accepted as not too high a figure for the net reaper stock in 1858.

But, it is necessary to compare both the net and the gross stock estimates with the *national* wheat harvest, rather than with the Western wheat harvest as Rogin does. Taking the average national wheat yield per acre as 11.4 bushels in 1859 (a figure computed by weighting regional yield estimates given in Table 5 of Parker, *op. cit.*), and following Rogin's procedure of comparing the wheat acreage harvested, as estimated from the Census of 1860 ouptut figure and the yield per acre, with that acreage which could be cut by the stock of reapers if each machine were worked at the normal seasonal capacity rate of 100 acres, one obtains the following estimates as alternatives to that given by Rogin. At a maximum, if we accept the gross reaper stock figure, 48 per cent of the 15 million acres of wheat harvested in the U.S. in 1859 was cut by machines; at a minimum, if we accept the net stock figure, 33 per cent was thus harvested. Rogin's figure of 70 per cent seems somewhat exaggerated for the West, since even were the entire stock of reapers (implausibly) thought to have been located west of the Alleghenies, the above revisions of the reaper stock figure would suggest that the proportion of wheat acreage in the West cut by horse power at the end of the 1850's lay somewhere between 70 per cent and 50 per cent.

rather ambiguous about the lines of causation linking dear labor, high grain prices, expanded production acreage, and the spreading use of the reaper must, with all diffidence, be attributed to the ambiguities of the literature from which the statement itself has been constructed. *Vide* Bidwell and Falconer's classic work on northern agriculture prior to the Civil War:

> During the early fifties the reaper was gradually supplanting the cradle in the wheat fields of the country, but as yet the acreage in grain in the Western States was largely limited to the capacity of the cradle. . . . Moreover, in a large part of the West there was little incentive to produce large amounts of wheat on account of the lack of markets and low prices. Rising prices of wheat caused a "boom" in agriculture from 1854 to 1857 and caused almost universal demand for reapers in the wheat-growing regions.[17]

P. W. Gates' recent study of ante-bellum agriculture proceeds in much the same general vein:

> With wheat well above the dollar mark from 1853 to 1858, Illinois, Wisconsin, Iowa, and Minnesota farmers enjoyed real prosperity and were in a position to buy and pay for reapers . . . . Since the amount of wheat a man could sow was limited by the short period in which it had to be harvested and by the man-days of labor required to cut it, it can readily be seen how much the reaper expanded the possibilities of wheat growing.[18]

Comparable passages of other contributions to American economic history could be examined without finding any clear views as to whether it became profitable for farmers to adopt the mechanical reaper only when they found it profitable to increase the acreage of wheat sown per farm, or whether it was the expansion of grain cultivation in Midwestern agriculture as a whole that led to a general substitution of machinery for labor in harvesting operations. The literature is no less ambiguous in the answers it offers to two closely related questions. Did the adoption of mechanical reapers make rapid expansion of grain cultivation in the Midwest possible by raising the scale on which it could be profitably grown (and harvested) by individual farming units? Or, was it simply that the widespread substitution of the reaper for the grain cradle alleviated the scarcity of agricultural labor which otherwise would have restricted wheat production in the newly developing western regions to appreciably lower levels?

There is no question that mechanical reaping effected a saving in harvest labor requirements; the evidence marshalled in Leo Rogin's pathbreaking work, *The Introduction of Farm Machinery in its Relation to the Productivity of Labor,* is nothing if not conclusive on that point.[19] Yet,

---

[17] Bidwell and Falconer, *op. cit.,* p. 293.

[18] Gates, *op. cit.,* p. 287.

[19] See Rogin, *op. cit.,* pp. 125–137, and the discussion of Rogin's conclusions in Appendix A.

to the writer's knowledge, no systematic attempt has been made to compare the magnitude of the savings in wage costs with the capital costs of a reaper to Western farmers during the first decade of the machine's widespread adoption. It is therefore not surprising that the accounts cited fail to divulge whether [or not] the new harvesting technique proved more profitable than grain cradling under all plausible relative factor prices, or whether [or not] it was economically superior to cradling for all scales of farm operations.

These are, indeed, crucial questions. If the answers are in the affirmative, then the rate at which the reaper replaced the cradle in Western grain fields during the 1850's depended solely upon the capacity of the agricultural machinery industry; Bidwell and Falconer's assertion that "Reapers were introduced as fast as they could be manufactured" (*op. cit.*, p. 293), would be more than a mere figure of speech. It would be literally true and would carry the implication that the replacement of hand-harvesting methods would have occurred much earlier in American history were it not for technically unsolvable problems of designing and manufacturing a reaping machine. One would then have to find more convincing technical obstacles than are discussed in the authoritative works on the reaper to account for the lag between the first sale of Hussey's machine in 1833, the filing of the original McCormick patent in 1834, or even the first sale of McCormick's machine in 1840, and the eventual adoption of the innovation in the 1850's.[20] If the mechanical reaping technique actually was superior to hand-harvesting with the cradle, regardless of relative factor prices or scale, this would also pose something of a problem for those writers who, like H. J. Habakkuk, regard the mechanization of agriculture in the United States as an "obvious" illustration of the labor-saving bias of American technology fostered by nineteenth century conditions of relative labor scarcity.[21]

It is quite clear, however, that the traditional accounts of the introduction of the reaper do not entertain such notions. By placing emphasis on the effects of rising grain prices and the extension of wheat production, they imply that altered demand for agricultural products was of fundamental significance in determining the rapid rate at which the innovation supplanted hand methods of harvesting small grains in the Midwest during the 1850's. This line of explanation, taken broadly, would suggest that the sudden growth of the market for the reaper—coming nearly two decades after the machine first began to be sold—was a consequence of the specific conditions surrounding midwestern agricultural development

---

[20] See Hutchinson, *op. cit.*, Chs. 5–10, *passim;* and Rogin, *op. cit.*, pp. 72–75, 85–91. It is not, however, necessary to depend upon a completely supply-determined explanation of this lag.

[21] H. J. Habakkuk, *American and British Technology in the Nineteenth Century*, Cambridge University Press, Cambridge, 1962, pp. 100–102 especially.

towards the close of the late ante-bellum era. Even had the rise of the market for farm machinery not provided significant impetus to the initial industrialization of the region, the implications of this hypothesis for our general view of the process of the diffusion of technology would make it important to try to formulate the economics of the traditional account in a fashion sufficiently precise to permit its re-examination in the light of pertinent evidence.

Suppose, for the moment, that it is justifiable to assert that the saving of labor achieved with the mechanical reaper was not so great as to render cradling an inferior technique in all relevant factor price situations. It may then be argued that mechanization of reaping spread through the agricultural sector as a result of an alteration in factor prices which accompanied the expansion of grain cultivation in the West.[22] In other words, the standard versions can be read as saying that the "agricultural boom" set in motion by rising grain prices in the mid-1850's added to already existing pressures upon the available harvest labor force in the region, drove up the farm wage rate relative to the cost of harvesting machinery, and, thereby, created a situation in which it became profitable for farmers to substitute machinery for labor in harvesting small grain. This argument requires the not unreasonable assumption that the supply schedule of harvest labor facing the farm sector in the Midwest was less elastic than the supply schedule for agricultural machinery; otherwise, the outward shift of the demand schedules would not have resulted in the relative price of harvest labor being raised to a level at which continuing substitution of machines for cradlers would take place. Granting that assumption, the argument may be completed by noting that as the availability of the new method of harvesting rendered the demand schedule for labor more elastic

---

[22] It is sometimes argued that the rate of growth of an industry is an important determinant of the extent to which it adopts new techniques of production (see, e.g., P. Temin, "The Relative Decline of the British Iron and Steel Industry" in this volume, Chapter 5), because with equipment of given durability the rate of growth of the industry will affect the equilibrium age of the capital stock and, therefore, the extent to which the capital stock embodies the newest techniques. This line of reasoning, which would connect the rising demand for wheat and the rapid growth of the Midwestern agricultural sector in the 1850's with the adoption of the reaper on a large scale in that part of the country—even if mechanical reaping was an unambiguously superior technique—does not carry much force in the present context. The reason is simply that the "older" technique (i.e., cradling) of cutting grain was not embodied in any fixed capital on farms; since they had virtually no sunk costs connected with the old method, established farmers would not *on that account* find it more expensive to switch to mechanical reaping than would new entrants to the industry or farmers who were making significant increases in their productive capacity. In explaining the adoption of the reaper in Midwestern agriculture it therefore does not seem important to concentrate on any distinction between new and old farms in the industry.

than would otherwise have been the case, substitution itself tended to check the extent of the actual rise in relative wages caused by the expansion of aggregate grain production. In this manner, the use of the reaper throughout the grain regions held down the total cost of production, although it could not prevent some rise in costs, and made possible a large volume of total output at any given level of grain prices.

For this analysis, in which mechanization appears as a change "imposed" upon grain farmers by the general expansion of Midwestern agriculture, the relative inelasticity of the farm labor supply schedule is crucial. The greater the emphasis that is placed upon the role of related competitive demands for labor, such as regional railroad construction, to cite but one significant source, the less thoroughly tied to exogenous events (e.g., the Crimean War) affecting world grain prices is the explanation offered for the timing of the adoption of mechanical reaping.[23]

In the picture just presented, *the individual farmer's* desire to increase his acreage under wheat does not appear as influencing his decision to purchase a reaper and dispense with the services of cradlers. Nor can the personalization of the collective market process described be justified with any plausibility. Since there is no reason to suppose that the labor supply schedule facing the individual farmer was less elastic than the supply curve for agricultural machinery that confronted him, why should there be any connection between *the individual farmer's* decision to sow more wheat and his choice of the new reaping technique? Yet, the literature is replete with statements suggesting such a connection: "When the wheat from an acre of land would sell for more than the price of the land, it was considered a safe investment to sow more land in wheat and by a reaper";[24] ". . . Americans also had a very strong incentive to develop machines which would enable farmers to cultivate a larger area. The alternative was to leave land uncultivated."[25] If such statements represent something more than illustrations of the ease with which efforts to write economic history as the intended outcome of purposive individual actions, rather than their interplay in impersonal markets, can lead to what may be called "fallacies of decomposition," their authors must have in mind a set of considerations influencing the introduction of mechanical reaping which is quite distinct from the process of market-imposed adjustments already set forth.

To put it most simply, these statements may be taken to imply either

[23] See, David, *op. cit.,* Ch. 5, for discussion of the competing sources of demand in the Midwestern labor market during the 1850's, in which it is argued that the effects of urban construction and internal improvements activity in creating a relative scarcity of unskilled labor in the region should be accorded more importance than they usually receive.

[24] Bidwell and Falconer, *op. cit.,* p. 293.

[25] Habakkuk, *op. cit.,* p. 101.

that there were significant economies of scale associated with the use of the reaper, or that diseconomies of scale existed in the use of labor for cradling grain that were not encountered with the mechanized technique in the range of farm size relevant to the ante-bellum Midwest.[26] Both situations would arise from the presence of indivisibilities among the inputs of the microproduction function for harvesting small grains.

In the apparent absence of feasible cooperative arrangements for sharing the use of harvesting machinery among farms, at this time the reaping machine itself constituted an indivisible input for the farmer.[27]

---

[26] It must be confessed that what Habakkuk has in mind in this connection is less than completely clear, and that some doubt remains whether the rationalization put forward in the text is appropriate. The last sentence of the quotation—i.e., "The alternative was to leave land uncultivated"—does suggest that the American farmer had a passion for cultivating all available land without consideration of profitability and that a machine permitting greater acreage to be cultivated with a given amount of labor would be adopted by the farmer under any product and factor price conditions. The former part of this view is perhaps shared by other writers. Of the American farmer, Hutchinson, *op. cit.*, pp. 50–51, says, ". . . environment compelled him to be acquisitive, and he was prone to add more acres to his freehold than he could well keep under cultivation." Yet, to proceed along these lines is to turn the question of the choice of harvesting techniques into one more properly dealt with by psychologists and sociologists, whereas, as will be seen, a satisfactory explanation can be provided in traditional economic terms.

[27] See Fred A. Shannon, *The Farmer's Last Frontier: Agriculture 1860–1897* (The Economic History of the United States, Vol. V), Farrar and Rinehart, New York, 1945, pp. 329–348, for farm groups' efforts at cooperative manufacture and large-scale purchase of agricultural machinery after the Civil War. Such cooperative ventures did not emerge prior to the War, nor are they equivalent to the cooperative use of farm machinery. There is little evidence of commercial renting of reaping and mowing machines, or commercial grain harvesting by horsepower, such as developed in connection with the use of the large breaking-plows on the prairies during the 1850's. Neighbors may well have shared the use of a reaping machine owned by one farmer, compensating the owner on an informal basis, but, some inquiry into contemporary accounts, farm newspapers, and such sources does not suggest that this was common practise. It certainly does not appear to have been as characteristic a feature of inter-farm relations as was the joint use of corn shellers, threshers, and other equipment used in *post-harvest* tasks. The foregoing impressions are, perhaps, not sufficiently firmly established to demand a hypothesis which would account for the absence of commercial renting of early reapers and the lack of arrangements for sharing the use of jointly (or singly) owned machines. Nor are we able at this point to offer more than a possible line of explanation. The fact that the maximum cutting capacity of the early machines was not very large, especially when the time constraint on harvesting in any given locale is taken into consideration, coupled with the high costs of overland transport for a bulky machine weighing upwards of half a ton, would appear to have militated against operating a profitable itinerant commercial reaping enterprise during the ante-bellum era. The time constraint seems the crucial factor, since it was not present to the same degree either in prairie-breaking operations or in post-harvest tasks such as threshing and

Since he typically had to purchase it, rather than rent it when it was needed, the relevant cost of using a reaper in harvesting was the average annual cost over the life of the machine. Within a particular season, however, the cost of a reaper per acre harvested would fall as the acreage was increased. It would continue falling to the point at which the cutting capacity of a single machine during the feasible harvest was reached. By contrast, given a perfectly elastic supply of labor and no diseconomies of scale in its use, the saving in wage costs obtained by substituting the mechanical reaper for cradlers would remain constant per acre harvested. It is possible, therefore, that below some level of acreage to be harvested —which we shall call the "threshold" farm size—the total capital cost of a reaper (or of more than one reaper) exceeded the potential reduction in wage costs, making its adoption unprofitable in comparison with the method of cradling.

Exactly where the threshold point was located in the spectrum of farm acreage devoted to the small grains was determined by relative factor prices. The saving of labor achieved with the reaper being essentially technologically fixed per acre harvested, a doubling of the total yearly reaper cost relative to the money wage cost of harvesting an acre with the cradle would double the number of acres that would have to be harvested before the costs per acre would be the same with either technique.[28] While it is conceivable that so great a saving of labor was effected by the reaper that the costs per acre harvested by machine were lower for any finite total acreage, so long as both the money wage rate and the cost of a reaper were positive and finite, the existence of *significant* economies of scale associated with mechanical harvesting cannot be taken to have been a purely technical matter; relative wage rates must not have been so high that it was profitable for the farmer to adopt the new method at any level of grain production.

In principle, the existence of diseconomies of scale in the use of labor for harvesting grain with cradles would operate in the same manner as

---

corn shelling; the former became established on a commercial basis, while sharing of equipment among neighbors was not unusual in the latter cases. Furthermore, as a consequence of the time constraint, the problems of deciding who was to have priority of use of a jointly owned reaper would have required the owners (users) to form some compensation arrangement, equivalent to an output pool or a profit pool. The economic, not to mention the political and sociological consequences of a reorganization of independent small farms into such pooling arrangements would have profoundly altered the course of agrarian history in the United States.

[28] The relationship between the relative price of labor, vis-à-vis the reaper, and the threshold size is developed formally in Appendix A. Even without that derivation it is readily seen that if the labor cost per acre harvested by cradle is constant, threshold size must vary in direct proportion to the *relative* cost of capital.

economies of scale associated with the mechanical reaper. Harvest workers required a certain amount of supervision to maintain their efficiency, and the addition of hands required to cut the grain on a larger acreage presumably taxed the farmer's supervisory capacities. The harvest had to be carried out in a limited number of days lest the ripe grain be lost through shattering or spoilage. It was therefore not feasible simply to employ the optimum number of hired hands that could be supervised at any one time for as long a period as it would take to cut the grain. Assuming that the average productivity of cradlers would begin to decline when the amount of supervision they received fell below some minimum, we may say that the manpower requirements per acre would have been greater for larger acreages. Consequently, savings in labor obtained by switching to mechanical reaping would tend to rise as the acreage to be harvested increased. Even if the capital costs of a reaper were constant per acre, this could define a threshold size beyond which farmers would find it advantageous to mechanize.

Although there is evidence of considerable contemporary dissatisfaction about the quality of hired help on farms during the first half of the nineteenth century, and notwithstanding the comments of American farmers on the need to supervise temporary help in order to keep them on the job and careful in their work,[29] it is difficult to gauge the extent to which the inferior quality of hired help failed to reflect itself in the general level of farm wages. Moreover, among the complaints registered by farmers are those specifically citing the carelessness of hired hands with machinery. If there were diseconomies of scale in the use of harvest labor, we do not know that these were restricted to the employment of cradlers rather than labor in general, and that they did not simply place a limit on the scale of farm operations in the free states.[30] It therefore seems justifiable to restrict the discussion of scale effects to consideration of those which arose from spreading the fixed cost of harvesting machinery over large grain acreage.

Figure 1 depicts the hypothesized situation in terms of alternative long-run unit cost curves for hand methods and machine methods of grain harvesting on independent farms. The supposed existence of some fixed

[29] See, e.g., Gates, *op. cit.,* pp. 272, 275 and also the passage cited from Edmund Ruffin's essay on "Management of Wheat Harvest," *American Farmer,* n.s., 6 (June 1851) in Rogin, *op. cit.,* p. 131. One of the state sales agents employed by the McCormicks in the 1850's took it as the object of his work to "place the farmer beyond the power of a set of drinking Harvest Hands with which we have been greatly annoyed," Hutchinson, *op. cit.,* pp. 355–356.

[30] Monographic studies of the effects of mechanization in agriculture, such as Rogin's, make no mention of increases in labor productivity associated with the reaper having been influenced by the size of the farm on which the machines were used.

costs with either process causes both the hand-method cost curve, $C_H C_H$, and the machine-method curve, $C_M C_M$, to decline over a range of total harvested acreage, but, because of the *additional* fixed cost entailed by the reaper, the curve $C_M C_M$ goes on falling after the hand method unit costs begin rising. The rise in unit costs results from the limitation on the total supervisory capacity of the farmer, a restraint which eventually also causes the $C_M C_M$ curve to turn upward at a larger scale of operations. In the situation shown, the representative farm operating with the hand method of harvesting is taken to be in equilibrium at size S_0, with the market price of grain (per acre harvested, assuming constant yield per acre) equal to minimum units costs at P_0. Beyond S_0 lies S_T—the threshold size at which unit costs with the hand method are equal to those with the machine method—whose location is determined by the factors influencing the relative positions of the two curves.

The argument that the individual farmer's decision to adopt mechanical reaping was tied up with a simultaneous decision to expand his grain acreage, the latter being prompted by a rise in the relative price of grain, may now be quickly restated in terms of Figure 1. If there were no initial costs involved in increasing grain acreage under cultivation, with the market price at P_0 it would clearly pay to abandon the hand method of harvesting and expand the representative farm from S_0 to S_M. However, the costs of acquiring, clearing, and fencing new land, or simply of preparing land already held, were hardly insignificant even on the open prairies. If these costs, relative to the market price of grain, were sufficiently large to prevent expansion beyond S_T, they would have effectively blocked the concomitant adoption of the mechanical reaper.[31] The significance of the rise in grain prices during the 1850's in bringing about widespread introduction of the reaper accordingly was, that by lowering the relative unit costs of expansion, higher prices induced the typical farmer to increase his grain acreage beyond the previous threshold size. In so doing, the farmer would take advantage of the $C_M C_M$ cost curve.

The presence of scale considerations in the choice between hand method and machine method of harvesting grain was not explicitly recognized in setting forth our earlier argument, in which the change in tech-

[31] On clearing and fencing costs, see Allan G. Bogue, "Farming in the Prairie Peninsula, 1830–1880," *Journal of Economic History,* March 1963; Clarence Danhof, "Farm-Making Costs and the Safety-Valve': 1850–1860," *Journal of Political Economy,* June 1941; Gates, *op. cit.,* pp. 34, 186–188; M. Primack, "Land Clearing under Nineteenth Century Techniques: Some Preliminary Calculations," *Journal of Economic History,* Vol. XXI (1962), 484–497. In terms of Figure 1 we can say that, spread over the total acreage to be harvested, the unit costs of expanding farm acreage beyond S_T was at least equal to the difference between P_0 and the $C_M C_M$ cost curve at S_M.

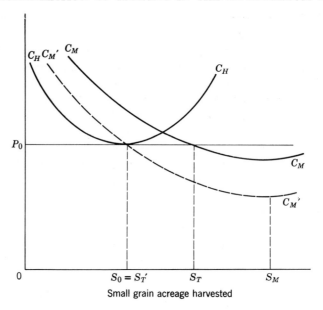

FIGURE 1 Hypothetical long-run average cost curves for harvesting.

nique was depicted as an adjustment imposed by the relative inelasticity of the aggregate supply schedule for farm labor. That hypothesis may, nonetheless, be quite readily stated within the framework of the micro-analysis summarized by Figure 1. The contention is simply that because the threshold point will move inversely with changes in the price of labor relative to the cost of the reaper, the relative rise in farm wage rates (resulting from the collective response to higher grain prices in the mid-1850's) drove the threshold size downward to the point at which adoption of the reaper became profitable even on farms that had not enlarged their cultivated acreage. This is shown in Figure 1 as a downward shift in the position of the long-run machine-method cost curve relative to $C_H C_H$, lowering the threshold size (S_T) to the optimum acreage (S_0) established under the regime of the older harvesting technique.[32]

IV

On formal grounds our two versions of the switch to mechanical reaping thus turn out to be entirely compatible; they merely stress what

---

[32] Note that the downward shift in $C_M C_M$ is equivalent to a rise in the market price of grain being accompanied by an upward shift in the $C_H C_H$ cost curve which is not matched by a rise in unit costs with the machine technique.

may have been different aspects of a single story—one directing attention to forces working to push farms across the old threshold point, and the other emphasizing that an alteration in relative factor prices may have brought the threshold down to the vicinity of previously established farm size.

The empirical requirements of these two hypotheses are equally apparent. To credit either version we must at least have some evidence that at the beginning of the 1850's the threshold size for adoption of the reaper lay above the average small grain acreage on Midwestern farms, not only in the region as a whole, but in those areas especially devoted to these crops. Once that is established, further evidence of a substantial decline in the threshold size *as the result of an alteration in relative factor prices* during the decade would lend credence to the view that the adjustment in technique was imposed by the inelasticity of the labor supply, whereas acceptance of the pure individual farm-size adjustment view would hinge on a finding that over the course of the 1850's average grain acreage on Midwestern farms rose to the neighborhood of the threshold size that had existed at the opening of the period.

Appendix A provides a detailed discussion of the evidence assembled and the way it has been used in calculating the threshold acreages for adoption of mechanical reapers by grain farmers in the Western states during the period under study. The computations are readily made by linearizing the cost functions for the hand and machine methods of harvesting. It is sufficient here to consider the results of those calculations in conjunction with such information as is available regarding actual small grain acreage on the average Midwestern farm.[33] This may be done with the aid of Figure 2, which depicts the relationship between threshold size and relative costs of labor and capital for the basic hand-rake reaping machine on the assumption of linear cost functions.

Figure 2 also shows the threshold function for the self-raking type of reaper which, by mechanically delivering the cut grain to the ground beside the machine either in gavels or in swath, dispensed with the need for a man to sweep the grain from the platform of the hand-rake machine. However, since self-rakers did not win popularity in the Midwest until the latter half of the 1850's, well after the initial acceptance of the

---

[33] It should be noted that although the traditional accounts consider the introduction of the reaper only in connection with the harvesting of wheat, the Midwest's principal cereal and leading commercial crop at the time, the discussion here has been phrased in terms of the small grains—wheat, oats, and rye, all of which were harvested with the cradle and could be cut with the early reaping machines. (See Bidwell and Falconer, *op. cit.,* p. 353 and Hutchinson, *op. cit.,* p. 310.) This means that calculated threshold sizes for adoption of the reaper must be compared to estimates of average small grain acreage, rather than average wheat acreage alone. See Appendix A, Section 3.

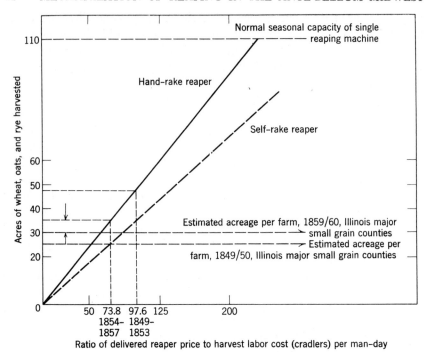

FIGURE 2   Threshold functions for adoption of the reaper. *Source.* See Appendix A, Tables A1, A2.

basic hand-raking machines manufactured by the McCormick Co., the discussion will focus on the pioneering hand-rake model.[34] Our conclusions, therefore, relate to the influence of alterations in market forces on the adoption of the basic reaper during the 1850's, rather than to the role played by the continuing technical refinement and elaboration of the device.

At the daily wage rate paid grain cradlers during the harvest and the average delivered price of a McCormick hand-rake reaper that prevailed in Illinois at the end of the 1840's and early in the 1850's, specifically in the period 1849–1853, the purchase of a reaper was equivalent to the hire of 97.6 man-days labor with the cradle. From Figure 2 it is seen that these factor prices established a threshold level at 46.5 acres of grain. Where it was possible to hire cradlers on a monthly basis, instead of by the day, and therefore to pay the lower per diem wages implied

---

[34] The McCormicks did not manufacture a self-rake model until the introduction of the "Advance" in the post Civil War period. See Appendix A for further discussion of the self-rakes and of the combined reaper-mowers which came into use in the Western states before the war.

in typical monthly agreements, the abandonment of cradling in favor of mechanical reaping would have reduced harvesting costs only on farms with more than 74 acres of grain to be cut. Hiring all the labor required for the harvest on a monthly basis was, however, generally not worthwhile for the farmer, so the lower threshold level is more relevant to the problem at hand.

Although there are no direct statistics for the average acreage sown with wheat, oats, and rye on Midwestern farms at the beginning of the 1850's, from the available data pertaining to average yields per acre and to the number of bushels of grain harvested per farm it is clear that a 46.5 acre threshold still lay well above typical actual acreage, even in the regions principally devoted to small grain cultivation at the mid-century mark.[35] It is estimated that at the time of the Seventh Census (1850) the farms in Illinois averaged from 15 to 16 acres of wheat, oats, and rye. In the 16 leading grain counties (of 99 counties in Illinois) which as a group produced half of the state's principal cereal crop at that time, the average farm land under wheat, oats and rye ran to approximately 25 acres. Among these major small grain counties, Winnebago County in the northernmost part of the state is representative of those with the highest average small grain acreage per farm, while Cook County was one of those having the lowest average acreage. Yet, on the 919 farms in Winnebago County the average worked out to 37.2 acres of small grain, still 10 acres under the threshold level, and in Cook County the 1,857 farms averaged but 18.6 acres apiece.

Two closely related points thus emerge quite clearly. First, in the years immediately surrounding the initiation of reaper production in the Midwest (1847) and the establishment of the McCormick Factory at Chicago (1848), the combination of existing average farm size and prevailing factor prices militated against widespread adoption of the innovation. The admonitions appearing in Western agricultural journals during 1846 and 1847 against purchase of the new reaping machine by the farmer "who has not at least fifty acres of grain," would appear in the light of the considerations presented here to have been quite sound advice.[36] Secondly, observations of the sort made by a reliable contemporary witness, Lord

---

[35] See Appendix A, Section 3, for discussion of this data and the acreage estimates in Table A2 on which the present statements are based.

[36] See quotations from the *Ohio Cultivator,* October 1, 1846, 147, April 15, 1847:64; and *Chicago Daily Journal,* July 2, 24, 28, 30 and August 15, 1846, abridged in Hutchinson, *op. cit.,* p. 234, n. 15. Note that, as one might expect in view of the upward trend of relative farm wages from the trough of the depression of the 1840's, the 46.5 acre threshold estimated here to be appropriate for the period 1849–1853 lies very close to, but slightly *below* the 50-acre threshold level implied by the advice to farmers in the years 1846–1847.

Robert Russell, who travelled in the prairie country in 1853, that "the cereals are nearly all cut by horsepower on the *larger farms* in the prairies,"[37] become understandable simply on the grounds of the scale considerations affecting the comparative profitability of the reaper. It is not necessary to explain them by contending that the larger farms were run by men more receptive to the new methods of scientific farming or less restrained by the limitations of their financial resources and the imperfections of the capital market, however correct such assertions might prove to be.

An initial empirical foundation for the plausibility of both our hypotheses having thus been established, we turn now to consider the evidence relating to the character of the adjustments themselves. During the mid-1850's, as the aggregate labor supply constraint hypothesis suggests, the price paid for harvest labor in Illinois did rise more rapidly than the average delivered price of a hand-rake reaper; in the period 1854–1857 a McCormick reaper cost the farmer, on average, the equivalent of only 73.8 man-days of hired cradlers' labor, compared with 97.6 man-days in the preceding period 1849–1853. In consequence, as Figure 2 shows, the threshold point dropped from over 46 to roughly 35 acres. By the middle of the decade, then, the average small grain acreage above which it paid the farmer to abandon cradling had fallen below the average acreage that had existed in a leading grain-producing area like Winnebago County, Illinois, at the beginning of the decade, and lay only 10 acres above the average on the 21,634 farms in the state's leading grain counties in 1849/50.

At the same time, there is some evidence pointing to a rise in the average grain acreage harvested per farm, such as is proposed by the individual farm-size adjustment version. Just how large an increase in average acreage occurred during the 1850's in the specialized small grain regions of the Midwest is difficult at present to say, for the simple reason that the Census of Agriculture in 1860, unlike the previous Census, neglected to publish the statistics of the number of farms on a county-by-county basis. In Illinois as a whole, however, the number of acres of wheat, oats and rye harvested per farm is estimated to have been roughly 19 per cent higher in 1859/60 than it had been ten years earlier. Of course, it is possible that in the transition from cereal to corn and livestock production that was under way in the state during this decade, specialization in small grain

---

[37] *North America, Its Agriculture and Climate,* London, 1857, p. 114, quoted in Rogin, *op. cit.,* p. 79. Italics added. Rogin says he regards this statement as "more in accord with the facts" than are claims that in the early 1850's cereals as a rule were cut by machinery but, he offers no further evidence or reasoning to support this judgment.

cultivation became more concentrated and, therefore, that the increase in the typical farm acreage sown with those crops in the leading regions of their cultivation was considerably greater than 19 per cent. But, such evidence as can be brought to bear on the matter does not point in that direction. Broadly speaking, small grain cultivation was spatially no more concentrated in Illinois at the end of the 1850's than at the beginning, and wheat production became, if anything, geographically more dispersed.[38] It is therefore not wholly unreasonable to assume that small grain acreage per farm in the areas especially devoted to those crops increased at the same rate as it did in Illinois as a whole. On that basis one may conjecture that the number of acres under wheat, oats and rye on a typical farm in the state's leading small grain regions increased from 25 to 30 in the course of the 1850's.

The story of the adoption of the mechanical reaper in the years immediately before the Civil War should thus be told in terms of the effects of both an expansion of grain acreage sown on individual farms and the downward movement of the threshold size as a result of the rising relative cost of harvest labor. But, of the two types of adjustment taking place during the 1850's, the former must properly be accorded lesser emphasis. As Figure 2 reveals, on farms in the leading grain regions of Illinois the estimated increase in average small grain acreage was responsible for less than a third of the subsequent reduction of the gap existing between threshold size and average acreage at the opening of the decade. Moreover, among the Midwestern states experiencing rapid settlement during the 1850's Illinois was singular in the magnitude of the expansion of its average farm size.[39] Elsewhere in the Midwest, the relative rise in farm wage rates is likely to have played a still greater role in bringing the basic reaping machine into general use during the decade preceding the Civil War.

[38] Whereas only 16 counties made up the group producing half the total wheat crop, and 19 counties accounted for half the total number of bushels of wheat, oats, and rye harvested in Illinois in 1860, it took 21 counties to account for 50 per cent of the wheat and 19 counties to account for 50 per cent of the three small grain crops harvested at the end of the decade. See J. D. B. DeBow, *A Statistical view . . . Compendium of the Seventh Census of the United States,* 1854, pp. 21–27; *U.S. Eighth Census* (1860), "Agriculture," pp. 31–35.

[39] Between 1850 and 1860 improved total acreage per farm increased from 66.2 to 91.3 in Illinois, from 53.4 to 62.4 in Indiana, from 55.6 to 62.1 in Iowa, and from 51.8 to 54.0 in Wisconsin. Illinois average farm size was thus not only growing more rapidly than that in the surrounding states, but was initially larger. (See *U.S. Eighth Census* (1860), "Agriculture," p. 222.) On these grounds alone, Cyrus McCormick's decision to move his base of operations from Rockbridge County, Virginia, in 1847 and embark upon manufacturing the reaper at Chicago during the following year proved extremely cogent.

V

Although the questions considered in the preceding pages are very specific, we have arrived at answers with rather broader implications. Historians of United States agriculture have maintained that during the nineteenth century the transfer of grain farming to new regions lying beyond the Appalachian barrier played a significant part in raising labor productivity in agriculture for the country as a whole. The connection between the spatial redistribution of grain production and the progress of farm mechanization figures prominently among the reasons that have been advanced to support this contention. Some writers suggest that inasmuch as heavier reliance was placed on the use of farm machinery in the states of the Old Northwest before the Civil War, and, similarly, in the Great Plains and Pacific Coast states during the last quarter of the century, the geographical transfer of agriculture into these areas was tantamount to a progressive shift of grain farming towards the relatively capital-intensive region of the technological spectrum.[40] But, the mechanism of this putative interaction between spatial and technological change has not been fully clarified, and as a result, important aspects of the interrelationship between the historical course of industrialization and the settlement of new regions in the United States remain only imperfectly perceived.

To make some headway in this direction it is necessary to distinguish two possible modes of interaction between spatial and technological changes in United States agriculture: one involves adjustments of production methods in response to alterations of relative prices that were associated, either causally or consequentially, with the geographical relocation of farming; the other turns on purely technological considerations through which regional location influenced choices among available alternative techniques. Now, the general statement that the conditions under which farmers located in the country's interior carried on grain production especially favored the spread of mechanization is sufficiently imprecise to embrace both interaction mechanisms, the influences of market conditions as well as those of technological factors peculiar to farming in the different

---

[40] As an indication of the extent of the geographical redistribution of grain farming prior to the Civil War, it may be noted that Pennsylvania, Ohio, and New York were the leading wheat growing states in 1849/50, but, a decade later roughly half the total U.S. wheat crop was raised in Ohio, Indiana, Michigan, Illinois, and Wisconsin—i.e., in the Old Northwest Territory. See Everett E. Edwards, "American Agriculture—The First 300 Years," *Yearbook of Agriculture 1940*, G. P. O., Washington, 1940, p. 203. Among recent explicit treatments of this question, Parker's (*op. cit.*) offers a set of calculations designed to gauge the impact of regional shifts in the pattern of production on the productivity of labor in small grain farming, and attributes much of the "region effect" (on national productivity) to the interaction between location and the degree of mechanization.

regions. One may well ask whether such ambiguity is justified. Without establishing the dominance of purely technical considerations it would be unwarranted to suggest that shifts of small grain farming away from the Eastern seaboard automatically, in and of themselves, accounted for increases in the extent to which that branch of United States agriculture became mechanized.

In the case of reaping operations, it is certainly true that there were technical features of Midwestern farming which in contrast with those characteristic of the Eastern grain regions proved inherently more congenial to the general introduction of ante-bellum reaping machines. On the comparatively level, stone-free terrain of the Midwest, the cumbersome early models of the reaper were less difficult for a team to pull, less subject to malalignment and actual breakage; because the fields were unridged and crops typically were not so heavy as those on Eastern farms, the reapers cut the grain close to the ground more satisfactorily, and the knives of the simple cutting mechanism were not so given to repeated clogging.

Yet, despite the relatively favorable technical environment (and larger average small grain acreages on farms) in the Midwest, we have seen that the prevailing factor and product market conditions during the 1840's and early 1850's militated against extensive adoption of mechanical reaping equipment even in that region. Against such a background the fact that a large-scale transfer of small grain production to the Old Northwest Territory took place during the 1850's does not appear so crucial a consideration in explaining the sudden rise in the proportion of the total American wheat crop cut by horse power between 1850 and 1860.[41] Instead, it seems appropriate to emphasize that during the Midwestern development boom that marked the decade of the 1850's the price of labor—as well as the prices of small grains—rose relative to the price of reaping machines, and that the pressure on the region's labor supply reflected not only the expanded demand for farm workers, but also the demand for labor to build railroads and urban centers throughout the region—undertakings ultimately predicated on the current wave of new farm settlement and the expected growth of the Midwest's agricultural capacity. If one is to argue the case for the existence of an important causal relationship between the relocation of grain production and the widespread acceptance of mechanical reaping during the 1850's, the altered market environment, especially the new labor market conditions created directly and indirectly by the quickening growth of Midwestern agriculture, must be accorded

[41] This proportion rose from a negligible level at the beginning of the decade to somewhere between 33 and 50 per cent by the close of the 1850's. At the latter date the proportion of the trans-Appalachian wheat crop cut by horse-power was appreciably higher than that for the nation as a whole. See footnote 2 of this chapter for the sources and some discussion of these estimates.

greater recognition, and the purely technical considerations be given rather less weight than they usually receive in this connection.

There is, however, a sense in which the decline in the cost of reaping machines relative to the farm labor wage rate may be held to have reflected the interaction of the technical factors favoring adoption of the early reapers in the Midwest with that region's emergence as the nation's granary during the 1850's. The rising share of the United States wheat crop being grown in the interior did mean that, *ceteris paribus,* a larger proportion of the national crop could be harvested by horse power without requiring the building of machines designed to function as well under the terrain and crop conditions of the older grain regions as the early reapers did on the prairies. For the country as a whole, as well as for the Midwest, this afforded economies of scale in the production a simpler, more standardized line of reaping machines. It thereby contributed to maintaining a situation in which the long run aggregate supply schedule for harvesting machinery was more elastic than the farm labor supply. Thus it may be said, somewhat paradoxically, that the movement towards regional specialization in small grain farming directly made possible greater efficiency in manufacturing and thereby promoted the simultaneous advance of mechanized agriculture and industrial development in the ante-bellum Midwest.

APPENDIX A: Threshold Farm Size

The element of fixed cost present with the mechanical reaping process for harvesting grain makes it necessary to take account of the scale of harvesting operations in cost comparisons of hand and machine methods. One means of doing this would be to stipulate the acreage to be harvested and then proceed to ask how the profitability of mechanical reaping compared to cradling was affected by the prevailing level of factor prices. This appendix tackles essentially the same question by posing it in a slightly different way. The question can be put as follows: given alternative sets of factor prices, at what alternative scales of harvesting operations would it be a matter of indifference (on cost grounds) to the farmer of the 1850's whether he adopted the reaper or continued to rely on the cradle? The answer is to be found from a computation of that acreage, called the threshold size, at which the total costs of the two processes were just equal and beyond which abandoning the cradle would become profitable, other things remaining unchanged.

1. THE FORM OF THE CALCULATION

It is not, however, necessary to calculate the total cost of harvesting an acre of grain at different scales of operation, as depicted by the long-run unit cost curves of Figure 1. In the first place, as will be seen, the activities of the harvest other than the actual cutting of grain—raking, binding, and shocking—may be omitted from consideration as not significantly influencing the choice between machine and hand reaping. Secondly, all that is required is the computation of the total *saving* of money wages effected by adoption of the mechanical reaper and the *additional* fixed capital charge that the farmer would incur in order to have the machine at his disposal during the harvest season. What must be known, therefore, is:

L_s : the number of man-days of labor dispensed with by mechanizing the cutting operation, per acre harvested;
w : the money cost to the farmer of a man-day of harvest labor;
c : the fixed annual money cost of a reaper to the farmer.

From this information the threshold size, S_T, in acres to be harvested, can be determined, since, *ceteris paribus,* total costs of cutting the grain are the same for both processes when

$$(1) \qquad c = \sum_{i=1}^{S_T} L_{si} w,$$

where the index i designates the acre in the sequence of acres ($i = 1, \ldots, S_T$) harvested.

Actually, the problem can be further simplified. From the available information it appears justifiable to assume that within the range of normal daily cutting capacity of the reaper there were no economies or diseconomies of scale in the use of labor in cradling, and that the saving of labor effected by the mechanical reaper per acre harvested was a technically determined constant. In a word, the cost functions for the two processes may be taken as linear over the relevant range of operations. Consequently, we may replace equation 1 with the much simpler expression,

$$(1a) \qquad c = S_T L_s w.$$

The average annual capital cost, or effective rental rate on a piece of durable equipment may be reckoned as the sum of the annual depreciation of the equipment and the annual interest cost on the capital invested in it. One can think of the latter as an opportunity cost, since for half the year, on average, the owner's funds are tied up in the machine instead of being lodged elsewhere at interest. Alternatively, the interest cost is to be thought of as the actual charge made for a loan of the purchase price of the equipment. Strictly speaking, in calculating the interest cost of a mechanical reaper, allowance should be made for the fact that funds were locked up in these machines for periods longer than a year; it is known that Midwestern farmers purchased reapers on credit during the 1850's and paid them off only over an extended period of time.[42] Yet, within the range of accuracy we can hope to attain in the present calculations, the niceties of compound interest may be foregone and the interest cost computed on a simple basis. The half life of reapers was not, in any case, so long as to render this a serious omission.

[42] See, e.g., Hutchinson, *op. cit.,* pp. 368–369.

An equivalently liberal attitude is warranted regarding the question of depreciation charges. Rather than play with formulas that attempt to take into account the actual time pattern of loss of value through wear and tear and obsolescence, straight-line depreciation over the physical life of the machine will be assumed.

As a result of the foregoing simplifications, the average annual gross money rental charge is quite straightforwardly given by

$$(2) \qquad\qquad c = [d + 0.5(r)]C,$$

where $d \equiv$ the straight-line rate of depreciation,
$\quad\quad r \equiv$ the annual rate of interest,
$\quad\quad C \equiv$ the purchase price of a reaper.

Putting this together with equation 1a, we have the relation defining the threshold size in terms of the prices of harvest labor and reapers, the rate of interest, and the "technical" coefficients L_s and d:

$$(3) \qquad\qquad S_T = \left(\frac{d + 0.5r}{L_s}\right)\left(\frac{C}{w}\right).$$

From the form of equation 3 it is apparent that, given the rate of interest, the threshold for harvesting machines of specified durability and labor-saving characteristics is directly proportional to the relative price of the reaper (C/w). Thus, the threshold functions shown in Figure 2 of the text appear as positively sloped rays from the origin of a graph of acreages against the ratios of reaper prices to wage rates. In the following section we proceed first to consider the evidence that establishes the slope of the threshold function, and then to take up the question of the relevant range of variation of factor prices in the Midwest during the period preceding the Civil War.

2. PARAMETERS AND VARIABLES

2.a. Labor Savings

The reduction in harvest labor requirements achieved by the introduction of the mechanical reaper is perhaps the single most widely cited instance of the improvement of agricultural technology in small grain production during the ante-bellum era. Various estimates of the magnitude of the saving in labor appear in the secondary literature and the economic history texts, but virtually all of them derive from the evidence and conclusions presented in Leo Rogin's pioneering study.[43] A crucial issue that arises in this connection is one that is frequently overlooked, namely, the amount of grain that the mechanical reaper could cut in a normal day's work. Notwithstanding the fact that during the 1850's the McCormick reapers were warranted to cut 15 acres of wheat in a 12-hour day and that frequently mentioned records set in reaper trials

[43] See, e.g., Bidwell and Falconer, op. cit., pp. 293–294; Gates, op. cit., p. 237; Robertson, op. cit., p. 258; and Danhof, in Williamson, op. cit., pp. 145–156.

cite 15 as the acreage cut in a day, Rogin's survey of the evidence leads him to conclude that 10 to 12 acres per day was closer to normal practise even on the broad prairies of Illinois:

. . . the foregoing rate is the one most frequently mentioned in other contemporary accounts and may be taken to represent the average performance with the hand-rake reaper after it came into prominence, as well as with the self-rake which superseded it.[44]

Following Rogin, then, 11 acres per day may be taken as the average cutting rate with the reaper during its first decade of widespread use.

The significance of establishing the normal daily rate of harvesting with the reaper lies in the fact that the information available on the labor requirements of the hand method of cutting grain comes in the form of statements about the number of acres that it was common for a man working with a cradle to harvest in a day. In Rogin's judgment, "there appears . . . . . to have been a norm of performance for the country as a whole which approximated two acres" per man-day,[45] despite regional and local variation in speed caused by differences in the heaviness of the grain. If an allowance of a 10 per cent difference in speed above the national average is made in recognition of the lighter yields in small grains typical in the Midwest,[46] we are led to conclude that during the 1850's a mechanical reaper cutting 11 acres accomplished the work of 5 man-days labor with cradles. Two men were required to operate the hand-rake reapers, whereas the self-rakers, first marketed commercially in 1854, needed but a driver. Therefore, in the cutting operation itself the use of the hand-rake reaper effected a saving of 3-man-days in cutting 11 acres, while the self-rakers saved 4 man-days.[47]

Although two other sources of economy are sometimes cited as associated with the mechanization of reaping, their inclusion does not seem warranted in the present connection. The reduction of losses due to the shattering of overripe grain by cradlers cannot be considered as anything more than a consequence of the saving in labor already mentioned: if this source of losses had proved sufficiently costly in the era prior to the introduction of the reaper, farmers would have found it worthwhile to hire enough cradlers to ensure

[44] Rogin, op. cit., pp. 134–135. The Census of 1860 also maintained that "a common reaper will cut from ten to twelve acres in a day of twelve hours." (U.S. Eighth Census (1860), "Agriculture": xxiii.) Bidwell and Falconer (op. cit., pp. 293–294), who base their discussion on the results of the Geneva, N.Y. Trials of 1852, where mechanical reapers were matched in competition with cradlers cutting 15 acres, point out that the latter "was a large area for an early reaper to cut in one day." See Hutchinson, op. cit., p. 336 for the McCormick warranties, and ibid., p. 73, for a characteristic example of McCormick advertising giving the savings achieved with the reaper, based on an assumed daily cutting capacity of 16 acres.

[45] Ibid., p. 128.

[46] See Parker, op. cit., Table 5, 14. Wheat and oats yields were higher in the Northeast and Middle Atlantic states.

[47] Rogin, op. cit., p. 135, gives the same savings in cutting 10 acres a day, but in some places says 10 to 12 acres per day.

that their grain was harvested before it became especially prone to shattering.[48] The second point is somewhat more complex. Both the hand-rake and the self-rake models left the grain swept into gavels, or lying in swath, for the binders who followed behind the machine. Rogin[49] notes that binding behind machines was done at a faster rate than when the binders followed cradlers through the fields, and allows an additional saving of labor (amounting to two binders per day in harvesting 10 to 12 acres) on this account. This leads him to state that the total saving in labor connected with the use of the reaper amounted to 5 man-days, instead of just 3 in the cutting operation itself. However, it is pointed out that the reduction in the labor requirements for binding that accompanied the mechanization of grain-cutting may be attributed to the increased pressure put on the binders to get the grain out of the way of the machine, and the consequent adoption of the system of "binding stations" in place of the traditional practice of permitting binders to range over the field at their (comparative) leisure.[50] Since it would appear that the "saving" of the hire of two binders per 10 to 12 acres was achieved by having those employed behind the reaping machines work at a faster pace, the binders thus engaged would ask a higher daily wage, and, so long as there was work available for those who preferred the less demanding task of binding for cradlers, the differential wage would have to be paid. Thus, in terms of the cost of labor to the individual farmer, the greater efficiency exacted in binding by the introduction of the reaper cannot be considered to have resulted in any further economies. Indeed, on this account the reaper may have entailed additional monetary costs for the farmer, since when the system of binding stations was employed the use of women and children was precluded by the pace of the work.[51]

[48] Note that there is no evidence of smaller losses from shattering resulting from machine cutting as contrasted with hand cutting of *equally* ripe grain. Yet the tradition has grown up in the secondary literature of treating the reduction of shattering losses owing to more rapid harvesting as distinct and supplementary to the reduction in labor requirements with the mechanical reaper. See e.g., Bidwell and Falconer, *op. cit.,* p. 294; and Robertson, *op. cit.,* p. 258, where specific mention is made of the reduction of output losses due to damage from the elements as a further benefit bestowed on the farmer by the reaper. This would be justified if, for purely technical reasons, expected post-harvest yields, as well as harvest labor requirements per acre were different with the two methods.

[49] See, Rogin, *op. cit.,* p. 136.

[50] See Rogin, *op. cit.,* pp. 103 and 136, n. 339.

[51] *Ibid.,* p. 103, n. 179. Even if the reduction in manpower requirements for binding were due to purely technical considerations, e.g., the way the grain was delivered from the machines, it would be necessary to take account of the lower daily wage rates typically received by binders, compared to cradlers. In Ohio during the harvest of 1857 binders were paid roughly two-thirds the rate received by cradlers. (See *Ohio State Board of Agriculture Report,* 1857, pp. 181–182.) With this as a basis for weighting the reductions in labor requirements by relative wage rates, Rogin's procedure should give a total saving in labor with the hand-rake machine equivalent to 4.33 cradler man-days, on 10 to 12 acres, rather than the 5 (heterogenous) man-days saving frequently mentioned in the literature.

In summary, for a normal day's work cutting 11 acres, the saving in labor per acre (L_s) with the hand-rake reaper is estimated at 0.273 man-days hire of cradlers services, whereas with the self-raker introduced in the latter half of the 1850's the saving amounted to 0.364 man-days.

2.b. Durability and the Interest Rate

Information as to the average length of life of the reaping machines produced in the Midwest prior to the Civil War is very scanty. Yet those statements regarding durability that have come to light agree in placing the useful life of a reaper at close to ten years.[52] This figure apparently assumed good care and normal use of the machine. Just what constituted "good care," and how closely such a standard was approached by the notoriously casual practices of American farmers during the nineteenth century in the maintenance and storage of equipment, is extremely difficult to say.[53] What "normal use" entailed is somewhat clearer; for, as a rule, the rate of ripening of the grain confined the feasible period for the harvest of small grain crops to roughly a two-week interval, with 10 full working days.[54] Thus, approximately 110 acres of wheat would represent the annual normal use cutting capacity of a reaper. On the assumption that the life of the machine would not be prolonged beyond ten years by utilization at rates below the capacity level imposed by custom, the available hours of daylight, and the length of the period within which the grain could be safely gathered, we shall take the annual straight-line depreciation rate as $d = 0.10$.

Selection of an appropriate rate of interest proves to be quite simple. It appears that the McCormick Company charged farmers a standard rate of 6 per cent on the unpaid balance of their reaper notes throughout the 1850's[55] Even if the farmer was able to secure a higher rate of return by placing his funds elsewhere than in a reaper, the 6 per cent rate is nonetheless appropriate from an opportunity cost viewpoint; so long as the McCormick Co. was willing to encourage sales by foregoing the opportunity to earn more than 6 per cent on its funds, the farmer who purchased a reaper would find it profitable to borrow at that rate and free such capital as he had for investment at higher rates of return.

Combining the 10 per cent depreciation rate and the simple interest cost, according to formula (2), we estimate the annual average rental rate of a reaper at 13 per cent of its purchase price.

2.c. Threshold Functions and Relative Factor Prices

The data assembled in the two preceding sections define a pair of functions relating threshold size to the relative price of reapers—one for the choice between cradling and hand-rake reaping machines, the other for the choice be-

[52] See Hutchinson, *op. cit.*, pp. 73 and 311, and Rogin, *op. cit.*, p. 95.

[53] See Harry J. Carman, "English Views of Middle Western Agriculture, 1850–1870," *Agricultural History*, January 1934, 13; and, Hutchinson, *op. cit.*, p. 365.

[54] See Rogin, *op. cit.*, p. 95.

[55] See Hutchinson, *op. cit.*, p. 337, 369, n. 31.

tween cradling and self-rakers. With the parameter values substituted for d, r, and L_s in equation 3, the functions are found to be,

$$\text{hand-raker versus cradle:} \quad S_T = 0.4765 \, \frac{C_{\text{HR}}}{w},$$

and

$$\text{self-raker versus cradle:} \quad S_T = 0.3572 \, \frac{C_{\text{SR}}}{w}.$$

Both functions are shown in Chart 1, but, since the self-raker was introduced in the Midwest only after 1854 and the reapers for which reliable price information is readily available are those of the hand-rake type manufactured by C. H. McCormick in Chicago, rather than the Wright-Atkins self-raking variety, the present discussion has been restricted to consideration of the threshold levels for adoption of the hand-rake machine.

We have also chosen to avoid the complications that would arise in attempting to work out the threshold function for the basic McCormick reaper with the mower attachment (perfected in 1855) that enabled the machine to cut grasses as well as grain. The technical advance embodied in the reaper-mowers obviously contributed to the abandonment of the cradle by permitting the fixed cost of the machine, which was sold either with or without the mower attachment, to be spread over a greater total (grain and grass) acreage harvest. It thus became profitable to use the reaper on farms with small grain acreages too low to justify the expense of a machine that could not also be converted to cut grass crops.[56] Similarly, since the advent of the self-raker did not drive the McCormick hand-rake machines out of the market, it must be inferred that the former were not less expensive than the hand-rake model on which McCormick continued to rely until after the Civil War. Instead, they must have been priced low enough to drop the threshold grain acreage at which their introduction as a replacement for the cradle was profitable to a level under the hand-raker threshold.[57]

The Price of a Reaper. From 1849 through the harvest of 1853 the price of the McCormick hand-rake reapers actually sold to farmers averaged 113 dollars plus freight charges, whereas the average unit price, also f.o.b. Chicago, for the period 1854–1858 was 133 dollars.[58] Comparable average figures for

[56] On the mower and the reaper-mower, see Hutchinson, *op. cit.*, pp. 309–316 and Rogin, *op. cit.*, pp. 96–102.

[57] From the threshold functions given above, one would surmise that, at a maximum, the self-raking machine could have carried a delivered price as much as a third higher than that of the hand-rake reaper, and still have been competitive with the latter, i.e., $(C_{\text{SR}}/C_{\text{HR}}) = (0.4765/0.3572) = 0.33$.

[58] Average unit prices, reflecting the proper mixture of cash and credit prices on actual transactions have been computed from financial data of the McCormick Co. presented in Hutchinson, *op. cit.*, p. 369, n. 60. The figures given above agree fairly closely with the announced f.o.b. prices of 115 dollars prior to 1854 and 130 dollars for the harvest of 1854 (*ibid.*, p. 323).

it would be cheaper for the farmer to hire a worker by the month only if his services were needed for 17 or more out of the 26 working days in a month, that is, for a period considerably longer than the average 10 working days within which small grain crops like wheat could be safely harvested on a single farm. Farmers undoubtedly hired some hands on that basis, and we shall therefore make use of the lower rates to compute the relative price of a reaper when labor was hired by the month. Nevertheless, it is more reasonable to suppose that the marginal workers replaced in the harvest by the mechanical reaper were those that would have been taken on at the higher daily wage rates just for the duration of the harvest.

3. Estimates of Threshold Size and Actual Small Grain Acreage

In Table A1 the delivered prices of reapers and the alternative wage rate data developed in the preceding section have been brought together to provide a set of estimates of the relative price of a hand-rake reaper for the early and middle years of the 1850's. Columns 3 and 6 of the table present the corresponding threshold acreages at which the costs of harvesting with cradles and with the reaper would have been exactly equal. The latter are computed from the threshold function for the hand-rake reaper given in Section 2.c of the Appendix, and provide the basis for the discussion of Figure 2 in the text.

The acreage figures in Table A1 are discussed in conjunction with estimates of the actual average acreage sown with small grain crops on farms in Illinois during the 1850's, which are presented in summary form by Table A2. A few words about the sources of the latter figures are therefore in order.

The estimates for the harvest of 1849–1850, in Panel I of Table A2, are based on the statistics given in the Census of Agriculture for 1850 on the

TABLE A1. Threshold Grain Acreage for Adoption of Hand-Rake Reapers in Illinois

Terms of Hire of Farm Labor	Period: 1849–1853			Period: 1854–1857		
	(1)	(2)	(3)	(4)	(5)	(6)
	w	$\dfrac{C_{\text{HR}}}{w}$	S_T	w	$\dfrac{C_{\text{HR}}}{w}$	S_T
	cradlers, in current dollars	in man-days per reaper	acres harvested	cradlers, in current dollars	man-days per reaper	acres harvested
Day	1.27	97.6	46.5	1.87	73.8	35.1
Month	.80	155.0	73.8	1.18	117.0	55.6

TABLE A2. Average Acreage per Farm in Illinois

Region	Number of Farms	Wheat Acreage per Farm	Total Wheat, Oats and Rye Acreage per Farm
I. Harvest of 1849–50			
State	76,208	11.0	15.4
Major Wheat Counties*	21,634	19.3	25.2
Winnebago Co.	919	30.4	37.2
Cook Co.	1,857	11.4	18.6
II. Harvest of 1859–1860			
State	143,310	14.6	18.3

* The group of leading wheat-growing counties which accounted for 50 per cent of the total wheat production in the state.

volume of wheat, oats, and rye harvested and the number of farms in each county of Illinois, as well as in the state as a whole.[67] From this information, the bushel harvest per farm of wheat, and of oats and rye (combined) were obtained and then converted into acreage estimates per farm for these crops by employing coefficients of the average grain yield per acre. For the harvest of 1859–1860 (in Panel II) only the estimate of the state average is given, since the Census of 1860 does not supply statistics of the numbers of farms on a county basis.[68]

Fortunately, the choice of appropriate average grain yield coefficients for Illinois at the beginning and end of the 1850's is immensely simplified by the availability of William Parker's recent exhaustive research on the problem of wheat and oat yields per acre in nineteenth century America. In comparison with oats, the rye crop of the Western states was insignificant prior to the Civil War; application of the yield estimates for oats to the combined oats and rye output statistics—figures for the harvest of these crops not being given separately on a county basis by the Census of 1850—should not, therefore, introduce serious error into the acreage estimates.[69] In constructing the acreage figures shown in Table A2, the yield of wheat in Illinois from the harvests of 1849–1850 *and* 1859–1860 was taken to have been 11.3 bushels per acre. The yield of oats we take to have been 30.5 bushels per acre. The following evidence, drawn from Parker's work, may be adduced in justification of these coefficients:

[67] J. D. B. DeBow, *Compendium of the Seventh Census,* pp. 21–27.

[68] See *U.S. Eighth Census* (1860), "Agriculture," pp. 31–35.

[69] In Illinois the number of bushels of rye harvested was a mere 0.8 per cent of the oats harvest of 1849–1850, and even after rapid expansion during the decade the rye harvest of 1859–1860 amounted to but 6 per cent of the volume of oats produced. See Bidwell and Falconer, *op. cit.,* pp. 350–356 for summary tables.

1. Between 1849 and 1859 the average yields of wheat and oats in the region comprised of Ohio, Indiana, Illinois, Missouri, and Iowa were virtually unchanged; the wheat yield dropped from 12.4 to 12.1 bushels per acre, and the oats yield rose from 29.3 to 30.4 bushels per acre. (Parker, *op. cit.*, Table 10, p. 32.)

2. From the U.S. Department of Agriculture revised data on acreage yields in the period 1866–1875 it is found that the wheat yield in Illinois was slightly below the typical yields in the Midwestern region, whereas the yield of oats was virtually the same as that for the region as a whole. The Illinois yield of wheat per acre was 11.3 bushels, compared with the mid-range figure of 12.2 bushels per acre for the group of states mentioned above, while the Illinois oats yield was 30.5 bushels per acre compared with the mid-range figure of 30.3 for the region. (Parker, *op. cit.*, Table 1, p. 4.)

Since the Department of Agriculture regional yield data for 1866–1875 agree so well with the regional data for 1849 and 1859, the U.S.D.A. data on Illinois were accepted as appropriate for the decade of the 1850's.

The average yield coefficients employed for Illinois may be, if anything, somewhat low for the major grain regions of the state.[70] Consequently, if the derived acreage estimates do contain a bias, it is certainly not one which would favor our conclusion that a considerable gap existed between the threshold size for adoption of the hand-rake reaper and the actual average small grain acreage per farm in the early 1850's.

[70] A sample of Illinois county estimates drawn from different dates in the period 1843–1855 gives a median wheat yield of 16 bushels per acre, and a median yield for oats of 40 bushels per acre. See Parker, *op. cit.*, Table 3, p. 8.

THE AMERICAN COMMON
SCHOOL REVIVAL:
FACT OR FANCY?

Albert Fishlow
University of California, Berkeley

Within the past decade economists have begun to rediscover the role of human capital as a factor of production. The rapid recovery of the war stricken nations of Europe and that of Japan, in sharp contrast to the growing pains of the newly developing states, gave hint of the significance of an educated populace. More direct research has since confirmed the existence of positive economic returns that can be attributed to further years of schooling. One need not literally accept the claim that education was responsible for 42 per cent of the increased labor productivity in the United States between 1929 and 1957 to concede its importance.[1]

Horace Mann, more than a century ago, argued the precise point. One reason to promote free, universal education was its function "as the grand agent for the development or augmentation of national resources; [it was] more powerful in the production and gainful employment of the

● I wish to acknowledge the generous financial support of the National Bureau of Economic Research, where this ongoing project on the historical influence of education on economic development originated, and to the Institute of Business and Economic Research, University of California, Berkeley, for subsequent assistance.

[1] See Edward F. Denison, *The Sources of Economic Growth in the United States,* Supplementary Paper No. 13 of the Committee for Economic Development, New York, 1962, pp. 67–79. In his review of the book, Abramovitz correctly points out that the consequences of education are more than doubled by assuming increased attendance within a school year is equivalent to extension of the number of grades completed. He also focuses upon other weaknesses of the calculation [*American Economic Review,* LII (1962), 765–771]. But note that T. W. Schultz obtains comparable results, approaching the problem in a rather different way in his "Education and Economic Growth," in N. B. Henry (ed.), *Social Forces Influencing American Education,* Chicago, 1961, pp. 73–82.

total wealth of a country than all the other things mentioned in the books of the political economists."[2] Through information from employers he sought (as did John Eaton, the second Commissioner of Education, in 1870) to ascertain the productivity differential associated with further training—a line of inquiry the Census Bureau unfortunately did not pursue until 1940. Their estimates that schooling could account for employee wage differentials of between 25 and 50 per cent within manufacturing establishments testify to the historical importance of education on the American scene, as much as do the comments of perceptive contemporary visitors.

Impelled partially by such logic, but undoubtedly even more by the currents of social and political reform then in the air, the United States experienced before the Civil War a great crusade for popular education.[3] Led by Mann and Henry Barnard in New England, but with equally fervent espousal in other regions, the conception of state directed and supported systems of education had largely triumphed before the Civil War. Eighteen-hundred and fifty is typically viewed as the turning point; the Census results of that year imply that "publicly supported schools had already assumed the primary burden of the formal education of the American young."[4]

Histories of American education have given considerable emphasis to this ante-bellum emergence of the common school, and this for a variety of reasons. At one level, it commemorates the victory of the fondly held principle that a democratic polity requires a public form of education. At another, because educational history has been written primarily for the educator, it represents the emergence of state administrative centralization, a subject occupying a central place in education curricula until recently. In the background, less stressed, but more relevant to the student of American economic history, is the apparent revolution it wrought in the level of educational activity. As a late nineteenth century report of the Commissioner of Education put it:

A careful estimate of the entire amount of schooling obtained by the average person in 1800 shows that it did not exceed 82 days of school instruction during his life. . . . In 1840, . . . the total amount of schooling for each inhabitant had risen to 208 days; and according to the Census of 1850 the average amount of schooling had increased to 420 days, for this decade was a period of agitation on the part of Horace Mann and his disciples. A great

[2] Mary Mann, *Life and Works of Horace Mann,* Boston, 1891, III, p. 111.

[3] F. T. Carlton in his "Economic Influences Upon Educational Progress in the United States, 1820–1850," *University of Wisconsin Bulletin,* Economics and Political Science Series, Vol. IV, No. 1, considerably overstates the role of purely economic factors, undoubtedly as an overresponse to treatment totally ignoring them. Lawrence Cremin, *The American Common School,* New York, 1951, provides a more balanced picture of the circumstances of the reform movement.

[4] *Ibid.,* p. 179.

revival in common-school interest extending through the thickly populated sections of the country had produced this great change in the ten years, 1840–1850.[5]

Such a sharp increase in the educational attainments of the youth of school age in the decade of the 1840's could not help rapidly augmenting the embodied capital of the labor force in the 1850's and beyond. Since Denison finds so large a return for the more modest evolution of secondary education in the post-World War I era, it is tempting to speculate upon the contribution of primary education to the quickened pace of ante-bellum economic activity. However, that ultimate task lies beyond the intent of this present essay. Before calculating its effect, it is necessary first to analyze the dimensions of this common school revival itself. In particular, the claims of vast and immediate progress in formal education during the 1840's seem to be much exaggerated. Moreover, much of the change that did occur was due to the initial dissemination of mass schooling to the West and the South, not to an uplift in the East where the reformers' attentions were concentrated. Successive sections of this paper now take up these two fundamental questions: the progress attained in formal schooling before 1860 and it unequal regional diffusion.

I

The scope of educational energies in the first half of the nineteenth century is largely an unknown quantity. Not until 1840 were formal census inquiries instituted on a national level, and before the expanded role of state supervision in the same decade, that potential local source is absent as well. Nonetheless, what scattered reports are available suggest a more optimistic evaluation of the state of educational facilities prior to the reform efforts of the 1830's and 1840's that culminated in free public education in the North and West.

Table 1 records for selected states, principally those of New England, comparable ratios of school enrollment to population for 1830 and 1840. With due disparagement for the quality of the earlier data, the conclusion that little change occurred between the two dates—at least for this sample—seems amply justified. Indeed, in the instance where the information is perhaps most accurate and comparable, the New York rates, their difference is in favor of an earlier advantage. Where the most marked increase occurs, in Virginia, it is the consequence of a larger enumeration of poor children eligible for free schooling rather than a shift in their en-

[5] *Report of the U.S. Commissioner of Education for 1900–1901,* Washington, 1901, p. xviii.

TABLE 1. Enrollment Rates, 1830 and 1840

State	Ratio of Enrollment to White Population 5–19	
	1830	1840
Maine	70.3	87.7
New Hampshire	74.8	85.6
Massachusetts	72.9[a]	68.9
Connecticut	83.9	65.3
Rhode Island	51.9	49.4
New York	73.8	69.4
South Carolina	8.5	8.1
Virginia	5.4	9.8[c]
	(51.3)[b]	(56.7)[b]
Kentucky	15.5	10.6

[a] 1832

[b] Ratio of enrolled pauper students to total number of poor children 8–15.

[c] 1841

Source: Attendance, 1830: for Maine, N.H., Conn., R.I.: *Statistical View of the Population of the United States from 1790 to 1830 Inclusive*, 23rd Congress, 1st session, Washington, 1835, pp. 190, 209, 214. The total for New Hampshire was obtained by increasing the sample returns by the ratio of sample tax revenues to the estimated total; for Massachusetts: Partial report for 1832, reprinted in *American Almanac*, scaled upward by ratio of reporting population to total; for S. Carolina: Pauper school returns summarized in Edgar W. Knight, *The Influence of Reconstruction on Education in the South*, New York, 1913, p. 62; for Virginia: Pauper students for 1830 reported in *American Almanac* (1834) 208; for Kentucky: *American Almanac* (1834), 236–238.

Attendance, 1840: all except New York, South Carolina, and Virginia: 1840 *Census* results reprinted in J. D. B. DeBow, *A Compendium of the Seventh Census*, Washington, 1854, pp. 150–151; New York and South Carolina: same as 1830; Virginia: *American Almanac* (1843) 245.

Population 5–19, 1830, 1840: *Compendium of the Seventh Census*, p. 52.

rollment rate; to this the figures in parentheses testify. Since free schools were only a fractional source of education in the South, a corresponding increase in total enrollment rates is by no means necessary.

Some 40 per cent of the 1830 school age population is comprehended in the relatively firm statistics of Table 1. This alone sets a considerable constraint upon any assertion of substantial change between 1830 and 1840. In addition, for two other populous states, Pennsylvania and Ohio, it is possible to infer in less rigorous fashion what order of increase might have occurred during the decade.

A committee agitating for public schools in the former state in 1830 could claim no more than that

> . . . there are at least four hundred thousand children in Pennsylvania be-tween the ages of five and fifteen. Of these, during the past year, there were not one hundred and fifty thousand in all the schools of the state. Many counties, townships and villages have been taken indiscriminately from all parts of the state, and been examined by your memorialists, and the average proportion of children educated in any one year . . . appears to be but one out of three.[6]

Adjusted for a larger population base inclusive of ages 5 to 19, the ratio becomes 23 per cent, compared with 31.7 per cent in 1840. At worst, then, the 1830 Pennsylvania enrollment rate stood at no less than 70 per cent of its later value.

For Ohio, our evidence is almost wholly qualitative and is based on continuing legislative enactments in favor of public education.[7] Taxation for district schools was authorized as early as 1821, and the school law of 1825, entitled "An act to provide for the support and better regulation of common schools," made such provision compulsory. Subsequent action in 1829 increased the county tax from one-half to three-fourths mill in recognition of the larger financial needs of the system. It is inconceivable therefore that, in 1830, Ohio's enrollment rate did not exceed the 1840 rates of 18.8 and 20.6 per cent for Indiana and Illinois, both more rural than 1830 Ohio, without public support for schools, and with illiteracy rates twice as large. This 1830 floor of around 20 per cent provides scope for substantial increase to the recorded 1840 rate of 38.4 per cent; the divergence between maximum and actual changes in this instance is probably quite large, however.

A final supplement to the 1830 evidence derives from subsequent literacy rates. Literacy, of course, encompasses a wide range of educational attainment—from a few meager years of primary schooling through college attendance and beyond; that is, it encompasses a large proportion of the frequency distribution of years of education. A given literacy rate is therefore consistent with quite different levels of years of schooling and thus of enrollment rates, but to the extent that achievement of literacy requires some minimal amount of education, such information can define

[6] Quoted in J. P. Wickersham, *A History of Education in Pennsylvania,* Lancaster, 1886, p. 300.

[7] For these and further details, see *A History of Education in the State of Ohio,* Columbus, 1876, Ch. I; also the *Report of the U.S. Commissioner of Education for 1894–95,* pp. 1525–1535.

a *lower* limit to enrollment rates.[8] Thus, although the group aged 20 years in New Jersey and New York in 1850 possessed identically low illiteracy rates of 6 per cent, the 1840 enrollment rates in the two states were a disparate 43.3 and 76.7 per cent respectively.[9] If we presume, however, that three years of enrollment and consequently about one and a half years of attendance are necessary to be able to read and write, we could have predicted an average enrollment rate over the period 1835–1849 for these two states of *at least* 19 per cent. Such a prediction is in fact borne out by the data, but to little avail; minimum and actual attendance are too widely divergent.

As this example illustrates, literacy rates transmit useful information only when educational levels are so low that literacy and educational achievement are practically synonymous. Such a circumstance seems to have prevailed for the great bulk of the ante-bellum Southern white population. The reported enrollment rate for Southern whites in 1840 is a scanty 14.5 per cent, and not much greater in 1850. Yet among the group of age 20 in 1850, 80 per cent were recorded as able to read and write. In turn, invoking the assumption of three years minimum schooling, enrollment rates of 16 per cent would have been expected over the interval 1835–1849.[10] Such a prediction is consistent with actual circumstances. Now since illiteracy in the South, among those whites aged 20 in 1840, was limited to 18 per cent, by the same logic enrollment

---

[8] The formula relating minimum enrollment rates to literacy rates is as follows:

$$\text{min. enrollment rate} = \frac{\text{Lit. rate} \times \text{min. years of schooling required}}{\text{No. of years eligible for schooling}}$$

The enrollment rate is calculated on the same school age base that determines the time interval over which education for literacy can be attained.

[9] Here and subsequently in this section, 1840 education statistics are taken from *Compendium of the Seventh Census*, Washington, 1854, pp. 150–151, and illiteracy data for a special study published in the *Report of the U.S. Commissioner of Education for 1870*, pp. 467–502.

[10] The choice of three years as a minimum is corroborated by evidence presented in E. H. Bernert and C. B. Nam's "Demographic Factors Affecting American Education," in Henry (ed.), *op. cit.* They point out: "It is well to bear in mind the clear relationship between years of schooling and literacy. . . . About 74 per cent of the population with no schooling cannot read and write in any language; the corresponding percentages are 59 per cent of those with only one year of school, 33 per cent of those with two years of school, 17 per cent of those with three years, 5 per cent with four years, and 2 per cent with five years." (p. 111). The average time required to attain literacy according to this distribution is 3.2 years. If one presumes that the standards of literacy have increased proportionally with improved and longer schooling, this result is directly appropriate; even if not, it still sets a lower limit for the earlier time value.

rates over the period 1825 to 1839 would have had to be something like that same 16 per cent, or greater than the recorded 1840 result. We can conclude, therefore, that enrollment rates in the South in 1830 could not have been lower than those achieved in 1840; indeed, if the literacy statistics and the experience of Kentucky reported in Table 1 are reliable indicators, they might have been greater.

The upshot of this discussion is that a national enrollment rate of as much as 35 per cent apparently had been attained by 1830. New England, New York, and the South together exhaust two-thirds of the population. These are the areas where 1830 enrollment almost certainly was equal to or greater than the rates reported in the 1840 Census. Among the other states Pennsylvania and Ohio are by far the two most important; yet in these very instances the evidence suggests relatively modest change. Accordingly, the 1830 rate could not have been much smaller than the 38.5 per cent returned by the 1840 Census.

To go back farther to the turn of the century is more hazardous; it is probable, however, that education was being prosecuted with comparable vigor over the whole period. New England's provisions for popular, if not public, education date to the seventeenth century and especially to the Massachusetts legislation of 1647 requiring communities to educate their youth in schools, under penalty of fine. Although the standard interpretation of the post-1790 period through 1840 is one of the steady decline and degeneration, this view—originally advanced by Mann and Barnard—is perhaps as much the product of the subsequent bias of historians of education as reality.[11] Because they viewed the subject as professionals, they were united in their espousal of public education under centralized, state administration. During this interval in New England, however, districts became the unit of authority, semiprivate school societies arose to administer state funds in Connecticut, and private academies partially replaced the previously mandatory town grammar schools. For these reasons, but apparently few other, this period saw the "low-water mark" of New England education.[12]

In fact, it is likely that enrollment maintained itself at the high levels attained earlier and later. Connecticut established in 1795 a generous school fund derived from the sale of the Western Reserve in Ohio. So liberal were the dividends that taxation ceased after 1820, and with it, perhaps, some local interest and initiative. The lament of Governor Wolcott in 1822 for the decline of the "old habit of 11 months' school in

[11] For an illustration of this interpretation, see the still influential book by Elwood Cubberley, *Public Education in the United States,* Cambridge, Mass., 1934, p. 110.

[12] George Martin, *The Evolution of the Massachusetts Public School System,* New York, 1901, p. 92.

every town" relates only to the recent past and is an indirect indication of the continued advanced state of Connecticut education in the nineteenth century rather than of its steady decline.[13] Another contemporary, writing in the *North American Review* of 1823, bemoans the potential accomplishment lost because the income from the School Fund was not supplemented by taxes, but sees no retrogression.[14] All other New England states, too, have left record both of general school laws after the Revolution and of means for support. In those, as well as in Connecticut, there is no evidence of a radically weakened educational resolve over this period 1800–1830, except in relation to a substitution of private for public effort.

For the state of New York, fortunately, it is possible to be more precise. Its schools do show an increase in enrollment rates of some 25 per cent from 1815 to 1830 while expenditures per pupil remain approximately constant.[15] Note, however, that by 1823 the 1830 level had already been reached and that as early as 1798 a partial enumeration of school attendance suggests no great difference from the 1815 level. Moreover, at the earlier date, expenditures of public funds per student were somewhat greater.[16]

Finally, the South could hardly have enjoyed less schooling previously than it is credited with in 1840. More than 80 per cent of the entire white adult population at that date could read and write. Over the period 1800 to 1839, then, an average enrollment rate of some 16 per cent must have been achieved. The fact that the literacy rate of new adults in 1840 was no different from that of the previous generation bespeaks this continuity. Neighborhood field schools, denominational efforts and academies were substituted for the more universalistic practices to the North, with the consequence of lesser, but nonetheless existent, enrollment rates. Lack of statistics or of sympathy with the educational philosophy should not obscure an ongoing process of instruction in the Southern states.

All in all, then, the 154 per cent increase in days attended per person between 1800 and 1840, advocated in the previously quoted report of the Bureau of Education, must be regarded as highly exaggerated. The days-

---

[13] *Report of the U.S. Commissioner of Education for 1894–95,* p. 1583.

[14] *Report of the Connecticut Superintendent of Common Schools for 1853,* pp. 148–150.

[15] S. S. Randall, *The Common School System of the State of New York,* Troy, 1851, p. 91.

[16] *Ibid.,* p. 7; *Report of the U.S. Commissioner of Education for 1895–96,* p. 221. The expenditures here are not deflated since teachers' wages apparently did not fluctuate anything like the changes recorded in the Warren-Pearson price index; nor are constant dollar expenditures employed in later comparisons since price changes over one relevant interval were not large enough to affect any conclusions.

attended statistic is obtained by multiplication of enrollment rates, average daily attendance rates, and average length of the school year. The first of these has been shown to vary within narrow limits over the period. Neither average daily attendance rates nor length of school year is likely to have shown rapid change. The rigorous standards of the early New England legislation and the comparable sums spent per pupil early and later in the century convey this impression. Thus, Massachusetts required a minimum of six months' schooling in 1789; the average length of school term in 1840 extended slightly beyond seven. The Connecticut School Fund paid average annual dividends of 35,000 dollars in the first decade of the nineteenth century, amounting to 40 cents per person of ages 5 to 19; in addition there were tuition payments and the receipts from taxation. In 1840 the dividends amounted to just about 1 dollar per child with very little supplement beyond.[17] It is doubtful there was much difference in expenditure, and hence length of school year. There is less evidence on average attendance rates. Yet, there was some tendency for average daily attendance and length of school year to be negatively associated during this period: the longer the school year the less likely were students to attend with regularity.[18] This type of offset has the effect of making changes in enrollment rates the major factor in increasing the days-attended statistic. In any event, so large an increase as the implied minimal 40 per cent gain in each of the two components seems wildly improbable since between 1861 and 1900 they moved through quite a narrow range.[19]

The fact of the matter is that from the very beginning, the inhabitants of the new world attached considerable importance to education. Mulhall's conjectural 1830 enrollment rates place the United States second only to Germany, and well beyond France and the United Kingdom; an adjustment to reflect education of whites alone, as an allowance for the institutional barrier slavery imposed upon education of Negroes, would place America

---

[17] Data from *Third Annual Report of Massachusetts Board of Education, for 1839–40;* for Connecticut School Fund, *American Journal of Education,* VI (1859); for population, *Compendium of the Seventh Census.* (The average 1800 to 1810 population ages 5–19 was estimated by using the 1830 ratio of this age group to total and applying it to the average of Connecticut population of 1800 and 1810.)

[18] In 1861, for 15 Northern and Western states, Spearman's *rho* was equal to −0.09 when average daily attendance and length of school year were correlated. Eliminating Connecticut, Massachusetts, and Rhode Island, which enjoyed high values for both variables, *rho* diminishes to −0.50, which is significantly different from zero at the 0.95 significance level.

[19] This 40 per cent change in average daily attendance and length of school year presumes as large a change as 30 per cent in enrollment between 1800 and 1840. As Table 4 later reveals, 1861 average daily attendance relative to enrollment stood at 56 per cent and length of school year at 124 days. Comparable 1900 statistics are 69 per cent and 144 days. (*Historical Statistics,* GPO, Washington, 1960, p. 207)

in the first rank. *The Compendium of the Seventh Census* reflected this same leadership in an international comparison made 20 years later. Literacy rates tell the same tale.[20] It should come as no surprise that even earlier in the nineteenth century the United States probably was the most literate and education conscious country in the world. Whatever the accomplishments of the common school movement, we cannot neglect its firm and long standing foundation.

II

So far we have not touched directly upon that educational crusade itself; in this section we do so, through an examination of the changes wrought between 1840 and 1860. It will be seen that although much that was beneficial occurred in the sphere of education over this interval, present accounts tend to distort the accomplishment. They emphasize New England and the 1830's and 1840's to the exclusion of both the significant quality improvements of education in the 1850's and the rapid increase in formal education in the West and South.

Table 2 provides a useful focus for the discussion. What it shows unequivocally is a rapid increase amounting to almost 60 per cent in the national enrollment rate between 1840 and 1860. The division of growth

TABLE 2. Enrollment Rates,[a] 1840–1860

Regions[b]	1840	1850		1860	
	(1)	(2)	(3)	(4)	(5)
New England	81.4	76.1	79.0	73.8	75.0
Middle Atlantic	54.7	61.9	63.6	61.3	64.6
South Atlantic	16.2	29.7	38.6	31.4	42.5
North Central	29.1	52.4	58.8	69.4	65.6
South Central	13.4	31.0	45.4	38.6	45.9
Total	38.4	50.4	56.5	57.0	59.9

[a] Total number of pupils, primary, academy, and college, divided by white population 5–19.

[b] Census regions excluding territories as of the date taken.

Sources: Cols. 1, 2, 4. Census of Schools, 1840, 1850, 1860, as reported in the *Compendium of the Seventh Census*, pp. 141–143 and 150–151, and *Eighth Census*, II, pp. 505–506. Cols. 3, 5. Census of Population, 1850, 1860, as reported in the *Compendium*, p. 144, and *Eighth Census*, II, 507.

[20] Michael G. Mulhall, *The Progress of the World*, London, 1880, pp. 88–89; *Compendium of the Seventh Census*, p. 148. Denmark is ranked slightly ahead of the United States in 1850.

between the two decades is only slightly more problematic, although it does depend on whether one accepts the returns from the direct count of schools or prefers the response from individuals themselves regarding attendance. Consistency requires the former, at least between 1840 and 1850, and results in a 31 per cent increase between those two dates, and a lesser 13 per cent between 1850 and 1860. The later figure is further reduced to 6 per cent if the individual attendance tallies are used. Regardless, it is clear the educational gains of the 1840's dominate.[21]

But note where they are concentrated: the South and the West (North Central states), and to a lesser extent the Middle Atlantic region, primarily Pennsylvania. There were in fact *two* processes at work affecting formal education during the decade. One was the common school revival centered in New England with its emphasis upon free, public education, higher standards, and increased state supervision. The other was an initial diffusion of education to the new states of the West and the laggard South; it was this that had the greater impact.

Moreover, for the West, this increase in enrollment rates was largely disassociated from the free school ideals of the reformers. Rather, it was the 1850's that saw their legislative and administrative aims realized—*after* the significant progress of the previous decade. Thus in Ohio, "the great principle of free common-school education was put into operation under the school law of March 14, 1853." In Indiana, the "wave of the great revival" did not strike until 1851. Illinois lagged until 1854; in 1847 the Secretary of State, ex officio superintendent of schools, "exposed what was still, after the great revival of the common school had been ten years on its triumphant progress in the East, the feeble condition of public instruction." In Iowa, private rate bills to supplement public funds continued until 1858; earlier legislation in 1849, subsequent to statehood, had organized the system effectively in the first place. Wisconsin, also admitted to the Union late, entered in 1848 with a forthright declaration for public education in her constitution. It is difficult to believe that the more than doubling of the enrollment rate between 1840 and 1850 in these states can be attributed to the short period under liberal statutes rather than to the earlier period of territorial laws permitting rate-bill payments—taxes levied on parents of school children—and private subscriptions. Michigan, too, despite its early provision of state supervision and its high enrollment rates, deferred free schools even longer. Not until 1869 were rate-bills abolished, but again the first efforts in that direction can be traced to the 1850's. In 1850 the Michigan Constitution required the legislature to make provision within five years for a system which would include a school in each district open at least for three months without payment of tuition; this imperative was in fact ignored.[22]

[21] For evaluation of these Census statistics see Appendix.

[22] *Report of the U.S. Commissioner of Education for 1900–01*, p. 147; *Report*

The advances of the 1840's preceded these gains achieved by the reformers. They occurred within the familiar legislative context of mixed public and private support that had evolved from the beginning of the century. Public funds were necessarily an important element in Western education because the generous gift of the sixteenth section of every township created state monies for distribution. These, not taxes, remained the dominant source of support. As late as 1850, taxes accounted for only a third of total income in the public schools. The capital in the school funds accumulated rapidly during the 1830's, both as land was sold and also as sizable parts of the Surplus Revenue of 1837 were dedicated to educational purposes in Ohio, Illinois and Indiana.[23] The increased availability of appropriations from this traditional tap was undoubtedly a factor in the enrollment growth of the subsequent decade.

Important, too, however, was the changed character of the western population itself. Rapid Western growth between 1830 and 1840 had induced migration from the East in unprecedented amount. The immigrants transmitted personally the educational heritage that had been theirs years earlier and immediately set about to duplicate a previous environment. Those states of the region with the greatest proportion of native New Englanders and New Yorkers in 1850 also tended to have the highest 1850 enrollment rates:[24]

State	Enrollment Rates	Proportion of Non-native Population from New England and New York in 1850
Ohio	66.4	19.7
Indiana	42.3	7.8
Illinois	38.9	20.4
Michigan	74.3	64.1
Wisconsin	58.7	39.4
Iowa	40.3	9.6

The disproportionately low value for Illinois in 1850 was reversed in the next decade when that state achieved the highest rate of growth of en-

---

of the U.S. Commissioner of Education for 1898–99, pp. 375, 382, 433; J. W. Stearns, The Columbian History of Education in Wisconsin, Milwaukee, 1893, pp. 15–23; Arthur R. Mead, The Development of Free Schools in the United States, New York, 1918, p. 93 and p. 220 for the amount collected in the 1840's in Michigan by rate-bills.

[23] F. W. Swift, A History of Public Permanent Common School Funds in the United States, 1795–1905, New York, 1911, pp. 75, 77.

[24] Enrollment rates are based upon the Census of Schools, as reported in the Compendium of the Seventh Census, pp. 141–143; the nativity of the residents of the states was calculated from the same source, pp. 116 and 117.

rollment rates in the group; the higher value for Ohio is indication of its longer length of settlement and more substantial economic position: its wealth per capita was almost double that of Wisconsin.

To be sure, other influences also made themselves felt. The rapid growth of the 1830's increased population density and hence the ability to utilize district schools. It also brought a measure of economic surplus that could be employed for educational ends; equally relevant were the more permanent character of the population and the lesser degree of new settling. Whatever the shape of the total constellation of causes, the important point is that the increased interest in free schools, state supervision, and direct state taxes waited upon the earlier, independent growth of attendance.

The similar expansion of formal education in the South in the same period is less easily explained. Interestingly enough, although the educational revival is most frequently ascribed to the 1850's there, it does seem that public initiative in the 1840's may have played a greater role in the South than in either the West or North. The distribution of the surplus revenue was a central factor in the two states experiencing the greatest advance in the decade—North Carolina and Tennessee. In the former, the school law of 1840–1841 grew directly out of availability of funds. Although it only established a school system on a permissive basis, the legislation led to a remarkable expansion in appropriations and enrollment by 1850. The usual opinion that appointment of a state school superintendent in 1853 initiated public educational efforts misses the point.[25] In Tennessee, provision for distribution of the interest from the public funds dates back to 1838 and the receipt of the surplus. That the office of state superintendent of education was abolished in 1844 serves again only as a misleading indicator. Judgments such as "the wave of educational enthusiasm which began in the early thirties . . . was spent," and "from 1844 to 1854 the poorly organized school system was little more than a name," ignore the evidence of enrollment rates.[26] Louisiana, the only state to adopt a free school law—in 1847—experienced the third largest gain. By 1850 these three states, North Carolina, Tennessee, and Louisiana, had greater proportions of the white population at school than the South as a whole: 52.2, 54.1, and 36.8 per cent respectively, compared with an overall 30.4 per cent, using the Census of Schools, but a lesser 46.8, 68.3, and 40.4 compared with an aggregate 41.7 per cent, if the Census of Population count is used instead. Note that they also obtained a larger proportion of educational expenditures from public sources than did the South as a whole: 45, 27 and 50 per cent versus a total of 24 per cent.

[25] Edgar W. Knight, *Public Education in the South,* Boston, 1922, p. 235.
[26] *Ibid.,* p. 239.

This is by no means a complete explanation. Although education in Alabama, Kentucky and Maryland was to have benefited from the distribution of the surplus revenue as well, evidence suggests that in the first two, at least, the funds were diverted to other purposes within the decade. And what of the accomplishments during the 1840's of Virginia, Georgia, South Carolina, Mississippi, states that did virtually nothing during the entire ante-bellum period for popular education? Their rates of increase concentrate between 34 and 42 per cent, a pace that perhaps may be regarded as the "natural" advance uninfluenced by the consideration already adduced. In part, these educational gains may be exaggerated by what appears to be an unduly small count in 1840; it will be recalled that the enrollment rates that year were actually below the minimum implied by the level of literacy in the region. Nonetheless, there would appear to be a strong, underlying upward tendency that historians of education might well seek to interpret in lieu of the usual tale of accomplishments of the common school revival in the North Atlantic states.

For, examined more closely, the effects within *that* region in the 1840's seem to have been substantially exaggerated. New York did not attain completely free schools until 1867, and the principle was accepted only in 1850, after which the largess of the state was more fully made available for educational needs. Barnard's own state of Connecticut did not enact a state tax for the support of schools until 1856, and did not abolish rate-bills until 1868. Ironically, the one large state completely to achieve the ideal of free education during the period was Pennsylvania—always regarded as a laggard—in 1834 and prior to the emergence of Mann and Barnard.

If free schools in the 1840's were not the creation of the revival, neither did the efforts of the reformers come to immediate fruition in objective indicators of educational progress. New England and New York enrollment rates stayed at the high levels that had been attained earlier. In Massachusetts the average length of school year stayed the same between 1840 and 1850, and the rate of average daily attendance was no larger at the later date. Annual outlays per student did rise from $3.76 to $5.01, or by a third. One's enthusiasm is tempered by the realization that the gain from 1832 to 1840 was a much more substantial 90 per cent; the decade 1850–1860 saw a larger rise as well. In other North Atlantic states the same modest advance in the 1840's was in evidence. Indeed, taken as a whole, regional expenditures per pupil seem not to have increased at all.[27]

[27] For six states, Maine, Vermont, Massachusetts, Rhode Island, New York and Pennsylvania, expenditures per pupil declined from an average of $2.33 to $2.17 between 1840 and 1850. The necessary information was secured from the *American Almanac;* R. S. Pitkin, *Public School Support in the United States During Periods*

Rather, the reform movement attained its greatest immediate success in the triumph of New England public schools over the flourishing private alternative. In Massachusetts between 1840 and 1850 the number of students opting for private education almost halved; aggregate expenditures for public schools doubled while tuition to academies hardly increased.[28] For New England as a whole, public enrollment grew by 10 per cent; academy attendance *declined* by 6. Nationally, and in the same vein, Cremin is heartened to find that by the century mid-point "over 90 per cent [of the students] were enrolled in some kind of public facility."[29] Actually, this measure exaggerates; the same 1850 Census report reveals that of the 16.1 million dollars expended for education in that year, less than half emanated from taxation and the interest upon state permanent school funds; even within the more limited domain of public schools, private payments provided one-quarter of the revenues.[30] By 1870 the situation was far different: two-thirds of educational outlay was public, primarily taxes; and more than 90 per cent of public school funds had a public source.[31]

Only if we make our criterion the type of education rather than the quantity or quality, can we consider the educational revival a positive factor in the 1840's. Yet, within the context of the ante-bellum period, it is not obvious that *public* education should rank as the supreme good. Free public education is probably indispensable to universal training of high quality in a heterogeneous community. Whether it was needed by 1860 to accomplish the same ends is open to doubt. In this sense, the reformers were in advance of their time. Nonetheless, the publicity of the educational revival was not without beneficial effects before the war. But, these can be found in the liberalized legislation that was instituted almost everywhere in the 1850's, and in the increased expenditures of that same decade, not in any remarkable renascence in the 1840's. Of the first, we have already spoken. For the second, it remains to recount the statistics.

---

of Economic Depression, Brattleboro, 1933; Massachusetts State Reports; Randall, *op. cit.;* Wickersham, *op. cit.,* and the *Compendium of the Seventh Census.* The general mild decline in teachers' salaries over this interval seems to confirm this trend.

[28] Data compiled from the annual reports of the State Board of Education.

[29] Cremin, *op. cit.,* p. 179.

[30] It is possible that this represents an understatement of private tuition payments, or rate bills, used to support public schools. Randall, *op. cit.,* p. 91, suggests a much larger sum for 1849 than does the Census, and there is no reason to expect a downward trend. The same is true of Michigan: see A. R. Mead, *op. cit.,* p. 220.

[31] Ninth Census, *Population,* II, pp. 450, 452.

TABLE 3. Educational Expenditures,[a] 1840–1860

Region	Total (Mill. Dollars)			Outlay per White Person, 5–19		Outlay per Pupil	
	1840	1850	1860	1850	1860	1850	1860
New England	2.7	2.9	4.4	3.32	4.60	4.23	6.25
Middle Atlantic	3.4	5.6	9.9	2.42	3.76	3.90	6.14
South Atlantic	1.1	1.9	3.7	2.48	3.69	8.34	11.60
North Central	0.9	2.6	10.0	1.28	3.07	2.44	4.50
South Central	1.0	2.7	5.6	2.63	3.86	8.46	10.00
Total	9.2	16.2	34.7	2.23	3.66	4.43	6.34

Source: 1840, calculated as product of number of pupils and 1850 expenditures per pupil; 1850, 1860, Census of Schools as cited in Table 2.

[a] Actually measured in the Census as income received.

Table 3 serves as a convenient summary.[32] It tells with certainty of a large increase in educational expenditures between 1850 and 1860, an increase that comprehends all regions. Similar Census statistics for 1840 are not available. Yet, because much evidence suggests that total outlay per pupil changed little during that first decade, it is possible to approximate expenditures at the early date. The constancy in the North Atlantic states has already been alluded to. Scattered evidence from Western and Southern states only reinforces it: expenditures per pupil in Michigan were almost the same in 1840 and 1850, declined somewhat in Ohio over the decade, and showed rather substantial deterioration in North Carolina.[33] Such lack of progress is hardly surprising in light of the very rapid enroll-

[32] The implicit GNP deflator that emerges from Robert E. Gallman's estimates of national product stands at 99, 96, and 101 for the three Census years 1839, 1849, and 1859. ("Gross National Product in the United States, 1834–1909," in *Output, Employment, and Productivity* in the *United States after 1800*, Vol. 30, *Studies in Income and Wealth*, New York, 1965.) Accordingly, deflation of these current dollar expenditures seems unnecessary for the analysis here.

[33] The Michigan finances and enrollment were taken from Mead, *op. cit.*, pp. 222 and 224; for 1840 and 1850 outlays per pupil were respectively $1.63 and $1.97. The Ohio data for 1839 and 1850 are for teachers' salaries per pupil and are to be found in *A History of Education in the State of Ohio*, pp. 446 and 449. The statistics are $1.54 and $1.50 at the two dates. North Carolina data refer to expenditures from the public funds which constituted the major source of support. Interest monies allocated for schools were $49,000 in 1841 and $161,000 in 1850 while enrollment more than quintupled. (E. W. Knight, *Public School Education in North Carolina*, Cambridge, Mass., 1916, p. 98.)

ment gain experienced in the Western and Southern states and, to a lesser extent, the Middle Atlantic. What is peculiar is the behavior in New England. Although already possessed of high attendance rates and enjoying a burst of industrial prosperity in the 1840's, that region too postponed more ample provision for education until the next decade.

The consequence was that educational expenditure during the 1850's grew much more rapidly than gross national product. Crudely, the income elasticity was 1.52, compared to a lesser 1.40 for the previous decade. Indeed, the relative pace of advance substantially overshadowed the gains accomplished in the last 30 years of the nineteenth century despite the simultaneous Southern educational recovery and improved quality of Northern education then.[34]

Here is another of the central, but unnoticed, features of the educational revolution that transpired before 1860. The greater outlays of the 1850's purchased substantially better education than had been available earlier; this is the purport of the increased expenditures per potential and actual pupil. Teachers' salaries everywhere experienced rapid rise; in turn, licensing requirements were much more honored by compliance than by breach. Especially helpful in this process of upgrading the professional status of teachers were the teachers' institutes that became widespread in the later 1840's and 1850's. These, like normal schools, were a direct outgrowth of the reform movement. By means of meetings lasting from one day to several, usually with outside lecturers, at least a modicum of pedagogical method was brought to the field, pending the ability of normal schools to meet the increased demand for skilled teachers. For prior to the Civil War the dozen existing institutions were quite unable to supply more than an insignificant fraction of current needs.

The increased expenditure of the decade reflected itself in a longer school year as well. This was particularly true in the West, where an extension of as much as 40 per cent was not unlikely. In Ohio and Wisconsin the gain was 40 per cent and more; by 1860 Illinois schools were open about seven months a year, longer than those in Pennsylvania and scarcely a month less than in Massachusetts. Even the latter state added a quarter of a month over this period.[35] Rising to the opportunities thus presented,

[34] Gross national product in current dollars was taken from Gallman, "Gross National Product . . ." The estimates of income elasticity are calculated simply as per cent change in educational expenditure divided by per cent change in national product. They are gross because other variables are excluded, and all change in expenditure is assumed proportional to income. From cross section data to be presented below, the calculated partial elasticities both for 1840 and 1860 are lower, as is not infrequent when the two alternative means of estimation are used; the elasticities at the mean then are close to, but less than, unity: in 1840 .79 and .78 in 1860.

[35] For the statistics cited on length of term, see the following: Wisconsin, *Tenth*

more ample curricula found their way into use; at the primary level, the traditional "3 R's" were supplemented by geography and grammar. Graded schools, and even public high schools became more than an oddity. During the period 1849–1860, 80 high schools were established in Massachusetts compared with 37 over the years from 1821 to 1848. Other New England states exhibited the same tendency, not to mention those of the West and New York.[36]

One of the important factors making for this advance in the 1850's was the return of prosperity to the West and South. Rapid prosecution of railways accelerated Western settlement and permitted commercial agriculture to prosper almost at once; continued high cotton prices and bumper crops created favorable conditions in the South. As can be seen from Table 3, Western and Southern aggregate expenditures climbed most rapidly. Note, however, that only in the West did per pupil outlays exhibit markedly faster rise than average. In this realm of quality improvement, the North Atlantic states participated as fully as the Southern. Much of this accomplishment was the logical consequence of the pioneering efforts of Horace Mann, Henry Barnard, and others. That should not be obscured, but it does little honor to those bold and far-seeing spirits to perpetuate in their behalf erroneous and exaggerated claims to fame.

Annual Report of the Common Schools (1858), 7; Ohio, *A History of Education*, p. 447, and *Twelfth Annual Report* (1860), 9; Illinois, *Fourth Biennial Report* (1862), 7; Massachusetts, *Twenty-fifth Annual Report of the Board of Education* (1862), 102, 104; Pennsylvania, see Wickersham, *op. cit.*, pp. 373, 549.

The additional observations supporting the contention of rapid increase in length of school year in the West are: for Indiana, R. G. Boone, *A History of Education in Indiana,* New York, 1892, p. 315, and Michigan, *Twenty-sixth Annual Report* (1862), 81.

[36] Data on New England secondary schools are conveniently compiled in E. D. Grizzell, *Origin and Development of the High School in New England Before 1865,* New York, 1923. For other regions one is forced to rely upon the extremely imperfect tabulation in the *Report of the U.S. Commissioner of Education for 1904,* II, pp. 1782–1789. This table purports to contain the data of establishment of high schools extant at the later date. The substantial variance with Grizzell for the New England states and with contemporary reports of others suggests that it is useful only for its rough indication of concentration of establishment and not for absolute quantities. As far as the former are concerned for New York and Ohio, the only other states besides Massachusetts with extensive public high school development before 1860, the results are as follows:

	Before 1840	1840–1849	1850–1860
New York	9	10	22
Ohio	0	5	37

III

The high degree of regional differentiation is one feature of the process of ante-bellum educational development that inevitably comes to the fore. In this section, in part through the use of cross section regression analysis, we extend the discussion to underscore two characteristics of this regionalism: the first is the persistence of such differences despite allowance for objective variables like income per capita and degree of urbanization; the second is the contrast between the rapidly merging identities of the North and West, and the continuing Southern inferiority in mass educational facilities.

Both observations are borne out by a simple comparison of regression equations explaining the enrollment rate in individual states for 1840 and 1860:[37]

$$\text{En Rt}_{1840} = 75.7 - 53.4S - 47.1W - 0.02Ur - 0.07Y/P \qquad R^2 = 0.74$$
$$\phantom{\text{En Rt}_{1840} = 75.7 -} (7.1) \quad\ \ (8.6) \qquad (.32) \qquad\ \ (.12)$$

$$\text{En Rt}_{1860} = 91.0 - 43.2S - \ \ 9.5W - 0.27Ur - 0.07Y/P \qquad R^2 = 0.71$$
$$\phantom{\text{En Rt}_{1860} = 91.0 -} (9.4) \quad\ \ (11.1) \qquad (.28) \qquad\ \ (.07)$$

In 1840 Western enrollment rates were on average 47.1 percentage points smaller than those in the East; in the South they were still lower, namely, by 53.4 percentage points. Both differences are statistically significant, whereas neither income per capital nor population density is. Indeed, the influence of the latter run in the wrong direction: greater population density and more income per capita reduce the enrollment rates.

Although the West and South in 1840 each shared the misfortune of lagging behind the East, it is useful to distinguish between them. In the former, the deficiency was a temporary phenomenon caused by tardy growth of educational facilities; in the latter, the difference was more persistent and symptomatic of a different educational philosophy. This dis-

---

[37] The independent variables are S, to indicate location in the South; W to reflect inclusion in the North Central region; Ur, percentage of urban population in the state, where urban includes places of 2500 inhabitants and above; and Y/P white income per capita. $N = 28$ in 1840, and 29 in 1860, and both relationships are statistically significant.

The income per capita estimates are based upon Richard A. Easterlin, "Interregional Differences in Per Capita Income, Population, and Total Income, 1840–1950," *Trends in the American Economy in the Nineteenth Century,* Vol. 24, of *Studies in Income and Wealth,* Princeton, 1960; and his "Regional Income Trends, 1840–1950," in Seymour Harris (Ed.), *American Economic History,* New York, 1961. For the South, slave income was estimated at $30 (maintenance), and the white per captia income calculated after this adjustment. For 1860, Gallman's national product estimates were distributed regionally by Easterlin's relatives; to obtain a state distribution, 1840 intraregional relatives were used. Other methods of distributing the regional income estimates were also tried, but with little difference to the final result.

tinction the 1860 results reflect. Although enrollment rates as a whole rose between the two dates, it was the West that achieved the truly spectacular gains. When basic enrollment had climbed from 28.6 per cent of school age population in 1840 to 81.5 per cent in 1860 the West as a whole could no longer be said to lag behind the Northern and Eastern states. What difference remains in 1860 is no longer statistically significant. The South, on the other hand—although also displaying enrollment gains, as we have seen earlier—was now the only region that stood apart with regional homogeneity and lower enrollment rates. Its advance was minimal. Even with the somewhat more favorable attendance statistics, less rapid Southern development and absolute inferiority remain—albeit with differences in levels some 10–15 per cent smaller.

The failure of income and urbanization to contribute to the explanation of enrollment rates before the Civil War is a consequence in part of an overlap between the regional and objective variables. Thus, the Western variable, in particular, corresponds to a significant step down in both income and urbanization from Eastern levels, and it is to such large differences that we might expect to find response.[38] When only the Southern regional indicator is introduced, therefore, both income and urbanization have the right sign, but still remain well below statistical acceptance levels. More fundamentally, however, state variations in enrollment were the consequence of a more complicated set of factors including nativity of population, structure of territorial or colonial laws, pace of settlement, and so forth, that are better represented by broad regional groupings than by the objective variables. *Within* the regions one can identify many of these same forces, as was noted above. Thus, the derivations from the 1840 regression equation in the West conform quite well with the divergent types of population bases: predicted enrollments for Ohio, Wisconsin, and Michigan fall short of the actual, whereas the reverse is true for Indiana, Illinois, and Iowa. However, by 1860, as a result of the flow of migration within the region and from the North, the differences among the states narrowed, and only Indiana, with its large Southern population, exhibited much deviation.

Yet, if the tale so far is one of Southern backwardness, the expenditure data place matters in a somewhat different perspective. Table 4 conveys some of the facts. Between 1840 and 1860 the relative amount of resources devoted to education doubled in the South, meanwhile actually *declining* in the North. From the standpoint of sacrifice, the region was

[38] The low per capita incomes in the West in 1840 may understate the higher real incomes due to low food prices attained within the region. Cincinnati, Charleston and New York prices were used to deflate the money incomes for geographic price variation, but without perceptible difference in the final results.

no laggard at all. This munificence was reflected in more ample provision per pupil. The cross-sectional analysis illustrates this well:

$$Ex/pupil_{1840} = -1.92 + 7.94S + 0.86W + 0.06Ur + 0.064Y/P$$
$$\qquad\qquad\quad (2.41) \quad (2.92) \quad\;\; (.11) \qquad\;\; (.04)$$
$$R^2 = 0.54$$

$$Ex/pupil_{1860} = -6.71 + 7.26S + 4.51W - 0.1Ur + 0.07Y/P$$
$$\qquad\qquad\quad (1.41) \quad (1.66) \quad\;\; (.04) \qquad (.01)$$
$$R^2 = 0.83$$

In both 1840 and 1860 Southern expenditures per student—apart from variations in per capita income and urbanization—were significantly greater than in any other area. In part this higher outlay is a reflection of the "elite" structure of Southern education, resulting in relatively larger academy and college attendance, both of which were more expensive; but in large measure it also derives from either a quality differential or cost disadvantage that prevailed at the level of the common school.[39] Both in 1850 and 1860 the South Central and South Atlantic regions ranked first and second respectively in expenditure per elementary student. Despite this apparent impressive showing, the *changes* between 1840 and 1860 are revealing about the process of ante-bellum educational development. First, the initial Southern advantage relative to the West was considerably eroded over the twenty-year period, virtually disappearing by the end; indeed, as Table 4 shows, the West exhibited the largest gain in expenditures and spent relatively more for education than any other region in 1860. Second, the 1840 expenditure gap between South and North of $6.02 per pupil gave way to one of only 55 cents in 1860. Accompanying this shift, income itself became a more cogent determining factor, and the South was destined to fall behind other regions in this regard—particularly after the Civil War.

Nonetheless, the fact of the matter is that the South was by no means unable to develop a respectable surplus for education before the Civil War. The abundance carried over even to the provision for potential students: the South in 1850 had more to spend per person aged 5 to 19, free *and* slave, than the West, and although by 1860 this was no longer true, the region was not grievously disadvantaged even then. Still, it never attained

[39] It is impossible to choose among these alternatives from the data themselves. All they do is establish the fact of Southern schools with many fewer pupils than in the rest of the country. This could involve diseconomies of scale, or better, more personal guidance. Qualitative descriptions tend to refute the latter hypothesis, however.

TABLE 4. Regional Educational Expenditures

	1840			1860		
Region	Educational Expenditures (Mill. of Dollars)	Gross Product	Expenditures as Percentage of Product	Educational Expenditures (Mill. of Dollars)	Gross Product	Expenditures as Percentage of Product
New England	2.7	267	1.0	4.4	594	0.7
Middle Atlantic[a]	3.4	644	0.5	9.9	1526	0.6
South Atlantic[b]	1.1	220	0.5	3.7	382	1.0
North Central	0.9	204	0.4	10.0	888	1.1
South Central	1.0	236	0.4	5.6	721	0.8
Total	9.2	1570	0.6	34.7	4240	0.8

[a] includes Delaware and Maryland

[b] excludes Delaware, Maryland, and District of Columbia

Source: Expenditures, see Table 3; Gross Product, see Gross national product estimates of Robert E. Gallman, allocated regionally using percentages developed by Richard Easterlin, in Harris (ed.), *American Economic History*, p. 535.

the high degree of popular education, even for its white population, that so indelibly marked the period. The universality of slavery and the plantation system is frequently cited as an explanation for the aristocratic Southern mentality. It is interesting to note, however, that the evidence for such an interpretation is almost exclusively limited to the observed differences between free and slave states. There appears to be, within the South as a whole, and even within individual states, no correlation between white school attendance and the prevalence or absence of large slaveholdings. Thus, for 1850 the rank correlation between state attendance ratios and the inverse of the slave ratio amounted only to +0.37, not significantly different from zero; after a further decade of educational advance—particularly noticeable in the plantation states—the relationship was diminished to +0.25. Samples of counties drawn from Virginia, Alabama, and South Carolina affirm the same lack of association within industrial states.

These findings do not preclude an important and adverse effect of that peculiar institution. The consequence of slavery may be independent of variations in its magnitude, just as enrollment differentials were partially conditioned by income, but not in a systematic fashion. Still, coupled with the generous regional expenditure, such a result reinforces the obvious necessity for more careful study of the extent and timing of the dissemination of education within the South. Indeed, more generally, this brief analysis of inter-regional differences perhaps best points up again the limited insights the traditional emphasis upon the reform movement of the 1840's is able to provide. Concentration upon New England is to miss the rapid change under way in the West and to fail to question the relative decline of the South.

IV

The Census enrollment and expenditure data, however useful for delimiting the outlines of educational history before the Civil War, fail to measure accurately all the dimensions of educational activity. In particular, they tell us nothing about average daily attendance or length of school year, both of which are vital to any assessment of the extent of the educational enterprise. In this section, therefore, we go beyond the confines of the Census material to extend the analysis to a measure of the number of days of school attended by each eligible member of the population. This statistic not only has the virtue of summarizing the three components of enrollment, average daily attendance, and the length of school year but also is directly comparable with later nineteenth and twentieth century measures.

Table 5 sets out the requisite information. For the Northern and Western states the material has been assembled from state reports either

TABLE 5. Educational Level, Public Facilities, 1861

Region	Enrollment Rate	Average Daily Attendance Rate	Average Length of School	Number of Days of School per White Person 5–19
	(Percentage)		(Days)	$(1) \times (2) \times (3)$
New England	62.8	74.9	135	63.5
Middle Atlantic	61.4	53.0	157	51.1
North Central	75.9	56.7	116	49.9
South	29.5	45.0	80	10.6
Total	57.4	56.2	124	40.3

Sources: For New England, Middle Atlantic, and North Central: State Reports, both directly and as reprinted in the *National Almanac*, 1863 and 1864; many small adjustments not worth reporting here were necessary. For the South: enrollment, see Table 1; average daily attendance and length of school, see text. Total: Cols. 1 and 4 weighted by size of regional populations, Col. 2 weighted by size of regional enrollment 5–19, Col. 3 weighted by size of regional average daily attendance.

directly or as reprinted in the *National Almanac*. For the South equivalent precision is impossible. It is fair to say, however, that the values selected for the region do not overstate the educational achievement, nor do reasonable variations much influence the final result.[40] If the South were presumed to have zero entries, the national total days attendance per white person ages 5–19 would drop from the tabulated 40.3 only to 37.3. Accordingly, we need not be overanxious concening the accuracy of the Southern entries.

These two months of actual school participation in 1861 refer only to public schools and do not allow for the substantial number of Southern Negroes growing up in ignorance. Both factors adjusted almost perfectly offset each other and produce a final statistic of approximately 40.2 days for all educational facilities and for members of the school age population.[41] Such a level is substantially above the 31+ days posited by late nineteenth century Commissioners of Education and requires a more favorable view of educational pursuits on the eve of the Civil War than seems to be widely held.[42]

The same observation applies equally well to the entire ante-bellum era. Extrapolation back from the 1861 bench mark implies an 1850 level

[40] Thus the enrollment rate selected is for common schools, and is taken from the Census of Schools, which for the South may mean an understatement of upwards of 20 per cent. The average daily attendance figure is selected on the basis of virtually no information. Yet in 1869, in the midst of the chaos, the rate was above this low level in all states reporting. The length of school depends upon the reported 4 months availability in North Carolina, the 59 days for the pauper schools of Virginia, and the observation of the *Compendium of the Seventh Census* that "the average annual time of attendance at school of each child is much larger in the Southern than in the Northern States . . ." (p. 149). Without giving full credence to this assertion, some allowance seems appropriate.

[41] The adjustment to accommodate slaves was made by using the ratio of slaves in the South to white population (0.55) to reduce the Southern enrollment rate proportionately. This also increases the relative weight of the Southern school age population and affects the national total in this fashion as well. The national enrollment rate is reduced from 57.4 per cent to 49.6 per cent, and the number of days of school for each person to 34.8. Note, however, that the average daily attendance rates and length of school day, because they are weighted by enrollments and attendance rates respectively, are unaffected.

To increase the scope of coverage of public (or in the South, common school) facilities to a comprehension of total education, the 1870 ratio between the number of days attended in both categories was used. This procedure may understate the pre-Civil War results, owing to the greater strength of private academies at the earlier date; the alternative was to assess the average daily attendance rates and length of school year for such facilities earlier. Although some distortion may be introduced, it is a relatively minor matter.

[42] The Commissioner's 434 days' total education in 1860 is based on multiplication by 13 of 33.4 days attended in 1860 by the population ages, 5–18. To make

of 26 days, 20 in 1840 and 14 as early as 1800.[43] The comparable Commissioner's series is 30, 15, and 6 days. Only in 1850 does the quasiofficial estimate exceed our own, and that by virtue of the educational gain presumed to be concentrated in the 1840's. In fact, the rate of growth of schooling in the eligible population emerges as slightly greater between 1850 and 1861 than in the decade 1840–1850 in the estimates presented here. This result takes cognizance of the increasing length of school year in the 1850's to compensate for lesser gains in enrollment. Reliance upon the common school revival, by exclusion of the drastic changes in the West and South, fails adequately to explain the educational gains of the 1840's: the consequences of the reform emerged only a full decade later when more abundant financial provision permitted substantial quality improvement.

Such a reappraisal of the extent of early educational facilities increases their potential role as a factor in nineteenth century economic growth. Accordingly, I must partially dissent from the recent view expressed by Stanley Lebergott:

It is a fair inference, therefore, that from 1800 to 1870 formal education per person in the U.S. labor force came to less than 2 months a year during their years of schooling. Nor could it have risen much above 3 months prior to 1900. It is scarcely likely, therefore, that the quantity of schooling compensated for limitations on its quality. Taken together they do not suggest that formal education was anything like a significant factor in raising the quality of the American labor force, or in stimulating economic growth.[44]

The absolute levels of education are correct; indeed, much too generous for the earlier years. Yet, is it not appropriate to remember that currently the standard is not much above six months? A factor of increase of three, separated a century apart in American development, is by no means great.

Nor does Lebergott take cognizance of the substantial growth in educational opportunity over the course of the century. The generation at-

---

the statistic comparable with our own, based upon a larger population, 5–19, the 434 days were divided by 14. This distorts the Commissioner's estimate slightly since the population aged 19 is somewhat smaller than that found in preceding ages: hence the 31+. The same qualification extends to the other statistics of the Commissioner quoted. It is not an important matter.

[43] These estimates were obtained by extrapolation upon enrollment rates. The 1850 figure is based on the assumption that length of school year and average daily attendance increased in sum between 1850 and 1861 the same 19 per cent that enrollment did. The 1840 figures assumes constancy of length of school year and average daily attendance at their 1850 level. The 1800 estimate continues to maintain constancy in these factors, but involves a 30 per cent decline in enrollment below its 1840 rate.

[44] These remarks come from his paper, "Labor Force and Employment, 1800–1960," to appear in Vol. 30 of *Studies in Income and Wealth*.

tending school in 1800 received but 14 days a year education on average, or a life total of perhaps 210. In 1900 the comparable levels were 70 and 1050 days. Whether the criterion be absolute or relative increase, the nineteenth century exceeds the first half of the twentieth. Another way of portraying this evolution is to consider the educational level of the population in 1860 and in 1900. At the former date, persons above age 14 had attained an average of 2.06 years of schooling of 1940 length; at the latter, the sum had increased to 4.96.[45] Such a gain exceeds the equivalent increment between 1930 and 1950, a period over which quality appreciation in the labor force due to education apparently figured substantially in national growth. Although it is not our intention to prejudice the results of future research, it appears that education will have to be reckoned as a considerable factor in nineteenth century economic development.

V

The analysis of the historical consequences of American educational investment is still in its infancy. Before it can proceed in any fruitful fashion, the facts surrounding the evolution of formal education must be clarified. That has been the intent of this paper for the ante-bellum period.

Although further research may qualify certain of these particulars, it is unlikely to alter the general conclusion that the common school revival has served as the wrong focal point for interpretation of that era. The movement for free schools was a fact, but that does not make it the transcendent feature of some six decades of educational experience. American efforts prior to the first such stirrings in the 1830's were exceptional by contemporary standards. When the great advance in enrollment rates occurred between 1840 and 1850 it was as much, or more, the result of independent forces making for educational diffusion in the South and West. Only in the subsequent decade were the ambitious ideals of the reformers more closely realized, and this both qualitative accounts and quantitative measures have obscured.

There are many features of this early educational development that need clarification. Particularly obscure are the factors underlying rapid Southern advance in the 1840's and the subsequent disappointing performance of the 1850's. Again, there is the timing of the increased educational

---

[45] These are preliminary estimates obtained by summing up the apparent lifetime education of cohorts a decade apart. Note that the 1900 estimate slightly exceeds T. W. Schultz's comparable statistic of 4.14. This may be due to insufficient allowance for the educational gain between 1850 and 1900. Schultz's principal source, Clarence Long, says : ". . . the standard of education changed relatively little between 1850 and 1890 . . . ," whereas our data suggest a more than doubling of level. (T. W. Schultz, in Henry (Ed.), *op. cit.,* pp. 64–73; Clarence D. Long, *The Labor Force Under Changing Income and Employment,* Princeton, 1958, p. 420.)

outlays of that latter decade. What does seem certain, however, is that Americans had attained a substantial gain in educational facilities in the two decades before the Civil War, an accomplishment not to be overlooked in examining subsequent economic growth.

APPENDIX: Some Remarks on Ante-Bellum Educational Statistics

A few comments upon the reliability of the Census data perhaps are in order. This is the more so in view of the official critique of the Census of 1840 by the American Statistical Association, published as Senate Document No. 5, 28th Congress, 2nd Session. Their conclusion that "the errors in regard to the common schools are the most striking" cannot be denied. Yet those errors primarily relate to the ambiguity of the category of "scholars at public charge," and the consequent inability to use it as a measure of public education at that date. Thus, in the state of Ohio, only a small fraction of pupils were so reported despite the universality of public facilities. A second valid objection is the reported excess of those at public charge over total number of students in a number of counties; this should have been impossible since the former is a subgroup of the latter. While conceding the implication of carelessness we should at the same time point out that the error it leads to in the aggregate enrollment ratio is only slightly in excess of 1 per cent! In Ohio, where the largest deviation is to be found, the understatement is less than 5 per cent. Such an approximation is in fact quite respectable, and it was both unnecessary and unwise to adjust the reported totals.

For all three Census dates it was possible to test the tabulated results against the independent State Reports of Massachusetts, New York, Pennsylvania, Ohio, and Michigan; North Carolina was entered with the later data as the only Southern state for which data could be obtained. These states account for some 50 per cent of common school attendance.

The comparison of enrollments is as follows:

	State Reports			Census of Schools		
	1840	1850	1860	1840	1850	1860
Massachusetts	136,788	185,374	212,637	160,257	176,475	206,974
New York	603,583	800,430	867,388	502,367	675,221	697,283
Pennsylvania	205,105	469,344[c]	645,669[c]	179,989	413,706	565,303
Ohio	254,612[a]	421,733	685,177	218,609	484,153	590,549
Michigan	51,245[b]	110,478	192,937	29,701	110,455	201,391
North Carolina			105,048			105,025

[a] 1839

[b] 1841

[c] original estimates exclusive of Philadelphia; adjusted upwards by 45,000 in 1850 and 60,000 in 1860 to measure total state.

In absolute terms, the Census tends to be somewhat low—but seriously only in New York; for all states together, the margin of difference is only about 10 per cent. This understatement may well reflect reports to the Census of a previous year's results since correct knowledge of current enrollment was necessarily lagged. Moreover, the relative change between the three dates is only moderately affected; the alternative percentage rates of growth (excluding Michigan in the first decade) between 1840 and 1860 are: Census, 100.5; State Reports, 104.9; between 1840 and 1850; 64.9 and 56.4; between 1850 and 1860: 31.0 and 21.6. Impressions of overall change, as well as its distribution between decades, are consistent between the two different sets of data, as are the rankings of the individual states. Acordingly, since it was desirable to retain consistency among states and regions, and because the State Reports themselves are neither entirely available nor without their own inaccuracies, the Census data were to be preferred.

Another check upon the Census of Schools in 1850 and 1860 derives from the returns to the independent query relating to school attendance found in the Census of Population in the same years. Nationally, the totals are some 10 per cent different in 1850, and still closer in 1860. The only region showing substantial deviation is the South, and for reasons quite understandable. This area possessed the least developed school system in the country, and education in private homes or schools of short duration easily were missed. In all of the discussion, this possible understatement of Southern education in the Census of Schools is taken into consideration.

The same general level of accuracy obtains for the income data as well. For the identical states treated above, expenditures reckoned from the State Reports are within a margin of -7 per cent in 1850, and $+8$ per cent in 1860. Given the basic differences between the income and expenditure approaches, as well as the difficulties of comparable coverage—particularly since they involve inclusion of capital outlays, such a small error, if it is one, is reassuring. Note moreover, that its effect is to diminish the rate of growth of outlays between 1850 and 1860 and thus only to reinforce the point made in discussion concerning the spurt of that decade.

Although a state by state review of the Census statistics before the Civil War undoubtedly would lead to many individual changes, for most purposes they seem to suffice in their present form. Specifically, their reliability is such that they support the analysis to which they are subjected here.

NO SAFETY IN NUMBERS:
SOME PITFALLS
OF HISTORICAL STATISTICS

Goran Ohlin
Development Center, OECD, Paris

Il est plus d'hommes qui savent calculer que raisonner.—Moheau, *Recherches et considerations sur la population de la France* (1778).

Nur in Ermanglung der Gewissheit gebrauchen wir die Wahrscheinlich-keit. Wenn wir zwar eine Tatsache nicht vollkommen kennen, wohl aber etwas *über ihre Form wissen.*—Wittgenstein, *Tractatus logico-philosophicus.*

In 1864, Quetelet published a paper *Sur les Indiens O-Jib-Be-Wa's et les proportions de leur corps* in which he concluded that their bodily propor-tions were almost exactly the same as those of Europeans.[1] This paper, one finds, was based on the study of a party of twelve Indians visiting Brussels, who had generously allowed themselves to be measured by him. A slender basis for inference, but social historians attempting to recon-struct the prestatistical past must, like Quetelet, squeeze information out of whatever evidence comes their way.

Fortunately, the processes of government and economic activity slough off a prodigious amount of material that can be used for statistical purposes, and many of the classical contributions to economic history have been based precisely on the compilation of statistics from institutional records, tax lists, and the like. As some innovators in the field of historical statistics have remarked, the enormous effort required to deal with data on a large scale has kept many such sources—and precisely the richest ones—from being used.[2] Here, as in so many other fields, the new tech-nology of electronic data processing has opened up a new era.

There is not always, however, an abundance of data awaiting their interpreter. Especially in preindustrial times, the problem facing the his-torical statistician is more likely to be that his samples are small, far from random, and perhaps only remotely related to what he is really interested in. The pseudostatistics compiled for purposes of primitive administration

---

[1] Joseph Lottin, *Quetelet, Statisticien et Sociologue,* Louvain and Paris, 1912, p. 176.

[2] Lance Davis et al., "Aspects of Quantitative Research in Economic History," *Journal of Economic History,* XX (1960), 542.

he can use only at his peril; the enumerations are deficient, errors of copy-ing, reporting, and arithmetic abound, and we may not even know what was being enumerated, as in the case of rolls of "adults."

Those who distrust historical statistics are right in doing so, but they would be wrong in rejecting them. In fact, any understanding of statistical information is founded on distrust, and the classical problem of statistics is that of making valid inferences from observations that are known to be poor. To abandon the scraps of quantitative insight into the past merely on the grounds of general suspicion would be as foolish as to regard them as wholly accurate.

The question at all times must be how great the uncertainty is and how seriously it affects the conclusions at stake. In the statistical, as in any empirical study of the world, "a reasonable probability is the only certainty." This is the problem to which the theory of statistical inference addresses itself; it can provide procedures for estimation and for the testing of hypotheses. Sometimes the application of such standard procedures to historical statistics serves little purpose, since the principal sources of error are not likely to be random and cancel out obligingly. Apart from that problem, however, these procedures do not in themselves tell us what con-stitutes a "reasonable probability." The modern theory of statistical deci-sion-making attempts to provide a rational criterion by assuming that the acceptance or rejection of a hypothesis leads to actions of consequence. Statistical inferences should then be made in a way that takes into account the gain from being right and the loss from being wrong.

Such rational action is not always easy, least of all in historical sta-tistical work. One naturally wishes to be as accurate as possible, to come close to the truth, but what are the consequences of being wrong? As long as one is inclined to regard it as a gain to have a statistical picture of the past at all, the dangers of being wrong seem small. Thus, little attention is usually paid in historical statistics to what the data themselves suggest about degrees of uncertainty, ranges of confidence, and levels of significance.

When systematic error is likely to be very great, classical statistical tests do not suffice. The tests of historical statistics must then be tests of consistency, compatibility, and common sense, with all the knowledge available brought into play. Population history furnishes many illustrations. For instance, enumerations, always incomplete, may really give more accu-rate clues about age structure and social composition than about total pop-ulation; growth or decline indicated by a series of censuses may be subject to internal checks which can be surmized if the censuses provide a break-down by age, for the survival of different age groups over, for example, a decade could not be entirely random. (Due account must of course be taken of known migration and other external factors.)

The more fragmentary the evidence itself, the more important the role of outside knowledge brought to bear on the problem. Thus, to take an example, the information on ages at death on Roman tombstones may constitute a fairly sizable sample, but it is evidently and for obvious reasons not representative even of the social groups that rated such honors; infants and children are absent or underrepresented. Only by analyzing this material against the background of what is known about mortality as a function of age in a great variety of human populations is it possible to put this evidence into proper perspective and draw any conclusions from it.[3]

In the following some other contributions to statistical population history will be scrutinized, partly as an attempt to revise them, partly to demonstrate some of the problems of uncertainty and plausibility in historical statistics.

J. C. RUSSELL'S MEDIEVAL DEMOGRAPHY

The Life Tables

Josiah Cox Russell's *British Medieval Population* (1948), which represented an ambitious inventory of English demographic conditions between 1086 and 1545, was based on a wide range of materials, many previously unused for such purposes. Among other things, Russell submitted detailed life tables purporting to represent the course of mortality in England between the thirteenth and fifteenth centuries. Historians, innocent of technical demography, were bound to seize on these calculations with pleasure and relief, and Russell's figures have been widely cited.[4] Precisely for this reason it is necessary to point out that they are not only afflicted with the uncertainties that beset all statistics but actually contain such curious elements of speculation and guesswork that they must regretfully be dismissed altogether.

However, a second reason to reconsider Russell's work is that his sources for the study of English mortality are of undisputable interest. The inquisitions post mortem on which this part of his work was based, state the date of death for owners of property as well as the age of the heir. They do not give the *age* at death, which can only be ascertained by the combination of two inquests, the first giving the date and the age of the heir, the second the subsequent date of his (or her) death.

The major difficulty lies in combining the documents properly. The

[3] John Durand, "Mortality Estimates from Roman Tombstone Inscriptions," *American Journal of Sociology,* LXV (1959–1960), 365–373.

[4] To take only one example, Arthur E. R. Boak in *Manpower Shortage and the Fall of the Roman Empire in the West,* Ann Arbor, 1955, assumes that Russell managed to calculate medieval life expectancy at birth "with reasonable certainty" and cites his figures to the second decimal (p. 11).

permanent surname was not yet established, and spelling vacillated among English, Norman, and arbitrary variants. The large material that emerged from Russell's painstaking labor is so far unique in its kind. It is of course drawn from propertied classes, although not so limited as are the records of the peerage. The class limitation alone suggests that one should approach it with caution, but there is some other evidence to suggest that the mortality of adults in the Middle Ages was not strongly affected by economic or social status. In any case, Russell's data should give an indication of minimum levels of mortality.

With the data derived from the inquisitions post mortem one could in principle proceed in two different directions. The first would be simply to note how many years an heir survived after his appearance in the records. This would provide direct observation of remaining life and thus of life expectation at the age when the heir was first recorded. As a matter of statistical procedure, however, it is advisable to take another path and compare the number of heirs known to have survived to a certain age with the numbers who died within a subsequent period of time, such as five years. In this way Russell calculated age-specific risks of mortality from which a life table could be constructed. From the inquests we learn nothing about infant and child mortality, but it is possible to estimate the expectation of life at some later age. Russell guessed at infant mortality and then completed generational life tables for eight different groups of English male heirs (Table 1).

The smallest group contains 343, the largest, 532 deaths; since all cases entered the samples only at the time of inheritance, there are rather few observations in young and old age brackets, and the sampling error is likely to be substantial. The standard deviations for the life expectancies at age 15 in Table 1 can be computed on the basis of Russell's material and turn out to be of the magnitude of 1.2–1.3 years, which is enough to deprive the minor variations of statistical significance. However, the broad contours of the table are not likely to be due to sampling error but —as we expected—to the plague.[5]

The age-specific mortality rates for the different generations can also be subjected to chi-square tests to decide whether they are actually significantly different. The chi-square test in this case posits hypothetically that the true death rates of the different generations were identical and aims to decide how likely it is that samples of the sizes actually drawn would show the observed discrepancies merely as the result of chance. It then appears that the variations for individual age groups could easily be due to chance in most cases, but the patterns as a whole seem to vary

[5] For the method of computing standard deviations for estimates of life expectancy, see Edwin B. Wilson, "The Standard Deviation of Sampling for Life Expectancy," *Journal of the American Statistical Association,* XXXIII (1938), 705–708.

TABLE 1. Life Expectation for English Male Heirs at Birth and at 15,
According to Russell

	Expectation of Life at:	
Generation Born	Birth	Age 15
Before 1276	35.3 years	32.7 years
1276–1300	31.3	28.6
1301–1325	29.8	26.8
1328–1348	30.2	25.1
1348–1375	17.3	25.2
1376–1400	20.5	22.9
1401–1425	23.8	29.4
1426–1450	32.8	30.9

Source: *British Medieval Population*, 1948, p. 186. To
take account of the plague, a dividing line was drawn at
1348 rather than at the end of 1350.

in a significant way. The plague hit different generations in different por-
tions of their life span, as shown in a comparison of the generations born
in 1276–1300 and 1348–1375. (Table 2). The generation of 1348–1375
was exposed to great hazards in its early years, and that of 1276–1300
only when its youngest members were close to 50. Thus, the change in
sign in Table 2. For ages below 25 and over 50, chi-square suggests that
the differences are significant, but that between 25 and 50 when neither
generation was exposed to the worst of the plague, the differences are
too small to be taken seriously. There would be a greater than even chance
for sampling errors alone to produce the small discrepancies in those age
groups.[6]

To distinguish the mortality in the period known to have been most
plague-ridden from that before and after, one may reorganize the material.
Instead of generational life tables one wishes to have tables that measure
the mortality in a given period. From the generation born in 1301–1325,
we might thus take the deaths of those between 50 and 55 which occurred
in the years 1351–1379 when the plague struck repeatedly. However, the
assignment of the age groups to the plague is not always obvious or precise.
Out of the same generation, for instance, those who died between 30 and

[6] Chi-square for the first four groups is 9.8, which with four degrees of freedom
suggests that the difference is significant on the 2 per cent level. Above the age of
50, chi-square for eight age groups is 18.1 and the difference is significant on the
same level. For the six age groups in between, chi-square is 5.2, and P over 50
per cent.

TABLE 2. Life-Table Mortality Rates for Males born in 1276–1300
and 1348–1375 (Per Thousand)

Age	Born 1276–1300	Born 1348–1375	Difference	Chi-square
5– 9	44	130	86	1.26
10–14	47	184	137	4.61
15–19	57	141	84	3.90
20–24	126	158	32	0.58
25–29	137	167	30	0.65
30–34	110	114	4	0.16
35–39	127	174	47	1.91
40–44	184	192	8	0.04
45–49	167	224	57	1.82
50–54	250	185	−65	1.78
55–59	257	147	−90	2.95
60–64	439	227	−212	9.85
65–69	394	371	−23	0.08
70–74	450	523	73	0.45
75–79	696	476	−220	2.27
80–84	714	636	−78	0.12
85–89	1000	750	−250	0.60
				33.63

35 died in the period 1331–1359, the first half of which was free from plague whereas the second includes the Black Death itself. If the material were more extensive, the groups with such mixed experiences could have been left out of account, but in the circumstances it seems best to assign the age groups from the various generations to three different periods depending on whether the majority of the deaths fell in the period 1348–1400, or earlier, or later.[7]

The result is shown in Table 3. For age groups under 15, the rates are erratic, and even the rates for 15–19 look suspicious, but between 25 and 50 where the samples are largest, the excess mortality of the second half of the fourteenth century is very marked. A chi-square test shows that the differences from the patterns of the other two periods (for age groups 15–19 and above) are significant on the 0.1 and 1 per cent levels respectively. The same test also indicates that the pre-plague and post-

[7] To illustrate, the average birth date for the generation of 1301–1325 is assumed to have been mid-1312; more than half the deaths that occurred between 30 and 35 would therefore have occurred before 1348. This method, to be sure, takes no account of the fact that the plague did not leave deaths evenly spaced, but systematic differences in mortality should nevertheless appear.

TABLE 3. Life-Table Mortality Rates ($5^q x$) for 1250–1348,
1348–1400, and 1401–1500 (Per Thousand)

Age	1250–1348	1348–1400	1401–1500	Middle Group Drawn from Generations Born
5– 9	21	96	13	1348–1400
10–14	29	134	111	1326–1400
15–19	39	113	129	1326–1375
20–24	100	161	150	"
25–29	128	181	137	"
30–34	95	133	110	"
35–39	140	190	143	1301–1375
40–44	163	192	141	1301–1348
45–49	153	216	183	"
50–54	240	247	181	"
55–59	284	252	247	"
60–64	337	356	273	1276–1348
65–69	420	406	354	1276–1325
70–74	493	443	455	"
75–79	514	645	576	"
80–84	647	625	643	"

plague patterns are significantly different. As the table shows, mortality after the plague seems to have been higher than before the plague for age groups up to 30, and lower for those over 50, whereas the rates criss-cross in the middle range. It would be rash to infer that this pattern has a meaning, but it is at least compatible with the assumption that mortality was rising in the fourteenth century before the plague—since this would raise the pre-plague curve in the higher age brackets—and declined only gradually in the fifteenth century. This would produce a lingering effect of the kind we have tried to eliminate by constructing nongenerational life tables.

Life expectation at 15 was several years lower in the plague periods than in the others (Table 4), and it also seems to have been lower in the fifteenth century than before the plague. Since we know that the plague did not vanish, this is in line with expectations. The standard deviations for these life expectancies are of the order of 0.7 years, from which we may assume that there is only a fairly small chance that the difference between 27.2 years (1401–1500) and 30.3 years (1250–1348) is due to sampling error. On the other hand, inspection of the rates in Table 3 shows that the drop is due almost entirely to the excess mortality in the groups between 15 and 24, and the pre-plague rates for the age group 15–19 look spurious. In fact, life expectancy at 25 was about the same

TABLE 4. Life Expectation at 15 and 25

Approximate Period	At 15	At 25
1250–1348	30.3 years	24.5 years
1348–1400	24.3	20.9
1401–1500	27.2	24.6

for both periods, and we cannot really say, then, that the material demonstrates that the fifteenth century was unhealthier than the thirteenth and early fourteenth.

Infant Mortality and Life Expectation at Birth

Russell made up hypothetical schedules for mortality in the first year of life, and between the ages of 1 and 4.[8] "Remembering the good economic conditions of thirteenth century England," he said, "it would seem that for the period before 1276 a mortality rate somewhat better than that of either China or India might be assumed."[9] He thought infant mortality might have increased gradually, reaching a peak with the Black Death, and then subsided, as in the following schedule:

Before 1276	140	1348–1375	300
1276–1300	150	1376–1400	260
1301–1325	160	1401–1425	200
1326–1348	170	1426–1450	140

The first thing to be said about this is that it is sheer speculation, and the next that it is also bad speculation. It is only necessary to consider infant mortality rates at various times and places to realize how unlikely it is that infant mortality could have been as low as 140 in the thirteenth and fifteenth centuries, even among fairly privileged groups. This would be even lower than the 165 computed for the English royal family between the eleventh and sixteenth centuries. As late as the last decade of the nineteenth century, Norway, Sweden, Scotland, and Denmark were the

[8] Almost all his tables suffer from mistakes in the calculation of the number of years lived in these intervals. The formula he used between one and four should be

$$l^L4 = 0.034\ l_0 - 1.184\ l_1 - 2.782\ l_5$$

and was used in that form in his Table 8.2. But the formula was misquoted with the first coefficient as 0.34 (p. 178) and this is the form in which it was used in the other tables. Similarly the separation factors used to estimate $_0L_1$ are actually not what they are claimed to be (0.8 and 0.2), but 0.812 and 0.208 which does not add up to unity. The resulting error is trifling but not confidence-inspiring.

[9] Josiah Cox Russell, *British Medieval Population*, Albuquerque, 1948, pp. 262–263.

only European countries that had reached such a level; in Western Europe infant mortality rates were generally between 150 and 200, and in Eastern Europe and Russia they were closer to 250.

A vague impression of social conditions is no help here. It is tempting, however, to explore the hypothesis that infancy and childhood mortality are sufficiently well correlated with mortality in higher age groups to make possible a statement about the former on the basis of the latter. This is the assumption underlying the United Nations model life-tables, which were used by Durand to estimate Roman life expectancy in the study cited earlier. The life expectations at 15 in Table 4 would actually then imply that infant mortality rates were already above 300 per thousand in the pre-plague period, and the model life-tables would suggest the following expectations at birth:

Approx. 1250–1348	21 years
1348–1400	14
1401–1500	17

These expected lives are as short as those Durand thought were indicated for the Roman Empire, but since he used essentially the same procedure this only means that adult mortality seems to have been much the same according to Roman tombstones and to English inquests in the Middle Ages.

The unpleasant fact, however, is that the correlation between infant and adult mortality is quite weak. In recorded demographic history it is easy to find instances of different societies with comparable mortality rates for adults but with infant mortality rates differing anywhere between a range of, for example, 150–350. Such a range corresponds to a difference of more than ten years in the life expectancy at birth, even if life expectancy at 15 is identical.

This is a range of uncertainty amounting to virtual ignorance. Infant mortality in British royal families and among the children of English ducal families studied by Hollingsworth was actually a good deal lower in relation to their adult mortality rates than predicted by the United Nations life-tables, which are based on modern evidence from high-mortality societies. Their life expectancy at 15 was of the same magnitude as that of Russell's heirs, and the life expectancy at birth of sons of dukes in the generation 1330–1479 was 24.0. Violent death, however, took a savage toll in the feudality, and, if it is disregarded, their expected lives were all of 31.0 years.[10]

---

[10] T. H. Hollingsworth, "A Demographic Study of the British Ducal Families," *Population Studies,* XI (1957), 8–9. Life expectations at 15 are given only for the generation of 1480–1679, but at age 20, the expectations for males born in 1330–1479 were 21.7 years; excluding violent deaths, they were 31.5 years.

In their adult years, the subjects in Russell's samples seem to have lived rather longer than the sons of dukes, but their infant and childhood mortality is unlikely to have been so low; the same must hold a fortiori for the population at large.

In the end, then, we cannot say much about the actual length of life in medieval England on the basis of the Russell material. If infant mortality was somewhere around 250, except in the most disturbed plague period, life expectation at birth would have been in the neighborhood of 25 years. Yet we cannot with any confidence say more than that it is likely to have fallen within the range of perhaps 22–28 years, and it might well have been lower.

The Black Death

Even if there is very little to be said about the absolute level of mortality, it may be possible to draw some pertinent conclusions about the excess mortality caused by the plague. In the absence of direct information about the losses of English population in the Black Death and the following epidemics, evidence on mortality assumes a special interest.

As we have seen, the expectation of life in the second half of the fourteenth century may have been some five or six years shorter than previously. This suggests something about the magnitudes involved, for it implies that the average death rate in that period was 7–16 points higher. If we disregard the problems of a changing age composition and assume that there was no change in the average birth rate over the period, the population shows a decline of 30–55 per cent by the end of the century.

Actually, the plague did not raise mortality gradually. It is true that it became endemic towards the end of the century, especially in the towns where it lingered for centuries. In *Piers Plowman* it was compared to the steady drizzle of the rain coming in through a leaky roof, and it must have contributed to mortality in the early fifteenth century—before 1450, Parliament was adjourned or moved four times for fear of it.[11] Yet, as we have seen in the preceding section, judging from Russell's material, this effect was slight. Demographically, it seems to have been the explosive outbursts of the plague in the fourteenth century that really mattered. Russell was able to present some extremely interesting evidence on the fatalities among property-holding heirs in the four most important attacks.

The Black Death of 1348–1349 was followed by a "second pestilence" in 1360–1361, and then by a third and fourth in 1369 and 1375. For each of these, Russell analyzed the impact on different age groups, and he also tried to estimate their combined impact, a project that is well worth doing, although his procedure was curious and at times clearly er-

[11] Charles F. Mullett, *The Bubonic Plague and England,* Lexington, Ky., 1956, p. 18.

roneous. To describe it briefly, he ascertained the rates of mortality in plague years; these rates were then applied to a life-table population in order to take approximate account of age distribution. "Normal" death rates were subtracted from the result, and the remainder was assumed to represent the plague loss.[12]

The deaths among the young were very few and the sampling error enormous. These groups, however, loom large in the age distributions, and the rates Russell assumed to be "corrected" were therefore only made more precarious. For the period 1348–1350, for instance, his cases include three heirs presumed to have been between one and five. Of these one died, indicating a risk of mortality of 0.33. This was taken as a measure of the force of mortality in the plague for the entire age group 0–4, in spite of the fact that it was hardly more than the average infant mortality rate Russell estimated for the entire generation born in 1348–1375.[13] The resulting death rate was 23.6 per cent, which Russell cites as evidence of the need for this kind of correction, since the crude rate from all his cases, regardless of age, was 27.3 per cent. If two rather than one of his young children in the 1–5 group had died, the rate of mortality for that age group would have been 0.67, and the corrected death rate would have jumped to 28.6 per cent. A procedure so vulnerable to chance is obviously not satisfactory.

It is not only in the case of the young that Russell's operations are dubious. He concluded from his mortality rates that the plague fell more heavily in older men than on the young and relied on this in his interpretation. But old age is always hazardous, and before we can say anything about the impact of the plague we must take more adequate account of the mortality that would ordinarily have occurred.

The refined procedures usually necessary to isolate the contribution to mortality of a single cause of death are not necessary in this case, for the plagues were sudden whirlwinds. Russell included in his plague mortalities for 1348–1350 and 1360–1361 all deaths in these periods and did the same for the single years 1369 and 1375.[14] To illustrate: of the 58

---

[12] Russell, *op. cit.,* pp. 216, 262–263.

[13] To make things worse, he grouped his plague cases in age groups 1–5, 6–10, etc., whereas his life tables were conventionally arranged in terms of 0–4, 5–9, etc. He thought "the results would probably not be sufficiently different to justify the effort of revising the data." Although this may be true for most other age groups, it cannot hold for the youngest where the absence of infants robs it of all significance.

[14] He did not state this explicitly, but he deducted twice the "normal annual mortality" from his death rates for the plague of 1360–1361 and slightly more from that of 1348–1350 which indicates that he included all deaths from the plague-ridden periods, and it is hard to see what else he could have done in the absence of reliable indications of the cause of death.

heirs between 46 and 50 exposed to the plague in 1348–1350, 17 died. Normally, however, we should have expected four or five of them to die in the course of slightly more than two years.

A primitive but in this case adequate way of separating plague fatality from ordinary mortality is simply to subtract, for each age group, the "normal" rate from that observed in the plague, remembering that the normal rate should be doubled for the two first epidemics. As "normal" rates we could use those estimated earlier for the century before 1348, but if those rates are plotted in a graph they show a most disorderly curve which cannot reflect a normal state of nature. The statistical impulse is to smooth it. This could be done in many ways; the simplest and most reasonable is to adopt the most appropriate of the United Nations model life-tables. Table 5 shows the plague fatality rates arrived at by this method. (Age groups under 15 for which the evidence is too sparse have been left out.) The residual plague fatality rates in the table show no convincing tendency at all to vary with age. They are erratic, as might be expected with samples ranging from 21 to 72, but especially in the first two epidemics they show a strong central tendency.

The simplest hypothesis not contradicted by this evidence is that in the devastating outbreaks of the plague, age made no difference to this particular risk of death. This is consistent with the general picture of a disease so devastating that, once contracted, it was almost always fatal. The risk of contagion would then be the only significant variable, and there is no reason to expect that to have been a function of age. Considering how ill understood was the nature of the disease, there is not much more reason to think that it was a function of social status, at least until it became a custom for the rich to flee to the country, as Creighton claims to have been the case after 1465.[15]

On this hypothesis, the best estimate of overall plague mortality in the various epidemics would be the averages of the last columns in Table 5. If younger age groups, including infants, were cut down at the same rate, the population declined by some 22 per cent in the first epidemic, 18 per cent in the second, 10 in the third, and 12 in the fourth.

Decimation on such scale must have given rise to some recuperative response. The vacancies of society must have stimulated early marriages; on the other hand, the mood of the times may have discouraged fertility. One advice, at least, was that in times of pestilence "every fleshly lust with women is to be eschewed."[16] In the end, we can only guess at the course of fertility. If we assume that in the long run it remained at the pre-plague level, the combined impact of the first four epidemics of the

[15] Charles Creighton, *A History of Epidemics in Britain,* Cambridge, 1894, I, p. 226.

[16] *Ibid.,* I, p. 213.

TABLE 5. Age Specific Plague Fatality Rates (Per Thousand)

Age	Normal Death Rate per Year	Death Rate in Plague Years				Plague Fatality			
		1348–1350	1360–1361	1369	1375	1348–1350	1360–1361	1369	1375
	(1)	(2)	(3)	(4)	(5)	(6)	(7)	(8)	(9)
15–19	12	200	171	140	110	177	148	128	98
20–24	15	197	225	30	160	167	195	15	145
25–29	18	188	220	140	160	153	185	122	142
30–34	21	283	134	20	60	241	92	0	39
35–39	25	333	233	150	130	283	183	125	105
40–44	31	210	225	210	70	148	163	179	39
45–49	39	294	333	120	30	216	255	81	—
50–54	47	344	182	140	120	250	88	93	73
55–59	58	456	413	50	150	340	297	—	92
60–	103	390	354	250	435	184	148	125	332
					Average:	216	177	96	118

Source: Col. 1. age-specific death rates corresponding to a life expectation at birth of 25 in the model life-tables, United Nations, *Methods for Population Projections by Sex and Age*, 1956, p. 72. Cols. 2–5. British Medieval Population, 1948, pp. 216–218. Cols. 6–9 are reached by subtracting the rates of col. 1 for 1369 and 1375, and twice those rates for 1348 and 1360–1361.

plague would have been to reduce the population in 1377 to roughly 51 per cent of its level in 1347 (0.78 $\times$ 0.82 $\times$ 0.90 $\times$ 0.88 = 0.51). This is lower than Russell's 60 per cent, but in view of his extraordinary method, it is surprising that the figures are as similar as they are. The margins of uncertainty are large enough to envelop both estimates charitably, and if we assume some positive fertility response between the epidemics it may even be reasonable to think that the drop between 1347 and 1377 was 40 per cent rather than 50.

Russell also cites evidence relating to the declining number of land-holders in various villages, but there is no particular reason to expect the number of homesteads or landholders to follow total population very closely. Then there is the matter of the high mortality recorded in ecclesiastical establishments during the Black Death. In the first onslaught, between 35 and 50 per cent of the clerics perished in most dioceses, and in monasteries too this seems to have been an average level, although some were virtually extinguished. If such rates were indicative of general fatality in the first epidemic alone, the total loss between 1348 and 1377 would necessarily have been even greater than just concluded.

Although institutional mortality would be expected to be particularly severe in any plague epidemic, the Black Plague rates reported from the dioceses are surprisingly high, especially since their mortality in the following outbreaks seems to have been commensurate with that of Russell's heirs. Only if the age of clergymen in 1348 was very high or if they were especially exposed to contagion are those figures compatible with our earlier inference. They are, moreover, based on larger samples although their age distribution is unknown.

With this and other caveats in mind, we might tentatively conclude that the Black Death and the succeeding three outbreaks of the plague reduced English population by 40 and perhaps even 50 per cent in the span of little more than a quarter of a century. What happened later— whether the population continued to decline and if so for how long— Russell's data cannot possibly be made to reveal.

LAMPRECHT AND THE MOSEL VALLEY

The thesis that European population expanded spectacularly in the three centuries before 1300 is widely respected and lends color to most accounts of the vitality of the High Middle Ages. It is actually only in Western Europe and Italy that there is evidence of such growth, and even there the indications are not compellingly clear except in the case of Britain. For France, Russell resorts to the device of premising that the rate of growth was the same as in England, and he is then able to extend a series back from Lot's estimate for 1328.[17] In Italy, city walls were expanded in the period 1100–1250, and there is a sprinkling of evidence about urban population at various times, but estimates of overall population are breathtakingly conjectural. German urbanization presents similar evidence. The medieval population of the Mosel Valley, however, was studied in detail by Lamprecht, some 80 years ago.[18]

"This meticulous study," as Russell calls it, probably the only source of actual growth rates for a Continental population in the High Middle Ages, and in consequence it is frequently cited. The idea that Europe's population trebled in these 300 years seems to have its origin here. However, Russell has also given currency to a complete misinterpre-

[17] Josiah Cox Russell, "Late Ancient and Medieval Population," *Transactions of the American Philosophical Society, N.S.,* Vol. 48, Part 3 (Philadelphia, 1958), p. 105.

[18] Karl Lamprecht, *Deutsches Wirtschaftsleben im Mittelalter,* 1886. See particularly Vol. I, pp. 161–164, and Vol. II, p. 20.

tation of it in his *Late Ancient and Medieval Population* and Lamprecht's procedure does not seem to be widely understood.

Lamprecht's idea was to rely on toponymical research and convert the documented emergence of new place-names into a picture of population growth. Although the difficulties of toponymical research are forbidding, the qualitative impression of rapid growth in the Middle Ages is based in no small measure on the profusion of new names. An attempt to lend precision to that impression is of obvious interest.

Lamprecht started from the population figures for the area in 1821 and 1828, which were 640,000 and 720,000 respectively. The rate of growth in this seven year-period was thus, he said, 1.4 per cent per annum (actually it was 1.6), and he extrapolated back to 1800 on the assumption that it had remained constant. The population at the end of the eighteenth century would thus have been about 450,000.[19]

He then introduced the place-name counts, and in a crucial but obscure passage he presented his results as follows:*

Die zwischen dem 13. und 18. bis 19. Jh. liegende Periode einer im ganzen weitgehenden Ruhe im Ausbau gestattet also sehr wohl, die Zustände am Anfange und am Schluss der Periode selbst zum Vergleich zu bringen. Betritt man nun diesen Weg unter Vermittlung der Ortsstatistik . . . so würde:

Im Jahre	800	900	1000	1050	1100	1150	1200	1237	1800	
einer Anzahl von ca	100	250	350	470	590	810	990	1180	2000	Orten seine
Bevölkerungsziffer von ca	20	60	80	100	140	180	220	250	450	Tausend Seelen.

entsprochen haben.[20]

From these figures he derived the rates of growth for the population:

800– 900	1.1 per cent
900–1000	0.3
1000–1050	0.45
1050–1100	0.7
1100–1150	0.5
1150–1200	0.4
1200–1237	0.35

I have retained the awkward form of Lamprecht's table in the above quotation in order to clarify Russell's misreading of it. According to him, "Lamprecht assumed that the average size of the villages increased greatly in the period A.D. 800–1300," and Russell presents the bottom line as estimates of the average village population: 20, 60, 80, etc.[21] He then proceeds to dispute these estimates by computing his own series for the

[19] *Ibid.,* Vol, I, p. 161.

[20] *Ibid.,* p. 163.

[21] Russell, *Late Ancient and Medieval Population,* p. 95.

number of villages and comparing its rate of growth with that of English population. (It is not clear why he does not use Lamprecht's middle line.) Because the rates of growth for the number of Mosel villages and the number of Englishmen were comparable, he infers that village size did not change.

But Lamprecht says nothing about village size, and the series that Russell quotes is the estimate of *total* population (in thousands). If he had meant what Russell thought he meant, he would have believed that the population of the Mosel valley in 1237 was 150 times as large as in 800, about 10 times as large as in 1000, and that the annual growth rate was over 1 per cent per annum. Actually, he thought it was one-half of 1 per cent which, sustained over such a long period, was high enough to be remarkable.

And what did Lamprecht assume about village size? In listing the place-names he included for each one its population in 1825–1828, a procedure suggesting that to Lamprecht each village had sprung up fully equipped with its nineteenth-century complement of inhabitants.[22] Actually, his procedure was even simpler. From the estimated population in 1800 he derived an average village size of 225, which he applied to the numbers of villages existing between 800 and 1237 A.D. That the ratios between his population figures and village figures are not constant but swing between 200 and 240 is all explained by the word "about" in his table. He rounded off his figures to the nearest ten and computed his growth rates on the basis of the rounded population figures. Because he rounded them to one or two digits, the growth rates for the population differ slightly from that of the number of villages, which creates the tantalizing suspicion that some inscrutably sophisticated technique was being used. In actual fact, however, nothing whatever besides the number of place-names was drawn upon.

What is one to make of this procedure? Two a priori considerations push in opposite directions. There can hardly be any doubt of the direction of the bias of toponymical statistics. We cannot from historical documents know of a village before it is founded, but we are quite likely to ignore it for a considerable period of time. Increasing literacy, pacification, and the consolidation of law and litigation all contributed to the likelihood that a village should come to our attention only in the course of the High Middle Ages although it might then have existed for some considerable time. The distinction between Roman, Celtic, and German names in the Mosel Valley makes it possible to avoid flagrant error, but the late appearance of certain of the older forms also points up the danger of the procedure. There can be no doubt that Lamprecht's figures overstate the rate of growth of village communities.

[22] Lamprecht, *op. cit.,* Vol. II, 20.

But how valid is the assumption of proportionality between villages and population? This question arises not only in the expanding phase of medieval history to which Lamprecht turned his attention, but also in the controversial fourteenth century where the continued abandonment of homesteads and villages has been interpreted as a sign of sustained decline in population. Serious doubts arise in both cases. Even in an orderly but imaginary process of settlement, in which every new village ceases to grow when it reaches a certain limit, there will be an approximate correspondence between the growth of villages and that of the population only if villages reach their limiting size very rapidly. Otherwise, the growth in size of the villages must obviously be added to that of their numbers. It seems unlikely that the new villages of medieval Europe immediately filled to the brim, although there are fair grounds to suspect that the oldest ones had filled up at the end of the period. Hallam's Lincolnshire censuses, to mention only one example, show spectacular growth in numbers of households between Domesday and 1287:[23]

	1086	1287
Spalding	91	587
Pinchback	57	646

If the toponymical basis of Lamprecht's estimates is sound, his figures would represent a lower limit, and the actual rates of growth of population should have been a good deal higher. They would thus be higher than those estimated for England before the Black Death on the basis of entirely different, and on the whole probably more reliable, sources.

This would not be outrageously implausible, but when the two sources of error—the inevitable toponymical oversights of villages, and the neglect of village growth—are simultaneously considered, one must conclude that Lamprecht's figures are fairly worthless. Those who use Lamprecht's work to illustrate the rate of medieval expansion should at least be aware that what he offers is the rate of growth of place-names, not of population.

THE HERIOTS ON THE WINCHESTER MANORS

Professor Postan and J. Titow have made ingenious use of records of certain medieval death duties to trace the course of mortality during the century before the Black Death.[24] The heriots were duties levied on

[23] H. E. Hallam, "Some Thirteenth-Century Censuses," *Economic History Review*, X (1957–1958), 340.

[24] M. M. Postan and J. Titow, "Heriots and Prices on Winchester Manors," *Economic History Review*, XI (1958–1959), 392–417.

holdings of customary tenants at the death of the tenant and were paid in animals or money. If the number of tenancies remained approximately constant, the number of heriots should reflect the course of the crude death rate among tenants.

The series of heriots that Postan and Titow extracted from the accounts of five of the manors of the Bishop of Winchester is of special interest when it is compared with the movements of grain prices. Deaths and prices were for the most part fairly well synchronized, though a few peaks of mortality in years of low prices suggest epidemics unaccompanied by poor harvests; after 1325 the correlation is much less impressive than at earlier times.

No doubt the contours of mortality are reflected in those figures. To derive a meaningful measure of it is none the less difficult. Postan affirms that the number of customary tenants must have been approximately constant at 1,725, the number of tenants liable to heriot in 1321. The annual number of heriots paid was high, particularly in the first half of the fourteenth century, for which the figures seem most accurate, and the crude death rate among tenants in that period approached 50 per thousand.

Customary tenants were, in general, male adults, and Postan therefore treats this figure as an estimate of the death rate of the population over 20. By comparison with other societies, particularly Russia around the turn of the century where death rates were considerably higher for the population under 20 than over 20, Postan-Titow arrive at the conclusion that overall death rates at Winchester must have been spectacular:

> If these differential death rates of the Russian adult population were used to convert the Winchester death rate of adults into those of the population as a whole, a crude rate as high as 70–75 per thousand would result. Somewhat similar results would emerge from the comparison of Winchester rates with the adult death rates of Indian population between 1890 and 1920. There is thus very little doubt that the mortality on the Winchester manors in the second half of the thirteenth and the first half of the fourteenth centuries was at least as high, and probably much higher, than the mortality in any other preindustrial society whose evidence is available to us.[25]

Indeed, death rates of this magnitude in an almost stationary population would be extraordinary. They would correspond to a life expectancy at birth of about 14 years, which is less than that of the unhealthiest metropolitan centers of the eighteenth century, and considerably less than that of primitive societies.

Temporarily, mortality rates may attain any level including total extinction, but an approximately stationary population must match mortality and fertility. No estimates of fecundity in the Western world in recent centuries would suffice to maintain a population at birth and death rates

[25] *Ibid.*, p. 400.

TABLE 6. Heriots and Mortality Rates of Customary Tenants
on Five Winchester Manors, 1245–1348

Years	Animal	Money	Total	Death Rate (per Thousand)	"Life Expectancy" of Tenants (Years)
1245–9	38	9	47	27	37
1250–9	38	10	48	28	36
1260–9	30	2	32	19	54
1270–9	32	14	46	27	38
1280–9	37	12	49	28	35
1290–9	33	28	61	35	28
1300–9	44	30	74	43	23
1310–9	49	57	105	61	16
1320–9	44	41	84	49	21
1330–9	38	47	85	50	20
1340–9	39	56	95	55	19

Source: Prepared from figures in Longden, "Statistical Notes on Winchester Heriots," *Econ. Hist. Rev.*, XI (1958–1959), 412–417.

around 70 per thousand.[26] This estimate of medieval mortality is therefore suspect from the outset. Actually, the Winchester heriots do not constitute evidence of such sensational rates of mortality.

The records may of course be less than perfect. The recorded number of heriots paid in money is assumed to have been seriously deficient in the thirteenth century, before it jumped to rough parity with those paid in animals. (Table 6) Money heriots were levied on holdings too small to pay in animals, and the collection or recording of such heriots apparently left out of account many of the poorer tenants in the first half of the thirteenth century. After 1270, we are told that the records appear complete, in spite of the continued rapid increase in money heriots. The annual death rates before 1300 were considerably below those of the fourteenth century, and it is tempting to conclude that mortality was rising around 1300. The authors, however, refrained from stressing this trend, but there is no particular reason for such reticence—one thing their material suggests very forcefully is an increase in secular morality.

[26] It is true that in recent years demographers have discovered African populations with birth rates far above the level around 50, which was long regarded as a maximum. Rates above 60 or even 70 have now been claimed. See Blanc and Théodore, "Les populations d'Afrique noire et de Madagascar," *Population*, XV (1960), 407–432.

But the crucial question is what the age distribution of the tenant population was like. It cannot have been that of an ordinary population as the authors imply. The Winchester customs for accession to property were undoubtedly complex, but we may be certain that the entry into tenancy occurred at an average age higher than 20. It is in error that the authors say:

> the death rates on the five manors, as measured by heriots, suggest that the expectations of life of the substantial tenants, i.e., the intervals between their accession at 20 and their death, should have varied from about 24 at the beginning of our period to just under 20 in the period following 1292.[27]

Tenants did not acquire their holdings at 20—indeed, the very next sentence mentions "uncertain guesses as to the average age of accession to property." The death rate (or its inverse, the "expectation of life") of these customary tenants can therefore not be compared with that of the age group over 20 in a regular population. A group of this kind, consisting of heads of households, may however be compared with other groups of similar nature. Death rates for such groups are usually not conceded any statistical significance and are therefore rarely published, but two cases will show that the death rate in such a group is not necessarily lower than that of the population as a whole.

In 1851, Farr investigated mortality in different occupations. He found the crude mortality rate of farmers over 20 to be 28 per thousand. This was a high rate—that of tailors was 20 per thousand. Yet his analysis showed that the age-specific mortalities of farmers were the lowest of any occupational group: they were "the oldest and the longest livers."[28] Farr suspected that the number of farms had been stationary for some years, and as the age group of 45–55 was greater than any other, it was clear that more men entered than left the group up to that age. Now, 28 per thousand was a high rate for Victorian England, and if we assumed that infant and child mortality, still extremely high at the time, should raise our estimate of overall mortality, we would be led in the wrong direction, for the overall death rate in England at the time was about 22.5 per thousand.

It would thus be quite possible that the Winchester population was not regularly subjected to the conflagration inferred by Postan and Titow. The overall death rate may have been lower or of the same magnitude as among customary tenants.

Between 1674 and 1742 in the parish of Crulai, in Normandy, which Gautier and Henry have subjected to intensive analysis, the average age at death of married men was between 50 and 55 (depending on the at-

[27] Postan and Titow, *op. cit.*, p. 395.

[28] William Farr, *Vital Statistics*, London, 1885, p. 395.

tribution of borderline cases). The average age at marriage for men was about 27 years, and the life expectancy at marriage would therefore have been about 25 years, which in a stationary population corresponds to a death rate of 40 per thousand for married men. For the population as a whole, the death rate is estimated at 31 per thousand, and the life expectancy at something close to 30 years,[29] In this case, then, the mortality of the population as a whole was lower than that of heads of households."

The customary tenants at the five Winchester manors were not identical with the population of married men; we are told there may even have been a few teen-age girls among them. But there can be no doubt that their age distribution must have been more like that of married men than like that of the population over 20. The manorial custom for accession to property did not lay down hard and fast rules; minors of both sexes sometimes succeeded to holdings, and "a surprisingly large number of successors were men who married the dead men's widows." Succession by a grown-up son (or son-in-law) will not always occur even where it is favored by law and custom. All possible permutations of family survivorship may occur at the death of a husband originally counted as the head of household; in slightly more than half the cases he will leave a widow who may be childless or not, whose children may be minors or not, and so forth. However, it is not unreasonable to assume that in many cases the accession to a tenancy was connected with marriage, which would make the tenants of the Winchester manors roughly comparable with the married men at Crulai. In that case, their rate of mortality was not startlingly high.

Over the whole century between 1245 and the Black Death, the heriot rate at Winchester was actually almost identical with the Crulai death rate of 40 per thousand. The heriots were fewer in the first half of that century—the rate was only about 27 per thousand for 1245–1299—and it was only in the second half that deaths of tenants were numerous enough to raise the death rate to about 50. Postan and Titow suspect that the records of money heriots are incomplete before 1270, but in the 1280's and 1290's the rates were still only 28 and 35 respectively. It is true that the proportion of money heriots was still curiously low, and Longden, who assisted them in the statistical analysis of the heriots, was apparently suspicious enough of that portion of the material to disregard the tenancies liable to money heriots before 1300. Instead, he assumed that the tenancies that paid their heriots in animals formed a constant share of the total number; he was thus able to extend the series of high death rates back into the thirteenth century (since the number of animal-paying heriots was roughly constant all the time).

[29] E. Gautier and Louis Henry, *La population de Crulai, paroisse normande,* I.N.E.D., Travaux et documents, Cahier No. 33, Paris, 1958, pp. 181, 191, 232.

This is questionable procedure. We are told that the records appear complete and "bear no trace of a change in the administration of the heriots," and the rise in money heriots would seem rather to call for an explanation than for the scrapping of the lower figures. Money heriots were paid by the tenancies that were too small to pay in animals, and subdivisions would appear to be a possible explanation. We are told that they were few, and that the total number of tenancies was more likely to decline than to increase.[30] It is worth considering, however, that an increase in the number of small tenancies would not only explain the anomalies of the money-heriot series but would also temper the exceedingly sharp rise in the turnover rate (i.e., the death rate) as calculated on the assumption of a constant number of tenancies. Subdivision would be an exceedingly probable phenomenon in the circumstances. For that matter, one can imagine an increasing tendency to pay heriots in money even on marginal tenancies. Money heriots, as Postan and Titow stress, in a number of cases also represented "anticipated death duties" levied on sales of land *inter vivos* sometimes paid by substantial tenants selling parts of their holdings, and in all such cases tending to understate the actual life of the tenant. Finally, one might consider the possibility that there was a rise in the death rate, as the authors very reasonably hold, and that it tended to hit poorer tenants much harder than substantial ones. This may go some way towards explaining why the annual rate of money heriots should have doubled or tripled around the turn of the century, but this part of the data remains troubling.

The rates from the fourteenth century are on firmer ground. They are perfectly compatible with a level of mortality for medieval society indicated by the discussion of Russell's material in the previous pages. There is no reason to believe that the overall death rate around Winchester was higher than that of the customary tenants. If it were roughly the same or slightly lower it was of the order of 40–50 per thousand, which corresponds to a life expectation at birth of 20–25 years. For a period that included one of the most devastating famines in European history, that of 1315, this is about what we should have expected. The Postan-Titow evidence also, interestingly enough, seems to point to a deterioration between the thirteenth and the fourteenth centuries. Such a deterioration has a place in the interpretation of the turn of events in the early fourteenth century, but actual statistical evidence of it is sparse.

EPILOGUE

It is possible to argue that to the progress of historical inquiry, the most important thing is not the historian's answer to some specific question

[30] Postan and Titow, *op. cit.*, p. 399.

but his unearthing of the sources, their processing, and presentation. As
G. N. Clark once remarked,

> even in the few instances where the answer is in such a form as "Yes"
> or "No" or "5½ million souls" or "£ 1,753,000," the most valuable part of
> the investigation will be not that conclusion but what has been ascertained on
> the way to it.[31]

The reasonable part of this proposition is clear enough. Yet there
is something not wholly satisfactory about the view that the conclusion
of an investigation is less valuable than the investigation itself, as if the
principal purpose were not to arrive at that conclusion. When the purpose
is that of ascertaining some isolated historical statistic, such a view may
be acceptable. What, indeed, does it matter whether the population of
England and Wales at the beginning of the eighteenth century was five
million, six, or 5.5?

The answer is that it acquires considerable significance when historical statistics are combined into a greater perspective of historical change.
The three problems of statistical interpretation that have been briefly considered here may in themselves seem trifling, but when the estimates of
mortality in medieval Europe are to be fitted into the picture of the evolution of Western mortality and when rates of demographic expansion become cornerstones in interpretations of the economic dynamics of preindustrial growth, it is more important to know the range of confidence of
such estimates and the reasons for that confidence. Statistical estimates
are not "facts" of history, first to be ascertained and then to be interpreted;
the estimation of historical statistics is merely an aspect of historical
interpretation.

[31] G. N. Clark, "History and the Social Sciences," in *The Social Sciences: Their
Relations in Theory and Teaching,* London, 1936, p. 89.

JAPAN'S TRANSITION TO MODERN ECONOMIC GROWTH, 1868–1885

Henry Rosovsky

Harvard University

. . . every excess causes a defect; every defect an excess . . . —Ralph Waldo Emerson

Where must an analysis of Japanese industrialization begin? Those countries trying at present to conquer economic backwardness know only too well that it takes time to get started. Decades of preparatory activity may be necessary before modern economic growth (or as we shall sometimes write: MEG[1]) can begin, and much of this activity will have to be outside the range of what is usually termed "economic." From a certain point of view the roots of growth can be extended backwards for centuries. The genesis of modern agriculture may, perhaps, be traceable to early medieval conditions, just as some aspects of the modern factory can be connected to the skills and techniques of organization which evolved in fourteenth century guilds. This somewhat superficial element of continuity is terribly

● I would like to express my deep gratitude, first of all, to Ohkawa Kazushi, habitual and generous collaborator, who has allowed me the use of research materials which will eventually appear in a jointly authored book, now in preparation. Simon Kuznets, David Landes, and Irwin Scheiner read the manuscript, and made many helpful suggestions.

[1] Modern economic growth in its technical sense is a term coined by Simon Kuznets. According to his formulation there are four major characteristics associated with this phenomenon. First, modern economic growth involves the application of modern scientific thought and technology to industry. Second, a country undergoing MEG has a sustained and rapid rise in real product per capita usually combined with high rates of population growth. Third, this type of growth is reflected in rapid rates of transformation of the industrial structure, essentially the movement of workers, capital, and entrepreneurship out of agriculture and into manufacturing and services. Finally, modern economic growth for any one country requires the presence of international contacts—it has never taken place in an area isolated from all outside contacts. See Simon Kuznets, *Six Lectures on Economic Growth,* The Free Press, Glencoe, Illinois, 1959, Lecture I.

bothersome for those whose primary purpose is the study of an industrial revolution. Is it really necessary to move back farther and farther in time in order to appreciate the significant dimensions of a recent and entirely different past?[2] We do not believe so, although we do believe that it is important to determine just how far back it is useful to trace the antecedents of modern economic growth. This function, we hope, can be performed by the concept of "transition."

In our sense, transition has a clear beginning and end. It is defined as that period which elapses between the time when MEG becomes a national objective and the time when MEG begins for the first time. The end of transition can present no particular analytical problems: the four major characteristics of MEG are empirically verifiable. When they can all be identified, transition has ended and MEG has begun. The beginning of transition is best understood in the Japanese context, although the ideas also apply to follower countries in general. A national objective directed towards economic development implies a level of consciousness typical of late industrializers. Usually this goes together with government's playing a vital role in bringing about growth. Vague desires for modernizing the economy can exist for decades and even centuries, but they will not become effective—especially in a relatively backward country—until growth becomes an avowed objective of those who can influence the course of national policy.

In Japan, transition begins with the Meiji Restoration of 1868 and terminates with the end of the Matsukata Deflation in 1885. This essay will therefore describe the history of a lag—that is, the lag between the time when MEG became a national objective and the beginning of MEG, a period of slightly less than twenty years. We will examine the evidence in two ways. First, we shall describe the "given conditions," meaning thereby the state of economy and society existing at the time when the new national objective first appears. Secondly, we must discern how the given conditions were shaped or changed—by public or private action—to bring about modern economic growth itself.

A final preliminary point relates to the use of dates. When we say that transition ends in 1885, what kind of meaning is intended for the specific year? Our aim is the analysis of trends, and especially those elements bringing about a change in the trend. Both in statistical and historical terms, this leads to the use of "smoothed" facts (in history) and numbers (in statistics). As such, each specific year, selected as a turning

---

[2] "The explanation of the very recent in terms of the remotest past, naturally attractive to men who have made of this past their chief subject of research, has sometimes dominated our studies to the point of a hypnosis. In its most characteristic aspect, this idol of the historian tribe may be called the obsession with origins." Marc Bloch, *The Historian's Craft,* trans. Peter Putnam, Vintage Books, New York, 1964, p. 29.

point, is both an average and an abstraction, representing a clustering of forces at that point. Therefore it is best to think of a selected point in time as representing a range of approximately plus or minus a few years.

THE GIVENS

Japan's economy in 1868 was relatively backward. No one will dispute this statement, perhaps because of its emptiness. A somewhat closer look may reduce the general level of agreement, at the same time that it enlarges the contents of our assertion. We wish to understand the givens for the economy at the time of the Restoration, but with what facet of the economy should we be concerned? We have chosen those variables which we know to be important in later years: per capita product, population growth, industrial structure, science and technology, and international contacts.

Real Product Per Capita and Population Growth

It is difficult to make precise quantitative statements about the Japanese economy during the 1860's. This is especially true if interest centers on national information. National income figures begin only in 1878, and the reliability of the earlier estimates is debatable. Population figures present similar problems: Japan's first modern population census was taken only in 1920. Nevertheless, let us begin with such information as is available and then attempt inferences about the unknown.

We may start with the level of real product per capita. Since reports for the period before 1878 are not available on a yearly basis, we begin by using a three-year average (1878–1880) in order to have a benchmark against which fragmentary evidence can be matched. At that time, the gainfully employed population was distributed as follows:[3]

	Agriculture	Manufacturing	Services
1878–1880	83%	5%	12%

This working population produced a gross national product according to these sectoral divisions:[4]

	Agriculture	Manufacturing	Services
1878–1880	65%	9%	26%

[3] Computed from Ohkawa Kazushi and Others, *The Growth Rate of the Japanese Economy Since 1878,* Kinokuniya Bookstore Co., Ltd., Tokyo, 1957, p. 145. These figures undoubtedly overstate the agricultural population. A gainfully employed proportion in agriculture of approximately 79 per cent seems closer to reality.

[4] Gross product estimates from Ohkawa Kazushi and Akasaka Keiko, "Kobetsu suikei no sōgōka" (Survey of Individual National Income Components), Hitotsubashi University, Institute of Economic Research, Rockefeller Project Preliminary Report Number D11. (Hereafter cited as Hitotsubashi D11.)

For the same period, average GDP was ¥627 million (current prices) while total population approximated 36.6 million, resulting in a per capita product of ¥18.7 (Per capita net national product was ¥16.5.) There is a strong temptation to convert this figure into present value. If this were possible, and if the results for other countries were accurate, we would be able to compare quantitatively preindustrial Japan with present-day underdeveloped areas. But this step is inadvisable on at least two counts: the index number problem precludes the historical conversion, and the ordinary techniques using exchange rates for international comparison yield equally misleading answers.

Early national income figures can be used to obtain an approximation of the sectoral productivity structure. Based on gainfully employed population these results appear for 1878–1880:[5]

	Agriculture	Manufacturing	Services	Total
Product per gainfully occupied person—current ¥	26.0	59.0	70.0	33.0
Relative product	79	179	213	100

These answers undoubtedly understate the labor productivity of agriculture, because many persons who were counted as gainfully employed on the land were actually employed in other sectors on a part-time basis. In spite of this, the relative productivity ordering can be safely assumed to be correct.

All this, however, does not bring us very much closer to the two major questions which should be answered: what was the level of per capita product in the 1860's (preferably at the time of the Restoration) and what was its rate of increase? Economic historians generally agree that the 1860's "was a decade of political and social dislocation in which the traditional economy was not functioning normally";[6] the economic level of that period probably lay below that of the 1850's. During these years Japan was just in the process of joining, *for the first time,* the community of nations. Some foreign representation had already arrived to watch the spectacle of the old order disintegrating. A variety of factions were struggling for power, and uncertainty must be the most descriptive word for the situation. The shogunate was uncertain about what policies might most effectively counter both foreign threats and domestic discontent; the imperial court was uncertain about where to exercise its limited influence; the opposition—mostly samurai—was split, rallying behind now one slogan and then another. Economic relations could not remain un-

---

[5] *Ibid.*

[6] E. S. Crawcour, "The Tokugawa Heritage," to appear in W. W. Lockwood (ed.), *The State and Economic Enterprise in Modern Japan,* Princeton University Press, Princeton, 1965.

affected—especially in an economy where authorities had traditionally exacted adherence to numerous rules and regulations. Peasants, merchants, and craftsmen could not but have a confused and anxious picture of the future. Some practiced economic caution and retrenchment; others engaged in reckless speculation, egged on by unscrupulous foreign merchants. The net effect on national income was almost certainly a decline in the 1860's—compared with either the early 1850's or late 1870's.[7]

Recently, E. S. Crawcour prepared an estimate of the average level of national income for Japan during the 1860's—he made no attempt to calculate yearly figures. These calculations necessarily involved heroic assumptions and indirect procedures, some more valid than others, and, as Crawcour admits without hesitation, the numbers cannot be very reliable. (Needless to say, we share some of these feelings as far as our own numbers go for the period 1878–1880.) He finds that national income (NNP) averaged between ¥383 and ¥418 million per year, whereas per capita income was between ¥13 and ¥14, all stated in 1878–1880 prices.[8] Let us, for the sake of argument, accept these estimates. What do they show? Assuming that these averages hold for 1860 and measuring the twenty-year period until 1880, one may say that per capita income before or at the time of the Restoration was rising at between 1.25 to 1.5 per cent per year, while national income was increasing at between 2 (minimum assumption) to 4 per cent (maximum assumption) per year. This is certainly a shallow and misleading interpretation.[9] The 1860's were a trough and cannot be used as a base from which to measure trend values. If we could measure income growth from the 1850's to 1880, the rates would have been a good deal lower. Moreover, once MEG begins, in the 1880's, even the upward-biased rates of the 1860's appear low. For example, toward the end of the 1880's and during the 1890's per capita product was rising at 3.1 per cent per year; between 1905 and World War I the rate rose to 4.8 per cent per year.[10]

We conclude that when the Restoration occurred per capita product was not rising at a rapid rate—with "rapid" understood in the comparative context of modern economic growth. Of course, there were in Japan at that time both rich people and relatively rich and advanced sections of the country. Nevertheless, the Japanese economy of 1868 was still typified

[7] Some official pronouncements, written at a later date, support this view. See, for example, Japan, Ministry of Agriculture and Forestry, *Kōgyō iken* (A Survey of Industries), 1933. This report was originally written in 1884, and in a great many places stresses the disorganization and economic distress of the 1860's.

[8] Crawcour, *loc. cit.*

[9] An interpretation implicitly condemned by Crawcour.

[10] See Ohkawa Kazushi and Henry Rosovsky, "A Century of Japanese Economic Growth," to appear in Lockwood (ed.), *op. cit.*, Statistical Appendix, Table 1.

by the small peasant cultivator working in many cases only slightly above subsistence levels. An impressive secular increase in the growth rate of national product per capita required significant improvements in *average* agricultural practice and the introduction of new industries. All this came only after 1868. It may well be true that in the 1860's—and perhaps as early as the 1830's and 1840's—we can see some of the "preliminary stirrings"[11] contributing to the eventual achievement of MEG. But, as has been pointed out earlier, the search for preliminary stirrings is likely to be endless.

Findings pertaining to population tend to support these views. Our knowledge about the demographic aspects of early modern Japan are a bit more detailed, and also reach back farther in time. Irene Taeuber's book, *The Population of Japan*,[12] has proven particularly useful at this juncture, and her conclusions have been adopted without modification. She based her findings on the work of Japanese demographers, such as Morita and Tachi,[13] and general agreement seems to prevail among the principal investigators.

According to Mrs. Taeuber, in 1852 the total population of Japan was somewhere between 29.4 and 32 million. A report for 1872 suggests a level of 34.8 million. "Thus the increase of population in these two decades of transition from seclusion to the modern era may have amounted to less than 10%; it certainly did not reach 20%."[14] In other words, population growth was rather slow. It is generally believed that the Japanese population began to grow again in the early 19th century—after nearly a century of stability—". . . but there is no conclusive evidence that the rate of increase quickened in the early decades after the opening to the West."[15] Mrs. Taeuber believes that in the 1870's rates of increase were of the order of ¾ of 1 per cent per year; no one would be disposed to call this an especially high rate of population growth.

Information concerning vital rates, if properly interpreted, supports the findings about total population. Mortality in 1868 must have been high, although it may have been slightly declining. The decline can be explained by an improved food supply, access to external markets, and the decreasing incidence of epidemic and endemic diseases. Contact with the West did bring new diseases such as cholera and bubonic plague, but public health programs were adopted early and probably more than counterbalanced these adverse influences.

[11] An excellent phrase originally used by Crawcour in a preliminary version of the article cited above.

[12] Princeton University Press, Princeton, 1958.

[13] *Ibid.*, p. 395ff.

[14] *Ibid.*, p. 44.

[15] *Ibid.*

In the 1860's population was growing slowly while the level of mortality remained high. This must have required high fertility, and Mrs. Taeuber suggests that a rate of 40 per 1000 is plausible. She concludes that in Japan early and sustained declines in mortality were followed by declines in fertility (in the twentieth century), with a consequent increase in the rate of growth of population during MEG. There is thus nothing particularly unusual about Japan's demographic transition, other than the possible impact of the cessation of infanticide. This manner of fertility control may have been more extensive in premodern Japan than in other Asian cultures, and the initial result of Western contact and consequent abandonment of *mabiki* (a Japanese euphemism for infanticide) could have precipitated a slight rise in fertility. No one really knows—but we do know that the balance of demographic changes was "normal."

Industrial Structure

What was the industrial structure of Japan when MEG became an objective of national policy? Once again the lack of sufficiently early macroeconomic series precludes direct answers. Perhaps the first bit of relevant information dates from 1874, with the publication of *Meiji shichinen fu-ken bussanhyō* (Prefectural Production in 1874), an official government survey designed to ascertain the national level of production. Experts believe that the results of this survey were quite accurate, and the *bussanhyō* combined with other fragmentary data yield a fairly detailed picture of the productive structure before industrialization began.[16]

According to the *bussanhyō*, the value of total gross output—*excluding services*—is divided into three categories:[17]

Value of agricultural output	62.0%
Value of manufactured output	30.3%
Value of "other" (*genshi*) output	7.4%
	99.7%

[16] We have relied on the interpretation of *bussanhyō* prepared by Yamaguchi Kazuo. See his *Meiji zenki keizai no bunseki* (An Analysis of the Early Meiji Economy), Tokyo Daigaku shuppankai, Tokyo, 1956, Ch. 1.

[17] *Ibid.*, p. 5. These percentages differ very slightly from Yamaguchi's results. See p. 18. At first glance these figures may appear completely inconsistent with the previously cited national income figures for the late 1870's. In the *bussanhyō* agricultural output is only about twice as large in value terms as manufacturing, whereas in the national income figures agriculture is over six times larger. However, it must be remembered that *bussanhyō* deals in gross value, whereas the GDP figures show only value added. Under realistic value-added assumptions the inconsistencies would be largely eliminated. See Ohkawa, *The Growth Rate of the Japanese Economy*, where the following net income ratios are indicated for the late 1870's: agriculture, 88 per cent (p. 62); factory manufacturing 25–27 per cent (p. 87); domestic manufacturing 60 per cent (p. 90). Also, see Crawcour, *loc. cit.*

TABLE 1. 1874: Value of Agricultural Products (%)

Rice	62.8
Wheat and barley	11.0
Soy beans	3.3
Other cereals	3.8
Potatoes and vegetables	5.1
Fruits	1.0
Special (tokushu) crops[a]	12.3
Others	0.7
	100.0

[a] Special crops are largely cash crops, such as cotton, silkworms, indigo, tobacco, etc. Among the other crops there was, of course, also a certain proportion of cash crops.

Source: Yamaguchi Kazuo, Meiji zenki keizai no bunseki, p. 6.

To eliminate one possible ambiguity at the outset, it must be understood that with the exception of mining, "other" or genshi output is largely agricultural or agriculture-related. "Other" is divided into these subcategories:[18]

Value of wood and wood products	53.5%
Value of marine products	26.6%
Value of mining products	14.0%
Value of animal products	3.7%
Total	97.8%

It is therefore correct to say that roughly 70 per cent of gross physical production was what is usually termed primary.

The distribution of major crops is shown in Table 1, and it contains few surprises. Rice was overwhelmingly important in agriculture, and consequently also in the general economy: it accounted for about 38 per cent of the value of all nonservice output.

With the bussanhyō of 1874 it is also possible to get a breakdown of manufacturing values as shown in Table 2. We are dealing here with a rather typical premodern manufacturing pattern, and only a few points require explicit comment. Textiles and food together accounted for over 70 per cent of total manufacturing output. Items classified under heading

[18] Yamaguchi, op. cit., Yamaguchi's calculations have been corrected with respect to animal products, because stock instead of flow values were used. Yamaguchi's original percentages are: Wood and wood products, 44.1 per cent; Marine products, 22.1 per cent; Mining products, 11.5 per cent; Animal products, 22.7 per cent.

VII—here called "capital equipment"—carry only moderate weight. The two most important manufactured items were the production of cloth and the brewing or distillation of alcoholic beverages (mostly *sake*). Cloth accounted for 15.5 per cent of all manufactured products and for 4 per cent of all physical output; alcoholic beverages were 16.8 per cent of manufacturing and 5 per cent of physical output. In fact, these two commodities ranked in importance immediately after rice, barley, and wheat. Among types of textiles, cotton goods led by wide margin (63.3 per cent), followed by silk (26.7 per cent), mixed cottons and silks (8.0 per cent), and linen and others (2.0 per cent).

Very little of this production took place in factories or even in sizable manufactories. In 1874 the typical enterprise was small, used little wage labor, and frequently represented a form of rural by-employment.

TABLE 2. 1874: Structure of Manufacturing Output

I. Textiles 27.7%
  Cloth
  Dyed products
  Ready-made clothes
  Raw silk
  Silk wadding
  Cotton thread
  Footwear
II. Food Products 41.9%
  Alcoholic beverages
  Shōyu (soy sauce)
  Miso (bean paste)
  Manufactured tea
  Salt
  Sugar
  Other foods
  Other beverages
III. House Accessories 1.7%
  Mats
  shoji screens
IV. Lamp Oil and Candles 6.3%

V. Utensils 7.7%
  Ceramics
  Lacquer ware
  Cabinets
  Wooden utensils
  Boxes
  Tubs
  Metal containers
  Reed and bamboo products
  Misc. items and toys
  Grass products
VI. Paper Products 5.2%
  Paper
  Stationery
  Books and printing
  Ink and paints
VII. Capital Equipment 5.9%
  Misc. machinery and tools
  Fertilizer
  Ships
  Nets

VIII. Medicines, etc. 3.6%
  Medicines
  Drugs
  Cosmetics
  Others

Source: Yamaguchi, *Meiji zenki keizei no bunseki*, p. 14.

TABLE 3. 1873 & 1875: Breakdown of Gainfully Occupied Population

	1873		1875	
Occupation	No. of Workers	%	No. of Workers	%
Agriculture	15,320,367	77.97	15,656,621	77.20
Manufacturing	688,964	3.55	748,596	3.70
Commerce	1,289,070	6.56	1,357,956	6.70
Misc. work	1,805,180	9.19	1,922,380	9.50
Fishing	3,558	0.01	27,206	0.01
Servants	445,242	2.26	417,534	2.00
Govt. officials	19,658	0.10	32,237	0.16
Priests	5,522	0.02	12,703	0.06
Soldiers	27,248	0.13	54,740	0.27
Teachers	8,565	0.04	12,141	0.06
Doctors	24,918	0.12	33,849	0.16

Source: Yamaguchi Kazuo, "Meiji jūnen-dai no shokugyōbetsu kaisōbetsu jinkō kōsei" (Occupation and Class Structure of the Population during the Second Decade of the Meiji Era), *Keizaigaku kenkyū*, No. 13, p. 36.

There were some notable exceptions such as the mechanical silk-reeling mills belonging to Matsudaira and Ōno, or the government mill at Tomioka, and the Satsuma mechanized cotton-spinning mill at Sakai—all founded before 1874. None of this, however, represented the average picture. This is borne out by the geographical distribution of manufacturing.

Both cloth weaving and especially *sake* brewing, the two most important industrial products, were widely distributed throughout the entire country, implying small units of production.[19]

Bussanhyō contains no information about tertiary production, and knowledge concerning this sector remains sparse well into the 1930's. Nevertheless, there may be some value in citing the results of one of the earliest breakdowns of the gainfully occupied labor force. For this we refer to Table 3, originally compiled by Hirano Gitarō for the years 1873 and 1875. His results are not above suspicion. The method by which the classification was obtained is unknown, and obvious errors are present. How else can one explain the ninefold increase in the number of fishermen

[19] What Paul Mantoux said about Great Britain before the Industrial Revolution seems to apply also to Japan in the 1870's: "One thing strikes us at once, namely, the great number of industrial centres and their dispersion, or rather their diffusion, over the whole country. The fact is more striking for us as nowadays, under the factory system, the opposite is the case. Each industry is highly centralized and controls a limited area in which its productive power is concentrated." *The Industrial Revolution in the Eighteenth Century,* Jonathan Cape, London, 1955, p. 49.

in two years? No doubt there must also have been unsatisfactory reporting of part-time and domestic occupations. During the Tokugawa and early Meiji periods, for example, fishing was primarily a local occupation in which home consumption was prominent. Consequently in both the *bussanhyō* and the Hirano survey this rather important economic activity does not pull its proper weight. And yet, for the most part, these figures are reasonable. They are consistent with the earliest national income estimates showing 12 per cent of the gainfully occupied population engaged in services. They are also consistent with the general economic level of Japan at that time: an overwhelming majority of farmers, relatively small numbers in manufacturing and commerce and government, and a rather large number of servants. One word of caution about the doctors: they were practicing non-Western medicine.

All this pertains to the first half of the 1870's. Was it any different in the 1860's or 1850's? Most probably not. Crawcour's estimates of the structure of national income in the 1860's (divided into agriculture, manufacturing, and services) tallies almost exactly with the results for the late 1870's.[20] There is no evidence which suggests that the industrial structure was changing rapidly any time before the 1880's. An economy whose agriculture remained heavily concentrated on rice growing, and whose industries were largely handicrafts catering to local needs—this remains an accurate description for the century preceding MEG.

None of this, however, should leave the impression that the Japanese economy was in a state of stagnation during the last hundred years of Tokugawa rule. Economic growth (to be sure not *modern*) could and was occurring—the opinions of many Japanese Marxists notwithstanding—and even though rates of progress were low, over long periods they cumulated into significant achievements. Recently, some economic historians have been impressed with the magnitude of changes in the first half of the nineteenth century. A number of factors are frequently discussed in this connection: growth of output in agriculture, commercialization of agriculture, diffusion of traditional industries, and the establishment by certain *han* (clans) of some Western industries. All these factors were present, but there remains room for differences of emphasis and interpretation.

Take the problems related to agriculture. Two of the most prominent Western students of Japanese history have, of late, suggested a revisionist point of view. T. C. Smith in his *Agrarian Origins of Modern Japan*[21] showed that the agriculture of certain regions became more productive during the late Tokugawa era. He cannot show similar increases in the

[20] Crawcour, *op. cit.,* Table 2.
[21] Stanford University Press, Stanford, 1959.

TABLE 4. Proportion of Crops Marketed in the Early 1870's (%)

Rice	15–20
Coarse grains, beans, potatoes	5–10
Industrial crops	80–90
Vegetables	20–30
Fruit	20–30
Total (All crops)	25–31

Source: Yamaguchi, *Meiji zenki keizai no bunseki*, p. 42.

national averages because adequate statistics are not available. There may be, and in our opinion there were, significant differences between regions and national averages, and these differences must be taken into account; they form areas for potential development. The same sort of problem comes up in connection with commercialization of agriculture. Crawcour feels that in the 1860's agriculture over most of Japan was basically commercial, that is, that the bulk of farm produce was grown for a market rather than for consumption by the cultivator.[22] This raises many questions. How do we properly define the commercial proportion of agriculture? This is not an unimportant consideration in Japan where the peasant, under the Tokugawa, had to deliver an average of 30–40 per cent of his rice crop in the form of taxes in kind to the daimyo. To be sure, a great deal of tax rice eventually reached the market because daimyo and samurai sold it to obtain cash, but from the point of view of the peasant this was not rice grown for commercial purposes. After all, if the grower had had a choice, he might have himself consumed a great proportion of the tax rice. Yamaguchi's calculations, shown in Table 4, which exclude tax rice from the commercialized segment, do not give a picture of an agriculture in which the bulk of produce reached the market. Most important, however, is the matter of regional differences. Unquestionably there were regions in the first half of the 19th century in which commercial agriculture predominated, such as Kinai and Tōsan. Just as clearly there were regions, perhaps larger in number, where subsistence farming was average practice, such as Kyushu, Shikoku, and Hokuriku. We need only point out that at present, long after World War II, about 75 per cent of agricultural output reaches the market, and this should place the premodern period in perspective.[23]

[22] "It seems safe to say that in Japanese agriculture as a whole over half and probably nearer two-thirds of output was marketed in one form or another [during the 1860's]." This *includes* tax rice. Crawcour, *op. cit.*

[23] "The rate of commercialization of agricultural products rose from 62 per cent in 1952 to 75 per cent in 1960." Ogura Takekazu (ed.), *Agricultural Development in Modern Japan*, Japan FAO Association, Tokyo, 1963, p. 93.

Turning now to the diffusion of industry, a few more lines from another Crawcour article are appropriate:

Industry had become widely diffused throughout most of Japan by the mid-19th century. This diffusion rather than any great technological progress was the main feature of industrial development in traditional Japan. At the beginning of the Tokugawa period in the early 17th century, when the mass of the population still lived by subsistence farming and demand for most industrial products was practically confined to aristocrats and feudal courts, industry was mostly of the craft type and existed only in a few centres such as Kyoto, and the castle towns. By the mid-19th century, however, industries, once the jealously guarded preserve of groups of craftsmen under imperial or feudal patronage had spread widely through towns and villages over most of the country. This spread was closely connected with the spread of the commercial economy.[24]

To a certain extent, this "diffusion" is analogous to the undermining of craft guilds in Europe, and the rise of cottage industry and the putting-out system.[25] In effect, it supports the notion of increased rural by-employments, also noticed by Smith and Japanese observers. It is evidence of changes in methods of production, but not of a transformation of the industrial structure.

Some scholars have attributed considerable importance to the establishment of Western industries by a few *han*. Since these were frequently connected with a desire to produce armaments, Norman went so far as to suggest that the "normal" pattern for an industrial revolution was reversed in Japan, with heavy industry preceding the development of light industry.[26] Smith takes a more temperate view:

. . . the Meiji Government owed much to the Tokugawa and *han* governments. It was not obliged to begin the process of industrialization from scratch. When the new government took power, it was already the prospective heir to several iron foundries and numerous scattered furnaces for smelting iron ore, a mechanized spinning mill, an important coal mine, scattered facilities for shipbuilding and repair, and a modest but substantial merchant marine. Not the least benefit of its inheritance was a group of persons who had acquired invaluable technical and managerial experience in starting these enterprises and upon whom it could draw for help. Thus by the end of the Tokugawa period

[24] E. S. Crawcour, "The Japanese Economy on the Eve of Modernization," *The Journal of the Oriental Society of Australia,* Vol. 2, No. 1 (June 1963), 37.

[25] See David S. Landes, "Technological Change and Industrial Development in Western Europe, 1750–1914," *Cambridge Economic History,* Vol. VI, Cambridge University Press, Cambridge, 1964, pp. 276–278.

[26] E. Herbert Norman, *Japan's Emergence as a Modern State,* Institute of Pacific Relations, New York, 1940, pp. 125–126. Alexander Gerschenkron has suggested a similar pattern of development for Germany and Russia. But conditions in these countries—especially as they pertain to the labor supply—were very different. See *Economic Backwardness in Historical Perspective,* Harvard University Press, Cambridge, Mass., 1962, Ch. I.

the first and in some ways most difficult step in industrialization had already been taken, that of overcoming inertia and making a start.[27]

No one will deny that these developments could have had an influence on subsequent growth, and Smith in emphasizing the training of even a few future leaders has placed the issue in the proper context. At the same time, isolated islands of modernity existed and exist in most backward countries; these should not be confused with the beginnings of an industrial revolution, the error made by Norman. A few spinning mills and iron foundries cannot be said to change the industrial structure of a country with a population of some 30 million people.

We conclude that in 1868 the industrial structure of Japan was not undergoing rapid transformation. There were changes, but their pace was slow and their impact highly limited.

Relation of Modern Scientific Thought and Technology to Industry

In the 1860's there was almost no modern technology or industry in Japan; consequently, modern scientific thought could not possibly have been involved in most of the productive process. Modern education and technology started to develop in earnest only in the 1870's and thereafter, and yet things are not quite so simple as that. Let us cite another couple of sentences from Smith: "Industrialization began earlier and proceeded more rapidly in Japan than elsewhere in the Far East. One of the reasons for this was that knowledge of the West, and particularly its technology, was more advanced in Japan than elsewhere almost from the beginning of Western intercourse."[28] Smith stresses the level of Dutch Studies (*rangaku*) spearheaded mainly by some of the largest *han:* Satsuma, Chōshū, Saga, Tōsa, and Mito. He notes that some of the schools in the early nineteenth century had surprisingly wide curricula, sometimes including astronomy, geography, physics, metallurgy, English, German, French, and Russian—in addition to Dutch. Smith also observes that some schools even operated laboratories with experiments in photography, cotton spinning, sugar refining, the plating of metals, and the manufacturing of acids, alcohol and glass. A few of the laboratories also built experimental models of reverberatory furnaces, steamships, and telegraph systems.

Our inclinations would be to discount these developments rather heavily as far as their relation to MEG is concerned. The examples are isolated, and while they may testify to considerable intellectual ferment within an extremely restricted sphere of society, this is not the stuff of which industrial revolutions are made. It would be almost like saying that

---

[27] Thomas C. Smith, *Political Change and Industrial Development in Japan: Government Enterprise, 1868–1880,* Stanford University Press, Stanford, 1955, p. 12.

[28] *Ibid.,* p. 1.

Leonardo da Vinci's experiments were a sign of the beginnings of the industrial revolution!

Even if the *han* factories and laboratories were of limited impact, there existed an element of much larger importance in late Tokugawa society—namely the level or stock of education. This was a "given" for the new regime, and may have played a vital role in the eventual adoption of modern scientific thought and technology. There are, in fact, many reasons for believing that Japan's stock of education—and human capital—was unusual by international standards.

The British sociologist R. P. Dore has examined some of these questions in a recent paper entitled "The Legacy of Tokugawa Education."[29] His opening sentences provide the theme: "Japan, we are frequently told in these days of growing punditry on the course and causes of economic development, is 'different.' And there is by now a growing awareness that one of the ways it differs from most other late-developing countries is in starting its career of forced-pace modernization with a widespread and well-developed tradition of formal institutionalized education."[30] One must ask questions both about the kind and amount of formal education that went on in premodern Japan. Dore believes that at the end of the Tokugawa era every samurai was capable of reading and writing his own language, and most of them knew some Chinese as well. Public provision for formal education was limited to the samurai class, but the lower orders, still according to Dore, provided very well for themselves.

In the towns a good proportion of the population could read and write Japanese. Parents bought such education for their children, voluntarily and with hard cash, from teachers who derived their total income from fees. In country districts, paternally disposed richer villagers did a great deal to supplement the operations of an otherwise private-enterprise system. At a very rough estimate it would seem that by the time of the Restoration forty to fifty per cent of all Japanese boys, and perhaps fifteen per cent of girls were getting some formal schooling outside their homes.[31]

If these estimates are to be accepted, they suggest a spread of literacy greater than in most currently underdeveloped countries, and greater than in any European country at a comparable stage of development, with the exception of Holland and Prussia. Certainly England and France were quite far behind.

There are independent estimates which tend to confirm Dore's conclu-

[29] In Marius B. Jansen (ed.), *Changing Japanese Attitudes Toward Modernization,* Princeton University Press, Princeton, 1965, Ch. iii. By the same author, see also *Tokugawa Education,* University of California Press, Berkeley, 1965, Ch. x. Also Herbert Passin, "Education and Economic Growth in Japan, 1850–1912" (mimeo.).

[30] Cited, with permission, from a preliminary version of Dore's paper.

[31] *Ibid.*

sions.[32] Late Tokugawa Japan had five major types of schools, with different functions and aims. Most important by far were the *terakoya* (Buddhist temple schools) operated on a private pay-as-you-go basis mainly for the benefit of commoners. The curriculum was normally confined to the local version of the three R's, and the period of attendance ran from three to seven years. (Women were not excluded, and samurai children sometimes attended.) In 1868 there were 12,000 to 13,000 *terakoya* with a total enrollment of 837,000 pupils. (Slightly more than 21 per cent of the students were women.)

A second type of school were the *hankō* or *han* schools. These had, in about 1868, about 85,000 pupils, mostly members of the *bushi* or samurai[33] class, although commoners were not always entirely excluded. (In fact, very few commoners attended.) *Hankō* were operated with public funds, and were designed to give an education to the upper classes. They were institutions of a somewhat higher level, and stressed subjects beyond the three R's: martial arts, Confucian learning, and sometimes even "modern" subjects. Some *han* made use of local *terakoya* and then transferred *bushi* pupils to *hankō* for purposes of higher education. Others forbade *bushi* children to enter *terakoya* and thus the *hankō* became more inclusive schools. Richer *han* had more children in school—this correlation is quite clear.

Some *han* also operated so-called *gōgaku*—really rural-based schools, specializing in secondary education and designed to be a bridge between *terakoya* and *hankō*. These, at the same time period, enrolled about 42,000 pupils.

There were also *shijuku*—private schools of higher education—with an enrollment of 107,000 and *bakufu* schools with about 70,000 pupils. What these particular schools really represented is hard to say. The former were forerunners of some of Japan's leading private universities, and the latter were irregular schools and a kind of adult education or indoctrination program operated by the shogunate.

Altogether, the totals for 1868 looked like this:

Terakoya	837,000 pupils
Hankō	85,000 "
Gōgaku	42,000 "
Shijuku	107,000 "
Bakufu gakkō	70,000 "

Total: 1,141,000 students in some sort of formal school.

[32] Sano Yōko and Hasegawa Tsuneo, "Estimated Number of Pupils in All Japan, 1864–1867 and 1868–1870" (Unpublished research report of the Keio University Institute of Industrial Relations).

[33] The term *bushi* is a synonym for samurai. Japanese historians generally prefer the former term.

These estimates are consistent with Dore's opinion that 40–50 per cent of the boys and 15 per cent of the girls received some formal schooling. Let us assume that the total population in 1868 was 34 million. For that time we do not know the age distribution—this information becomes available only in 1920. In 1920, 12.25 per cent of the total population was in the 5 to 9 age group (12.4 per cent of the men, and 12.1 per cent of the women). During the late Tokugawa this age group must have accounted for the bulk of school attendance because of the overwhelming importance of *terakoya*. If we apply the 1920 age distribution to 1868, the result is 4 million people in the age group 5 to 9—approximately 2 million males and 2 million females. Fifty per cent of the males and 15 per cent of the females would be slightly above our calculation of national school attendance. Given the nature of these "guesses," however, the correspondence is close enough.

The amount of formal education is one thing; the kind of formal education is another matter. We may take it for granted that the bulk of education concentrated on imparting the simplest skills—a minimum level of literacy. Higher education was characterized by excessive formalism in the form of memorization of Chinese classics, although sometimes modern subjects were taught. What good can this stock of education do for a country seeking economic growth? In this connection, Dore makes four points.

About the general impact of formal education, he says: "The picture was patchy; feudal separatism had produced wide regional differences in the spread of education and the prevailing enthusiasm for it. But the exceptional thing, compared with other societies at a comparable stage of economic development, is that the average level was so high. The ideological transition to an ambitious knowledge-seeking and qualification-seeking society had not only begun; it was well under way."[34] In other words, the rather widespread system of formal education ensured a positive attitude towards the process of deliberately acquiring new knowledge and also helped instill in the minds of most citizens the possibility of individual and national improvement.

Secondly, the content of samurai (leader) education had frequently moved out of the rut of Chinese learning.

Thirdly, the previous spread of education—together with its moral basis—made the concept of universal elementary education speedily acceptable in Japan. (In many countries this was not the case.[35]) By moral basis is meant the Confucian notion of acquiring "virtue" through education—in essence, in order to understand one's station in life. This was equally important for all orders of society.

[34] Dore, "The Legacy of Tokugawa Education," p. 102.

[35] Dore, *Tokugawa Education*, pp. 297–298.

And finally, Dore presents the following intriguing idea:

> Whatever might be said about its effects on curiosity . . . , the traditional education may have prepared its products for the acceptance of new knowledge in another way . . . . Had the Tokugawa schools been mainly concerned to "teach people to think", had they encouraged the free play of ideas between teacher and pupil on a footing of near equality, there might have been many more steamships whose boilers were ruined by men who thought they could run them by the light of pure reason before they got instructions in how to keep them filled with water.[36]

That is to say, in a backward country, discipline and docility may be more important than creativity, *when technology can be imported!*[37]

No doubt all of the assets described above helped in the eventual achievement of MEG. In 1868, however, they were largely potential forces.

International Contacts

There is a saying that when one is besieged in a castle, to raise the drawbridge is to imprison oneself and make it impossible to hold out indefinitely; and again, that when opposing forces face each other across a river, victory is obtained by that which crosses the river and attacks. It seems clear throughout history that he who takes action is in a position to advance, while he who remains inactive must retreat. Even though the Shogun's ancestors set up seclusion laws, they left the Dutch and the Chinese to act as a bridge [to the outside world]. Might this bridge not now be of advantage to us in handling foreign affairs, providing us with the means whereby we may for a time avert the outbreak of hostilities and then, after some time has elapsed, gain a complete victory?

These are the words of the Lord of Hikone, Ii Naosuke, written in 1853.[38] In the perspective of the long run, the senior councilor of the shogun made a great deal of sense, but for the next twenty years or so reestablished international contacts were to bring their share of grief to Japan. A bridge can be used for coming and going, and the arrival of the foreigner in Japan—especially after an absence of over 200 years—upset well-established political and economic routine in no small way.

Of all the attributes of MEG which have been considered, only the presence of international contacts was fully developed by the time of the Restoration. Commodore Perry arrived in 1853, and returned the next year to sign the Treaty of Kanagawa. This led to the establishment of an American consulate general in 1856, headed by Townsend Harris, followed by the United States-Japan Commercial Treaty of 1858. Similar arrangements were made with Great Britain, Russia, France and the

---

[36] Dore, "The Legacy of Tokugawa Education," pp. 109–110.

[37] An idea not infrequently stressed by Gerschenkron; see *op. cit.*, Ch. i.

[38] Cited in W. G. Beasley, *Selected Documents on Japanese Foreign Policy,* Oxford University Press, London, 1955, p. 117.

Netherlands. Foreigners were given the right to set up missions, to trade in certain specified ports, and were given extraterritorial protection. In addition, by arrangements concluded in 1865, Japan's power to levy tariffs was restricted: import duties could be no higher than 5 per cent ad valorem.

Diplomatic and economic arrangements were concluded during the 1850's. Trade and other economic activities began at the very end of that decade, but did not reach moderately sizable quantities until the 1860's. (For example, in 1859, total commodity exports and imports out of the three major trading ports—Yokohama, Nagasaki, and Hakodate— amounted to 1.9 million dollars. In 1867 the figure was 29.6 million dollars.[39]) It is very difficult to give a brief assessment of the immediate economic consequences of an open Japan. As seen with Japanese eyes, it must have been a mixed blessing. On the positive side, the leaders of Japan—at any rate those interested in change—must have realized that the possibility of economic modernization was uniquely tied to the expansion of exports and imports. Japan needed to import the know-how and commodities of the more advanced countries, and this required both diplomatic contact and exports with which to purchase foreign goods and services. Furthermore, Japan was no pauper. She had articles which foreigners wanted to purchase—for example, silk, tea, and fish-oil,—and a not inconsiderable bullion reserve. In the beginning, business was quite good, and the balance of trade was generally favorable until the Restoration; after that it turned sharply negative.

It is equally easy to point out the less pleasant aspects of foreign economic contact. Foreigners were a disruptive element in Japanese society. Their mere presence caused unrest, civil war, and armed retaliation by the Western powers. Cheap foreign imports ruined some traditional industries, such as cotton growing, and the behavior of foreign merchants created resentment. It was not easy to swallow extraterritoriality or the management of exports and imports by foreign hands; the feeling was strong that the foreigners absorbed more than their fair share of profits. The following quote from an official government report written in 1884 gives an idea of the emotions prevailing at that time concerning the "battle of foreign trade":[40]

Foreign merchants who came to our nation in the early years were never those who commanded large sources of capital. One can say that they were

[39] Hugh Borton, *Japan's Modern Century,* The Ronald Press Co., New York, 1955, p. 57.

[40] Japan, Ministry of Agriculture and Forestry, *Kōgyō iken,* pp. 113–114. However, see also John McMaster, "The Japanese Gold Rush of 1859," *The Journal of Asian Studies,* Vol. XIX, No. 3 (May 1960), who feels that foreign profits in bullion speculation have been much exaggerated.

a lot of cunning tricky speculators. They took advantage of our people's lack of knowledge of the actual condition of foreign trade. . . . Since then, the number of foreign merchants who have come to our nation has increased month by month and year by year, and now conditions are such that they have formed a residential area resembling a walled-in castle. At present there are in residence several hundred foreign merchants who support their families without inconvenience. They can do this because of the profit margins which they earn as go-betweens. It may be said that they are subsidized by our manufacturers and merchants. . . . The first commodities through which foreign merchants gained enormous profits were pure gold and silver coins. Next came silkworm egg-cards, silk, tea and other miscellaneous commodities. Imports began with medicines, followed by ships, machines, armaments, iron tools, and eventually cotton cloth, sugar, petroleum and miscellaneous items. We needed imports more than the foreigners needed our goods, and therefore they were stronger. In addition, both imports and exports required the services of foreign merchants in the port cities. It is natural then that most profits fell into their hands.

The Givens in Comparative Perspective

The state of the Japanese economy from the point of view of eventual MEG is comprehensible primarily in comparative terms. Japan is perhaps the classic example in economic history of a move into industrialization from an "in between" position. She was not so far along economically as the early industrializers of Western and Central Europe or the U.S.A. in their preindustrial phases, nor was she so backward as most of the countries of Asia and Africa today. This is an important point because of its relationship to the applicability of the Japanese experience to current problems. We shall pursue it briefly in accordance with a few generalizations proposed some years ago by Kuznets.[41]

The present-day developed countries of the world, before they began to industrialize in the eighteenth and nineteenth centuries, were by contemporary standards relatively advanced. They had experienced fairly sustained growth, were politically independent, and had all been participants in the intellectual, political, and geographical revolutions which engulfed Europe between the thirteenth and sixteenth centuries. Currently underdeveloped countries find themselves in a very different position: the great intellectual movements have passed them by; for centuries many of them had neither grown nor enjoyed political independence, and by contemporary standards they are backward. Where does one place Japan? Squarely in between these (ideal type) extremes. Japan was, by 1868, one of the oldest independent nations of the world. Although not affected by the major intellectual trends of the Western world, and undoubtedly

[41] Simon Kuznets, "Underdeveloped Countries and the Pre-industrial Phase in the Advanced Countries" in A. N. Agarwala and S. P. Singh (eds.), *The Economics of Underdevelopment*, Oxford University Press, Bombay, 1958, pp. 135–153.

relatively backward by the standard of the second half of the nineteenth century, she nevertheless did not wallow in economic (or cultural) stagnation before the Restoration. Even Japan's relative backwardness must be treated carefully; the gap between the advanced and backward countries is much larger today than it was in the 1860's.

An accepted index of economic development is the proportion of labor force active in agriculture. Even though the measurement of this quantity poses fantastic problems, most investigators would agree that when the Western European countries began to industrialize they had a markedly lower percentage of the population engaged in agriculture than is now found in currently underdeveloped countries. For example, there is an estimate which places the proportion of the active agricultural population of France in 1789 at 55 per cent.[42] Gregory King suggests a level of 60 per cent for England and Wales in 1688.[43] More generally, Kuznets suggests that the older countries of Western Europe had reduced agricultural occupations to about 60 per cent by the first quarter of the nineteenth century, but that this took place earlier in England, France, and the Netherlands. Similar levels were achieved in the middle of the nineteenth century by the Scandinavian countries, the United States, Australia, and New Zealand. In contrast, most of Asia and Africa at present have upwards of 80 per cent of their populations gainfully employed (or underemployed) in agriculture. From this we may infer that per capita income levels in the older countries were relatively high before industrialization, because average productivity levels were higher in nonagricultural occupations. In this comparison, the national figures tell us that Japan resembles more closely the underdeveloped world: approximately 80 per cent of her gainfully occupied population was agricultural and, by inference, her per capita income levels were probably relatively low. Yet this conclusion cannot be accepted in an overly simplified manner. The figures for Japan tend to overstate the agricultural population,[44] and, to the extent that they do, the levels of per capita income are understated. It is impossible to measure the bias or to say whether this bias influences other countries to a similar degree. All we can do is to suggest great caution in interpreting the meaning of the 80 per cent actively engaged in agriculture. At the very least we would say that Japan was in an "in between" position.

The emphasis changes, however, when total population and population growth are considered. Two things stand out about the early industrializers: their total populations were rather small, and the natural rates of increase were moderate before the industrial revolution. For example,

[42] J. C. Toutain, *La Population de la France de 1700 à 1959*, I.S.E.A., Paris, 1963, p. 125.

[43] Cited in Kuznets, *op. cit.*, p. 143.

[44] But this holds for the statistics of all countries.

the population of England and Wales was between $5\frac{1}{2}$ and 6 million in 1700 and had reached 9 million by 1800. France's population between the same ten years grew from approximately 19 million to 30 million.[45] None of the pioneers of industrialization were giant repositories of people in the manner of China, India, and Indonesia, nor did any of them have rates of natural population growth close to the biological maximum. Japan's population of about 30 million was large but not gigantic, and her population was increasing rather slowly—in this again she resembled faraway Europe more than her closer cultural and geographical neighbors.

HOW THE GIVENS WERE CHANGED

In this section we shall examine some of the forces which led to the beginning of modern economic growth in 1886, and which began with the Meiji Restoration of 1868. Since the specific facets of a large topic which may be singled out for closer inspection are largely a matter of personal predilection, a few introductory remarks explaining our choices may be necessary. What follows begins with the Restoration and is in the main confined to two aspects of government activity: its principal socioeconomic institutional reforms and the creation of a modern financial and banking base in Japan.

Why the Restoration has been chosen as a symbol of the beginning of Japan's modernization has already been touched upon. There are dates similar to 1868 in world history—1066, 1776, 1789 and others—all forming major turning points. Eighteen hundred sixty-eight, however, is much more than a symbol. It is also a real beginning: the beginning of the end of the vacillation and confusion which had characterized Japanese policy ever since the foreign threat first materialized. Imperial Restoration ended the two and one-half centuries of rule by the Tokugawa family, brought to the throne a new emperor (Meiji), and, most important, catapulted into power a new group of determined young leaders—Okubo, Kido, Iwakura, and others—who shared the view that Japan would have to modernize or go under. It was not the end of confusion, disputes, vacillations, and temporary setbacks, but it was the beginning of the end.[46] The real end, as far as economic policy is concerned, comes only with

[45] For England and Wales: B. R. Mitchell and Phyllis Deane, *Abstract of British Historical Statistics,* Cambridge University Press, Cambridge, 1962, p. 5. For France: E. Levasseur, *La Population Francaise,* 3 vols., Paris, 1889–1892, Vol. III, table facing p. 232.

[46] See, for example, Sidney Devere Brown, "Okubo Toshimichi: His Political and Economic Policies in Early Meiji Japan," *Journal of Asian Studies,* Vol. XXI, No. 2 (Feb. 1962), especially 184.

Matsukata's deflationary policies in the 1880's, and the years of transition are really the history of the government's trying to gain control over an explosive situation.

Primary focus on government activity during transition can be justified. Comparative economic history tells us that countries beginning industrialization in a setting of relative backwardness require leadership and strong action to get started. More or less spontaneous modern economic growth may have been the case in Great Britain, but it is difficult to find elsewhere. Government, and to a greater or lesser degree private or semi-private banks, supplied the necessary push in Prussia and Russia. This alone would warrant a close look at what the government was doing in Japan, but the situation goes deeper than that. The genesis of Japanese industrialization naturally coincides with events which affected other aspects of society: a new political system, a new class structure, and participation in international affairs. Especially during the years of transition, when changes came in rapid succession, the private sector—individuals without a policy—played a less active role. It tried to keep its head above water in a stormy period, and this alone was no easy task, but the main impetus for action had to come from the government. None of this means that in viewing a century of modern economic growth one should ascribe all success to government and a minor and inactive role to the private sector. It does mean, however, that in the very early stages of growth government performed the more important tasks.

During transition, government in Japan carried out a multitude of policies. It operated factories, subsidized certain industries, imported technicians, and sent students abroad. It also invested quite heavily in human capital. We will allude to these activities only in passing for two reasons. First, they have been well described elsewhere,[47] and second, they seem to us of lesser long-run significance than institutional reform and financial policies.

Major Institutional Changes Initiated by the Meiji Government[48]

1. One of the first tasks undertaken by the Meiji Government was a reform of the Tokugawa class structure. Until 1869, the population of

[47] For example, Smith, *Political Change and Industrial Development in Japan,* Emi Koichi, *Government Fiscal Activity and Economic Growth in Japan,* 1868–1920, Kinokuniya Bookstore Co., Ltd., Tokyo, 1963; and W. W. Lockwood, *The Economic Development of Japan, Growth and Structural Change,* 1868–1938, Princeton University Press, Princeton, 1954.

[48] In this section we have relied very heavily on Yamaguchi Kazuo, *Nihon keizaishi kōgi* (Lectures on Japanese Economic History), Tokyo Daigaku Shuppan-kai, Tokyo, 1960, pp. 103–135.

Japan was officially divided into five major groups, in order of precedence: *kuge* (the small and relatively unimportant court nobility), *bushi* (the ruling warrior or samurai class), *nōmin* (the farmers), and finally the *kō-shō-nin* (the commercial and craftsmen groups sometimes called by the collective name *chōnin*). In addition there were also small outcast groups, among whom *eta* were the most numerous. Membership in these classes was determined by birth, and, at least in theory, people could not move from one class to another. There was, in fact, only little upward or downward mobility. We are not entirely certain how the population was distributed among these classes, but there is little doubt about the general order of magnitudes. Approximately 80 per cent of the population were farmers, and the remainder must have been split more or less evenly between *bushi* and *kuge* on the one hand and *chōnin* on the other; roughly 7 per cent *bushi* and *kuge,* and 13 per cent *chōnin*. Each class, with the possible exception of *kuge,* performed a specific economic or administrative task. Farmers provided the nation with essential food and therefore, in keeping with Confucian or more familiar physiocratic prejudices, ranked above the city dwellers who performed "mere" services. Warriors who had fought no battles for over two hundred years were supposed to rule and administer the country, and in return for this were supported by the farmers. Members of the *bushi* class were not permitted to engage in agriculture or commerce—indeed, no member of one class could perform the function of the member of another class.

It must have been obvious soon after the Restoration that this class structure was a major obstacle to modern growth. It was too rigid and froze society in an agricultural mold; it was a wasteful arrangement in that the best educated and most able section of the population was largely underemployed.

Between 1869 and 1871 the government forced through major changes. As a result, three new official classes emerged: the *ka-zoku* (the former *kuge* group and a few top-ranking members of the *bushi* class), the *shi-zoku* (the ex-*bushi* class), and the *heimin* (including all the rest of the population). *Ka-zoku* became the new nobility, an open-ended class which successful businessmen, statesmen, and military leaders could eventually hope to join. Membership conferred no specific economic privileges. *Shi-zoku* was merely a courtesy designation indicating former *bushi* status.

A simple listing of the decrees does not do justice to the resentment, conflict, and confusion which these measures must have caused. For example, in October, 1871, the *Outline of the New Criminal Law* entirely omitted mention of the recognized Tokugawa Era practice that allowed samurai freely to cut down a commoner on grounds of rudeness; persons wearing swords were no longer permitted to ride the ferries in Metropolitan

Tokyo free of charge, and anyone was permitted to ride a horse.[49] An Imperial Edict of 1872 added insult to injury:[50]

> Those who have worn two swords during the Tokugawa regime have been known as *bushi,* and in their bearing they have been obdurate, they have lived at the expense of others, and in extreme cases, they have put people to the sword; their crime being regarded by officials as no offense. . . . No such practice prevailed in ancient Japan. After living a life of idleness for generations, the samurai have had their stipends reduced and they have been authorized to take off their swords so that all strata of the people may finally gain their rights to liberty. By these innovations the rulers and ruled will be placed on the same basis, the rights of the people will be equal, and the way will be cleared for the unity of soldier and peasant.

A final blow came in March of 1876 when, in accordance with a decree suggested by War Minister Yamagata Aritomo, a ban was placed on the wearing of swords.[51] It does not require a great deal of imagination to realize how even slightly conservative *bushi* must have felt about the forcible removal of their main status symbol.

More or less at the same time, between 1868 and 1873, other administrative and economic changes gave meaning to the new class structure. Farmers, craftsmen, and city dwellers were permitted to move freely within the country (see below) and to change the nature of their work. Equally important, members of the former ruling classes, the *ka-* and *shizoku,* could now participate in agriculture, industry, or commerce. There were a number of other major and minor changes: the *kabunakama*— restrictive guild organizations—were dissolved, and long-term apprenticeship contracts and various forms of hereditary servitude were abridged.

2. Before the Meiji Restoration both internal and external travel and commercial communications were under severe control. Together with the class reform, the government also loosened these restrictions. These measures began in 1868 with the abolishment of *sekisho,* the checkpoints located along all major roads through which one could pass only after proper identification and in possession of the requisite pass. Now it became possible for all citizens to travel freely and to select their place of residence at will. Other measures followed in the next few years, all designed to free the internal market from previous "feudal" restrictions. Among the more effective, were the end of the *tsuru* system which had prevented

---

[49] But "the practice of leniency under criminal law for the peers and persons of samurai stock was preserved until the end of the year 1881." Ishii Ryosuke, *Japanese Legislation in the Meiji Era,* trans. William J. Chambliss, Pan-Pacific Press, Tokyo, 1958, p. 104.

[50] *Ibid.,* pp. 723–724.

[51] *Ibid.,* pp. 102–103. Swords were permitted as part of dress and police uniforms.

the movement of rice and some other grains across *han* boundaries, and the discontinuation in 1871 of the government-operated horse-relay system along the principal roads. In order to use these horses it had been necessary to secure permits, another restrictive control device.

Restrictions on external economic relations were also lifted during the early years of Meiji. The government opened the ports of Yokohama, Nagasaki, Hakodate, Kobe, Osaka, and Niigata to foreign ships. At the same time, the export prohibitions on rice, wheat, copper, and raw silk were done away with, and foreign trade became nearly entirely free.

3. Owing to the class reform, the former *bushi* class was now permitted to engage in any economic activity. Their energies need no longer be reserved for ruling the country, an activity which only a minority of this class had performed anyway. There remained, however a major problem for the new rulers: how to dispose of the continuing economic burden which the *kuge* and especially the *bushi* (now *ka-shi-zoku*) represented. Under the Tokugawa, *bushi,* were, in some sense, a *rentier* class. Their income derived from rice stipends of widely varying amounts which they received from their respective lords (daimyo). In turn, the lord received his income from taxing the peasantry of his domain, largely by appropriating a share of the rice crop. It was then the lord's responsibility to support his retainers. To call most of these retainers *rentiers* is accurate because, frequently, they no longer performed substantial services in return for stipends. Originally a group of warriors, the *bushi,* by the time of the Meiji Restoration and after 200 years of peace, had lost their function in society. With the Restoration, however, the *bushi* became a financial responsibility of the new government, since it was intent on abolishing daimyo rule and responsibility. Approximately 6–7 per cent of the population were members of the *bushi* class, and continuing their stipends consumed about 30 per cent of ordinary government revenue in 1868 and 1869.

How the government actually unburdened itself of this great financial and social burden is an incredibly complicated story. Simple repudiation of *bushi* economic claims was impossible, and a final settlement was not reached until 1876. The details which led up to the settlement need not concern us now, although we will return to this subject later. In essence, the stipends were abolished, and as compensation the former aristocracy received government commutation bonds. Approximately 313,000 heads of households were involved, and the average payment amounted to ¥548. Altogether the settlement cost the government over ¥170,000,000 in bonds, and over ¥730,000 in cash. These sums were not small for either party—let us recall that per capita product at that time was only slightly above ¥18. But on the whole, the advantage was clearly on the side of the government and the nation. Japan had, through the bonds, divested itself of a perpetual obligation, and subsequent inflation considerably light-ened the burden of the bonds. The old aristocracy was—in the short run at least—appeased, and for some the transformation to the new conditions was eased. Most of them, it must be said, did not have much luck with their bonds. Inexperience in business and in handling money in general wiped out much of their capital in relatively short order.

4. Perhaps the major institutional reform of Meiji times took place in the realm of agriculture. Agriculture had in Tokugawa times been the main source of national revenue, and it was to retain this position through-out the Meiji era. (It was not, it must be added, an adequate source of national revenue. Throughout most of the Meiji period the government had to indulge in considerable deficit financing, as we shall see in the next section.) That is why the institutional changes in the agricultural sec-tor were of extreme importance.

The feudal land tax, which operated before the Restoration, was mainly based on payments in kind, the rate varying with different *han* and in accordance with the state of the harvest. Its incidence fell most heavily on the rice crop. From the point of view of a government interested in fostering MEG, this was an inefficient arrangement. Meiji leaders wanted a uniform national tax which was both monetized and unrelated to the state of the harvest.

Reform began gradually in 1870, and by 1873 the major outlines of the settlement were clear. We can only summarize the very major issues and solutions. First of all, land tax payments were made payable to the central government instead of to the *han*, and payment in kind was turned into a uniform money payment. As a consequence, the major tax revenues of the government no longer depended on the price of rice (as it did when collections were made in kind), and the farmers were placed in closer contact with the money economy. Secondly, the land tax was levied directly on landowners—they were the ones who were held responsible for the payments. At the same time, in 1872, the Tokugawa prohibition against land sale was abolished. (This applied also to urban land.) Thus, the Tokugawa peasant-cultivator was transformed into an owner-cultivator to whom land titles were issued, and who could transfer and sell his land at will.[52] A modern system of private property had been established.

Thirdly, whereas the feudal tax had been imposed on the harvest,

[52] Of course this only applied to peasants who could establish ownership rights to the land. Although exact figures are not available for this period, it is generally conceded that tenancy was relatively widespread. Quantitative estimates usually show about 30 per cent of the arable land cultivated by tenants. For example, see M. Fesca, *Beiträge Zur Kenntniss Der Japanischen Landwirthschaft,* Berlin, 1890, Vol. I, p. 158, and Japan FAO Association, *A Century of Technical Development in Japanese Agriculture,* Tokyo, 1959, p. 29.

the new land tax was based on the value of land. This involved a number of steps. The output of specific fields was converted (for an average period) from quantity units (*koku*) into money. Certain expenses, such as seeds and fertilizers, were deducted from the money value of output, and the remainder was considered the farmers' rent from the land. This remainder or rent was capitalized at rates of interest that usually lay between 4 and 6 per cent, a procedure which yielded rather high land values. On the one hand, the deductible expenditures were usually underestimated by the farmers; on the other hand, the rate of interest used for capitalization purposes was on the low side.

The actual tax rate was initially established at 3 per cent of assessed valuation—on a national basis. In addition, farmers were obliged to pay a surtax to local authorities amounting to 30 per cent of the land tax payment. It has been estimated that the tax and surtax, at first, amounted to 34 per cent of the rice crop, and therefore represented no radical departure from average feudal levels. This is a complicated and controversial issue; Tokugawa tax rates varied widely over time and place, and under these circumstances an average level is not meaningful.[53] It does, however, seem safe to assume that initially there really was no radical departure in either direction. However, the early Meiji rates were not maintained. In 1877 the land tax was lowered to 2.5 per cent of land value and the local surtax was reduced to 20 per cent. Even greater relief was provided, in later years, by a secular inflation which significantly lightened the burden of assessed valuation.

5. Another problem confronting the government during the earliest years of Meiji related to currency and banking.[54] Before the Restoration, the state of the currency—both coins and paper money—was chaotic. Many types of coins were in circulation; their relative value fluctuated considerably; and calculating proper rates of exchange and assuring wide acceptability of the coins was a major problem as well as a full-time occupation. The Meiji government established its mint in 1869, and began to issue national coins at that time. Old Tokugawa coins and monetary units were abolished, and in their place a decimal system was adopted, creating the Yen, Sen, and Rin. By 1874 the unification and adoption of new coins was more or less completed. Much the same fate awaited the some 1600 varieties of Tokugawa paper money in circulation at the time of the Restoration. These were generally retired by 1880.

The government also attempted to encourage the establishment of a modern banking system, and some aspects of this development will be

[53] See W. G. Beasley, "Feudal Revenue in Japan at the Time of the Meiji Restoration," *Journal of Asian Studies,* Vol. XIX, No. 3 (May 1960).

[54] On this general subject see Hugh T. Patrick's excellent essay, "Banking in the Early Stages of Industrialization: Japan, 1868–1914" (mimeo.).

discussed in the next section. It may, however, be desirable to be explicit about an obvious point: Tokugawa Japan had nothing resembling a modern banking system. To be sure, there were pawnbrokers (large and small), money changers, and money lenders, and their activities were typically preindustrial. They specialized in consumption loans at relatively high rates of interest, and to some extent in short-term business loans and "court finance" if we can attach that label to their relation with the *bushi* class. How could it have been otherwise? The development of a modern banking and credit system arises as a response to the needs of modern economic growth and not vice versa. In Japan, we may consider the formal beginnings of a modern banking system to be the National Bank Act of 1872 which eventually led to the establishment of over 150 banks largely founded with capital supplied by *bushi* commutation bonds. We now turn to this subject.

FINANCIAL ASPECTS OF TRANSITION

Some of the terminology currently in use by analysts of economic planning can be of help in achieving a better understanding of governmental policies and problems in Meiji Japan. Five concepts are especially appropriate: objectives, targets, resources, means of implementation, and boundary factors.[55]

Objectives

The long-run objective of the new government was to maintain and, if possible, increase the power and prosperity of the Japanese nation. This required modern economic growth which can therefore also be called a long-term objective. As a short-run objective, the government had to create the conditions which made MEG a realistic possibility. The latter implied negative and positive action: first the abolition of certain hampering institutions, followed by the creation of minimum conditions which would permit MEG to begin.

Targets

This term is used to designate certain specific short-term objectives. As we shall try to show, two must have had top priority during transition, and both were financial: the creation of a sound budget system, together with modern currency and banking institutions. It is a characteristic of Japan's transition that the reaching of these targets involved considerable trial and error—perhaps not such an uncommon phenomenon in early phases of industrialization.

[55] The use of these concepts was first suggested by Ohkawa Kazushi.

Resources

Action is only rarely costless. To carry out its economic objectives and targets, the government required funds. As we have previously pointed out, in spite of severe resource limitations Japan was not a pauper nation. The central authorities had four principal sources of funds in the very late 1860's: inherited assets from the Tokugawa, foreign borrowing, increases in domestic output, and redistribution of the income flow and capital stock. There was much overlapping between these categories, and yet each one is a bit different. Inherited assets mean the stock of funds—private and public—on which the government could somehow lay its hands. For example, there existed a big hoard of specie; Japan exported ¥23.7 million of gold and silver during 1868–1871.[56] Domestic borrowing, forced or voluntary, were methods employed to tap this resource. Foreign borrowing was limited by the uncertain credit worthiness of a "new" nation, and perhaps even more by Japan's own fear of domination by Western Powers. Increases in domestic output (if achievable) and redistribution of current income and assets had to rely on the power to tax. Two general considerations characterized all of Japan's resources. For one thing, they were limited; for another, most credit items were accompanied by debits. The latter was especially true of inherited assets. There were, as will be discussed in detail, very heavy, inherited, pre-Restoration liabilities.

Means of Implementation

Limited by available resources the government had to select means of implementation which were both "economic" and "feasible." Feasibility raises a particularly interesting set of problems. In analyzing historical problems we sometimes tend to forget how much things have changed. What is possible for a government today was frequently out of the question in the nineteenth century, and when we talk of the relative importance of government in Meiji Japan this cannot be forgotten. From the end of the Tokugawa until now Japan has always been an essentially free economy. The government could and did at times plan, act as an entrepreneur, subsidize, favor, discriminate, etc. Its powers of direct control, however, were limited; it had to work by economic means within the market and not by direct decree as in some underdeveloped countries today. Japan's situation as a free market economy affected means of implementation. Specifically it meant that currency and banking manipulations were both means and ends. It was necessary to work through the note issue and

---

[56] An estimate made by Y. Horie, "Japan's Balance of International Payments in the Early Meiji Period," *Kyoto University Economic Review,* Vol. 24, No. 1 (April 1954), cited in Hugh T. Patrick, "External Equilibrium and Internal Convertibility: Financial Policy in Meiji Japan" (mimeo.).

banking regulations in order to achieve a sound flexible money supply and a responsive banking system. This program of implementation, however, led to a variety of shocks in the economy, resulting in inflation and deflation. Both were the direct consequence of government programs designed to stimulate the beginnings of MEG.

Boundary Conditions

We have already suggested that government activity was circumscribed by some economic limitations such as the need to economize resources and the necessity to work within a free market. There were other limitations as well, and these, usually of a somewhat broader nature, are referred to as boundary conditions. With the financial targets kept in mind, any number of boundaries must be considered during the 1860's and 1870's. Of extreme importance was the element of time; targets had to be reached within a reasonable number of years because delays would have made more serious internal and external threats. Japan felt that simply to maintain her independence a considerable increase in national power based on a modern economy was an absolute necessity. If this could not be accomplished in time, foreigners might decide that the Japanese melon was also ripe for slicing. Time was equally precious at home, for here too inaction might have given the opposition a chance to regroup. Many powerful segments of the population were, or believed they were, adversely affected by the Restoration. There were those who had remained loyal to the House of Tokugawa. There were samurai who saw their privileges abolished and who could visualize no future in the rapidly changing new society. There were merchants whose close ties to the *bakufu* now spelled ruin. Forces of discontent were widespread, and only the speedy initiation of a new program (of course not entirely confined to the economy) could maintain the Meiji government in power.

What has been said indicates that the power balance between government and antigovernment forces was a delicate matter, and this formed another boundary closely related to but separate from the question of time. Time means that things had to be done in a hurry: ". . . that great delays in industrialization tend to allow time for social tensions to develop and to assume sinister proportions."[57] Power balance meant that too much hurrying might prove dangerous. If the new government moved too rapidly in any one direction it might thereby mobilize antigovernment forces. The pace of change had to be just right.

Choice among a variety of possible economic policies was also restricted by Japan's somewhat unusual status in the world community. Western Powers had taken away tariff autonomy, and the great majority

---

[57] Gerschenkron, *op. cit.*, p. 28.

of exports and imports were in the hands of foreign merchants. According to the provisions of the 1868 treaty with the United States, Japan was committed "to a system of free international trade, unrestricted inflow and outflow of gold and silver, and unrestricted domestic circulation of foreign gold and silver coins comparable to Japanese coins."[58] Convertibility was a virtual imperative.

The years of transition, as might be expected, were none too peaceful, and this formed the final boundary. When the Meiji Government assumed power in 1868, memories of civil strife and foreign intervention were fresh. Satsuma and Shimonoseki had been attacked by Westerners in 1863–1864, and in 1865–1866 the Tokugawa had fought a civil war with the Chōshū clan. In 1877 the last and most dangerous challenge came with Saigō's Rebellion. Minor incidents arose with alarming regularity. The new government had to control a restless country and potentially aggressive foreign states. Measures of control entailed outlays which were sometimes in competition with expenditures designed to further economic development.

This is the framework. Let us now see how it fits the events of history.

Passive Stability, 1868–1876. Japan's period of transition into modern economic growth, short as it was, forms two distinct subperiods: an interval of passive stability from 1868 to 1876, and an interval of great shocks from 1876 to 1885. During the earlier subperiod, in spite of chaotic political and social conditions, the economy remained remarkably stable as evidenced by the very moderate fluctuations of commodity prices. By contrast, between 1876 and 1885 Japan was shaken by sharp inflation and deflation. This contrast deserves attention. It seems to us that stability was a product of relative governmental passivity combined with an essentially preindustrial economy. The ferment of the late 1860's and early 1870's was primarily institutional and did not greatly affect the daily economic life of the people. Stability was followed by great shocks, reflecting not only stronger actions of the government, but also stronger reactions of the economy to the new policies.

Tokugawa Keiki, the last shogun, relinquished power in November 1867. On January 3, 1868, the formal Imperial Restoration took place. In August 1871 the clans (*han*) were abolished by Imperial Decree. In 1872 Japan's first railroad line, linking the 18 miles between Tokyo and Yokohama, was completed. This somewhat random listing of events should serve to indicate the fullness of these years; the new central government which assumed power with the Restoration was not at all well prepared to shoulder the burdens. It had no systematic financial program and meanwhile was saddled with heavy burdens by the departed Tokugawa. Many of the difficulties, as usual, had to do with expenditures and revenues. Large sums were needed to vanquish rebellious remnants of Tokugawa

---

[58] Patrick, "External Equilibrium and Internal Convertibility."

loyalists, to provide annual pensions for the former warriors since this obligation had now been assumed by the central authorities, and also to service the considerable debts (domestic and foreign) of the clans. Sources of funds were limited, and the financial position of the Meiji Government was unenviable; from September 1868 through December 1872, total expenditures were ¥148.3 million against revenues of only ¥50.4 million.[59] Given the level of administrative inexperience which must have prevailed, one wonders how the government managed to survive.

Three main methods were employed by the government to meet its early deficits: the issue of paper notes (¥68.4 million were in circulation by 1872), loans from well-to-do merchants (the government owed them ¥23.2 million in 1872), and foreign borrowing (this liability stood at ¥4.9 million in 1872).[60] The new note issue was inconvertible and took its place side by side with already existing *han* currency. Popular confidence in the eventual success of these procedures was limited, as shown by the rapid depreciation of government notes vis-à-vis specie. Meiji paper notes began life at discounts of 55–60 per cent relative to specie. Initially some inflation occurred, but by 1870 the situation was well under control. Inflationary pressure abated, while the government's announcement of its intention to redeem notes in the near future stemmed the tide of depreciation. By 1872, also, the government was actively redeeming clan currency with its own notes at market rates, a significant step in the direction of currency unification.

Quantitative information for these years is, of course, scanty, but what exists is consistent with the interpretations offered here. The facts themselves are quite clear. Their interpretation is another matter. Why did the considerable increase in inconvertible note issue not bring about inflation? We can only suggest a few possible explanations. Between 1868 and 1872, Japan's total deficit in her international accounts has been estimated at ¥30.2 million, and this must have created a downward pressure on the price level because the deficit had to be covered by export of specie (a very rough estimate because there exists no exact record of the outflow of gold and silver to foreign countries). We also speculate that the velocity of circulation might have been declining—in some senses the economy was still too backward to respond in the expected manner.

[59] Emi Koichi and Takamatsu Nobukiyo, "Meiji ikō zaisei shūshi no sukei, 1868–1929" (A Survey of Tax Revenues and Expenditures since Meiji), Hitotsubashi University, Institute of Economic Research, Rockefeller Project Preliminary Report, Number D18. (Hereafter cited as Hitotsubashi D18.)

[60] Currency figures from Ōuchi Hyoe (ed.), *Nihon keizai tōkei-shū* (Collected Japanese Economic Statistics), Nihon Hyōronshinsha, Tokyo, 1958, pp. 194–195. Figures for loans from Kimura Motokazu, *Conditions for Direct Taxation and Other Essays*, The Science Council of Japan, Tokyo, 1958, Ch. iii, p. 73.

TABLE 5. Passive Stability (I)

	Wholesale Price Index (1868 = 100)	Interest Rate (%)	Government Paper Money (Million ¥)	Total Inconvertible Notes in Circulation (Million ¥)	Specie + Convertible Notes to Total (%)
1868	100.0	14.0	24.0	65.4	75.1
1869	123.0	14.0	50.1	94.4	66.2
1870	109.4	13.5	55.5	103.2	62.1
1871	113.2	13.8	60.3	108.5	57.0
1872	104.5	14.6	68.4	102.7	53.1

Source: The wholesale price index and interest rates are cited in Tsuru Shigeto, *Essays on Japanese Economy*, pp. 150–151. The interest rate is the annual average for loans between ¥1000 and ¥10,000 in Tokyo. Government paper money and total inconvertible notes from Ōuchi, *Nihon keizai tōkei-shū*. Specie and convertible note ratio to total from Patrick, "External Equilibrium and Internal Convertibility."

So far we have dealt with the first half of the stable years. From 1873 to 1876 things continued in a similar vein, even though the government inaugurated somewhat stronger policies aiming in the direction of previously described targets. These were the years of land tax implementation, of paper money redemption, and of the foundation of national banks. Perhaps the most successful of these policies was the land tax. It was put into effect speedily and effectively, and certainly by 1875 the government had assured itself of large revenues from the agricultural sector. Currency and banking policies did not move forward equally smoothly.

Redemption of paper notes proceeded only slowly owing to a variety of difficulties. The government offered bonds in exchange for its notes, but these carried unattractive interest rates. Bond interest was 6 per cent whereas the market rate was above 10 per cent. Another method was tried with the creation of the national banking system in 1872. It was hoped that the banks would create a money supply responsive to the requirements of industrialization. More specifically, however, the desire was to reduce the quantity of inconvertible government notes and to replace these by convertible national bank notes. There was also the expectation that the new banks might help to reduce the high rate of interest. What actually happened is well summarized by Allen:[61]

According to the Regulations issued in 1872, a national bank was to deposit Government paper money equal to three-fifths of its capital with the

[61] G. C. Allen, *A Short Economic History of Modern Japan*, George Allen & Unwin, Ltd., London, 1946, p. 38.

Treasury, and to hold gold equivalent to two-fifths of its capital as a reserve. The Treasury handed to the banks Paper Money Exchange Bonds bearing 6% interest in return for the notes deposited with it, and the banks were then permitted to issue their own notes redeemable in gold up to the amount of the security which they possessed. In this way it was expected that part of the Government's inconvertible note issue would be replaced by notes convertible into gold, and that effective banking machinery to serve the needs of the new economic system would be brought into being. The operations of these banks, it was also hoped, would lead to a fall in the rate of interest which, since 1868, had apparently ranged between 13 and 14% per annum.

These expectations were not realized. Only four national banks were established under these regulations . . . . Their actual note issue never exceeded 2,300,000 yen. The reasons for the failure of this experiment are not difficult to discover. The relatively low rate of interest paid on the Government bonds, which the banks received in exchange for the Government paper money deposited with the Treasury, made investment of this kind unprofitable. Further, the banks found difficulty in keeping their notes in circulation. Since these notes were convertible into specie, whereas the Government paper money of the same face value was at a discount, merchants who had to pay for imports naturally found it profitable to present the bank notes at the issuing bank and so to obtain gold for their foreign payments. In this way the national banks were drained of their reserves.

In fact, the supply of government paper notes continued to rise because deficits remained large and revenues were too small. By June 1876, ¥105 million were in circulation. The source of the trouble can be easily identified in Table 6. Despite increases in revenues, fiscal problems were still far from solved. In essence they all revolved around the burden of transfer payments, namely the burden of the former *bushi* stipends. A high ratio of transfer payments reflected the continuing influence of the

TABLE 6. Government Current Expenditures and Transfer Payments

	(1) Total Current Expenditures (Central & Local) Million Yen	(2) Transfer Payments Million Yen	(3) Ratio 2/1
1872 (Jan.–Dec.)	45.1	16.1	35.3
1873 "	53.3	18.2	34.1
1874 "	67.6	34.3	50.4
1875 (Jan.–June)	60.8	32.5	53.3
1875 (July–June)	62.5	25.4	40.6
1876 "	51.1	17.9	35.1

Source: Hitotsubashi D18.

TABLE 7. Passive Stability (II)

	Wholesale Prices (1868 = 100)	Interest Rates (%)	Total Inconvertible Notes in Circulation (Million ¥)	Tokyo Wholesale Prices		
				Rice (koku)	Ginned Cotton (60 kg.)	Iron (100 kg.)
1873	95.8	12.8	104.5	¥4.80	¥26.80	¥11.27
1874	101.5	12.9	98.9	7.30	23.52	12.02
1875	95.4	11.8	101.9	7.13	21.92	11.0
1876	111.9	12.1	109.1	5.13	21.12	9.14

	Government Paper Money (Million ¥)	Specie + Convertible Notes to Total (%)
1873	88.3	44.7
1874	101.8	42.4
1875	100.6	41.2
1876	105.1	40.3

Source: See Table 5. Tokyo wholesale prices from Ōuchi, *Nihon keizai tōkei-shū*, p. 254.

premodern distribution of income. This burden had to be eliminated before the government could fruitfully concentrate on modern economic growth.

And yet—notwithstanding the unsettled currency and banking problems, continued increases in government spending, the expenses of the Saga Rebellion and Formosa expedition of 1874—there was still no inflation. Instead, government notes actually reached par with specie in June of 1876, and some commodity prices even showed a certain amount of "softness."[62]

We must again ask, why so little upward pressure on prices? One definite anti-inflation factor continued to be the international trade deficit; ¥31.8 million in gold and silver flowed out of Japan during this period. Two other somewhat more speculative factors may be added. The land tax, which had to be remitted in money, no doubt raised the transactions demand for money, and at the same time output—especially marketed output—of the traditional industries rose vigorously.

We can now summarize the major points of this period of passive stability. The economy remained stable in spite of preliminary policies in the direction of the two specified targets: the budgetary and the currency

[62] Perhaps the prevailing world depression also exercised some downward pressure on Japanese prices.

and banking reforms. As far as resources went, the government depended heavily on inherited assets. Issuance of large quantities of inconvertible paper notes without the creation of disorder, loans from merchants, outflow of gold and silver—all were relying on the political and economic stock left by the Tokugawa. One should not, of course, ignore the role of foreign borrowing and increased output in resource mobilization, but at this stage we would rather stress the inheritance.

To be sure, the inheritance had good and bad features. Government was plagued by an exorbitant level of transfer payments, and these were a direct liability passed on by the old regime. In a broader sense, the weight of this burden was a symptom of even more serious boundary factors. The power balance between supporters and enemies of the Meiji rulers remained precarious, and the biggest and final armed challenge was yet to come. Time was needed to consolidate the central government's strength, in particular the nine years between 1868 and 1876. Furthermore, it would be incorrect to give the impression that economic passivity adequately describes all governmental activity. Capital formation in the form of social overheads and model factories had begun, but investments were still below 10 per cent of budgeted expenditures.

Great Shocks, 1876–1885. The calm ended very suddenly. Two events, closely linked in origin and consequence, rocked Japan in 1876 and 1877. First came the compulsory commutations of *bushi* stipends. After attempting a variety of voluntary schemes without sufficient success, the government finally decided that a sterner compulsory measure was needed to lift an intolerable burden. Stipends were replaced by commutation bonds (*kinroku kōsai*) amounting to ¥172.9 million, and carrying interest rates of 5, 6, 7 and 10 per cent. Compulsory commutation was followed within less than a year by what the Japanese call the Seinan War and what Western writers have usually referred to as the Satsuma Rebellion. The importance of this conflict is widely recognized. It was a last desperate attempt to gain power by those who opposed the new regime. It also was the first victory of a newly created conscript army largely manned by peasants over the old knightly class. It was a rebellion led by one of Japan's most romantic heroes, Saigō Takamori, who took his own life in bitter defeat. Saigō's fellow rebels, mostly former Satsuma warriors, had many grievances, and one of them was a profound dislike of compulsory commutation. The civil war was won by the government, but only at considerable cost. Its entire army of 32,000 men, plus a reserve of 10,000 men, and numerous national police had to be committed before Saigō was driven to *seppuku* at Kagoshima in September of 1877. Expenditures were also high. To pay the bills, the government was forced to issue another ¥27 million in notes and to borrow ¥15 million from the Fifteenth National Bank.[63] To repeat once more, not only were the war

[63] Kimura, *op. cit.,* p. 78.

TABLE 8. Great Shocks (I)

	Gov. Paper Money (Million ¥)	National Bank Notes (Million ¥)	Total (Million ¥)	Increase (Decrease)	Specie & Convertible Notes to Total (%)
1876	105.1	1.7	106.9		40.3
1877	105.8	13.4	119.1	12.2	35.2
1878	139.4	26.3	165.7	46.1	25.6
1879	130.3	34.0	164.4	−1.3	25.7
1880	124.9	34.4	159.4	−5.0	23.4
1881	118.9	34.4	153.3	−6.1	19.1

Source: See Table 5. National Bank notes from Ōuchi, *Nihon keizai tōkei-shū*, p. 194. Total notes and deposits from Fujino Shōzaburō, "Kaheiryō, Māshyaru no 'k', yokin kaitenritsu no suikei, 1877–1940" (A Survey of the Quantity of Money, Marshall's 'k', and the Turnover-Rate of Deposits), Hitotsubashi University, Institute of Economic Research, Rockefeller Project Preliminary Report Number D13. (Hereafter cited as Hitotsubashi D13.)

and capitalization of pensions connected causally, there were also events of similar origin. Both were costly and necessary expenditures to wipe out feudal privileges and antigovernment ferment.

It could have come as no surprise to the authorities that compulsory commutation was extremely unpopular with the ex-clansmen. Voluntary commutation had gotten nowhere in 1874 and for good reasons; after a few years, the value of these pensions bonds was discounted by 40–50 per cent. Motives for resistance to these schemes go all the way from concrete economic self-interest to deep psychological feelings. To begin with the concrete, interest rates attached to the commutation bonds (voluntary and involuntary) were too low. One could, perhaps, argue that the pension bonds should have been issued at market rates of approximately 12 per cent rather than at average rates much closer to 5 per cent, but this would have made commutation more than twice as expensive and was not a realistic possibility. Even at the low interest rates, servicing the bonds ate up 26 per cent of total government expenditures between 1877–1880.[64] A greater burden could not be assumed.

There were additional problems. The quantity of pension bonds which any head of household received varied according to his pre-Restoration status. Former daimyo, for example, were given considerable fortunes; the same was true of other high-ranking *bushi*. Ex-*bushi* of lower rank ob-

[64] Hitotsubashi D18.

TABLE 9. Great Shocks (II)

	Wholesale Prices (1877 = 100)	Interest Rate (%)	Paper Money/ Silver[a]	Commodity Prices (Yen)		
				Rice (Koku)	Ginned Cotton (60 kg.)	Iron (100 kg.)
1877	100	10.0	1.033	5.34	21.12	8.39
1878	108	10.4	1.099	6.39	20.0	8.39
1879	130	12.0	1.212	7.96	21.28	8.67
1880	148	13.1	1.561	10.57	23.84	8.20
1881	164	14.0	1.696	10.59	33.76	8.39

[a] In 1878 the silver yen became legal tender with the government adoption of the bimetallic standard. Therefore, paper money/silver represents the rate of paper note depreciation vis-à-vis silver.

Source: See Tables 5 and 6. Paper money/silver ratio from Hitotsubashi D13.

tained only small sums, and many felt that they had been unfairly treated. Perhaps the psychological burden was the most serious of all. After forced commutation all semblance of previous privilege had been surrendered by the old ruling class. Not only was government support a thing of the past. Now proud warriors brought up to despise money and trade had to move into a more active economic life or be reduced to even more severe poverty—a poverty which had lost both its gentility and virtue.

The authorities were aware of these problems, but their own ability to act was limited by a set of boundaries. Officially compulsory commutation was justified on two counts. According to Ōkuma,[65] who instigated the policy, pension bonds were designed both to create means for former samurai to find new employment and to stimulate the economy simultaneously, by making available more venture capital, lessening the tightness of money, and (it was hoped) leading the economy into an upswing. These announced intentions, coupled with an obvious desire to lessen the transfer burden, may very well have been sincere. However, the real point is that the policy misfired by precipitating, for a while, a violent inflation which endangered the totality of government targets, and the government itself. It was necessary for the government to create additional incentives to make pension bonds acceptable. These incentives caused a great deal of trouble and illustrate how the latent power of the old aristocracy affected economic policy.

[65] Allen, op. cit., pp. 38–39.

One month before the adoption of compulsory commutation, in August of 1876, national bank regulations were amended, and it was a device to make pension bonds more desirable. According to the new rules, the specie reserve requirement for note issue was abolished, and national banks were allowed to issue notes against pension bonds deposited with the Treasury up to 80 per cent of their capital. In this fashion, ex-samurai received a ready-made profitable outlet for their bonds; meanwhile the convertibility of notes was sacrificed. Quite suddenly many new national banks were established. There were four national banks in 1874, responsible for a note issue of about ¥2 million. By 1880 their number had reached 148, and the total note issue amounted to ¥34 million, which was the legal maximum. Together with the expenses of the Seinan War, the economy had sustained another large injection of inconvertible paper currency. Only now the Japanese economy reacted very sharply, as Tables 8 and 9 show. Prices in many instances responded in kind.

No one has to our knowledge succeeded in explaining precisely why very similar circumstances precipitated inflation after 1877 but not before. Tsuru believes that the earlier expansionary impulses were "localized owing to the immaturity of the capitalistic milieu within the country," and perhaps one cannot say much more;[66] clearly the impulses had become less localized. The inflation certainly had a number of interesting features; for example, commodity prices rose unevenly. By representing 1877 as 100, we see that in 1881 rice stood at 198, ginned cotton at 160, and iron at 100. Furthermore, there seems to have existed a two-year time lag between the injection of additional inconvertible currency and the rise in prices. Wholesale prices, interest rates, and paper money depreciation all reached peaks in 1881. Actual net increases of paper notes were, compared with those of the late 1860's and early 1870's, relatively moderate: between 1876 and 1880 a rise of ¥60 to ¥70 million, as against an increase of ¥40 to ¥50 million from 1868 to 1872. We must also note that between 1877 and 1881 the foreign trade deficit continued as before, the outflow of gold and silver amounting to ¥38.3 million (though in 1881 it amounted to only ¥1 million).

Among its many repercussions, the inflation particularly affected traditional production—agricultural and related activities. A doubling of the rice price combined with a fixed land tax created large windfall profits for the landowners. They quickly became more prosperous and began investing more actively in diverse small domestic industries. Some even

---

[66] Tsuru Shigeto, *Essays on Japanese Economy,* Kinokuniya Bookstore Co., Ltd., Tokyo, 1958, p. 125. Patrick also makes the valid point that much of the earlier note issue, between 1871 and 1874, served to replace Tokugawa currency. This might have lessened its inflationary impact. See "External Equilibrium and Internal Convertibility."

turned their attention to the manufacture of import substitutes, largely Western consumer goods. In 1884 the government published a list of 128 newly produced commodities varying all the way from hats and shoe polish to cigarette cases and Western liquor, and concluded that "80 to 90% of these commodities are luxuries, imitating foreign products, and made with imported raw materials. The manufacture of these contributed but little to increase national power."[67] In other words, the inflation was not doing much for industrialization; profits were moving into the wrong hands. In fact, factory industry was experiencing no particular boom in spite of considerable government encouragement. What happened with the cotton-spinning industry can serve as an example. In 1877 the government imported two spinning machines from England and offered them to any enterpriser willing to start a mill. No one accepted. In 1879 the government imported ten additional machines in the hope of forming new spinning mills. Money was also lent to three private entrepreneurs for the purchase of machinery. None of these endeavors was successful during the inflationary period.[68]

In many ways the most adverse effects of the inflation were felt by the government especially because of the fixed proceeds from the all-important land tax. The entire purpose of the tax was endangered. While the real purchasing power of its proceeds was falling drastically, the government had no power to siphon off the landowners' windfalls. A reduction in assessment from 3 to 2.5 per cent of land value in 1877 only aggravated things, and a sharp increase in rates was out of the question. It would have led to too much rural discontent and confusion. A crisis, in large measure the product of the government's own action, was somewhat mitigated by the introduction of new taxes on *sake* and tobacco. But this was not sufficient. Drastic reductions also had to be made in the amounts allocated for the advancement of modern industry; between 1872–1876 and 1877–1880 nonmilitary government investment fell from ¥11.1 million to ¥5.5 million *in current prices*.[69] The plans and ambitions of the Meiji Oligarchs were in difficulties, and some slight efforts were made to regain control of events. It is doubtful, however, whether the seriousness of the crisis was fully understood.

No wonder that the new bureaucrats had been caught by surprise. Up to 1876 the economy had behaved very differently faced with similar provocation. There must also have been disappointment in the results

[67] Japan, Ministry of Agriculture and Forestry, *Kōgyō iken*, p. 109. Obviously the additions to output which the new commodities brought were not considered very valuable by the authorities.

[68] Tsuru, *op. cit.*, pp. 128–129.

[69] Henry Rosovsky, *Capital Formation in Japan, 1868–1940*, The Free Press of Glencoe, New York, 1961, Tables VII–1 and VIII–1.

achieved with the revised national banks. It had been expected that they would contribute materially in the formation of modern industrial capital. This proved to be another miscalculation. Who were the new national bankers? Largely, these were former samurai without business experience, unable to differentiate between commercial and industrial capital requirements. They did only little to further the latter.

Inflation distorted the central government budget and the currency; by 1880 the specie reserves had dropped to 6 per cent of note circulation. The seriousness of economic conditions must be thought of in terms of the key role which the government had to play. If the economic strength of government was sufficiently undermined, the chances for MEG were nil. Significantly enough, foreign observers at this time were extremely pessimistic. With considerable complacency they wrote:[70] "Wealthy we do not think it [Japan] will ever become: the advantages conferred by Nature, with the exception of the climate, and the love of indolence and pleasure of the people themselves forbid it." Or, "The national banking system of Japan is but another example of the futility of trying to transfer Western growth to an Oriental habitat. In this part of the world principles, established and recognized in the West, appear to lose whatever virtue and vitality they originally possessed and to tend fatally towards weediness and corruption." Admittedly this sounds pretty amusing today, but the prediction might have been justified if the government had not been able to assume control.

A country is fortunate when in times of emergency a capable leader is waiting in the wings, or on the *hanamichi*.[71] In October 1881 a most remarkable man became Finance Minister of Japan. He combined firmness and wisdom with a strong belief in financial orthodoxy, and succeeded by 1885 in regaining control of the economic situation. He cleared the decks, and made it possible for modern economic growth to begin. We are referring, of course, to Matsukata Masayoshi (1835–1924), who began his career as a sword-wearing page of Lord Shimazu of Satsuma and ended it as a prince of the new Japan. His life, in many ways, is the story of Japan's awakening.[72] Matsukata's rise to prominence started in

---

[70] Both quotes are from *The Currency of Japan* (A Reprint of Articles and Reports) published by the *Japan Gazette,* 1882; cited by Allen, *op. cit.,* p. 41.

[71] *Hanamichi:* the "flower way"; a stage passage running through the audience on which important solos are performed in the *Kabuki* drama.

[72] On the career of Matsukata, see *Keizaigaku jiten* (Dictionary of Economics), Heibonsha, Tokyo, 1955, p. 1565; Tsuchiya Takao, *Nihon shihonshugi shijō no shidōshatachi* (Leading Entrepreneurs in the History of Japanese Capitalism), Iwanami shinsho, Tokyo, 1939, pp. 51–74. Also Tokutomi Iichirō, *Kōshaku Matsukata Masayoshi den* (The Biography of Prince Matsukata Masayoshi), 2 vols., Tokyo, 1935.

1868 through the good offices of Ōkubo Toshimichi, a fellow Satsuma clansman and one of the three or four most important leaders of the Restoration. Ōkubo appointed Matsukata governor of Hida Prefecture on Kyushu (presently Fukuoka Prefecture) where, by all accounts, he performed well, and was particularly remembered for the vigor with which he attempted to eradicate *mabiki* (infanticide). In 1871 he joined the new central government in the Financial Section of the Department of Civil Affairs. There, working under Ōkubo, he was active in drafting the land tax reform. Between 1875 and 1878, as a member of the Ministry of Finance, Matsukata's attention was focused on the central economic problems of the day: financing the Seinan War, reform of the fiscal year, national bank promotion, and paper money issues. Opportunity for foreign travel came in 1878 when Matsukata went to Europe as Japan's delegate to the International Exhibition at Paris. The sojourn was not lengthy since Matsukata returned to Japan in 1879, but it had considerable intellectual consequences. In France he encountered and conferred with Léon Say (1826–1896), grandson of Jean Baptiste Say, at that time French Finance Minister and a well-known name in economics and public affairs. Judging by Matsukata's subsequent actions, Say must have also been a persuasive advocate of his own ideas.

One wonders today why Say's ideas managed to appeal to Matsukata. Léon Say was a great believer in free trade, a system with which Japan had to live, but he was also anti-*étatiste,* and felt that it should be the main business of economists "to refute socialist doctrines and to combat the atrocious fallacies implied in all plans of social reform and of state interference of any kind."[73] The exact relationship between Say and Matsukata is not clear, but we can guess that there were other aspects of Say's ideas which particularly impressed the Japanese visitor. Say had been, between 1872 and 1879, "the autocratic ruler of French finances,"[74] and these had been difficult years. Not only did France at this time recover from her defeat at the hands of Prussia, but she also paid a £200 million indemnity to the victor in record time. How was this accomplished, Matsukata might have wondered? One can imagine the general lines of Say's answer: most vital is a sound convertible currency backed by gold; it establishes the credit and respectability of the State. France was able to pay an indemnity to Germany because the domestic and international credit of the State was excellent—all she had to do was to issue bonds, to have people fighting for their possession. Another important principle applies equally to the private and public sectors: live within your means. Govern-

[73] Joseph A. Schumpeter, *History of Economic Analysis,* Oxford University Press, New York, 1954, p. 841.

[74] Article on Léon Say in *The Encyclopaedia Britannica,* Eleventh edition (1910–1911), Vol. XXIV, p. 275.

TABLE 10. Public Finance Under Matsukata

	(1) Current Expenditures	(2) Current Revenues	(3) Gov. Savings (2) − (1)	(Unit: Million Yen) (4) Gov. Cap. Formation	(5) Surplus (3) − (4)
1881	67.1	101.4	34.3	12.6	21.7
1882	79.1	108.4	29.3	15.8	13.5
1883	83.1	106.5	23.4	15.4	8.0
1884	82.9	108.7	25.8	14.5	11.3
1885	61.1	88.8	27.7	15.9	11.8

Source: Hitotsubashi D18.

ment can tax heavily, and it can borrow, but on current account it should aim at balanced budgets. International bankers approve of convertibility and conservative finance. Japan must follow the general rules of behavior in the civilized world, otherwise she cannot expect to succeed.

Whether or not Say told all or part of this to Matsukata we do not know. We do know, judging by Matsukata's actions, that he believed these ideas and applied them when his hour came. In 1881, with his appointment as Finance Minister of Japan, there occurred a sharp change in government policy: convertibility once again became an aim, and in order to achieve it the government brought about austerity and deflation. Matsukata's policies jolted the economy, precipitating social disorder and political instability, but for five years he stayed on the same road, and by then the original government targets—adequate revenues, sound currency, modern banking—were safely and permanently achieved. The Matsukata deflation was strong medicine, but in our view it had life-saving qualities.

Budgetary reform formed the first prong of Matsukata's attack. A favorite prevailing government policy of establishing and financing model factories and mines was discontinued, and for the most part the existing establishments were sold to private individuals. On the revenue side, taxes on tobacco and *sake* were raised again, and many additional indirect taxes were instituted. A sinking fund was established for the anticipated surplus in order to bring about the redemption of the public debt; in 1880, this amounted to ¥245 million or three times the annual revenue of that year. Redemption was accomplished in ten years. In 1886 the authorities also managed to convert all public bonds carrying rates of 6 per cent and over to new issues at 5 per cent, thereby creating further savings.

In the figures for central and local government expenditures cited in Table 10 we can find some measure of Matsukata's achievements.

For these years the government saved 28 per cent of its current revenues, and after allocating half to the urgent needs of capital formation there still remained a sizable surplus. This was a remarkable achievement of the austerity program, especially because bond interest still amounted at that time to 18 per cent of current expenditures.

These attainments rested on a set of somewhat unusual circumstances. Retrenchment and austerity on the part of the government not only halted the inflation of the 1870's, but also turned the tide towards deflation. Actually this was to be the most severe deflation of modern Japanese economic history, and yet, because of the fixed land tax, it was very favorable to government revenues. Inflation had led to windfalls for the landlords, and now deflation, by raising taxes in real terms, was creating similar windfalls for the public sector. In spite of a sharp decline in the price of rice (see below), tax collection from the land remained constant even though landowners suffered a great fall in disposable income. The government, however, was also actively seeking a larger share of national resources in other sectors of the economy. This becomes clear in Table 11, which compares 1877–1880 with 1881–1885.

Although there were large increases in total taxes, land tax revenues remained more or less the same throughout. Obviously it was non-land taxes that were rising. Comparing 1878–1880 with 1882–1884 we can see that the land tax ratio to the net output of agriculture remained nearly the same (10.6–10.2 per cent), whereas there was a definite increase in the ratio of total taxes to NDP (5.6–8.3 per cent). In fact, between the

TABLE 11. Government Tax Revenues

	Land Tax Revenue	Total Tax Revenue	(Unit: Million Yen) NDP	NDP of Primary Sector
1877	39.5	51.5		
1878	40.5	54.5	405	248
1879	42.1	59.2	616	397
1880	42.3	59.3	805	536
1881	43.3	66.2	819	524
1882	43.3	70.9	719	426
1883	43.5	70.4	580	328
1884	43.4	71.5	498	245
1885	43.0	56.4	628	350

Source: Land tax from Ōuchi, *Nihon keizai tōkei-shū*, p. 226; total taxes from Hitotsubashi D18; NDP from Ohkawa, *Growth Rate of the Japanese Economy*, p. 247.

two groups of years the land tax declined from 77.2 to 64 per cent of total tax revenues. No doubt, partly as a result of Matsukata's efforts, the tax structure was in process of changing. It is true that proceeds from urban land taxes are included with the totals, and that peasants were also subject to non-land taxes. The main outlines of what was happening are, however, unmistakable. While maintaining the land tax as the major component of revenue, the government was getting increased taxes from non-agricultural sources.

Let us now examine the quantitative indicators of the deflation.

TABLE 12. The Matsukata Deflation

	Interest Rates (%)	Wholesale Prices (1877 = 100)	Tokyo Wholesale Prices		
			Rice (Koku)	Cotton (60 kg.)	Iron (100 kg.)
1881	14.0	164	10.59	33.76	8.39
1882	10.1	155	8.81	35.36	7.82
1883	7.9	131	6.31	20.80	7.37
1884	10.1	123	5.29	19.52	5.95
1885	11.0	128	6.61	22.72	6.05
1886	9.1	132	5.99	20.32	5.20

	Quantity of Money (Million ¥)	Paper Notes (Million ¥)	Notes/Silver	Specie & Conv. Notes/Total (%)
1881	192.8	153.3	1.696	19.1
1882	189.9	143.8	1.571	19.9
1883	166.1	132.3	1.264	20.4
1884	164.6	124.4	1.088	20.3
1885	154.7	122.5	1.006	21.5
1886	151.2	136.9	1.000	41.1

Source: See Tables 5, 7, and 9.

These figures reveal what Matsukata's tactics accomplished. A tight money policy decreased the quantity of money by some 20 per cent between 1881 and 1885. Commodity prices fell; rice prices were cut almost in half, and cotton and iron dropped by 25–30 per cent. The general price level dropped to 75 per cent of the 1881 level in 1884. Interest rates also declined, and notes were virtually at par in 1885. On the international scene things were also quite different. From 1881 to 1885 foreign payments were in the black except for a very minor deficit in 1881, the total gain amounting to ¥32.3 million, including a specie gain during 1882–1885 of ¥7.9 million. This was the first such experience since the Restoration, and it was not to be repeated frequently in later years.

All this gave the necessary stability for the creation of a convertible currency and reform of the banking system. Some of these events take us beyond 1885 and the end of transition; an indication of the main happenings will suffice. Based on Matsukata's memorandum of 1882, the Bank of Japan was founded in 1885 and replaced national banks by becoming the bank of issue. Its notes were convertible. National bank reserves were transferred to the Bank of Japan, and the national banks had to make annual payments into a Bank of Japan fund for the purpose of redeeming their previous note issue. Complete redemption of inconvertible government and bank notes took until 1899 and 1904 respectively, but the effects of a working central bank and reformed currency were felt much earlier. Thus, by about 1885/1886 the main targets of the government, first set in 1868, were in hand: a central bank was functioning, currency, purged of inconvertible paper, had become "respectable," and revenues were consistent with expenditures. It took the government nineteen years to accomplish this; from that time the economy was free to move progressively.

Some may feel that we have exaggerated the importance of financial factors and particularly the role of the inflation-deflation sequence. In studies of the economic history of Western countries, it would indeed be a rarity to find specific short-run monetary factors singled out for similar attention. Our emphasis in explaining transition, however, is not primarily monetary. What happened to the money supply and prices was indicative of more fundamental economic forces, and in this sense there can be no question of exaggeration. Let us abandon chronology for a moment and skip into the future.

The point has already been made that the Matsukata Deflation was exceptional in duration and especially in sharpness—this statement is true for the entire period 1868 to 1965: in terms of the General Price Index, post-Matsukata deflations were mild. Quantitatively they looked like this (1934–1936 = 100):[75]

		Price Decline
1890–1891	One year	29.0 to 27.3
1900–1901	One year	44.9 to 40.9
1907–1910	Three years	59.3 to 55.7
1913–1915	Two years	65.4 to 58.2

Price declines between 1886 and World War I were slight and of short duration. Between World War I and today, there existed only one deflationary period. The price level reached a peak in 1920 following the

[75] Hitotsubashi D11.

World War I boom, and it then took eleven years for prices to reach a trough in 1930. This was, compared to the boom, a drop in the price level of 47.5 per cent, even though the trough value (91.3) was still considerably higher than the average price level prevailing immediately before World War I (60).[76] The government never again followed any drastic and prolonged deflationary policy.

Matsukata's deflation was therefore a unique event in Japanese economic history, and a bold attempt to create a setting in which MEG could begin. The inflation which preceded it was equally unique. Post-Matsukata inflations can be traced to a range of circumstances, but generally they stem from credit creation to modern industry. In other words, the inflations were part of the growth process. This was not the situation in the late 1870's. That inflation was the financial result of disturbances and hindrances to growth which the leaders of the Restoration had inherited. At least in the eyes of the government, Japan was not on the right track in the 1870's, and part of the problem lay in its own actions. Private enterprise needed a more rational and elastic currency, and government had to have adequate revenues; both aims were materially advanced through Matsukata's efforts.

One final point about this entire episode. Matsukata's policies of the 1880's were unpopular with large segments of the population. Farmers suffered special distress, and many were reduced to tenant status after forced sale of their land.[77] A student of the currently underdeveloped world might ask: how did the government get away with it? Two elements must be considered in any answer. To begin with, boundary conditions themselves were subject to change. By the 1880's, those who represented potential antigovernment leadership were very much weaker. The rank and file of the samurai, who had received bonds, were largely ruined by the inflation of the 1870's. The value of their bonds had declined, and most of them had to sell bonds in order to stay alive. One can, perhaps, say that under Matsukata the former samurai had been divided into two groups. One group had sunk to a lower economic level and was trying somehow to make ends meet in an unpleasant and unfamiliar new world. The other group, much smaller to be sure, was rising to higher levels, drawn by the new career opportunities in private business and the bureaucracy. Neither group had the appetite for revolt: the sinking samurai were defeated, and the rising samurai were victorious. Another aspect of government strength, distinct from changing boundary conditions, lies in the differences between the economy and polity. The economy was, as we have said, quite free, but the polity was controlled. Japan was not a democracy,

[76] The same is true of the Matsukata Deflation.

[77] For example, between 1883 and 1887 the proportion of land cultivated by tenants rose from 35.9 to 39.3 per cent. Yamaguchi, *Nihon keizaishi kōgi*, p. 162.

and from the Restoration to the end of transition, each year the military and police power of the state increased. After the Satsuma Rebellion the Meiji leaders were firmly in the saddle. Lastly, we should also take into account an important characteristic of Japanese economic life: the people work hard and continue to produce, no matter what happens. Despite the dislocations occasioned by inflation and deflation, aggregate output almost maintained itself. GDP, in 1934–1936, prices, shows the following annual averages: 1879–1880, ¥2.4 billion; 1881–1885, ¥2.2 billion; 1886–1889, ¥2.9 billion.[78] This was an important asset.

[78] Hitotsubashi D11.

THE RELATIVE DECLINE OF THE BRITISH STEEL INDUSTRY, 1880–1913

Peter Temin

Massachusetts Institute of Technology

I

Britain's loss of preeminence in the production of steel during the decades before World War I represented a dramatic reversal of fortune for the world's industrial leader. Great Britain was first among the world's producers of steel in 1880. By 1890 she was second, and by 1900 she was third. In 1913, Britain produced less than half as much steel as Germany and less than one-fourth as much as the United States.[1] The decline of Britain's share in world trade was equally dramatic, if a little less rapid. Britain had supplied over three-fourths of the world's exports of iron and steel in the years before 1880. By 1913, she supplied less than one-third—less than one-fourth if exports of steel alone are considered.[2]

Explanations of this phenomenon have not been lacking. The Tariff Commission of 1904 reported that "It is in the organisation and policy of foreign countries, combined with the British policy of free imports [which allows dumping], that we find the explanation of the difficulties from which British trade is suffering at the present time."[3] Later investigators have rejected the reasoning of the Tariff Commission in favor of arguments stressing the difficulties of expansion in Britain. These investi-

• I would like to thank Charles P. Kindleberger, Wassily W. Leontief, and Robert B. Zevin for help in the preparation of this paper.

[1] Table 1.

[2] T. H. Burnham and G. O. Hoskins, *Iron and Steel in Britain, 1870–1930*, George Allen and Unwin, London, 1943, p. 30, Table 1.

[3] Tariff Commission, *Report*, Vol. I. *The Iron and Steel Trades*, P. S. King and Son, London, 1904, para. 54. The connection with dumping is made explicitly in para. 86.

gators agreed with the Tariff Commission that the retarding factors were not related to resource availability. Instead, the retarding factors, they said, were those characteristics of the British steel industry that prevented it from using the most efficient technology and the cheapest resources—notably the low-grade iron ores of Britian's East Midlands. Burn found these characteristics primarily in the " 'imperfections' of competition, which though universal were peculiarly significant for the British industry, and the structure of the British capital market."[4] Burnham and Hoskins found the difficulty in a failure of "entrepreneurship" in the British steel industry: "If a business deteriorates it is of no use blaming anyone except those at the top, and if an industry declines relatively faster than unfavorable external and uncontrollable factors lead one to expect, the weakness can only be attributed to those who are in control of its activities."[5] Later writers have generally accepted the reasoning of these writers.[6]

The purpose of this essay is to take issue with these writers. I shall argue that the decline in Britain's share of world steel production and trade was a natural result of two developments of the late nineteenth century unrelated to imperfections or irrationalities in the British industry:

1. The rapid growth of the demand for steel in the markets of Germany and the United States from which the British steel industry was barred by protective tariffs.

2. The approximate equalization of resource costs in the three major steelmaking countries as a result of the exploitation of previously unknown or unusable iron ore deposits.[7]

[4] D. L. Burn, *The Economic History of Steelmaking, 1867–1939*, Cambridge University Press, Cambridge, England, 1940, p. 263.

[5] Burnham and Hoskins, *op. cit.*, p. 271.

[6] See, for example, Walter Isard, "Some Locational Factors in the Iron and Steel Industry since the Early Nineteenth Century," *Journal of Political Economy,* 56 (June 1948), 203–217.

[7] A direct cost comparison such as this is, of course, irrelevant to the course of trade under the assumptions of the traditional theory of international trade which deals with comparative advantage, not absolute advantage. The justification for a direct cost comparison is the presumption that the exchange rates of the late nineteenth century were an accurate reflection of the average costs of production of the countries in question. A direct comparison of costs in a single industry in two countries then serves as a short way of comparing the costs of the industry in each country with costs in other industries in that country and then comparing the two relative prices. This is true because the denominator is assumed to be the same in both relative price calculations.

It is possible, of course, that this presumption is wrong, and that the relative costs of making steel in, say, Germany and Britain did not reflect the relative comparative advantages of the two countries in the production of steel. If this presumption is wrong, however, the implication of the overall pattern of British trade is that the Pound was overvalued at the end of the nineteenth century and therefore

I would like to stress the word "approximate" in the statement of the second development, since the precise relative costs of the competing resources in use at the end of the nineteenth century are still a moot point. Britain's relative decline was a startling phenomenon, however, and it was not the result of small changes in relative costs. In fact, it was inevitable—given the tariff policies of the major steel-producing countries—when steelmaking resources became available in those countries at roughly comparable costs. The growth of demand in the United States and Germany was more rapid than the growth in the rest of the world combined. The steel industries of these countries supplied this demand, and—when their costs approached those in Britain—they also exported steel to other countries. Competition in the export trade led to a lower rate of growth in Britain than in the United States and Germany because the British steel industry did not have a rapidly growing home market reserved for its product. The British steel industry had access to a market for steel that was growing less rapidly than those served by its competitors; its rate of growth was consequently less.

This slower rate of growth would have produced an older average age of capital in Britain than in Germany or the United States, even if all other things were equal. This in turn would have led to higher costs of production in Britain if technological change was embodied in capital equipment, even if resource costs were equal in all three countries. The higher costs of production in Britain noticed so prominently by comtemporary and later observers may, therefore, have been a *result*—not a cause—of Britain's relative decline. These higher production costs would of course accentuate Britain's decline, but they would not have initiated it. The argument of previous writers, in other words, is stood upon its head.

In the next section I shall describe the two developments listed above and show how they led to the reduction of Britain's share of world steel production and trade. In the following section I shall relate this discussion to previous descriptions of the British steel industry and draw some conclusions from the discrepancy between the present and past discussions of this problem.

II

The rapid growth of demand in the protected markets of Germany and the United States is a well-known feature of the late nineteenth century. The United States had begun to construct its protectionist policies

---

that the cause of Britain's relative decline in the production of steel was the result of excessive inflation. This is an interesting argument which is not precluded by anything said in this paper. It is also, it should be noted, a very different argument from those advanced by Burn or Burnham and Hoskins.

TABLE 1. Volume of Steel Production and Exports
(million tons)

	United Kingdom		Germany		United States		World	
	Produc- tion	Ex- ports	Produc- tion	Ex- ports	Produc- tion	Ex- ports	Produc- tion	Ex- ports
1880	1.29		0.69		1.25		4.18	
1890	3.58		2.10		4.28		12.28	
1900	4.90		6.36		10.19		27.83	
1910	6.37		12.89		26.09		59.33	
1913	7.66	2.74	17.32	4.52	31.30	2.54	75.15	12.03

Sources: Production: *Iron and Coal Trades Review*, Diamond Jubilee Issue, 1927, p. 130. Exports: United Nations, Economic Commission for Europe, *Statistics of World Trade in Steel, 1913–1959*, Geneva: United Nations, 1961, pp. 2–13.

during the Civil War; the Germans raised their tariffs to protectionist levels in 1879.[8] By 1880, therefore, when the introduction of the basic process expanded the list of available steel resources, the British steel industry was forced to look elsewhere for its customers. British steel was sold in Germany and America in special circumstances and in times of extraordinary demand, but the bulk of demand in these countries was to be satisfied by a native industry.

How rapidly was the demand for steel in these regions growing? Precise information on the growth of demand is lacking, but an estimate of this growth may be constructed from the data on production and trade shown in Table 1. Production for home consumption may be taken as a good measure both of consumption and of demand in the protectionist countries.[9] This type of production increased by a factor of 23 in the

[8] Tariff rates on iron and steel for 1904 are given in Tariff Commission, para. 153. Both countries used specific tariffs, but the rates on rails in 1904, for example, were close to 30 per cent (for prices, see Burn, *op. cit.*, pp. 101–115).

[9] The use of consumption to represent demand is fraught with difficulty. The justification for the procedure adopted here is, that the price of steel did not change greatly after the early 1880's, and that therefore the expansion of consumption shows the expansion of both supply and demand at roughly constant prices.

Production less exports is a good measure of home consumption for Germany and the United States because their tariffs precluded a large volume of imports. Exports may also be neglected for 1880 since almost all trade was still in iron, not steel. For 1880, see Fritz Kestner, "Die deutschen Eisenzolle, 1879 bis 1900," *Staats- und sozialwissenschaftliche Forschungen*, 21 (1902), tables on pp. 124, 126; American Iron and Steel Association, *Statistics of the American and Foreign Iron Trade*, 1880, pp. 51, 53. For 1913, see the source for Table 2.

United States between 1880 and 1913, and by a factor of 19 in Germany. The production of steel for consumption outside both the United States and Germany increased by 15 times in these years, or somewhat slower than production for consumption inside these countries. The British steel industry would have had to *increase* its share of the markets in which it could sell if it was to match the growth rates of the American and German industries. The British steel industry produced slightly over half of the steel consumed outside the United States and Germany in 1880; it would have had to produce three-quarters of this steel in 1913 for the growth of steel production in the three countries to have been equally rapid. To do this, the British steel industry would have had to prevent the American and German steel industries from selling outside their protected home markets and the smaller steel industries of other countries from growing as rapidly as their domestic demand.

Neither of these achievements, however, was within reach of the British steel industry. A result of the rough equality of resource costs in the major steel-producing countries was that all of these countries were active in world trade, and the same conditions that produced this rough equalization also led to a cost structure that facilitated the growth of less important steel industries in countries like Belgium, France, and Russia. From these developments, the relative decline of the British steel industry followed.

To demonstrate this point, it is necessary to contrast the location of the resources for making steel with the location of the demand for this product. The resources in question are primarily coal and iron ore, for although other materials were used in the fabrication of steel their costs were not an important element in the total cost.[10] We therefore need to consider the locations of coal, iron ore, and demand.

The availability of coal may be described easily. The coal deposits at Connellsville, Durham, and the Ruhr—in the United States, Britain, and Germany, respectively—produced coking coal of recognized high qual-

---

[10] The list of other materials used in making steel would include limestone, manganese and scrap, none of which represented an important part of steelmaking costs. A more important class of inputs to the making of steel is composed of the inputs usually included in "value added."

It is conceivable that the services of labor and capital were sufficiently cheaper in Britain than in the United States or Germany to make the costs of production of steel lower in Britain than in these other countries even if the materials for steelmaking were more expensive. But value added is a less important part of the cost of making steel than it is of many other products; if capital and labor were cheaper, relative to the cost of materials, in Britain than in Germany or the United States, Britain would have had a comparative advantage in the production of goods other than steel. If the absolute cost of making steel in Britain was then less than in the United States and Germany, it would mean that the Pound was undervalued. (See Burnham and Hoskins, *op. cit.,* pp. 62–64, on the trend in Britain toward production of more highly fabricated goods even within the steel industry.)

ity. To their comparability of quality was added comparability of cost, providing equal opportunities for three iron and steel industries based on them. Smaller deposits, less specifically suited to use in the iron and steel industry, were also available in Wales, Scotland, Belgium, and France, providing only slightly less inviting opportunities in these locations.[11]

The availability of iron ores is a more complex question. Iron ores are typically graded according to their phosphorus content. After the introduction of the basic process, however, almost any amount of phosphorus was permitted in an ore used to make steel, and we may classify ores instead on the basis of their iron content. High-grade ore, which had an iron content of 50 per cent or more, was valuable in relation to its weight and could be transported economically over long distances. Low-grade ore, on the other hand, had to be used much closer to the mines or quarries from which it was taken.

The two most important deposits of high grade ore used in this period were found in Spain and northern Sweden.[12] Their location at the northern and southern ends of the Atlantic coast of Europe contrasted with the East-West orientation of the European coal fields, with the result that the distance from any coal deposit to the ore deposits was approximately the same. Because the coal deposits were located near the Atlantic Ocean or the Rhine River, comparable distances could be translated into comparable costs of transportation.[13] The British preference for Spanish ores and the German reliance on Swedish ores are peculiarities still to be explained.[14]

[11] J. S. Jeans, The Iron Trade of Great Britain, Methuen, London, 1906, pp. 17–18, 114; Norman J. G. Pounds and William N. Parker, Coal and Steel in Western Europe, Indiana University Press, Bloomington, Indiana, 1957, pp. 127–246.

[12] The hematite ores of Cumberland and Lancashire were important in the establishment of the British steel industry, but imported ore was being used on Britain's Northwest coast by the turn of the century. See Howard G. Roepke, "Movements of the British Iron and Steel Industry, 1720–1951," Illinois Studies in the Social Sciences, Vol. 36, University of Illinois Press, Urbana, Illinois, 1956, p. 77.

[13] In the 1890's for example, Swedish iron ore traveled 1680 miles to reach Cleveland (on the British coast) and 1690 miles to reach Dortmund (in the Ruhr). J. Head, "Scandinavia as a Source of Iron Ore Supply," Journal of the Iron and Steel Institute, I (1894), 47–67. Extra transportation costs to the German works as a result of their inland location were offset by the German government's policy of subsidizing railroad transportation by means of "through rates" on goods crossing the German border. See Great Britain, Royal Commission on Shipping Rings, Report (1909), para, 131.

[14] There are three possibilities. Small differences in relative distances may have been important. The receptivity of the Spanish government to British investment, which contrasted sharply with the Swedish attitude, may have directed the attention of British steelmakers toward the South. And the contrast between the British production of acid steel and the German production of basic steel may have made a difference, although the Swedish mines produced ore suitable for both the acid and the basic processes, and the Spanish ore was used in both Britain and Germany.

Low-grade ores were typically used in the country in which they were found, and their diversity of chemical content makes a detailed comparison difficult.[15] The Lorraine ores of Germany and France are often paired with the ores of Lincolnshire and Northamptonshire, in England, as the best of the low-grade ores. This assertion may be accepted for the moment.[16]

The conclusion from this short discussion is that Britain and Germany could assemble the resources for making steel at costs that were not too different. Similar considerations imply that costs in Belgium were in the same range and that those in France were not too much more. The United States did not use European ore, but the ores of Lake Superior were similar to the European high-grade ores, both in their chemical composition and in their distance from coal deposits. Resource costs in the United States were consequently near the European level. Greater accuracy is not needed for this discussion.

It was shown above that the British steel industry could have grown as fast as the German and American industries only if it could have increased its share of markets outside these two countries. But the British could not even have retained the share of these markets they had in 1880 under the conditions just outlined. For one thing, the Americans were bound to supply the rapidly expanding market in Canada if their costs were anywhere near the European level. For another, the German industry was similarly destined to be the primary supplier of the countries along the Rhine if its costs were close to those of its rivals. Finally, the industries of other countries were in a position to help supply some of their native demands, and of these, Belgium was able also to compete in the export markets.

By 1913, Britain supplied only 23 per cent of the steel used outside Germany and the United States. A similar proportion (21 per cent) was supplied by exports from Germany and the United States, and the remainder (56 per cent) was supplied by the industries of other countries.[17] Could Britain have supplied a larger share of this market?

Actions by the British steel industry probably could not have reduced

---

See J. Head, *op. cit.;* A. F. Rickman, *Swedish Iron Ore,* Faber and Faber, London, 1939; Norman J. G. Pounds, *The Ruhr: A Study in Historical and Economic Geography,* Indiana University Press, Bloomington, Indiana, 1952; Michael W. Flinn, "British Steel and Spanish Ore, 1871–1914," *Economic History Review,* Second Series, 8 (August 1958), 84–90; "Scandinavian Iron Ore Mining and the British Steel Industry, 1870–1914." *Scandinavian Economic History Review,* 2 (1954), 31–46.

[15] Chemical analyses of the various ores in question are given in Burnham and Hoskins, *op. cit.,* pp. 296–297.

[16] It is explored further in Section III.

[17] Calculated from the data in Table 1.

the production of steel in other countries for consumption in these same countries. The smaller steel industries of the era before World War I were based on local resources and local demand. Even in those areas where tariffs would have permitted it, increased competition from Britain would not have made large inroads.[18]

On the other hand, lower costs of steel production in Britain probably would have altered the location of production of that steel sold outside the country in which it was made. We may attempt to estimate the magnitude of the possible shift in location in an effort to discover how far a reduction of British steelmaking costs could have gone toward equalizing the rates of growth of steel production in the three major steelmaking nations.

Approximately 40 per cent of all steel traded across national boundaries in 1913 was sold in Europe; the remainder was divided evenly between the British Empire and other countries. Table 2 shows the origins of the steel imports of various countries; the proportion of world trade in steel accounted for by the imports of any one country is shown in parentheses after the name of the importing country.

The steel imported into the British colonies other than Canada came mostly from Britain in 1913. A cost reduction in Britain might have increased the amount supplied from Britain, but the scope for improvement was not great. The large market in Canada was almost exclusively supplied by the United States, and would be so under almost any possible cost configuration. The other, smaller markets listed with the British Empire in Table 2 were similarly immune to the effects of changes in relative costs.

The countries of Western Europe reveal their proximity to Germany in the composition of their imports. A cost reduction in Britain would have greatly reduced the volume of British imports and also diverted some of the other trade from Germany to Britain. But the central location of Germany would have preserved for the Westphalian industry a large share of the trade to continental countries unless costs were markedly lower in Britain; the distribution of resources outlined above precluded this.

The "neutral markets" of the third group in Table 2 are those markets, primarily in South America and Asia, that were equally accessible to the exporting nations by virtue of their policies and locations. The composition of their imports was responsive to changes in costs, and lower costs in Britain would have secured a larger proportion of these markets for British steel producers.

---

[18] Steel production outside of the United States, Germany and Britain in 1913 was as follows (in millions of tons): Russia-Poland, 4.75; France, 4.61; Belgium-Luxembourg, 3.74; Austria-Hungary, 2.58; Canada, 1.04; Italy, 0.92; Sweden, 0.58; Spain, 0.38; Japan, 0.24. Of these countries, only Belgium was an important exporter of steel. From the same sources as Table 1.

TABLE 2. Distribution of World Trade in Steel, 1913
(percentages)

	Exporters					
Importers	Belgium	France	Germany	Sweden	United Kingdom	United States
British Empire, etc. (33.4)						
Brit. Empire excl.						
Canada (18.1)	10.6	—	16.0	0.2	63.4	9.7
Canada (11.9)	1.0	—	4.8	0.1	8.3	85.7
Cuba, Mexico &						
Panama (2.5)	5.2	0.1	4.8	—	5.5	84.5
Algeria & Fr. W.						
Africa (0.9)	1.1	97.1	1.3	0.2	—	0.3
Western Europe (39.7)						
U.K. (15.0)	22.6	0.7	58.4	5.1	—	13.2
Netherlands (5.2)	16.3	—	71.6	0.5	10.0	1.7
Scandinavia (4.5)	7.3	—	71.6	3.5	14.5	3.1
Belgium-Luxembourg (4.3)	0.1	40.7	48.5	1.0	5.6	4.0
Switzerland (2.6)	1.0	14.0	78.2	0.3	6.1	0.3
Italy (1.5)	11.8	2.1	63.7	3.6	16.8	2.1
Germany (1.2)	6.7	7.9	—	38.5	43.3	3.6
Other (5.4)	25.4	0.4	47.9	4.1	19.9	2.1
"Neutral Markets" (27.0)						
Argentina (5.6)	16.9	1.7	42.7	—	27.8	11.6
Brazil (2.7)	26.6	4.1	28.6	0.2	20.6	19.8
Chile (1.5)	11.2	0.2	35.3	—	19.7	33.7
Other Latin Amer. (1.7)	6.3	0.1	25.1	—	22.0	46.4
Japan (4.6)	9.7	0.1	40.4	1.2	23.0	25.6
Other (10.9)	13.4	3.5	42.9	4.7	27.3	8.2
Total (100.0)	12.3	3.8	37.6	2.3	22.8	21.2

Source: United Nations, *Statistics of World Trade in Steel, 1913–1959*, pp. 2–13.

If the costs of making steel in Britain had been lower than the costs in Germany, the shares of the "neutral markets" held by these two exporting countries might well have been reversed. Adding a change of this magnitude to those possible in the earlier groups of countries, we can estimate that lower British costs could have increased the production of steel in Britain by approximately 20 per cent of world trade in steel, or about 2.4 million tons.[19]

[19] This is derived as follows: half (10 per cent) is assumed to come from a reduction of British imports by two-thirds, the final third of British imports being assumed to stay as a result of the British policy of free trade. The other half is the result of increasing Britain's share in exports to various markets by the difference between the British and German share of the "neutral markets" (14.3 per

The average annual increase in British steel production after 1890, when the rates in Britain and Germany began to diverge, was 3.4 per cent, which may be contrasted with the 9.6 per cent average growth rate achieved in Germany in the same years.[20] If the increased production that would have followed from the hypothetical changes in world trade outlined above is assumed to date from 1890, the average annual growth rate in Britain after 1890 would have been increased to 4.6 per cent a year, compared with a German rate of 9.0 per cent.[21] Even if the cost of steel production in Britain had been lower than in Germany, the rate of increase of British steel production would only have been one-half the rate in Germany, and the volume of British production in 1913 would only have been two-thirds of the volume of German production. It was not possible, therefore, for the British steel industry to match or even approach the growth of the German and American industries. This conclusion is reached by studying the locations of the demand and the resources for making steel; it has nothing to do with the rationality or the lack thereof of British steelmakers.

But, it will be argued, the high costs of production and the antiquated equipment of the British steelworks that are usually used to explain the slow growth of the British industry surely indicate a lack of rationality and effective competition in the British industry. I suggest that they can be explained as a logical result of the slow growth of the British steel industry, which was determined by the causes outlined above, and that they imply nothing about the nature of competition or competitors in Britain.

If all other things are equal, except that one industry grows slower than another, then the industry that grows more slowly will have older

---

cent). This assumes that lower costs could have reversed the British and German position in these markets, and effected a shift of the same absolute—not relative—magnitude in other markets. The other markets affected are the British Empire excluding Canada and the countries of Western Europe other than the United Kingdom. Multiplying the share of world trade affected (69.8 per cent) by the proportion shifted (14.3 per cent) gives the other 10 per cent of world trade assumed to be supplied by British production.

[20] The rates of growth in Germany and Britain began to diverge at the point when the Swedish iron ores become available in these countries. The possible causal link deserves to be explored.

[21] The rates of growth have been calculated from the volumes of production in 1890 and 1913 as shown in Table 1. The German rate of growth after the hypothetical change in world trade just outlined was computed by assuming that British imports from all countries were reduced by the same proportion and that the diversion of other trade was a simple replacement of German exports by British. This implied a reduction of German steel production in 1913 by 1.9 million tons, and a reduction of the rate of growth of German steel production to 9.0 per cent.

capital equipment than its faster growing cousin. If technological advances are embodied in the capital stock, this older capital will be less efficient, and the slowly growing industry will have higher costs than the rapidly growing one. The application to the problem at hand is obvious.[22]

The magnitude of this effect may be estimated by means of a few assumptions. Under certain equilibrium conditions, the average age of capital in an industry is equal to the reciprocal of the sum of the rate of growth of the industry and the rate of depreciation in force, both being constant exponential rates. This formula may be used to approximate the ages of capital in the British and German steel industries. If the rate of depreciation was 5 per cent a year in both countries, the formula indicates an average age of twelve years for the capital in the British steel industry and seven years for the capital in the German industry.[23]

If the rate of embodied technological change were about 3 per cent a year, a five-year difference in the average age of capital would mean a difference of costs of about 15 per cent. The difference in costs between the German and British steel industries is not known with any accuracy, but it was probably in this range.[24] The argument then shows that the higher costs of the British steel industry can be explained as a result of the slow rate of growth in Britain. To show that they were in fact a result of the rate of growth would imply a more complete discussion of the technology of making steel than can be given here. The nature of the tech-

[22] The theoretical point was made by Robert M. Solow, "Investment and Technical Progress," in Kenneth J. Arrow, et al., (eds.), Mathematical Methods in the Social Sciences, 1959, Stanford University Press, Stanford, 1960. The application to this problem was made by D. J. Coppock, "The Climacteric of the 1890's, A Critical Note," Manchester School of Economic and Social Studies, 24 (January 1956), 1–31.

[23] The formula given above is true in an industry in which investment has been growing forever at a constant exponential rate, and in which a constant exponential rate of depreciation has always been in force. (It is assumed that the capital-output ratio stays constant.) The age of capital in a constantly growing industry that started a finite time ago approaches the age given by the formula as it continues to grow at a constant rate. If the growth rate has changed in the recent past, the current growth rate is the most important rate for the determination of the average age of capital.

The average rate of growth of the British and German steel industries in the 1880's was very similar, and close to the overall German rate from 1880 to 1913. The difference between the average age of capital in the two industries to be expected from their differing rates of growth then grew from near zero in 1890 to about five years in 1913 as a result of the slower rate of growth in Britain after 1890.

If a lower rate of depreciation were used, a longer average age of capital would result, increasing the difference between the average ages in the two countries.

[24] The export prices for rails, shown by Burn, op. cit., p. 103, may be used as a rough indication of relative marginal costs. They tend to stay within about 10 per cent of each other.

nology, however, is such that most of the technological advances of this period were embodied in the capital equipment.[25]

The slow rate of growth of steel production in Britain is usually explained as a result of the high cost of steel production in Britain, which is then attributed to other causes. The argument here has shown that the rate of growth of steel production in Britain had to be lower than the German or the American, once costs became roughly equal in the three countries (taking the tariffs in force as data). This slower rate of growth in Britain then produced a technological lag, relative to the German and American industries, which may have been large enough to account for the observed differences in costs. High costs in Britain appear, therefore, as a result of slow growth, not its cause. And the explanation of this rate of growth is found in the nature of resource costs and tariff policies in the three large steel-producing countries, rather than in the conditions of competition in Britain or the competence of British steelmakers.

III

Does this mean that the British steel industry had to grow as slowly as it did? Is this an assertion that British steel producers were producing as efficiently—and therefore as much—as possible? These questions cannot be answered from the information already considered. It has been shown that lower costs in Britain could have increased the production of steel in Britain by as much as one-third by 1913. This would not have changed the main outlines of history as we know it, but it would have been a benefit to the British economy.[26] We may ask whether a cost reduction of the necessary magnitude was within the reach of the British industry.

It must be remembered that the British industry labored under the handicap of older capital equipment, imposed by the slower rate of growth in Britain. This handicap meant that British resources had to be cheaper than the German resources, not just equivalent, to enable British steel to be produced at the same cost as German. The expansion of British trade anticipated as a result of lower costs in Britain in the preceding discussion would not have removed this handicap. The difference in ages between the capital equipment of the two countries would only have been lowered to about three years, which could imply a difference of costs of as much as 10 per cent.[27]

[25] This can be seen from the emphasis in all discussions of the steel industry in this era on the nature of the plants and equipment in use, as opposed to the methods of working with this equipment.

[26] See Jeans, op. cit., p. 221.

[27] The average age of capital in Britain would be lowered to about 10 years; the average age in Germany would only increase by about 0.3 years.

The assertion that costs were higher in Britain than was necessary rests on the observed inefficiency of the British steelmaking plants and the restricted use of the low-grade iron ores in Lincolnshire and Northamptonshire. It has already been shown that British capital was bound to be older, and hence less efficient, than the German; we now consider the "comparative neglect" of the native British ores, "the most amazing feature of British steelmaking," according to Burn.[28]

The use of these ores was expanding after 1890; between 1890 and 1913 it grew at an annual rate in the neighborhood of 3 per cent.[29] This could only be an amazingly slow rate of growth if there were overwhelmingly persuasive reasons why the ores of these counties should be mined at a faster rate. These have not been demonstrated. The cost calculations usually given do not claim that the British ores were substantially better than the Lorraine ores, that is, enough better to overcome the handicap of older capital equipment.[30] In addition, technical difficulties inherent in the use of these ores are mentioned but not included in the cost calculations.[31]

The technical difficulties were probably sufficient to discourage faster exploitation of these ores. But even if we assume away all technical difficulties, there is little evidence that the British ores were markedly superior to the Lorraine ore. The costs of mining were approximately equal, as were the costs of bringing coal to the mines.[32] The cost of transporting the iron or steel made to markets was also probably a comparable barrier to the use of either type of ore.[33] British steel production using the low-grade native ores probably would not have had lower costs than the German production, and consequently would not have been able to compete on the export market. As a result, the incentives for using these ores were

[28] Burn, *op. cit.*, 167. The argument of Burnham and Hoskins is similar to that of Burn. See Burnham and Hoskins, *op. cit.*, pp. 120, 180.

[29] B. R. Mitchell, *Abstract of British Historical Statistics,* Cambridge University Press, Cambridge, England, 1962, pp. 129–130.

[30] Burn *op. cit.*, pp. 170–172, argues by comparison with an English firm that was in financial difficulty after 1900; Burnham and Hoskins, *op. cit.*, p. 114, do not claim great accuracy for their calculations or great supremacy for British ores.

[31] Burn even says that the question of whether the Northamptonshire ores could have been used successfully at any price before the first World War is still an open one. See *op. cit.*, p. 169 n., and the references cited there.

[32] Jeans, *op. cit.*, pp. 14, 114. (See also Tariff Commission, para. 1131, for a comment by Jeans on the complexity of comparing ore costs.)

[33] Pounds, *op. cit.*, pp. 110–111; Burn, *op. cit.*, pp. 179–181. Shipping costs to overseas markets were the same from British and continental ports; the cost of transporting German steel to the seacoast was partly paid by the German government through railroad subsidies. Great Britain, Royal Commission on Shipping Rings, paras. 62, 131, 207.

not very strong, nor would their exploitation have greatly increased the production of steel in Britain.

The impediments to the use of the British ores that have been discovered by earlier investigators may now be seen in their proper perspective. Since the opportunities for the expansion of British steel production have been exaggerated, the reasons previously advanced to explain the backwardness of the British steel industry may be expected to be exaggerated also. We may examine the traditional arguments, four of which should be considered: dumping, "imperfections" of British competition, the structure of the British capital market, and the weakness of British entrepreneurship.[34]

The dangers of dumping, by which contemporaries meant selling in foreign markets irrespective of costs, appear to have been grossly exaggerated. An industry will only sell consistently at prices that are unremunerative if it hopes to regain the profits foregone at a later time through monopolization of the market in question. Britain, as a free trade country, was a part of the world market, and it would have been necessary to have a monopoly of the world's supply of steel to have a monopoly of the British market for steel. The German steel industry could not possibly have planned to destroy the British steel industry beyond hope of recovery, form agreements with all other existing steel producers in the world, and arrange prices to discourage potential steel producers from entering the market. The risks of such an undertaking were far too great to justify the costs of selling at a loss in the British market to bankrupt the British industry.

If the Germans were not hoping to monopolize the British market, they would sell there on the same basis as everyone else: to maximize profits. If the cartel arrangements permitted by German law enabled them to have a monopoly of the protected German market, they would have different prices for their home and foreign markets to maximize profits.[35] Their prices in foreign markets would depend on their costs in the same way that the British prices did, and lower prices there would indicate lower costs.[36]

Burn asserts that the "imperfections" of British competition and the

---

[34] These are taken from the brief discussion of section I, above, and the sources cited there.

[35] In other words, they would act as "discriminating monopolists."

[36] The tariff could have lowered the German costs below the British costs if it enabled the German industry to realize economies of scale that were not open to the British industry. It would appear, however, that the British industry was large enough to enjoy any economies of scale that derived from the size of the industry. The size of individual firms is a separate matter, which was probably independent of the German tariff.

structure of the British capital market were "the most fundamental influences likely to cause a divergence of British and rival growth."[37] However, as Burn himself notes at the beginning of his discussion of these matters, they were the results, not the cause, of the slow rate of British growth. In Burn's words: "Great new plants could emerge in Germany and the States without other plants being stationary, let alone shrinking or disappearing; in Britain that was possible to a very limited degree, if possible at all."[38] The divergence between competitive conditions in Britain and those in Germany and the United States was a function of the differing rates of growth in these countries, which was in turn caused by the factors outlined above. The difficulties of initiating change in Britain were probably no greater than in any industry with similar opportunities for growth.[39]

Burnham and Hoskins isolated entrepreneurial failure as the cause of the British relative decline by a process of elimination.[40] In view of the availability of other explanations for this decline, their reasoning must be rejected. The problems retarding the use of the Lincolnshire and Northamptonshire ores have already been mentioned. Cost calculations for the other technical changes which the British industry is accused of neglecting are lacking, and it is not known how many of the alleged failings of the British industry were a result of the older age of capital resulting from a lower rate of growth. It would seem unlikely, though, that the production of basic steel in Britain was limited by a prejudice against basic steel by Lloyd's or the Admiralty in light both of the successful competition of German steel—mostly basic—in Britain and of the sale of much of British steel in export markets.[41] It is unlikely, also, that the

[37] Burn, *op. cit.*, p. 263.

[38] *Ibid.*, p. 240.

[39] The difficulties in starting new plants and raising new capital that Burn notices are best seen as a reaction to the lack of profit opportunities in the steel industry, given the slow rate of growth of demand. As Burn does not argue comparatively for the most part, there is little evidence that the British were in fact responding to their environment differently than any other nation would have reacted to a similar environment. It seems unlikely in particular that capital was unavailable for profitable undertakings in view of the large size of the London capital market and the low rate of interest prevailing. See Coppock, *op. cit.*, p. 26; Mitchell, *op. cit.*, pp. 455, 462.

[40] Burnham and Hoskins, *op. cit.*, *passim*.

[41] Jeans, in Tariff Commission, para. 1011, and J. C. Carr and W. Taplin, *History of the British Steel Industry*, Harvard University Press, Cambridge, Massachusetts, 1962, pp. 156, 217, explain the British production of acid steel by means of this prejudice. Burn, *op. cit.*, p. 112, makes the point that German basic steel competed successfully in Britain despite any prejudice against basic steel. He also, pp. 174–178, says that British basic steel was inferior to the German. To the extent that this was due to impurity of British resources, it meant that it was more expensive to get an equivalent grade of steel from British than from German resources.

progress of the British steel industry was hampered by inadequate information about the changes occurring in other countries,[42] and it is undeniably
true that technical progress in Britain was being made in some areas.[43]
It is not possible to say at this point whether the British steel industry
was operating with the most efficient techniques available to it, but since
any possible change would not have greatly altered the fortunes of the
British steel industry relative to its rivals in Germany and the United
States, the cost of this inefficiency in terms of production foregone was
slight.

The question to be asked, then, is this: If the costs of the British
steel industry were not a very important factor in its relative decline before
World War I, why have investigators occupied themselves with controversies about them? The argument presented here is neither complex nor
dependent on obscure data. If it is correct, there is little reason to give
prominence to the inadequacies of British industry or industrialists in an
explanation of the fortunes of the British steel industry.

The answer is probably that the investigators quoted here were not
primarily concerned with economic issues. They were anxious to explain
the failure of British prestige in the late nineteenth century. The leader
of the world was falling behind. The economic aspect of this decline—together with other aspects—was seen as a failure of leadership, as the
fault of specific people; it was too difficult to see it as the result of the
natural progress of technology and production. In the steel industry, the
suggestion that British resources were not adequate to ensure world dominance for the British industry was uniformly rejected. The actions of ma-
levolent foreigners were the first targets for blame in the search for villains
that resulted from the denial of natural causes. When the difficulties of
the initial, naive arguments were revealed, an equally naive denunciation
of the British participants was produced.

It is not to be denied that there were stupidities or failings in the
British steel industry before World War I. Nor is it asserted here that
government policy was particularly enlightened after the War. But it would
seem obvious that the relative decline of the British steel industry in the
years before 1913 was a straightforward result of the location of usable
natural resources, the location of the demand for steel, and the tariff policies of Germany and the United States—all of which were independent
of the conditions of competition in the British steel industry.

[42] There was a lively periodical press, and the *Journal of the Iron and Steel
Institute* published a regular review of articles on the iron and steel industry of
many countries that is impressive in its coverage.

[43] See W. A. Sinclair, "The Growth of the British Steel Industry in the Late
Nineteenth Century," *Scottish Journal of Political Economy*, 6 (February 1959),
33–47.

PART TWO

INDUSTRIALIZATION IN PLANNED ECONOMIES

Neither the great landmarks in the economic history of the Soviet Union over the past 35 years nor the specific institutional arrangements which are characteristic of the Soviet economy need be explained by recourse to Marxism. Rather, it is much more plausible to explain both the formidable changes that have taken place and the modus operandi *of the Soviet economy in part as a recurrence of a traditional pattern of Russian economic development: in part as stemming from the exigencies of a given situation and, most of all, as emanating from the mechanics of power politics—that is to say, essentially as necessitated by the desire of a dictatorial government to augment and to perpetuate its power position.*

Alexander Gerschenkron
Soviet Economic Growth

THE ECONOMICS
OF OVERTAKING AND SURPASSING

Joseph Berliner
Brandeis University

In the beginning there was England. And contentment vanished from the world. For the appearance of highly developed countries creates in others a condition of "tension between the actual state of economic activities in the country and the existing obstacles to industrial development, on the one hand, and the great promise inherent in such development, on the other."[1] The existence of such tension is the dominating fact in the economic and political programs of many countries of the world. But although the basis of the tension is economic, economic theory has not proved conspicuously successful in providing guidance for the removal of the obstacles and the progress toward sustained economic development.

The reason is in part that the cultural, political and social characteristics of underdeveloped countries are usually very different from those in countries in which economic theory has flourished. But another reason is that economic theory has been concerned primarily with what might be called "inner-directed" development. The tensions of backwardness, however, suggest that what is required is a theory of "other-directed" development. In the former, the rate and pattern of development are determined by the interaction of large numbers of producers and consumers each with his own product and time preferences; there is no particular social goal in view. In the latter, development is consciously directed toward

● The writer wishes to express his debt for the valuable criticism of an earlier draft by Herbert Levine, Peter Wiles, Abram Bergson, and other colleagues who were kind enough to comment on it.

[1] Alexander Gerschenkron, *Economic Backwardness in Historical Perspective,* Harvard University Press, Cambridge, Mass., 1912, p. 8.

the goal of imitating the attainments of other countries that are regarded as more advanced.

It is plausible to expect that, in principle, the character of self-generated behavior ought to be different in significant ways from that of imitative behavior. That there are differences in practice as well has been argued by Alexander Gerschenkron in his proposition that "in a number of important historical instances industrialization processes, when launched at length in a backward country, showed considerable differences, as compared with more advanced countries, not only with regard to the speed of development (the rate of industrial growth) but also with regard to the productive and organizational structures of industry which emerged from those processes."[2] It is the purpose of this essay to demonstrate that imitation is a fruitful concept for exploring some old notions and generating a few new ones about the process of emergence from economic underdevelopment.

VARIETIES OF IMITATIVE DEVELOPMENT

Charles Lamb tells us that roast pig was first invented in China when a cottage burned down with a pig inside, and for centuries thereafter, his apochryphal Chinese roasted their pigs by building and burning down their cottages. Few would hold with a pure roast-pig theory of imitative development, although East European copies of the Soviet model during the Stalin period came astonishingly close. Part of the problem is precisely to discover what parts of the process to imitate without having to burn down a whole cottage.

The character of the process of imitative development depends on at least two policy decisions. First, one must establish precisely what aspects of the economy of the advanced country are to be imitated. And second, one must determine the desired time-rate of approach to the state of the imitated economy.

The Ends of Imitation

In his discussion of "conspicuous consumption" Veblen introduced a decidedly imitative form of behavior into social analysis. But the interdependence of consumer preferences implied in the behavior of "keeping up with the Joneses" was rather a nuisance for the main body of economic theory which was built upon the assumptions of "inner-directed" rather than imitative behavior. It was not until Duesenberry developed a method

---

[2] Gerschenkron, *op. cit.,* p. 7.

along the path traversed earlier by their advanced forerunners. However, such theories are not optimistic enough, certainly not enough to satisfy the imitative objectives of Stalin or Chen Yi, for whereas the underdeveloped country is assured that one day it will begin moving along the path of the forerunners, nothing is said about the time-rate of movement along that path. And without the specific inclusion of time-rates, nothing can be said about the possibility of overtaking and surpassing the advanced countries.

We may distinguish three requirements of successful imitation. The first and weakest requirement is that A commence a process of sustained development like that experienced earlier by B. The second is that at some future date A attain the level of development *presently* held by B. The third and strongest requirement is that at some future date A attain the level of development of B on the same date.[10] If for some reason B's development should cease, the last two requirements merge into one. Some underdeveloped countries may be content with an imitative process that satisfies only the first or second requirement. It is enough for them that per capita incomes begin an uninterrupted and modest rise; an evolutionary or stage theory, perhaps of the Marxian variety, would satisfy their aspirations. On the other hand, those who wish to overtake and surpass the leaders insist on the third requirement for which simple evolution will not do. Something must be added to an evolutionary theory, something which will support the possibility that the development of those who come later may be more rapid than that of those who came before.

Evolutionary and stage theories stress the similarity in paths of development, the principal differences among countries being found in the historical time periods in which they traverse the successive stages. But mere similarity of development does not necessarily imply that any conscious imitation occurred, any more than the similarity of physical development of successive generations of organisms implies that the offspring imitated the parent. The classical stage theory of cultural evolution (savagery to barbarism to civilization), for example, does not depend on savages imitating barbarians.[11] Marx, however, does suggest that the development of the lagging countries is conditioned by their awareness of the experience

[10] During the catching-up period, B may alter its path in a direction that A may choose not to follow. In that case A's growth is no longer "imitative."

[11] The concept of imitation played a central role, however, in the great debate among anthropologists about the relative importance of "diffusion" and "independent invention" in explaining the similarity of culture traits in different societies. Diffusion is, of course, pure imitation. Imitation has also played a role in sociology (in child "socialization") and in psychology (in learning theory). Economic theory is rather underdeveloped among the social sciences in its analysis of imitative behavior, perhaps because innovative behavior is so much more interesting.

of the forerunners: "The industrially more developed country presents to the less developed country a picture of the latter's future."[12] By including some such notion as the forerunners "holding up a mirror" to the followers, an evolutionary theory can be made to include a specifically imitative element. In pursuing the implications of the latecomers' opportunity to imitate, we can find the special features that create the possibility of "overtaking and surpassing" the advanced countries.

One such feature emerged in the later debates among the Marxists about the possibility of skipping the stage of capitalism. Those who held to the purist position that stages could not be skipped were arguing, with a faint aroma of roast pig, from an organic model; children cannot skip the puberty stage by imitating the parent in the adult stage. Those who argued that latecomers could skip or foreshorten stages were presenting an instance of the case that imitative development may differ in a significant way from the development patterns of the forerunners.

Another special feature of imitative development was introduced by Veblen in his discussion of borrowing of technology. The imitator can adopt the most advanced forms of technology, which were not available to the forerunner when it was at the imitator's present position. It is therefore plausible that the imitator can cover the ground between its present position and that of the forerunner more rapidly than the corresponding ground had been covered by the latter in an earlier period.

Although the presence of such special features of imitation as stage-skipping and technology-borrowing is a necessary condition for overtaking the forerunner, it is not a sufficient condition. For if the forerunner continues to develop, the imitator will not necessarily ever catch up, even though his initial growth rates exceed those of the forerunner in the earlier period. To establish the sufficient conditions would require a double-dynamic analysis, that is, it would have to deal with the path of a moving point trying to catch up to a moving target. The analysis to be presented below has a more modest objective. We shall deal only with the second requirement of successful imitation, that the imitator attain the *present* position of the forerunner. Some part of Stalin's and Chen Yi's stated aims can be captured by adding the requirement that the target be attained in the minimal period of time. We decline the challenge of dealing with the pursuit of a moving target. Hereafter, the concept of overtaking and surpassing will be understood to mean the attainment of the present position of the forerunner in the shortest possible time.

We have now identified two possible commodity-objectives and two possible time-objectives of imitative growth. The commodity-objective may consist either of consumer goods or of military and heavy-industry goods; the time-objective may be merely to follow the path of the advanced coun-

---

[12] Quoted in Gerschenkron, *op. cit.*, p. 6.

try without specific regard to time or to overtake and surpass the present position of the advanced country. A general theory of imitative development would have to deal with processes described by all four combinations of these two sets of objectives. For the following discussion we shall be concerned with only one of the four combinations, that which characterizes the goals of Soviet-type imitative development set forth by Stalin and Chen Yi: to overtake and surpass the military-heavy industry attainments of the advanced countries.

SOME PATTERNS OF IMITATIVE DEVELOPMENT

The proposition to be investigated is that there are properties of the development process of an imitating economy which are different from those of the forerunner and which, moreover, make it possible for the imitator to overtake and surpass the military and industrial production capacity of the forerunner. In order to study structural growth patterns as well as aggregate growth rates, a model is required that lends itself to the analysis not only of the consumption-investment decision but also of a variety of substitution possibilities between factors and commodities. This could be accomplished by introducing several sets of variables representing different factors, consumer goods, and producer goods, but the number of variables would be awkwardly large. However, the same results can be obtained with only two variables by the ingenious device developed in the literature on efficient capital accumulation programs, namely, by ascribing to the goods the properties of both consumption and investment. That is, the goods are both factors and commodities, and can either be consumed directly or combined to produce new stocks of the two goods (rather like coal or electric power). Goods of the more familiar kind that are used exclusively for consumption or investment may thus be treated as limiting cases.

We assume an economy, then, with two factors or commodities, X and Y, stocks of which are available initially in quantities represented by P_0 in Figure 1. The stocks are used up in the first period in the process of producing new and expanded stocks of X and Y at the point P_1 on the transformation curve T_1.[13] A certain portion of the new stocks, represented by C_1, is consumed, and the balance used during the second period for the

[13] Commodities like machinery that outlast one production period may be handled by assuming "that a machine tool produces not only fabricated metal products but also a one-period-older machine tool." See p. 282 of Robert Dorfman, Paul A. Samuelson, and Robert M. Solow, *Linear Programming and Economic Analysis,* McGraw-Hill, New York, 1958, from whose work this model and the diagrammatic representation are adapted.

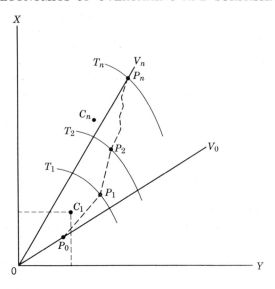

FIGURE 1

production of new stocks at the point P_2 on the second-period transformation curve T_2. In this way the economy moves along the indicated path
until at some time it arrives at P_n. In the course of the entire period it
has been transformed from an underdeveloped to an advanced economy.
The degree of development is reflected not only in the increase of product
from P_0 to P_n but also in the change in the composition of its stocks from
assortment ray OV_0 to OV_n.

Now another economy which has remained underdeveloped is seized
by the tension generated by the development of the first, and sets about
to imitate it. Suppose, for simplicity, that its stocks at time t are P_0, the
position occupied by the developed economy t years earlier. Its objective
is to attain P_n in the shortest possible time. Our task is to investigate
those properties of imitative development which may cause the development pattern of the imitator to differ from that of the forerunner. Four
such properties will be examined, having to do with the rate of investment,
the borrowing of technology, the design of the capital plant, and the time-
path of development.

The Rate of Investment

When the forerunner was at P_1, the amount of consumption C_1 was
determined by the incomes, tastes, and time-preferences of that period.

The location of the second period's transformation curve depended on how much was consumed of the first period's outputs. The smaller the consumption subtracted from P_1, the further to the northeast is the transformation curve T_2.

If the imitator at point P_1 is motivated by the "demonstration effect" it will strive to imitate the consumption standards attained by the forerunner at time t. But the volume of consumption of the forerunner at time t is quite large, perhaps at the point C_n, well beyond the initial production possibilities of the imitator. Even if the consumption levels of the forerunner cannot be fully attained, consumer preferences and political necessity are likely to lead to a higher level of consumption than that of C_1 which was attained by the forerunner years ago when it was at the same stage of development. Hence, smaller stocks will be available for further production, and the second period's transformation function will lie below and to the left of T_2. It will therefore take the imitator more than t years to attain P_n.

But if the imitator is motivated by the desire to overtake and surpass the forerunner, it will keep consumption down to a level lower than C_1. Its second-period transformation curve will lie therefore to the northeast of T_2, and since the same argument will apply in successive periods, it will attain P_n in a shorter period than t years.

This second case describes the conditions of Soviet growth. During the Five Year Plans consumption was held down to levels well below those in advanced countries at the same time, for the sake of rapid accumulation of production stocks. Indeed the harsh conditions of Soviet growth have sometimes been justified by pointing to the conditions under which industrialization began in the capitalist countries. Both the classical economists and Marx regarded it as an appropriate assumption that real wages were maintained at subsistence levels, and this is probably a fair approximation of Soviet conditions also, at least during the 1930's. Ignoring the fact that the conventional concept of minimal subsistence levels has changed, we may regard C_1 as the subsistence consumption level of both the forerunner at time 1 and the imitator at time t. How then can the rate of investment be higher for the imitator than for the forerunner?

Three factors provide the answer. The first is the fact that in the advanced countries the volume of consumption rose above subsistence levels as output increased. All that is required is that the imitator keep consumption from rising over time at the same rate as that earlier experienced by the forerunner. In fact, Soviet consumption per capita rose during the period 1928–1955, according to Bergson's calculations at 1937 prices, at 1.7 per cent per annum, or at 2.0 per cent if one considers only the peacetime years. In the U.S. during the period 1869/78–1899/1908, the annual rate was 2.6 per cent at 1929 prices; it would have been appreciably greater at mid-period prices. Moreover, most of the Soviet growth occurred during the 1950–1955 subperiod; in the 1928–1940 subperiod per capita consumption declined at an annual rate of 0.6 per cent. Although consumption levels fluctuated in the United States also, there was no decline quite so extensive.[14] Hence by keeping the rate of consumption from rising as rapidly as that of the forerunner, the U.S.S.R. was able to marshall larger proportions of its stocks for further production.

The second factor is that the imitator will mobilize its resources for a more intense rate of utilization than the self-generating economy did. The given stocks of labor or capital can thus be made to yield larger flows of factor services per period, and the transformation curve generated by a given set of stocks will therefore lie further to the northeast. Not very much evidence is available on capital services, but most analysts accept Soviet claims that the rate of utilization of capacity is greater in the U.S.S.R. than in the United States.[15] With respect to labor, if the total population is regarded as the stock, 53 per cent of the Soviet population was in the labor force in 1939, compared with 32–33 per cent in the United States during the period 1870–1900.[16] However, Soviet workers probably worked fewer hours per month than United States workers did in the late nineteenth century.[17] In this case the "demonstration effect" combined with socialist ideology to deprive the imitator of an advantage enjoyed by the forerunner.

The third factor deals with the commodity structure of consumption. Two baskets of goods which may be equally satisfactory in terms of consumer preferences or subsistence levels, will leave different quantities of stocks available for production in the next period. Each such set of stocks will yield a different transformation curve in the next period. In Figure 2, CC is an indifference curve (representing perhaps the subsistence level) of consumption mixes that may be selected out of stocks P_1. If C_1 were consumed, the stocks left over would yield transformation curve T_2, but if C_1' or C_1'' were consumed, the transformation curves would be T_2' or T_2''.

[14] Abram Bergson, *The Real National Income of Soviet Russia Since 1928*, Harvard University Press, Cambridge, 1961, pp. 284–288.

[15] See Alexander Erlich's remarks in Abram Bergson (ed.), *Soviet Economic Growth*, Row Peterson and Co., Evanston 1953, pp. 93–94. The statement does not necessarily apply to U.S. capital utilization in the nineteenth century.

[16] Warren W. Eason, "Labor Force," in Abram Bergson and Simon Kuznets (eds.), *Economic Trends in the Soviet Union*, Harvard University Press, Cambridge, 1963, p. 57.

[17] Janet Chapman, "Consumption," in Bergson and Kuznets, *op. cit.*, pp. 251–252. Also Walter Galenson, *Labor Productivity in Soviet and American Industry*, Columbia University Press, New York, 1955, pp. 52–55.

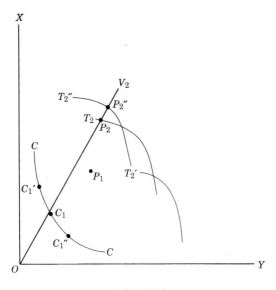

FIGURE 2

Now, an "inner-directed" economy exercising no control over the composition of consumption, would be led by consumer preferences to select some combination such as C_1 and to produce a second-period output such as P_2, whereas if the imitator has the power to control the composition of consumption, it has an additional degree of freedom. If it should wish to maximize output along the ray OV_2, it can provide consumers with a consumption-mix representing the same level of subsistence or welfare as C_1, but which would use up less of the resources that promote growth in the desired direction. It would thus adjust prices so as to induce consumption-mix C_1'', yielding transformation curve T_2'', and producing at P_2'', which represents a higher rate of growth along OV_2 than does P_2.

In the case of the Soviet economy the policy of restricting the consumption of residential housing and consumer durables may be interpreted as having had the purpose of reducing the consumption-drain of those resources having the largest-growth-inducing effect. Mr. Khrushchev's intention to restrict the development of the Soviet automotive economy to dimensions more reasonable than those of the capitalist countries may have a similar effect.

Thus, even if the imitator were confronted with the same set of technological alternatives as the forerunner faced in the corresponding period, it may be expected to grow more rapidly because of its control over the rate and composition of consumption.

Borrowed Technology

However, the technology available to the imitator is not the same as that employed by the forerunner *t* years ago, and this is another factor enabling the former to maintain a higher rate of investment than the latter during its development period. The path of the forerunner is strewn with the rusted remains of innovations that hadn't worked but which had consumed resources in the process of being proved unworkable. The imitator is spared this waste of resources, which may not have been a "waste" to the forerunner, since in the absence of less-than-perfect foresight, there is a necessary cost in discovering workable, to say nothing of optimal, forms of technology.

Consider a proposal by an imaginative engineer for an elaborate new process of mining coal. The obvious condition that the proposal must satisfy is that the production of one ton of coal not require a direct input of more than one ton of coal. Less obvious is that the direct *and indirect* (in the input-output sense) requirement of coal not exceed one ton. It is at least plausible that a technically elegant and complex process may consume a greater quantity of value than it produces. One way of testing the innovation is to apply the Hawkins-Simon conditions in the context of an input-output model.[18] Another is to estimate costs on the basis of present and anticipated market prices. With less-than-perfect knowledge and foresight, one must expect that some estimates will be inaccurate, and innovations will be undertaken that should not have been. The market casts them off, and the forerunner has, in effect, borne the cost of eliminating the more grossly inefficient innovations that failed to satisfy the Hawkins-Simon condition.

Of the past innovations that did satisfy the minimal tests of economic efficiency, there is a larger subgroup that was invested in by unfortunate entrepreneurs only a short time before a more productive process was invented. These too clutter the historical path of the advanced country with costs of development that must be borne by the forerunner but are spared the imitator.[19]

The imitator thus has available to it a basket of technologies that have survived to time *t* and that have been preselected by the forerunner out of its historical experience. However, the forerunner's selection process has also eliminated other technological variants which neither consumed more value than they produced, nor were superseded by improved processes, but which were simply less efficient than the accepted ones, given the conditions of the forerunner's economy. Some of these eliminated vari-

[18] Dorfman, Samuelson, Solow, *op. cit.,* pp. 215–219.

[19] See note 21.

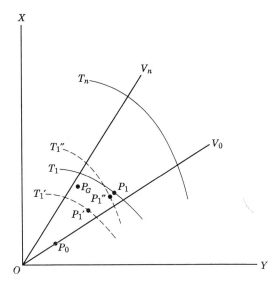

FIGURE 3

ants may be more efficient than the accepted ones under the conditions of the imitator's economy, and therefore, if the imitator confines the range of choice to the variants currently employed in the advanced economy, that imitation may take on the form of the roast pig. When the state of the imitator's economy is very far behind that of the advanced country, a direct imitation of the most advanced technology may result in a less-than-maximal rate of growth.

The argument is a variation of the factor-proportions problem.[20] In Figure 3, P_0 represents as before the current stocks of the imitator and the stocks of the forerunner t years ago, and T_n is the current transformation curve of the advanced country incorporating the most modern technology. If the imitator borrowed the most modern technological variants incorporated in T_n, with its initial stocks P_0 its transformation curve would be T_1''. Hence its output (P_1''), would be greater than that of the forerunner t years ago (P_1') and it would grow more rapidly. However, the most modern technological variants had been designed for a developed country,

[20] Richard S. Eckaus, "The Factor-Proportions Problem in Underdeveloped Countries," *American Economic Review*, September 1955. In Eckaus' Figure 4, process Oef may be regarded as the old technology and process Oab as the newest. If the existing factor endowment happens to be in the neighborhood of Oef, then a greater output could be obtained by redesigning a new technology such as process Ocd, rather than employing the most capital intensive process Oab.

with stocks of factors available in the proportions OV_n. By redesigning and adapting the newest technology to its own factor proportions, the imitator can achieve a transformation curve that would yield a higher output such as P_1, greater than either $P_1{}'$ or $P_1{}''$.

Was Veblen wrong, then, in ascribing Germany's success in overtaking England to the adoption of England's most advanced technology? Not if Germany's factor proportions were in the neighborhood of England's, such as at P_G. In that case the direct imitation of England's most advanced technology would have been appropriate, for that technology had presumably been designed to maximize output with factor proportions in the neighborhood of OV_n.[21] Thus the closer the imitator's factor proportions are to those of the forerunner, the smaller are the differences in design of the optimal variants of the newest technology in both countries. The existence of such differences between the more and the less developed imitator is suggested in Gerschenkron's proposition that "the extent to which these attributes of backwardness occurred in individual instances appears to have varied directly with the degree of backwardness. . . ."[22]

The evidence of Soviet practice in this respect is inconclusive. Granick has made a strong case for the view that, at least in the important instance of the metalworking industries, Soviet planners did adapt Western technology to their own factor proportions by substituting labor for capital wherever possible.[23] Even enterprises like the Gorky Automotive Plant, which was built on the direct model of the Ford River-Rouge plant and with the assistance of Ford engineers, was redesigned in significant ways in the light of special Soviet conditions.[24] Where Western technological equipment was used, the Soviets accommodated to their lower level of labor skills by redesigning job descriptions, so that several specialized Soviet workers performed tasks that in other countries were carried out by individual skilled workers. There is, moreover, the evidence of "dualism" in the economy which suggests that something like a redesigning of borrowed processes did take place. For example in many plants it is common to find basic processes highly mechanized whereas supplementary processes such as materials handling are carried out with large quantities of labor. The equivalent picture in agriculture is of the monstrous combine-harvester

---

[21] Veblen's chief point, however, is that Germany's transformation curve was superior to England's because the latter's capital stock consisted of units of various ages, whereas the imitator's capital stock consisted entirely of the most modern.

[22] Gerschenkron, *op. cit.*, p. 7.

[23] David Granick, "Economic Development and Productivity Analysis: The Case of Soviet Metalworking," *Quarterly Journal of Economics*, May 1957.

[24] David Granick, "Organization and Technology in Soviet Metalworking: Some Conditioning Factors," *American Economic Review*, May 1957.

followed about the fields by troops of elderly peasant women. At least we can say that there is no roast-pig imitation here, and indeed Granick has shown that perfect imitation is quite impossible, if only because of large differences in social organization.

On the other hand, while the Soviets have evidently taken advantage of the opportunities of improving on the directly imitative transformation curve T_1'' in the light of their own factor proportions, it is unlikely that they moved to the fully optimal T_1. It is difficult, for example, to dismiss entirely the prolonged official criticism of what Stalin dubbed "giganto-mania"—the view that the best must be the largest. In the case of the huge Magnitogorsk works, the Soviet planners overrode the advice of their American consultants and designed their blast furnaces substantially larger than the largest their consultants thought prudent.[25] To some extent, the selection of capital-intensive designs reflects the absence of an interest charge for capital, which is itself evidence of insufficient awareness of the significance of factor proportions. There are also indications that equip-ment design, particularly that of imported equipment, was rather more advanced than was warranted by existing levels of technical skills. Stalin, however, operated on the basis of a singular learning theory that had a certain plausibility from the point of view of dynamic efficiency. "We pro-ceeded openly and consciously to the inevitable outlays and overexpendi-tures associated with the shortage of sufficiently trained people who knew how to handle machines. True, we destroyed many machines at the same time, but at the same time we won the most important thing—time—and we created the most precious thing in the economy—Cadres."[26]

We may interpret Stalin's words as a decision to "trade-off" scarce physical capital for even scarcer human capital. There is a basis in ra-tionality for this decision for, as Gerschenkron has pointed out "Creation of an industrial labor force that really deserves the name is a most difficult and protracted process."[27] If the length of the process can be reduced by introducing the raw labor to the most modern of technological equip-ment, then the factor-proportions argument for using less capital-intensive equipment is somewhat weakened.[28] The argument is further weakened

[25] M. Gardner Clark, *The Economics of Soviet Steel*, Harvard University Press, Cambridge, Mass., 1956, pp. 65–66, 84.

[26] *Pravda*, December 29, 1934.

[27] Gerschenkron, *op. cit.*, p. 9.

[28] Peter Wiles has commented that breaking an expensive machine would seem to be less efficient than "not breaking a cheap one." This would be correct unless (a) the expensive machine is more productive during its brief but noble lifetime than the cheap one during its long but humble lifetime, and (b) the worker's skill rises more rapidly in learning to operate and maintain the expensive machine than in the case of the cheap one.

when one considers another difference between self-generated and imitative growth that bears on the design of fixed plant.

Flexibility of Fixed Plant

We owe to George Stigler the distinction between adaptability and flexibility of fixed plant.[29] A given stock of capital is adaptable if it can be combined with varying amounts of the variable factor, like the ten shovels that can be combined with eleven ditchdiggers by a suitable metamorphosis. The stock of capital is flexible, if it approximates the best technology for a broad range of output, although for no level of output does it incorporate the very best technology; approximate efficiency over a broad range of output is achieved at the cost of attaining perfect efficiency at no level of output. Flexibility is built into plants to offset the consequences of imperfect adaptability, for with imperfect adaptability any output other than the optimum either would involve prohibitively high marginal costs or would be highly unprofitable.

It is rational for an enterprise in a self-generating (market) economy to pay the cost of building flexibility into the plant,[30] for the characteristic of such an economy is uncertainty about the future level and composition of output. To design a plant which would give rock-bottom average costs only at the optimal output would expose the plant to immediate collapse if economic conditions should change and the optimum should shift to another level of output. The firm in an imitating economy, however, need not have the same concerns, in part because the imitating economy is likely to introduce large doses of economic planning, which ideally should be expected to reduce uncertainty. But more than the mere existence of economic planning is involved, for a planned economy need not be goal-oriented; it might be content to permit consumer sovereignty to determine the composition of the national product, including the division between consumption and investment. The crucial point is that the imitating economy has an end-in-view, and therefore need have less concern for unanticipated and uncontrolled variations in output or demand.

Consider an economy that wishes to change the composition of its stocks in the shortest possible time from OV_0 to that of the forerunner, OV_n. What will the shape of its transformation curve be at the end of the process? The economy of the forerunner, consisting of firms that have

---

[29] George Stigler, "Production and Distribution in the Short Run," *Journal of Political Economy*, June 1939; reprinted in William Fellner and Bernard F. Haley (eds.) *Readings in the Theory of Income Distribution*, Blakiston, Philadelphia, 1946.

[30] "Flexibility will be added until the 'accumulated' marginal cost equals the discounted marginal returns from savings due to that additional flexibility." *Ibid.*, p. 131.

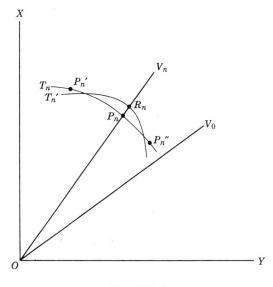

FIGURE 4

built flexibility into their plant, will have a transformation curve like T_n in Figure 4, which is drawn with slight curvature to reflect a relatively high elasticity of transformation. The flexibility is necessary because the firms cannot know at the time their plant is designed whether the optimum will be P_n or at P_n' or P_n''. The imitator, however, knows precisely that the end-in-view lies along OV_n. Hence, it does not need to reduce its capacity to produce along OV_n for the sake of the relatively greater efficiency with which it might produce P_n' or P_n'' if it had to. Its transformation curve will have the shape of T_n' and its output will be R_n, greater than the output P_n which a non-goal-oriented economy would select. Therefore, the imitating economy ought to experience a more rapid rate of growth than the self-generating economy of the forerunner.

Have the Soviets taken advantage of this opportunity for catching up? Stigler notes that there are two principal techniques for building flexibility into plants: divisibility, and low fixed-to-variable cost ratios. The aforementioned practice of "gigantomania" suggests that in the choice of the size of blast furnaces, for example, the Soviets preferred the productivity gains of an indivisible plant with a few large units, over the flexibility advantage of a divisible plant with many small units. It also suggests that they preferred the lower optimal-output costs that could be attained with higher fixed-to-variable cost ratios. In special instances, the Soviets did build flexibility into plants; in the tractor industry the possibility of conversion to military tanks was provided for, but the motive here was military rather than economic. By and large, however, the evidence seems to support the conclusion that the Soviets did take advantage of the imitator's opportunity to avoid the costs of flexibility.

Perhaps they went too far. Our proposition about the imitator's opportunity to avoid the costs of flexibility was abstracted from such nuisance considerations as imperfections in planning and changes in objectives. These unfortunate facts of the real world suggest that flexibility ought not be dispensed with as cheerfully as theoretical considerations direct. Nevertheless, the direction of the argument remains valid though its force is reduced from a bang to a whimper.

Imitation and the Turnpike Theorem

Suppose the imitator and the forerunner were alike with respect to all the factors discussed thus far; the consumption basket is fixed at the subsistence level in both (so that we may assume a "consumptionless" economy), the same technology is available to both, and both start with the same production stocks. There is one final reason why the imitator may be expected to grow more rapidly. The argument is based on the conditions of efficient capital accumulation.[31]

Consider a self-generating economy with initial stocks P_0 and transformation curve T_1, as in Figure 5. Any point on T_1 is efficient in the sense that no other output could be produced that would contain more of both X and Y. Suppose that P_1 were chosen. After subtraction of the fixed consumption basket once more, T_2 is the second-period transformation curve and P_2 is an efficient point on T_2. Note that within each period production has been perfectly efficient. Nevertheless, the path may be an inefficient one for the whole time span. How can it come about that a path which is efficient within all periods may nevertheless be inefficient over the whole time span?

The argument is based on the fact that the position and shape of the transformation curve in any period depends on the choice of product mix of the preceding period. The position of T_2 is based on the choice of P_1 in the preceding period. But if P_1' (or P_1'') had been chosen instead, the transformation curve would have been T_2' (or T_2''). There are as many second-period transformation curves as there are points on T_1. By a familiar line of reasoning the locus of all second-period efficient points is the envelope E_2 to the second-period transformation curves. As can be seen in

---

[31] The following discussion is based entirely on Chapter 12 of Dorfman, Samuelson and Solow, op. cit. Needless to say, they bear no responsibility for this interpretation.

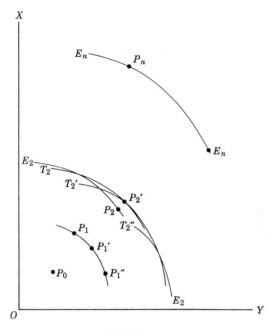

FIGURE 5

the figure, for example, if the economy wished its output in the proportions represented by P_2, it would have done better to produce at P_1' than at P_1. Then its second-period transformation curve would have been T_2' and its output P_2', greater than P_2. Therefore P_1 was not intertemporally efficient, even though it was located on the transformation curve.

Since the product mix at any time is the starting point for the production of the next period, there will be a family of envelope curves for all succeeding periods. Of all possible paths of getting from P_0 to some subsequent P_n, "only those paths which hop from envelope to envelope have any claim to efficiency."[32] Two intertemporally efficient paths have been represented in Figure 6, paths 1 and 3. Between P_0 and any point on E_n one and only one (intertemporally) efficient path can be drawn. Path 2 is an example of a path which may be efficient within each period, but which is not intertemporally efficient. It would take longer to get from P_0 to P_n by path 2 than by path 1.

Now suppose we have given the historical data on the path actually traversed by a self-generating economy during the period in which it was transformed from P_0 to P_n. Is the path likely to have been the unique

[32] Dorfman, Samuelson and Solow, *op. cit.,* p. 315.

efficient one? The answer depends, as in most economic theorems, on how "perfect" the economy was. In this case, if there were perfect competition, and if there were constant returns to scale, and if there were perfect certainty (so that "ex ante expected prices or rates of change of prices . . . correspond exactly to ex post observed prices,"[33]) then competition would lead the producers inevitably along the efficient path. Competition would pick, out of all sets of prices over time, precisely that unique set of prices such that profit-maximizing entrepreneurs, producing with marginal rates of transformation equal to price ratios, would produce the appropriate product-mixes on the envelope curves at all points. Any other set of prices could not endure, because arbitrage-through-time would restore prices to the optimal set, thus violating the assumption that ex ante prices always correspond to ex post.

The very strictness of the assumptions necessary to yield this result suggest the answer to the question about the self-generating economy. The likelihood that it was characterized by perfect certainty is small indeed. Hence, even if perfect competition ensured that the economy was on its transformation curves at all times, it is most unlikely to have been on its efficiency loci as well. However, perfect certainty is only one device that can guide an economy to the prices needed to place it on its efficiency loci. An alternative device is the possession of "vision at a distance."[34] That is, if the society has reason to know the capital stock it wished to attain at time t, it has sufficient information (given knowledge of the production functions) with which to calculate the prices or product-mixes needed to hop from envelope to envelope along its efficient path. Neither perfect certainty nor "vision at a distance" are characteristics likely to be found in the self-generating forerunner, but the very essence of imitation is the possession of a vision of what one wishes to attain, namely, the capital stock attained earlier by the forerunner at P_n. Since either an end-in-view or perfect certainty are required for the attainment of an efficient program, and since the imitator possesses the former by definition whereas the forerunner is unlikely to possess either, other things equal, the imitator is more likely to follow an efficient path from P_0 to P_n than is the forerunner.

Did the Soviet economy in fact make use of this potential advantage of imitative development? One would need much more detailed data about Soviet production functions than could possibly be had if the properties of the optimal path were to be calculated. But if we make one more rather heroic assumption about the Soviet economy, then an important property of the optimal path may be deduced, which moreover can be subjected

[33] *Ibid.*, p. 319.

[34] *Ibid.*, p. 321.

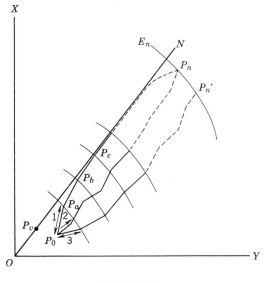

FIGURE 6

to a rough statistical test. It has been assumed in the preceding discussion that the economy is "consumptionless" in the sense that consumption is fixed at the minimal level needed to sustain the labor force and provide for its natural growth. We now add the requirement that labor (and land), like all other commodity-factors, be both an input and an output and that its rate of growth be proportional to the inputs used in its production. This additional requirement is not so unrealistic as it may seem at first glance, for if the labor unit is adjusted for levels of skill and incentives, then increased inputs of education and consumer goods may be expected to lead to an increase in labor so defined, though perhaps not proportionately. In like fashion, the "output" of land will increase in response to increased quantities of quality-improving inputs.

To the extent that the Soviet economy satisfied the conditions specified above, if its growth path had been efficient, it should have exhibited a certain property. This property may be described by noting that a ray drawn at random from the origin would represent a "balanced growth" path; that is, both stocks would increase at the same rate. Each of the one-parameter sets of rays would represent a different time-rate of growth. One such ray would represent the maximal growth rate that could be attained by balanced growth. Let that path, which has been named the von Neumann path, be represented in Figure 6 by ON. The von Neumann path is distinguished from all other balanced-growth paths by two properties:

(1) by the aforementioned fact that it is the maximally rapid balanced-growth path, and (2) by the fact that although all other balanced-growth paths are intertemporally inefficient, it alone is efficient in both the intratemporal and intertemporal senses. Thus, if by chance the initial capital stock happened to exist in the von Neumann proportions, such as at P_v, and if the economy wished to maintain these proportions indefinitely, the maximal time-rate of growth would be attained by shooting up ON.

In the general case, however, the initial stocks in the imitating economy are not likely to exist in von Neumann proportions, nor are the final stocks of the forerunner that the imitator wishes to overtake and surpass. The two stocks are more likely to be like P_0 and P_n, both off the von Neumann path. The interesting theoretical result is that even in this case the von Neumann path has a certain significance for the imitator. In the words of the inventors of the theorem:

> . . . if the programming period is very long, the corresponding optimal capital program will be described as follows: The system first invests so as to alter its capital structure toward the special von Neumann proportions. When it has come close to these proportions, it spends most of the programming period performing steady growth at the maximal rate (more precisely, something close to maximal steady growth). The system expands along or close to the von Neumann ray ON until the end of the programming period approaches. Then it bends away from ON and invests in such a way as to alter the capital structure to the desired terminal proportions, arriving at $[P_n]$ as the period ends.[35]

Let path 1 in Figure 6 represent the optimal path so described. The proposition has been termed the "turnpike theorem" because the growth rate along ON is maximally rapid, like the speed rate on a turnpike highway. If one wishes to travel from one point to another, neither of which happens to be on the turnpike, it pays *under certain conditions* to drive out of one's direct path toward the turnpike in order to take advantage of the maximal speeds that can be attained. The conditions are that the initial and end points should be not too far from the turnpike, and/or that the distance between them should be relatively great. Without knowledge of the position of the Soviet economy's von Neumann path, one cannot judge whether the first of these conditions holds. But with respect to the second, one can presume that the Soviet programming period should or could have been great enough that the initial and end points ought to be satisfactorily far apart. Moreover, the Soviet economy can be regarded as an approximation of a "consumptionless" economy in the sense described above, at least during Stalin's lifetime. Under these conditions, if the economy did capitalize on the imitator's advantage of having an end-in-view, then its growth pattern should have approximated a turnpike path.

If the Soviets did in fact succeed in attaining their turnpike path, then two characteristics of the growth pattern should be observable in the data (as necessary though not sufficient conditions). First, the degree of "unbalance" should have diminished from period to period as the stocks moved from P_0 to P_c toward the turnpike, after which a period of balanced growth should have ensued.[36] Second, the rate of growth should have increased as the turnpike proportions were attained and the maximal balanced-growth phase achieved.

With respect to the first test, the turnpike theorem is sometimes interpreted in terms of the distribution of national product between consumption and investment. In these terms the theorem is supposed to mean that initially investment grows more rapidly than consumption in order to build up the capital stocks at a maximal rate, and that after a time resources are finally shifted back again in the direction of a greatly enlarged output of consumer goods. This interpretation, which corresponds roughly to the Feldman model,[37] deals with the rate of investment, and was discussed above in that context; it is not however, a correct interpretation of the turnpike theorem. The turnpike theorem deals with a "consumptionless" economy; the subsistence minimum is treated not as final demand but as intermediate product, like fuel or animal fodder. No conclusions can therefore be drawn which include consumption as final demand. The stocks of commodities or factors that constitute the variables are both inputs and outputs; they exist in certain quantities at the beginning of a period, and, after being used for production, they exist in larger quantities once more at the end of the period after intermediate flows (including consumption) have been netted out. The peculiar appropriateness of the turnpike theorem to Soviet growth is that it deals precisely with those commodities that Stalin and Chen Yi had in mind in their justification of the motive to overtake and surpass the advanced countries, namely, stocks of productive resources.

It is in relative rates of growth of different productive stocks, then, and not in the difference between consumption and investment, that we

---

[36] It may be assumed that the economy has not yet reached the point of development at which it is prepared to veer off the turnpike toward its "final" destination P_n. A more general theory of imitation than that presented in this paper would deal with the problem of overtaking and surpassing a target that is moving. Such a theory would be more suitable to Soviet conditions, and the present theory dealing with an assumed fixed target would be a special case.

[37] Evsey Domar, *Essays in the Theory of Economic Growth*, Oxford University Press, New York, 1957.

should find our test of the extent to which an economy is approaching balanced growth. Balanced growth is a process in which the growth rates of X and Y are equal; that is, the ratio of growth rates $(\Delta X/X)/(\Delta Y/Y)$, is equal to unity (see appendix). In an economy approaching balanced growth as in the turnpike case, the value of the ratio in successive periods approaches unity. What we require then are data on the growth rates of different kinds of productive stocks for various periods.

The Soviets have recently published data which make it possible to compute the growth rates of stocks of fixed productive capital for seventeen industries, for the periods 1933–1940 and 1940–1955. Each industry was compared with all the others, yielding 136 pairs of industries in which relative changes in growth rates were observed; the details are explained in the appendix. In only 21 of the 136 cases did the pairs of stocks behave in both periods as if they were moving toward a balanced growth path. Moreover, the rate of growth of capital stocks was slower in the later period than in the earlier. Between 1933 and 1940 the capital stock increased by 157 per cent, whereas in the period 1950–1955 it grew by only 71 per cent. Thus, neither of the two characteristics one would expect to find in an economy following a turnpike path is observable in our data.

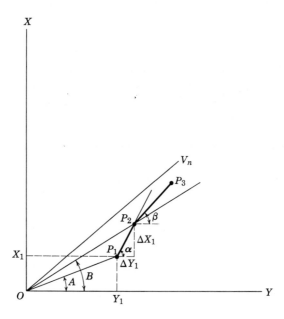

FIGURE 7

This conclusion is hardly likely to cause much surprise. For one thing, the data are very crude; at the least, one would wish to add inventories to fixed capital stocks. For another, even though some of the conditions for the turnpike theorem were present (an end-in-view, long-planning horizon, "consumptionless" economy, perhaps even constant returns to scale), others were not. Perhaps the major conditions not satisfied by history are constant technology and a fixed goal of desired stocks. In both instances, the fault is with the forerunner, which continued to innovate and grow. If the United States' economy had become a stationary state in the early 1930's, as some feared it might, the conditions for Soviet growth along a turnpike path would have been fairly closely approximated.

The turnpike theorem, then, deals with an advantage available to an imitator under certain conditions that are rarely realized. If the theorem were generalized to deal with such conditions as moving goals and changing technology, it would have more to say about the behavior of real imitators than it does in the present form. In general, the usefulness of a theory of imitative development like that presented here would be greatly extended if it were equipped with the tools to handle the process of overtaking and surpassing a moving goal.

APPENDIX: The Approach to Balanced Growth

Suppose an economy moves in one period from P_1 to P_2 (Figure 7). The ratio of the increments of X and Y is $\Delta X_1/\Delta Y_1$, or the tangent of angle α. The ratio of the initial stocks is X_1/Y_1, or the tangent of angle A. If the growth from P_1 to P_2 is balanced, angle α equals angle A, or $\Delta X_1/\Delta Y_1/X_1/Y_1 = 1$, or $\Delta X_1/X_1/\Delta Y_1/Y_1 = 1$. The numerator and denominator of the last fraction represent, of course, the growth rates of X and Y. If the ratio of the growth rates is not equal to unity, growth from P_1 to P_2 is unbalanced.

An economy approaching a turnpike would exhibit unbalanced growth initially; for example, α may be greater than A.[38] However, its movement in the next period from P_2 to P_3 would be confined within a certain range. P_3 would have to lie to the right of line $\overline{P_1P_2}$ extended, since the turnpike must be approached asymptotically. In addition, P_3 must lie to the left of $\overline{OP_2}$ extended, else the direction of unbalanced growth simply reverses.[39] The condition that P_3 lie within the permissible range is $\alpha \gtrless \beta \gtrless B$.

[38] The argument would apply with all signs reversed if initially α were less than A.

[39] Strictly speaking, the right boundary of P_3 is a line through P_2 parallel to OV_n. Since the position of OV_n is unknown, we have substituted the known OP_2. The effect is to extend the permissible range to include some growth patterns which are not consistent with movement toward the turnpike.

TABLE 1. Movement Toward Balanced Growth of Capital Stocks in the
U.S.S.R. 1933–1940 and 1940–1955

Industries	Engineering	Food	Iron and steel	Electric power	Chemicals	Light industry	Lumber and woodworking	Petroleum	Nonferrous metals	Coal	Other building materials	Other fuels	Paper	Printing	Rubber and asbestos	Cement	Glass and china
Engineering	▒	*											*		*		
Food	*	▒		*									*		*		
Iron and steel			▒		*												*
Electric power				▒					*		*						*
Chemicals	*				▒	*									*		
Light industry					*	▒											
Lumber and woodworking			*				▒										*
Petroleum								▒			*						
Nonferrous metals			*						▒		*	*					
Coal										▒					*		
Other building materials			*						*	*	▒	*					
Other fuels									*		*	▒					*
Paper	*	*											▒		*		
Printing														▒			
Rubber and asbestos	*	*				*							*		▒		
Cement									*							▒	
Glass and china			*	*			*				*						▒

The starred pairs of industries are those in which the changes in fixed capital stocks
during 1933–1940 and 1940–1955 were in the direction of more balanced growth.

The data are derived from the statistical handbook, *Industry in the
U.S.S.R.* (Promyshlennost' SSSR), Moscow, 1957, pp. 16–17. They consist of
the percentage distribution of the stock of fixed productive capital in seventeen
industries, at constant prices, for a series of years. Combined with the index
of growth of all fixed capital in industry,[40] they made possible the calculation
of growth indexes for the capital stock in the seventeen industries. The
most appropriate time periods for investigation afforded by the data were

[40] The index for 1932/33 was estimated as 125, in J. Berliner, "Capital Formation and Productivity in the U.S.S.R." *Special Publications Series, No. 14,* National
Academy of Economics and Political Sciences, June 1958.

1933–1940 and 1940–1955. To satisfy the requirements of the turnpike theorem, inventories should have been added to fixed capital, but the data were not available.

Ratios of the changes in capital stocks (α and β) and of the 1940 stocks (B) were calculated for all combinations of the seventeen industries taken in pairs. The data for each pair were examined to see if the condition formulated above was satisfied. Notwithstanding the 10 per cent margin of error allowed, the condition was satisfied in only 21 of the 136 pairs. The starred boxes in Table 1 are the pairs that moved together in a direction consistent with an approach toward a turnpike path.

Four industries (Food, Other building materials, Rubber and asbestos, and Glass and china) accounted for 15 of the 21 favorable cases. At the other extreme, Printing moved toward balance with no other industries. The reason is that although its first-period growth rate was near the median for all industry (157 per cent), its second-period growth rate was lowest of all (50 per cent). Coal and Cement moved toward balance only with each other. These two industries also exhibited erratic behavior; they were the fastest growing industries in the second period (467 and 373 per cents), but among the slower in the first period (133 and 88 per cents). If these three industries, which accounted for 9.1 per cent of the capital stock in 1955, are excluded from Table 1, the total number of cases is reduced to 91, and the number of cases of movement toward balance is reduced to 20. The results convey no suggestion of any general movement toward balanced growth.

Finally, if the economy failed to fulfill the requirement of being "consumptionless," one might wonder whether the consumer goods industries were disturbing the data. If Food processing and Light industry are removed from Table 1 together with the three erratic cases, the total number of cases is reduced to 66, and the number of movements toward balance is reduced to 14. Removal of the consumer goods industries thus fails to make a difference of any consequence.

ON THE THEORY
OF ECONOMIC ADMINISTRATION

Robert Campbell
Indiana University

Study of Soviet-type economies has progressed to a point at which those working on the subject seem to feel the need for some abstract, theoretical frame of reference for thinking about the planning and administration of this kind of economy.[1] This taste for theoretical generalization is, no doubt, partly a search for scientific respectability, but other considerations are also at work. For one thing, the anecdotal exposition of Soviet organizational behavior eventually palls. Too often our discussion of the Soviet economy goes along the lines, "this is the way they go about it" and "this is what happens," which eventually evokes the retort, "so what?" For another, it would be quite helpful if we could apply to the Soviet-type economy more of our traditional economic analysis. Coming fresh from graduate training in economics to the actual study of the Soviet economy, most of our fraternity experience a typical frustration in experience. Despite differences in institutions of the two economies, the basic fact of scarcity ought to mean that much of the logic of our model of allocation and rationality ought to apply even in the Soviet economy. But despite the logical relevance of this body of thought, the institutional peculiarities of the Soviet economy make it not very operational. Perhaps appeal to a higher level of generality will make it possible to see parallels better. It would be nice to be able to translate our professional expertise cast in the traditional jargon into insights about this new situation.

One reaction to this frustration is to consider the operation of the Soviet economy as a kind of Gargantuan management task and to examine

[1] See, for instance, David Granick, "An Organizational Model of Soviet Industrial Planning," *The Journal of Political Economy,* April 1959; and Gregory Grossman, "Notes for a Theory of the Command Economy," *Soviet Studies,* October 1963.

it either in terms of the lore, principles and theories of management, or in terms of organizational theory. Often this approach turns out to be equally unsatisfactory; applied to this particular organization, such a set of ideas is either too general to use productively the economic insights we already possess, or it is applicable to organizations on so obviously a smaller scale than the Soviet economy that it fails to consider many important economic questions. This paper is an attempt to organize some thoughts and reflections about the Soviet economy in a way that will be satisfyingly general, and, at the same time, more or less translatable into economics—to make a framework general enough so that we can consider many disparate ideas and points of view within it. And of course, the aim of any theoretical work should be not only to explicate—to accommodate what is known with a consistent conceptual framework—but to predict or turn attention to implications not already obvious.

The problem of administration to be discussed is the management of what might be called the state production establishment of the Soviet economy. Physically, this is represented by all the production facilities and the natural resources of the socialized economy. Although the production establishment draws on the services of households, the behavior of households is not part of the problem of administration. Their interactions with the operation of the production establishment are controlled essentially by market principles via a labor market and a consumer goods market. The boundary between households and the state production establishment is not actually quite that well delimited, of course, and in fact the Russians have often blurred it by injecting a measure of administrative direction into it; nevertheless, it is a sufficiently clear one for our purposes here. The relationship between agriculture and the state production establishment also is a peculiar mixture of administrative and market direction, but whether or not it should be considered part of the state production establishment does not need to be settled here. In those domains, because the theoretical concepts developed for the institutions of the market economy fit well enough to provide sufficient guidance for analyzing a problem and providing policy guidance, there is no need for any new ideas.

The task of economic administration is, therefore, the directing of this production establishment in the service of goals established by the leadership. The goal is to structure the environment of each decision-maker in the organization so that he makes choices and engages in actions that will maximize the attainment of the goals of the leaders of the organization. It is traditional to distinguish and discuss separately several different aspects of this problem, such as planning, control of plan-fulfillment, evaluation of executive performance, economic calculation, and so on; however, these are very closely interrelated. "Economic administration" as used here refers to the whole problem of running the organization. It is well to

reiterate that the problem embraces not only the current allocation problem, but also questions of technological change, growth, the long and the
short run, and decisions about ends as well as about means.

Three Structures of an Administrative Economy

In thinking about this problem it will be useful to try to distinguish
three separate structures.

Structure I. The first is the system of production possibilities as they
exist in reality. Underlying these are technology—all the interactions and
linkages that exist between different activities, production processes, and
sectors—and resource limitations. We are thinking of these primarily as
technological relationships, though it will doubtless sometimes be difficult
to draw the line between what are technological and what are human relationships. The laws of physics and chemistry, technology, human psychology, and so on set important limits to what is possible in the realm of
production, but within those laws there are an incredibly large number
of possible allocation and development patterns. This is especially understandable when it is remembered that this reality of production possibilities
has a dynamic aspect as well as a static one. The best way to describe
Structure I is as a catalogue of all the possible states of the production
establishement today, tomorrow, and for some appreciable time into the
future. This catalogue is so complex as to defy comprehension, but at
this point it is necessary only to affirm that it exists.

Structure II. The second is an organizational or administrative structure. It might be described as a network of supervisors or controllers,
making decisions and fixing some of the variables of Structure I. This
structure is conceived of here as represented for the most part by people,
although, at the most disaggregated level in a modern economy, many
interactions and decisions are coming to be controlled by machines. For
the moment we will not try to distinguish between the advisory and executive functions which these administrators perform. They may collect information only to aggregate it or pass it on, or they may perform a decision-
making role by taking incoming information and processing it into outgoing
information in the form of commands. Structure II does possess authority,
together with its role of communicating information.

Structure III. The third structure is a normative economic model.
The model has two distinct aspects—it models the production relationships
that exist in reality, and it contains some objective function that makes
it possible to distinguish more from less desirable states of the economy.
A criterion of rationality is thus expressed in it. It is important to stress
that this is a *model* of the production relationships in the economy, not
the reality itself. Gradations in goodness of fit between model and reality
might be distinguished, but it is almost inconceivable that the model should

ape reality perfectly. The more detailed the model and the better its fit to reality, the closer it comes to being what could be thought of as a control or regulator. By using its picture of the relationships between the variables of the system and by referring to its criterion for choosing between different states of the system, it would be possible to issue a set of commands concerning the choice variables that would constitute an optimum state.

Relationship of the Structures

One does not have to ponder very long on these three structures before doubts arise that such a differentiation is really possible, for all three structures are quite interdependent. Of the three, I and II, obviously, are not really separate, administration being an important influence on the possible states of the production system. The production possibilities are limited by what administrators' rules of behavior lead them to do, and what can be achieved depends very much on whether this administrative system receives and transmits information accurately, whether it uses its authority to innovate, whether the authorities in this structure economize—that is, make rational decisions concerning the use of resources and the choice of means. On the other hand structures II and III are clearly quite competitive with each other. The normative model may well take into account the actualities of II, but it is entirely possible to think of its having an existence apart from the way Structure II actually operates. For example, the idea of the perfect allocation of resources under idealized conditions, a concept in which the realities of institutionalized authority and decision making are ignored, is a thoroughly familiar one in Western economies. In fact, it is one of the most powerful ideas we have. In trying to visualize how, Structure II would operate, we see that the administrative system, in order to exercise its control functions, must resort to partial models of the economic system and local criteria. If the model is to be useful for anything, it should take account of what the institutional arrangements really are; even the model's criteria of rationality ought not to be completely at odds with the criteria that do, in fact, operate in the administrative structure. Thus there is something artificial in trying to distinguish these three structures, and we must acknowledge that their separate existence is an abstraction. The really important point about them is that they interpenetrate and constrain each other.

The interpretation of the market-organized economy in these terms is obvious. Such an economy involves such a high degree of isomorphism in the three structures that in their interpenetration they virtually collapse into a single system. (There might be some argument over whether "a high degree" is justified here, but to one who is familiar with the contrast afforded by the administered economy the phrase does not seem immoderate.) The institutional and organizational phase (that is, the market, the price system, and so forth) really do not much constrain the production possibilities, and the decentralized version of the objective function embodied in the decision-making behavior of the administrators is not much distorted by having been partialized. This kind of system has another interesting feature which should be mentioned for purposes of contrast with the administered system. Inasmuch as the objective function assumed in the model is built into the decision-making rules of the control apparatus, it is a consensus system. The social goals embodied in the model are not coercive, and we can think of them as being internalized in the decision criteria of the administrative structure.

The market economy in the real world does not fully justify this interpretation, of course, but by the same token its failures can be interpreted in terms of lack of isomorphism between the three structures. The monopolist (a phenomenon of Structure II) blocks off some of the production possibilities feasible in Structure I because the market system fails to make his decision model consistent with the normative aggregate model. Similar illustrations could be found in the area of dynamic problems.

Contemplation of the three structures suggests another model of economic organization which we might be tempted to call perfect administration. That is probably not a very good name for it since its essential feature is that it works by completely eliminating administration in the sense of Structure II, and achieves "perfection" by a high degree of isomorphism between a Structure I that has been mostly purged of administrative authority and Structure III. If it were possible really to model production relationships in disaggregated and explicit detail and to specify a clear-cut objective function, then the computer could be given the job of finding a solution, not only in the sense of the optimum output, but also in terms of detailed specification of the value of all the choice variables in the system. These variables could be communicated for execution to highly localized nodes in Structure I, represented by machines or individuals. In such a system, of course, people come to be essentially indistinguishable from machines in that the statement of what they are to do leaves no room for any initiative, action, or decision on their part. Note that such a model of economic organization is a complete antithesis of the perfect market economy in regard to consensus and internalization of values. Under perfect administration the local units do not have and do not need to have any values or criteria to which they ever appeal. There is no need for consensus, since the program removes all need for reconciliation of internalized values and the objective function of the normative model.

This kind of model is now being offered by some economists in the socialist countries as a possible vision for the future of their economic administration. This is essentially what Nemchinov means by "economic cybernetics," for instance. In this vision the extremities of *Gosplan's* neural net will extend to the machines themselves. The planners will have so precisely charted the interrelationships of all economic variables that computers at the center can be programmed to process this sensory input into detailed commands to be posted to the very workbench. It is to be like the automatic refinery drawn to the scale of a national economy.

They certainly do not have this kind of an economy now. Unlike the situation in either of the polar models described above, where the administrative structure is absorbed into either Structure I or the computer, the administrative structure is very much alive and consequential in the Soviet-type economy. It is in the deficiencies of this administrative structure that most of the troubles of Soviet-type economies lie. It is hypertrophied, imperfectly effective, independent, irrational, with its own criteria that do not necessarily conform to those of the top leadership. This administrative structure is congruent with either structure I, or III, and this breach of isomorphism is the main source of irrationality and inefficiencies in allocation and decision making.

This prompts some questions as to the "nature and necessity" of this administrative structure in Soviet-type economies, analogous to Schumpeter's exposition of the "nature and necessity" of a price system. Why is it there, and to what principle should it conform if it is to work effectively? Most of its deficiencies stem from the fact that it is hierarchical, in the sense that it converges to a relatively small set of nodes at the center. The hierarchical nature of the administrative structure is connected with its role as an aggregation device. The structure of III with which the leaders of the Soviet system operate is tremendously more gross than the structure of I, and the purpose of the administrative system is to reconcile the two. The need for aggregation is directly connected with the attempt to impose on the system a criterion and a set of objectives different from those which would be produced by consensus. This production system is like an organization whose leadership has set goals for it which differ from whatever personal goals the participants may have. In the literature on organization, there are two quite different points of view about organizations. The traditional view is that organizations have goals different from those of the participants and that hierarchy and organization were designed to coerce behavior toward these organizational goals. More recently many have seen organizations as coalitions, or as consensus aggregations in which administrative structure can be viewed as a political process for achieving consensus. For the particular organization considered here, the traditional view is probably more realistic. There is an implicit assumption in the coalitions approach that the organization is small in relation to the total environment, and that therefore, component interests have alternatives. It is therefore not really applicable to an organization which encompasses most of society, or to keep this within our present frame of reference, virtually all the production activity of the economy.

The imposition of an outside purpose makes aggregation necessary. It seems likely that in systems complex enough to possess anything that could be called will or consciousness, these aspects would have to be formulated on a much more aggregative scale than the actual activities they seek to manipulate. Certainly this is the case with human beings. Our perceptions, desires and willful actions are consciously formulated in an idiom which is very gross compared with the minutely detailed physical processes that effect them. For example, it is almost unthinkable that I should perceive, in the sense of Structure III, the typing of this paper in terms of the actual physiology (that is, I) of how it is accomplished. It is difficult to believe that the Lord notes every sparrow's fall, but if there is a divine will in the universe, it is easier to think of its being conceived and wrought not through a concern over the extinction and replacement of the individual sparrow, but through grosser mechanisms that assure the survival of the species. Just so, a regime that wants to impose its wishes on the production establishment of a national economy must formulate its goals and directives in aggregates and not in details. Like generals, chief executives must think big and concern themselves with strategy rather than tactics. The Soviet leaders must define the means toward their ultimate objectives in terms of the rate of growth of industrial output, the share of investment in national income and its allocation among branches, the emphasis to be assigned to research, and so on. There is nothing mysterious about this need for aggregation—it is simply a matter of the capacity of the human brain relative to the amount of information that the reality of a production system on the scale of a national economy contains. Thus, Structure III must be aggregative compared to I, and one of the main functions of the administrative system is to translate each into the other. Because of aggregation the two structures are not ostensibly isomorphic, and the goal is to make them so by a hierarchical administrative system.

Before considering the nature of this task, and the problems it involves, it may be useful to introduce another interpretation of the administrative system. In its role of mediating between the aggregative model of III and the reality of I, the administrative system works by disaggregating directives as to state and partializing the criterion which the central decision makers are using. The disaggregation process involves choice, and there must accordingly be some local criterion for decision making. Thus the central plan is disaggregated partly in terms of operational directives as to state, partly in the form of success criteria used in evaluating and controlling the current performance of the executors of Structure II, partly by enunciation of criteria for longer range planning and decision making. As Grossman has pointed out, for the administered economy, this blend of specific commands concerning economic variables and rules for making choices and evaluating success is equivalent to the price system in the market economy. It is a statement of the "terms on which alternatives are offered" to those who in the end will make decisions, and their responses to this price system constitute the actual state of the economic system.

Seeing this administrative system as a price system raises an interesting question. The virtue of the price system in market economies is not that it provides perfect indexes of economic value, but that it performs an equilibrating function. One would certainly not expect the price system constituted by the combination of physical directives and decision criteria that control the elaboration and fulfillment of a plan in a Soviet-type economy to be perfect on first elaboration and in all areas; there are two very great deficiencies in its equilibrating properties. First, it is not going to be very effective in correcting physical disequilibria. Equilibration in it generally takes place at fairly aggregative levels, and when disequilibria appear on the detailed level, it will be very difficult to correct them. Any perception of them or orders concerning their correction have to be filtered through the same communication channel that produced the error in the first place. Second, it is not going to be a very effective sensing mechanism even to disclose other kinds of disequilibria. Suppose that all activities are fairly well coordinated in the physical sense, but irrational in the light of overall objectives. There is not much in this "price system" to disclose the fact to anyone who would be interested in taking any action about it. There is an interesting difference here from the market form of organization. In the market economy, the executors of Structure II are generally distinct from the price system, so that it can guide their actions. In the administered economy, administration and the "price system" are more nearly synonymous. It is instructive to remember that whenever this happens in the market economy, as when monopoly power gives decision makers control over price, departures from rationality appear.

Criteria for Aggregation

To return to the main question, what principles and what kind of problems are involved in constructing an administrative structure to reconcile Structures I and II? To meet the requirements of isomorphism, the administrative structure must be built at its base on a template of technology, but it must converge at the top to a much simpler and aggregative structure. One familiar idea about organization is that aggregation should follow the rule of subjecting interactions to unified control. Moving upward, combinations should be established to combine under each node the people, activities, and processes that cooperate closely to produce some output. Looking downward, the hierarchy of the organization should correspond to successively finer partitionings of the total activity of the organization. These partitionings should be made according to the principle that activities are combined with or separated from each other in such a way as to maximize interaction within cells and to minimize it between cells.

However, this principle seems to break down in the specific context of administering production and growth on a national economic scale. The general admonition about partitioning to concentrate interactions within cells turns out to be very difficult to follow. This is contrary to the "nature of production," both as conceptualized in our economic models and as confirmed by experience. Research has generally shown, for instance, that input-output matrices are not triangular, which is a nice geometrical hint that the structure of production relationships is not hierarchical. Neither do these matrices reveal subeconomies which would give rise to corresponding nodes in an administrative structure. Exactly the same sort of thing appears in other relationships as well. The impact of some innovation in a particular industry may affect many other units of the system both upstream and downstream. Moreover, these are *ad hoc* groupings, different for each innovation.

Perhaps the emphasis should be on the aggregating aspect of the problem rather than on the partitioning aspect, and the best approach, to ask what are the valid principles of aggregation? The simplest answer would seem to be that aggregation requires that the addends be homogeneous with respect to the problem at issue, or that variables like input-output ratios be identical for all the constituents. Nodes should be established at any point where some variable can be fixed without much differentiation for a whole collection of subunits. The principle has been thought out for the input-output case. For example, it will be possible for the steel industry supervisors to settle satisfactorily with the tractor industry how much steel is to be supplied only if steel in this particular application is a more or less homogeneous commodity. If it is not, then the negotiation might as well be carried on directly between the producers and the consumers of the various types. Or it might make sense to have some supervisory agency for the pipeline industry that could negotiate with the steel industry and the equipment industry concerning the interrelated variables of pipe diameters and compressor specifications, since a limited number of these solutions could fit all situations. In short, there are many valid principles of aggregation; indeed the real problem is that there are so many.

Imagine that all the aggregations suggested by this principle were made and the corresponding supervisory authorities established. The result would not be a hierarchical administrative structure. Because there is aggregability along so many dimensions, the resulting system of administrative authorities would constitute a network rather than a hierarchy. The situation is like the familiar one in locational economics: one tries to deduce market areas in a uniform plane for various activities as the result of trading off transport costs versus economies of scale. There is no reason to believe that the resulting foci will fall neatly into a locational grid characterized by a hierarchy of economic centers. (This analogy suggests that a real structure will emerge as the result of agglomeration economics and of the accidents of order and priority in establishing transport routes in the one case and communication channels in the other.) One might ask, however, whether an administrative structure built in this way would not be isomorphic at the top with a rational planning model. The resulting administrative structure might be thought of as defining the planning model in the sense that each node should correspond to some indicator of the plan and some variable of the optimizing model. The answer obviously is that such a Structure III would not be aggregative enough. The administrative structure exists in the first place because the central planners can't handle that much detail.

The proposition that there is some basic incompatibility between the structure of production relationships in reality and a hierarchical administrative structure is also an induction from the experience of administered economies. In the history of the Soviet organizational structure, for instance, the partitioning of responsibilities has always left some crucial interactions without overseers. When administration was organized on a branch basis, many important interactions involving space got overlooked. Production was located wrongly; local agglomeration and cooperation were stultified. In the perspective of the leadership of the branch divisions these were subordinate responsibilities and were ignored. When responsibility for mineral exploration was divided among the various mining branches, there was much duplication of work, and no one undertook the general, regional geological work that would benefit all. Aggregations made according to one principle are inconsistent with those made according to another, as illustrated by the following instructive case described by an official in the oil-marketing organization. For good and sufficient reasons steel products have always been treated as "funded commodities," allocated via a material balance controlled at the highest level in the structure. This includes the grades used in the production of transformers. The same has been true for most oil products, but for minor or specialized ones, like transformer oil, the material balance was managed at the level of the oil industry. Plants producing transformers found it impossible to get consistent allocations of transformer oil and steel because there was no node in the allocation system to coordinate this particular interaction. The list of such examples could be made very long. Specific shortcomings can always be overcome by a reorganization and a redefinition of responsibilities, but that usually creates new gaps and new difficulties. After the 1957 reorganization of industry on territorial principles, new kinds of irrationalities emerged to take the place of those eliminated. When mineral exploration was made more centralized and focused in the Ministry of Geology and Conservation, the specific requirements of each kind of exploration were not given enough attention. There was little interest in proving up reserves, and the economic evaluation of newly discovered reserves was slighted.

There is an interesting parallel here with the external economies and diseconomies in market organized systems associated with benefits or costs to society that cannot be captured or charged for via market relationships. In the administered economy some costs or benefits to the regime from the activity of individual units are neither penalized nor rewarded by the system of administrative controls. In both cases these effects are therefore left out of account in decision making. In the market economy the solution is usually to supplement market indicators with direct administrative orders—"anti-smog devices must henceforth be provided on automobiles." This, incidentally, is an aggregable kind of phenomenon in the sense mentioned above—that is, a simple undifferentiated order applicable to everyone. Indeed it is because it is aggregable in that sense that it is not handled by the market. The rationality of the act cannot be calculated by the individual because its effect can be calculated only in reference to all auto users taken together. Considerations of symmetry suggest that in the administrative economy external economies and diseconomies are likely to arise in connection with fairly intimate interactions between units, not aggregable in the sense defined above, and that the remedy for them would be to allow more room for direct lateral interaction at the lower levels.

Some responsibilities do seem always to be cut adrift and some decisions made from too narrow a point of view, whatever principle is used in aggregating to make the hierarchy. What is suitable for one purpose is not for another. One possible answer might be to accept more multiple partitioning, and overlapping hierarchies. Nodes corresponding to particular aggregations and interactions could be established in the interstices of the dominant hierarchical control system, to handle problems otherwise ignored. In recent years the Russians have resorted more and more to this device. When some function gets overlooked by the regular organs they have set up a new agency to be responsible for it. A special organization, *Gossnab,* was created to establish input norms, and another, *Gosstroi,* to coordinate construction problems. The responsibility for looking at long-range aspects of plans has been given to organs distinct from those handling current planning, and a whole succession of agencies has been spawned to try to speed up the introduction of new technology. In each case the responsibility had already been assigned to the regular administrative structure, which had failed to give it full attention.

This approach must be used cautiously, for together with specifying responsibility more clearly, it also disperses power and confuses responsibility at lower levels. This can be best shown by an example. Since World War II the Soviet machinery industry has followed a policy of dieselizing equipment. The decision makers have done this in fulfillment of the responsibilities assigned to them. Undertaking to design power plants to do the assigned work at lowest cost, they performed their calculations and concluded that much of the work should be done by diesel engines. Meanwhile the administrators of the refinery industry simply produced outputs in proportions ordered from above, or, to the extent that they had some latitude for choice, referred choices to such criteria as "minimize costs," "economize on investment resources," or "maximize throughput from existing capacity." The outcome has been irrational in two senses. There has been a deficit of diesel fuel and a surplus of gasoline, and this disequilibrium would have been even greater except that they have permitted the quality of diesel fuel to deteriorate. Standards have been relaxed to take in both heavier and lighter fractions and permit an undesirably high sulfur content. Lowered quality has meant extra costs in the form of poorer performance and increased depreciation and repair of engines. They would probably have saved resources if they had gone less far in replacing gasoline engines with diesels and had moved toward higher compression ratios in gasoline engines, although this would have required that the refiners raise octane numbers from the prevailing 66-octane standard. Numerous examples of this kind of failure of coordination could be given.

It is easy to suggest in each such instance that the remedy would be the creation of a special agency with responsibility for the particular problem—in this case, coordination of the efforts of the engine builders and the refiners. However, that solution might have the effect of eroding the executive authority of the administrative hierarchy. Such an agency in the case just cited could have settled the issue in several ways. It could have studied the question and reported a recommendation to the highest levels which would then have issued specific orders about engine characteristics and refinery product mix, or it might have served as an informal mediation body between the engine industry and the refining industry. Whereas either of these roles would have been advisory, rather than executive, this body might alternatively be given authority to issue the necessary orders.

As stated above, executive authority given to these interstitial agencies turns out to be ineffective because people at lower levels find themselves subject to several masters who give them contrary instructions. In effect, this puts decision-making power into their own hands, since they must then take these decisions according to their own criteria. Giving such agencies an advisory role can be thought of as threading-in additional communication channels, collecting and integrating more information to rationalize interactions. Carried very far, this process would also destroy the executive power of the hierarchy because the executants lose their sense of what they are responsible for and to whom they are responsible. The administrative structure becomes a network rather than a hierarchy. The authorities of the oil industry would become involved in endless negotiations (that is, in *ad hoc* combinations) with fuel planners, with engine design planners, with steel planners, and many others, and in the end would not know whether they were responsible for saving metal by simplifying the refinery mix, for raising the octane rating of gasoline to permit higher compression ratios, for getting a higher share of diesel in refinery runs, or what. Authorities are transformed into errand boys for one another and in this welter of cross communication and cross responsibility the authority of all is mutually cancelled out. It migrates either to the top echelons, to which the disputed questions are referred for settlement, or to the bottom, when individuals are confronted with unresolved conflicts which they must decide by reference to their own internalized criteria. Rationalization of the administrative structure thus seems to mean a movement toward one or the other of our polar models. Which it will do depends on how well prepared the center is in terms of models into which the data can be fitted and in terms of computational capacity for coping with the decision problem. If it is ill prepared, then power goes by default to the bottom.

This, incidentally, clarifies somewhat the distinction between the "executive" and "advisory" roles in administration which, to the author at least, has always seemed very elusive. Executive decision making means acting on the basis of partial information, and according to your own lights. It means using simple-minded criteria rather than sophisticated ones, rules-of-thumb instead of elaborate calculations. One of the interesting things about the evolution of the Soviet system is the degree to which executive power has been aggrandized in the hands of advisory officials. Rationalizing efforts seem almost inevitably to have this result. All attempts to replace snap judgments with deliberation and to eliminate guessing by the creation of an adequate informational base inevitably diffuse power out of the hands of the nominal executives. The design bureaus have already usurped a lot of executive power by elaborating criteria for choice, such as those for capital intensity, but their definitions of concepts, and by the way they formulate problems of choice.

This raises an interesting question regarding the viability and vitality of the hierarchical control system, of the Communist Party, and of ideology as the Soviet system continues to evolve. It seems to me that efforts to improve economic administration are closely tied to the political evolution of the Soviet system. A characteristic feature of Soviet economic administration in the past has been the politicalization of economic decision making. The Russians have long been confused about the parallel distinctions between (1) ends and means and (2) politics and economics. Executive power in the hierarchy in the sense indicated above, that is, the right to make arbitrary decisions in the light of your own values on the basis of inadequate data, could be sustained only as the result of a confusion of political and economic authority. Erroneous decisions about location, about the desirability of hydroelectric projects, or about who is to own livestock were possible only because economic decision makers confused politics and economics. This confusion creates the conditions for the exercise of arbitrary, executive authority throughout the system; refinements in Structure III remove it.

Rationalization of the administrative structure inevitably means a movement toward one or the other of the polar models—the market economy or perfect administration. There are two possible chances for its survival—as a kind of human data-processing system, or as a decentralized repository of the goals of the regime, a network of people who have internalized the goals of the regime and whose authority is exercised in the application of these criteria in decision making. Neither seems very plausible. Human beings are not long fated to have a comparative advantage as data processors. Values can be internalized only imperfectly even in the aggregative terms of Structure III, and it is impossible to partialize these goals into usable criteria. The use of a price system and profit maximization as the criterion is the only way to do so, but that course would also eliminate the need for the administrative superstructure. This idea in its application to the Party structure and ideology has been extensively developed by Leonhard and Nove. For instance, Leonhard notes that the Russians have tried to revivify ideology by shifting from the past practice of defining it in terms of short-run means to phrasing it in terms of ultimate ends. Older definition betrays and wrecks it because the means change and people become cynical. Further, it is undesirable to internalize ideas about means since that would freeze the system, but it is quite difficult to raise enthusiasm or to control behavior by indoctrinating them with an ideology referring to vague ultimate ends.

Improvements in Economic Modeling

Another route to improving the effectiveness with which the economy can be bent to the will of the leadership is through perfecting Structure III. Not much can be done about I. Indeed, the exogenous tendency of this structure to become more complex with growth and modernity is the main background circumstance in the problem. The discussion above of ways of improving Structure II suggests that rationalization there calls for coordinate improvements in III. The imperfections of Structure III and indeed its very existence are testimony to the directors' clouded vision of what they are trying to do and of the nature of the mechanism they are manipulating to do it. The possibility of improvements in modeling has been much discussed of late, both by the Russians and outsiders. The emphasis has usually been on the technological aspect—on the capacity of computers to handle the volume of information involved. Although it is an important question, we have nothing to contribute, and prefer to dwell on other aspects of the problem.

The Russians have made notable progress in the area of economic model building in recent years, and are obviously counting on improvements in this area to achieve a breakthrough in effective control over their economy. In the past they have not really been much guided by economic theory. The Structure III which we have postulated did not even exist in a coherent form. What theory they had (that is, Marxian economic theory) was so abstract, lofty, and nonoperational that it had limited influence on their decision making. To the extent that they drew implications from it for strategic decision making at the level of central planning, as in the famous proposition that industry A had to grow faster than industry B, it was misleading.

If one set out to try to determine what normative economic model is implicit in the national economic plan document (the 1941 Plan, say), or in the behavior of the top level planners, he would find it rough going. Clearly it would be dominated by ideas of physical equilibrium and arithmetic consistency, with very little conscious optimizing. The national economic plan gives this impression partly because it is essentially a set of commands concerning the state, but there is little hint even in the categories of any conscious maximizing behavior. For instance, they are not at all explicit about what we would think of as end uses or what might be thought of as the income of the organization. It is a commonplace that Soviet planners at this level have often confused ends and means or have mistaken mediate ends for ultimate ends, as when Stalin equated the growth of steel output with growth in general. This was also obvious in the ubiquitous infatuation with gross output and the neglect of net output. Recall also the controversy over whether input-output planning should involve testing the feasibility of a final bill of goods, or a vector that included a number of gross outputs. A lot of Russians had a hard time seeing that the final bill of goods should be the maximand. The situation is analogous to the Pentagon before McNamara. There is plenty of data and plenty of calculation, but not organized in a way useful for economizing behavior.

One reason it is hard to discover optimizing ideas at the level of national economic planning is that much of the optimizing responsibility has seeped down the administrative structure to lower levels, and overall objectives have been partialized. To the extent that Structure III existed, it took the form of bits and pieces, applied parochially by each decision maker within his own bailiwick. They were operating on the premise that if each small decision maker would look out for the pennies, the nickels would take care of themselves. The trouble was that, whatever criterion of optimality may have been dimly perceived at the top, it was partialized very imperfectly. The capital allocation problem is a good illustration. For all the progress the Russians have made in understanding this issue, it still has the major defect that its prescriptions rule within too narrow jurisdictions. Only exceptionally do Soviet economists see how the main ideas of it can be integrated within the framework of a national economic optimizing model. Within specific areas it is very common for "effectiveness" to be pursued with a surprising amount of sophistication, but the insights derived are not applied across the board. The impossibility of applying them across the board is due to the existence of the administrative structure—the writ of the rationalizers runs only over small realms.

For instance, the history of the energy subeconomy shows really impressive achievements in economic sophistication by planners and economists working in its various branches. Indeed, the electric power branch has been the alma mater of some of the most perceptive economic theorists, and the oil industry has challenged some to impressive feats of economic analysis. But, however carefully they aimed at conscious maximizing within these separate areas, the energy subeconomy as a whole remained terribly irrational, because the administrative system was not structured to give anyone an information base to discern or the authority to enforce rationality throughout the whole. Niceties of economizing within each of its sectors were swamped by the tremendous loss from emphasizing solid fuels and neglecting oil and gas.

The politicalization of decisions and the failure to make any very clear-cut distinction between ends and means at the aggregative level are reflected at the micro level of theorizing, in the form of semantically tangled controversies which get nowhere because Soviet economists and planners have not been able to conceptualize an ultimate criterion of optimality. Thus one author formulates the "criterion of economic effectiveness" for projects to exploit oil reservoirs as "guaranteeing the assigned output levels at minimum capital and current expenditure with the maximum recovery coefficient." Even when some resolution is made among these contradictory goals, there is still much confusion engendered by uncertainty as to what can be taken as choice variables and what as constraints. The model which the theorist constructs may indicate that some variable should be treated as a choice variable, but administrative reality makes it either a constraint by assigning it from above or an objective by making it a success indicator in the system of administrative controls.

It is not necessary to say much about recent Soviet progress in model building, since the details are well known. To some extent this progress has come about simply from exposure to the world tradition in economics. Soviet economists may have posed the questions of model building and criteria more starkly than we customarily do, for the distinction between constraints and objectives has been made very clear to them by the linear programming form through which they have learned much of their economics. In speculating on the possible success of their model-building efforts, we should remember that their need is of a special kind, somewhat different from ours. Whereas the application of models in the market economy is usually for the general guidance of policy, the Russians, on the other hand, are trying to construct a III that will enable them to issue detailed, specific orders. Our need is probably less demanding concerning the realism of fit and degree of disaggregation. No one has even been concerned before to work out the kind of theory that is applicable to the problem the Russian theorists face. Since the tradition in economic theorizing is to abstract, simplify, and look at, some aspects of a problem and assume away others, the various parts of economic theory are not necessarily integrable. The micro assumptions of macro theories may be unreasonable, and there is a long-standing inconsistency between growth theories and the static theory of allocation that is only now beginning to be corrected following the path set by von Neumann. This gap, incidentally, is equally obvious in Marxian economics. One can generate a path of growth with Marx's expanded reproduction schemes only by violating the assumptions of his value theory. Our own experience suggests that lapses from rationality in a real economy often arise in the no man's land corresponding to the failure of closure between separate theories. It is when different, unintegrated theories have conflicting implications for some problem that we are at a loss to formulate remedial policy measures. It may be that failures of closure will be an even more serious problem in applied operational models than in policy guidance models.

Conclusion

The author's feeling on finishing this essay is that he has been defeated by a maze. The attempt to express in the language of economics the typical features and problems of running the administrative economy effectively does not change them enough to provide fresh insight. One can gain enlightenment from a dictionary despite the fundamentally tautological character of its propositions, but it may be that the conceptual dictionary of the economist is sufficiently circumscribed that he cannot compose an effective exposition of administrative economics relying on it alone.

The administrative economy seems an intractable problem for economics in its present form. The characteristic insights of economics are that everything depends on everything else and that economic life exhibits a duality feature which makes it possible to distinguish innumerable products, markets, processes, resources, and time periods but, at the same time, permits aggregation and comparison across the board through the instrumentality of price and value. Applied to the administrative economy this may be a mirage rather than an insight. The central institution of the administrative economy, the elaborate administrative system owes its existence to the fact that no one person can comprehend how everything depends on everything else. Its recalcitrance and inefficiency, together with the associated puzzle of a rational morphology for it, are witness to the irrelevance of the duality idea. If one could really find the kind of aggregating principles that would make it possible to bring all the separate *ad hoc* aggregations based on homogeneity with respect to a given variable together in a converging body of administrative bodies, the need for them would have vanished! It is probably necessary to go outside the language of economics to develop a generally useful theory of the administrative economy. Perhaps the specialists on the Soviet economy should take mass leave, and study cybernetics together for a year.

GOLD AND THE SWORD:
MONEY IN THE SOVIET
COMMAND ECONOMY

Gregory Grossman
University of California, Berkeley

«Все мое» — сказало злато;
«Все мое» — сказал булат.
«Все куплю» — сказало злато;
«Все возьму» — сказал булат. — Пушкин 1826.

"All is mine," said Gold;
"All is mine," said the Sword;
"I shall buy all," said Gold;
"I shall seize all," said the Sword.—Pushkin, 1826.

I

In Pushkin's quatrain, which was inspired by a traditional French epigram, *Le fer et l'or,*[1] the conflict between gold and the sword is as absolute as the stakes are unbounded, but the last word is the sword's. We can safely assume that the poem was familiar from childhood to the imaginary Russian student through whose eyes, opened after five decades of sleep "as the Kremlin chimes strike the first hours of the century's second half," Alexander Gerschenkron so masterfully surveys the reality of the Soviet economy.[2] Yet, with all his admiration for Pushkin's genius, the student may well have entertained some reservations about the poem's moral. Did not "the last word of science," which he, together with a large proportion of his university generation, most likely revered[3]—did not Marxism assert that gold had something to do with the "basis" of the

● The author is most grateful to Mr. E. Babitchev (New York), Professor A. Brzeski, Mr. P. Gekker, Mr. P. Ivory, Mr. J. A. Kirbyshire (London), Professors C. Landauer and R. Lang (Zagreb), and Dr. B. Levčik (Prague) for valuable comments on this or an earlier version of the essay. All responsibility remains with the author.

[1] The Russian word, "bulat," can mean either Damascus steel or the sword of which it is made—a felicitous ambiguity that permits us to translate the quatrain as we do.

[2] "Industrial Enterprise in Soviet Russia," in Alexander Gerschenkron, *Economic Backwardness in Historical Perspective,* Harvard University Press, Cambridge, Mass., 1962, pp. 270–271; originally published in Edward S. Mason (ed.), *The Corporation in Modern Society,* Harvard University Press, Cambridge, Mass., 1959.

[3] *Ibid.,* p. 272 n.

contemporary "social formation," whereas the sword belonged only to its "superstructure"? Was not gold clearly ruling the world then, at the turn of the century, and was it not forging its own swords in order to enhance its vast profits and to strike down barriers to the expansion of its dominion? Was not Russia's own history in the preceding decade, Witte's decade, ample proof that gold had the last word? Consider the adoption of the gold standard by dint of much popular privation, the copious inflow of foreign capital, the rise of the big banks, and all the rest. Like Eugene Onegin, the hero of his poetic masterpiece, Pushkin may have read a bit of Adam Smith, but—our student would muse—neither the greatest Russian poet of the nineteenth century nor the greatest British economist and moral philosopher of the eighteenth represented the last word of science on the intricate relationship between economic power and political authority at the threshold of the twentieth.

As Gerschenkron tells us with his wonted elegance and vividness, the imaginary student, just arisen in the new, socialist Russia after his long sleep, finds some of his discoveries pleasing to his radical tastes, others confusing and puzzling, still others shocking; he also stumbles upon much that is familiar. Among the last, we may add, is money. True, he observes only paper and small metallic coins changing hands; none of the heavy *imperialy* and other gold pieces with the likeness of Nicholas II on them. But then our student and his cronies had few of these jingling in their pockets in the old days anyway. If he were allowed to roam freely through the offices of the State Bank, he would overhear some new and strange accounting terms. He would disdain these as mere scribblers' jargon and would instead make a mental note of the highly familiar look of the physical setting—the abacuses, inkstands, blotters, desks, and stuffed chairs. But he would hardly be allowed to penetrate this far into the world of Soviet finance. More likely, his observations of Soviet money would be limited to the kind that passes from hand to hand in stores and open-air markets. He would note that goods bore prices (in rubles and kopeks at that!), and being an intelligent fellow he would also quickly infer that the people who bought these goods must be earning money wages. He might easily conclude that the Soviet economy was a money economy not unlike (apart from the important matter of property ownership) the one that obtained in "capitalist" Russia at the time of our imaginary student's retirement into his half-century long sleep, and with regard to the *household sector* he would be right.

What he could not readily discover from mere observation is that an ambivalent and at times hostile attitude towards money runs vividly through all of Soviet history. Useless in the millenial society of the future, a base survival from the sordid past, money has been the Cinderella of Soviet economics—an unrespected relation of sorts, a mistrusted servant, yet necessary for sweeping up the ashes under the noble flame of Soviet socialism. Its very existence has called forth repeated questioning over the decades. Its parentage has been most unconvincingly traced to gold, itself doomed to become, in Lenin's famous flight of derisive fancy, a mere construction material for public conveniences. Its function has been recently explained in terms of a so-called objective economic law, the Marxian law of value, whose relevance and meaning in the Soviet context are wrapped in considerable doubt. Finally, in everyday life in the production sector it has been treated as though its very moneyness were its paramount vice.

II

For our purposes it shall not be necessary to trace this history to the early, heroic era of War Communism, an era notable for the "colossal scale of its audacity"[4] in the virtual elimination of money from day-to-day use and by the theoretical debate, at once ingenious and ingenuous, looking forward to the perpetuation of this condition.[5] Both the state of virtual moneylessness and the attendant "theory [which] was a kind of 'child of despair' that, quite mistakenly, tried to change despair into a 'communist virtue' "[6] were soon superseded by the lusty commercialism of the New Economic Policy (NEP) and the fully consistent monetary and fiscal conservatism of the government in the middle 1920's.

Rather, our concern is with the place of money in the Soviet *command economy*. This term having now acquired considerable currency, its definition will not detain us long. A command economy is one in which, as a rule, the individual firm produces and employs resources primarily by virtue of specific directives (commands, targets) received from higher authorities. The firm's principal behavioral rule is therefore to execute the commands—in Soviet parlance, to fulfill the plan, for "the plan is law." Since the central authorities are normally also concerned with the coordination of productive activity, the directives presumably are based on a plan or set of plans that aim at balanced production. In the Soviet case, the directives to the enterprises are rigidly—but not always consistently— coupled to a system of materials allocation. Although enterprise managers

[4] Barbara Wootton, *Plan or No Plan,* Gollancz, London, 1934, p. 57.

[5] Though now little more than a historical curiosum, this debate has so far received less systematic attention in Western literature than it deserves. For useful brief summaries see R. W. Davies, *The Development of the Soviet Budgetary System,* Cambridge University Press, London, 1958, pp. 40–41, and Arthur Z. Arnold's enduring classic, *Banks, Credit, and Money in Soviet Russia,* Columbia University Press, New York, 1937, pp. 99–110.

[6] G. Sokolnikov quoted in Gerhard Dobbert (ed.), *Red Economics,* Houghton Mifflin, Boston and New York, 1932, p. 159 n.

are enjoined to carry out the commands without reservation—for the moment we will ignore mutually conflicting directives, which are in fact quite common—and are theoretically subject to penalties if they do not, they are also induced to do so by means of an elaborate system of bonuses and other incentives, both material and nonmaterial.[7]

The distinction between a command economy and a market economy is no less significant and useful for not being an "either-or" proposition in all the relevant respects. Elements of the command hierarchy and market mechanism can be and are found side by side in many economies, including the Soviet; in some examples the one shades into the other so that it is difficult to state categorically which "socioeconomic process," to use a Dahl-Lindblom generic expression, is actually in operation. This should not discomfit us. The same logical difficulty applies to such well-proven terms as, say, dictatorship and democracy.

In at least four instances in the Soviet economy, the market mechanism plays a predominant role: in the deployment of labor among jobs (especially after the *de facto* and, later, *de jure* abolition of some of Stalin's worst antilabor measures); in the distribution, though typically not the production, of consumer goods; in a part of the production and distribution of farm products on both private and collective account; and in certain minor, interstitial activities outside of agriculture, both legal (privately furnished services of physicians or tutors, some art) and illegal.[8] All these instances refer to relatively short-term decisions.

In regard to long-term economic decisions the situation may appear somewhat paradoxical at first glance. In a market economy, long-term investment decisions tend to be made less strictly on the basis of a "classical" profit-or-loss calculus than are short-term decisions. It is not that business enterprises are insensitive to the prospect of profits when contemplating long-term investments; surely they are, as a rule. Nonetheless, owing to the remoteness of the time-horizon and to the uncertainties attached to most prices and costs in the far future, long-term profit-or-loss calculations are quite imprecise and are therefore frequently buttressed by various macroeconomic considerations, such as the prospects of overall expansion of a national or regional economy, the likely fortunes of related industries, population changes, shifts in public policy, and the like. Although, these

---

[7] In this regard, the Soviet economy does not depend on the principle of command in the pure sense in which Dahl and Lindblom use the term, namely, on obedience alone without direct positive rewards for compliance. (Robert A. Dahl and Charles E. Lindblom, *Politics, Economics, and Welfare,* Harper & Bros., New York, 1953, pp. 106ff.)

[8] We may also make mental note at this point of the recent "economic experiments" in consumer-goods industries, possibly Liberman-inspired, to relate production more directly to consumer demand.

considerations supplemental to the "classical" calculus pertain primarily to the questions "whether, what, where, and how much to produce," they must also impinge on the question of "how to produce," that is on the choice of technology.

Now it is precisely in regard to the medium- and long-term choices of technology that the Soviets have lately come closest to the use of a fairly consistent economic calculus on a broad front. After a decade of lively debates, a standard methodology for project selection (where the different projects are distinguished from one another by technological differences, rather than by final output streams) has been officially promulgated in 1958. Not quite satisfactory from a theoretical standpoint and apparently not uniformly followed throughout the economy, the methodology nonetheless does legitimize what had already been fairly widely practiced earlier, namely, project selection according to the internal rate of return of marginal capital increments (the so-called coefficient of relative efficiency or its reciprocal, the "recoupment period"). For an ample discussion and analysis of this procedure the interested reader is referred to Professor Bergson's recent book[9] and to the now fairly extensive Western literature cited therein.

The paradox is readily resolved. In the case of long-term decisions in the market economy the deviation from "classical" profit-or-loss calculation is necessitated by the uncertainties surrounding the price and cost parameters, as we have just seen. In the Soviet economy, resort to an internal-rate-of-return calculation was prompted by the problem of designing numerous capital-intensive projects in the face of capital scarcity. The engineers and few economists who led this movement were at first severely rebuffed by the guardians of ideological purity, but the loosening of doctrinal orthodoxy that followed Stalin's death allowed rationality to prevail on this particular front. Yet even this partial move toward the "classical," market-like calculus was *possible* in the Soviet setting only because of two characteristics of this method of project selection: it does not invade the decision-making territory of the top planners and political leaders, and, pertaining to the long-term as it does, it does not run afoul of the tight and, if we may say so, jealous system of materials allocation. Indeed, later in this essay we shall have occasion to inquire into another situation involving relatively decentralized and standardized decision-making rules, namely, the financing of modernization by means of bank loans, where the experience in relation to the system of materials distribution has been of a rather different order. Lastly, we may ask why have not the uncertainties relating to future price and cost parameters impeded the adoption of the rate-of-return criterion or at least undermined confi-

[9] Abram Bergson, *The Economics of Soviet Planning*, Yale University Press, New Haven, Conn., 1964, Ch. 11.

dence in it. Only part of the answer is that the Soviet-type planned economy poses fewer such uncertainties over the long run than does a typical
capitalist economy. The rest of the answer is that the Soviet literature
dealing with this problem has simply not faced up to the question. The
early highly suggestive and much discussed article by Academician Strumilin[10] which tried to relate—theoretically quite unsatisfactorily—prospective
steady increases in labor productivity to the problem of project selection
attracted a good deal of attention in its time but virtually no follow-up
work that is known to us.

III

As we have already noted, the debate of the early 1920's revolved
around the question whether there was any place for money in the new
order even long before the advent of full communism. The question was
answered in the affirmative by the arrival of the New Economic Policy,
that is to say, more by the peasantry than by the theorists. Not until after
the XXth Party Congress—the de-Stalinizing congress—in 1956 did a new
debate concerning money in the Soviet economy break out.[11] This latter-day
polemic, still active at this writing if not quite so vibrant as a few years
ago, has been an integral part of the great and widely ramified debate
on the law of value. The problem this time, however, has not been the
"whether" of money (its necessity in this epoch of "full-scale construction
of communism" is not questioned by any opinion appearing on the pages
of Soviet journals,[12]) but the "why." This in turn has been reduced by
almost unanimous agreement to the "why" of the operation of the
(Marxian) "law of value" in the present-day Societ economy, and of its
implications and limits.

The Western economist who delves into the literature is likely to
be repelled by the mustiness of the intellectual atmosphere and bored by

[10] Strumilin, S. G., "Faktor vremeni v proektirovkakh kapital'nykh vlozhenii,"
Izvestiia Akademii nauk: Otdelenie ekonomiki i prava, 3 (1946), 195–216; in
English: "The Time Factor in Capital Investment Projects," *International Economic
Papers,* No. 1 (1951).

[11] The monetary *Dogmengeschichte* of the intervening 35 years is briefly summarized in two articles by Alfred Zauberman: "Economic Thought in the Soviet
Union," *Review of Economic Studies,* XVI, 40 (1949–1950), 102–116; and "Gold
in Soviet Economic Theory and Policies," *American Economic Review,* XLI, 5
(December 1951), 879–890.

[12] Let us remind ourselves that in his last work, *Economic Problems of Socialism
in the USSR,* 1952, Stalin predicted a gradual elimination of money from the
Soviet economy as it advanced on its way to full communism. This doctrine was
reversed soon after Stalin's death, especially after the XXth Congress, and the new
orthodoxy holds that "commodity-money relations" will continue to develop on the
way to full communism.

the verbosity of the polemics. And yet, although all too often arid, scholastic, and metaphysical, the issues cannot be readily dismissed as entirely inconsequential. The nature of the answer to the question "why value?" is likely to have a major bearing not only on the place and function of money in the Soviet economy but also, and more significantly, on the normative view of price formation and one's appreciation of the role of economic calculation in the Soviet economy. We shall briefly look at only three of the many distant positions on this issue.

The "juridical"[13] explanation, for which Academician Ostrovitianov has been the chief spokesman,[14] is essentially a reaffirmation of Stalin's argument in *Economic Problems of Socialism:* legal title to means of production is held either by the state or by cooperative (*kolkhoz*) entities; exchange between the two sectors involves transfer of legal ownership and is therefore "commodity exchange;" hence, there must be "commodity production;" hence, the so-called Law of Value "operates." The view is easily confuted. According to its logic one may expect that money, prices, and all other "value categories" would disappear overnight if all the remaining *kolkhozes* were suddenly transformed into state farms (as a substantial fraction of them indeed already have been since 1957), an hypothesis which is dubious at best.

A rather different explanation has been forcefully advanced by another (but much younger) leading economist, Ia. A. Kronrod,[15] who maintains that "commodity relations" are imminent in socialism for two reasons, because goods are necessarily produced for exchange, and because the exchange is "commodity exchange." In regard to the first, Kronrod argues that socialist enterprises enter into exchange with each other because they are autonomous, and, further, this exchange must be one of equivalents in order to afford material incentives to the enterprises and their workers. Concerning the second, he holds, rather metaphysically, that the exchange between socialist enterprises "necessarily creates and develops an internal, nonantagonistic, but very substantial contradiction in the directly social labor [which Kronrod insists, against the opinion of many of his colleagues, labor in the Soviet economy already is]—precisely a contradiction between aggregate [*sovokupnyi*] labor expended for the production of the social

    [13] The term is Mme. Lavigne's. Marie-L. Lavigne, *Le capital dans l'économie soviétique, SEDES,* Paris, 1961, pp. 37ff.

    [14] Reiterated by him in numerous places; e.g., recently in *Stroitel'stvo kommunizma i tovarno-denezhnye otnosheniia,* Moscow, 1962, pp. 34ff. His defense of the juridical position is so obdurate that one is led to wonder whether it was he, a prominent member of the Soviet economic profession long before Stalin's death, who may not lay claim to its parentage.

    [15] Kronrod—an even more prolix and repetitive writer than Ostrovitianov—has advanced his position on this matter on innumerable occasions, perhaps most fully in *Den'gi v sotsialisticheskom obshchestve,* Second, Revised Edition, Moscow, 1960, pp. 124ff.

product as a whole, on one hand, and individual and collective labor expended on the output of individual socialist enterprises, on the other hand" (p. 133). Although he concedes that the existence of a second form of property is another reason for "commodity production," it is to him only "supplementary" (p. 136). Kronrod's approach does not quite explain "value" or money in terms of the need to economize, but invoking as it does the autonomy of the economic unit and recognizing the importance of remuneration (material incentives), it seems to be less of an obstacle to a rationalist approach to monetary theorizing than the juridical explanation (which, however, does not prevent Kronrod from taking markedly orthodox positions with regard to other issues, such as price formation and the application of mathematics in economics).

A third view completely rejects for the Soviet economy the existence of "commodity production," which it identifies with the presence of private property. Although admitting that under socialism goods do have "value," this view ascribes its necessity to the practical (economizing) needs of the socialist economy. To I. S. Malyshev, one of its two chief proponents, " 'value' in the socialist society represents (*predstavliaet*) the social measure of labor expended in the production of the aggregate social product and of its separate parts. So defined, it will retain its significance under [full] communism as well."[16] V. A. Sobol', the other chief advocate of this view and, like Malyshev, a high official of the Central Statistical Administration, avoids defining value altogether and sees no place for the law of value—as distinct from a law of price formation—in the Soviet situation.[17] For their stands on "commodity production," the law of value, and money, Malyshev and Sobol' have drawn the concentrated fire of most of the big guns in the Soviet theoretical arsenal.[18] The vehemence of the critique suggests that the issue is more than academic, that the two authors have gone too far in their theoretical assaults on the conceptual pillars of the post-Stalin orthodoxy which at once provide the "objective" basis for erecting a doctrinally palatable theory of price and legitimize the actual policies pursued by the state during the "transition to communism." In the words of the statement cited in the last footnote: "The partisans of . . . Malyshev's and Sobol's views are few in number, but nonetheless the active propaganda of their ideas may cause harmful con-

---

[16] *Obshchestvennyi uchet truda i tsena pri sotsializme*, Moscow, 1960, p. 55.

[17] *Ocherki po voprosam balansa narodnogo khoziaistva*, Moscow, 1960, pp. 46, 64.

[18] See for instance Ostrovitianov, *op. cit.*, L. Gatovskii and M. Sakov in *Kommunist*, 15, (1960), 79–90; Malyshev's and Sobol's joint reply to them in *Kommunist*, 8 (1961), 82–88, followed by that authoritative journal's long editorial statement declaring them to be in the wrong; V. S. Nemchinov in *Voprosy ekonomiki*, [hereafter *VE*], 12 (1960), 89ff, English translation in *Problems of Economics*, IV, 3 (July 1961), 6ff; and G. Kozlov in *VE*, 11 (1960), 13–27.

fusion in theory and may reflect negatively on the practical solution of a series of important economic problems of communist construction. . . . [it is still] vitally necessary to use commodity-money relations most amply in the interests of communist construction." (p. 89). The stricture is less than fully just; at issue is not the "using of 'commodity-money relations,' " but the doctrinal legitimation of such use. On his own part, Sobol' replied caustically: "What kind of law of value in the socialist society is it if it fails to perform its basic function [that of resource allocation, as most Soviet economists assert—G.G.]? . . . Comrade Ostrovitianov would have it that the law of value is present in a socialist society but that its basic function is turned over to another, a non-capitalist law [the law of planful, proportionate development] . . . It is unthinkable that a socialist society would maintain unemployed capitalist laws [such as the law of value] on the dole (na soderzhanii)."[19]

That heresy respects few bounds is borne out by Sobol's equally iconoclastic assertion that the value of the ruble is determined not by the value of gold, as orthodox opinion has adamantly maintained since the initial stabilization of the ruble in 1922–1924, but "by the planned definition of the magnitude of labor expenditure in the monetary unit" . . . "not by the elemental forces of the market but by the planning organs of the state."[20] The crude metallism that has, in the face of the most overwhelming factual evidence to the contrary, completely dominated Soviet monetary theorizing for over four decades is indeed a remarkable demonstration of the survival powers of an archaic dogma in an ideologically charged scholastic atmosphere. Even Kronrod, whose basic orthodoxy has not prevented him (as we have already seen and shall see again) from occasionally adopting rather pragmatic views in monetary matters and who makes much of the conscious influence of planning on the value of the ruble (perhaps too much!), refuses to break the invisible mystical thread between Soviet money and gold.[21] However, in his conception, the causal nexus is in the reverse of that in Marx's capitalism: in the "who–whom" between Soviet money and gold it is the former that dominates, thanks to the planning power of the state behind it. The sword prevails. "In the course of the victory of socialism, gold as the monetary equivalent expressing socialist production relations *becomes entirely a planfully utilized equivalent.* . . . In the golden integument of Soviet money there swiftly develops the new socialist content."[22]

---

[19] *Op. cit.,* p. 46.

[20] *Ibid.,* p. 40.

[21] *Op. cit.* pp. 189–218.

[22] *Ibid.,* p. 218. The italics are ours; the Russian phrase is *"stanovitsia polnost'iu planomerno ispol'zuemym ekvivalentom."* For an extensive critique of the orthodox position on gold by the late Stefan Varga (Budapest) see his "Das Geld im Sozialismus," *Weltwirtschaftliches Archiv.* 78:2 (1957), 223–288.

IV

One of the consequences of the prevailing orthodoxy in monetary theory is that the scope of what constitutes money is defined in terms that were already too narrow even when Marx was writing on the subject. Gold, of course, is money, the money commodity itself, but gold does not circulate as a medium of exchange within the U.S.S.R. The concept is therefore effectively restricted to currency, which is said to represent the money commodity "symbolically." Other means of payment or liquid claims are generally denied the attributes of money. At bottom the question is more than definitional; it reflects a conceptualization of the economic process. But one should add in fairness that the *practice* of monetary management has certainly extended as well to means of payment, such as bank deposits, that are not accorded full rights of citizenship in doctrine. Not surprisingly, the planners have been more sensitive to instrumental realities than the theorists. Withal, as Garvy has recently reminded us:

> . . . the relationship between credit and money creation is still only dimly perceived by the majority of Soviet writers in the field; the view that the resources of the Gosbank determine its ability to expand credit is still widely held. Until very recently, Soviet economists denied the monetary nature of the deposits of enterprises. Most of them consider such balances to be merely a clearing fund, a liability of the Gosbank (State Bank of the USSR), or a potential claim of the depositor to currency.[23]

Garvy goes on to mention that the deviation from prevailing opinion advanced by Kronrod—namely, that balances held at the Gosbank represent "money of the banking circuit"—met widespread rejection by Soviet monetary economists. Kronrod argues that such balances perform the same functions as currency and, under appropriate conditions, are mutually convertible with currency. A failure to recognize this, he warns, may lead to the overextension of credit (to enterprises) and eventually to excessive currency issue.[24]

What in fact should be counted as "money" in the setting of the Soviet command economy surely depends on the specific financial and monetary arrangements that obtain there, the degree of liquidity of the various instruments and claims, and, last but not least, on the problem at hand. A careful study of the Soviet money supply in the prewar period by Raymond P. Powell lists the following components:[25]

[23] George Garvy, "The Role of the State Bank in Soviet Planning," Jane Degras and Alec Nove (Eds.), *Soviet Planning: Essays in Honor of Naum Jasny,* Blackwell, Oxford, 1964, p. 72.

[24] Kronrod, *op. cit.,* pp. 319ff. He claims to have first advanced this view in 1950 (p. 323m.) For polemics with his chief opponent see *ibid.,* and Iu. E. Shenger, *Ocherki sovetskogo kredita,* Moscow, 1961, pp. 119ff.

[25] *Soviet Monetary Policy* (doctoral dissertation), University of California, Berkeley, 1952, p. 128.

From the Gosbank: Treasury and bank notes; deposits of all kinds (except correspondent accounts of other banks;) accreditives, special accounts, bank transfers, accepted checks, and limited check books outstanding. From the Ministry of Finance: Coins. From the Savings Banks: All current accounts and an (unknown) part of other deposits. From the Special Investment Banks: Deposit accounts. From clearings mostly so-called Bureaus for Mutual Offset.[26]

All claims outstanding against clearings.

Hardly surprisingly, compared with what we find in an advanced capitalist country, the variety of instruments and claims that fall even within Powell's relatively generous definition of money is small in the Soviet Union.

More difficult is the question of liquidity. Money (in the Western conception) is something that has a high degree of moneyness, which in turn depends on the object's liquidity, that is, the ease and degree of certainty with which it can be converted into a generally acceptable payment instrument of a definite nominal value. Although this much is applicable to the Soviet case as well, we do run here into two thorny problems. First, for institutional reasons and for purposes of control by higher authorities, all Powell's money categories are subject to severe limitations, restrictions, and disabilities in regard to their use. Within its own sector currency in the hands of individuals remains the most usable, although even that cannot be spent in many ways normal in market economies lest the spender be accused of "speculation" or similar transgressions. In the state sector, the bank balances of enterprises are held down to strikingly low levels, and—in theory, at least—their uses must conform to the plans of the enterprises. The forced segregation of funds for specific purposes is common. Bank deposits are convertible into currency, almost exclusively for wage payment, only under stringent conditions. As Garvy writes (*op. cit.,* p. 64): " . . . in the Soviet banking system the absolute order to pay is unknown; payments from any account are made only if in agreement with the applicable rules and authorizations ('plan')"—though one might substitute "are supposed to be made" for "are made," since the banks' controls in this regard are notoriously imperfect. A very large proportion of interenterprise payments is carried out by the peculiar system of mutual offsets (*zachety*). These—and other—restrictions and devices are clearly intended to impair the liquidity of the individual means of payments and of the enterprises as such, and thereby to circumscribe the latter's freedom of action. We hasten to add, however, that in principle the phenomenon is hardly uniquely Soviet; it has analogues in all large formal organiza-

---

[26] In the later 1950's the Bureau for Mutual Offset virtually disappeared in favor of a system of "decentralized offsets" of payments among enterprises; see Shenger, *op. cit.,* p. 159.

tions in which the decentralized use of means of payments finds itself perforce in an uneasy compromise with the administratively expressed will of the top authority.[27]

A possibly even thornier problem in the interpretation of the liquidity of Soviet monetary instruments is posed by the prevailing seller's market. Once again, the problem is not uniquely Soviet; it is present in any repressed-inflationary situation. That the seller's market does obtain in Soviet-type economies even in "normal" times, in the household sector as well as within the production sector, is an elementary truth which hardly needs substantiation. Its basic causes are the strain placed on the nation's resources by the ambitiousness of the plans and by the structure of managerial incentives, the inefficiencies in goods' distribution, the relatively easy availability of bank credit for inventory acquisition,[28] and the fixity of official prices. Its visible manifestations in retail trade are more or less frequent queues, empty shelves, occasional informal consumer goods' rationing, and price differentials in favor of the open (*kolkhoz*) market in comparison with official stores; and, in the production sector, the tight allocation of materials, the "pushers," etc. Under such conditions, which in greater or lesser degree have persisted throughout the history of the Soviet command economy, actual cash balances of households and the cash resources (including availability of bank credit) of enterprises tend to exceed the desired or necessary levels—which in turn is of course the proximate reason for the seller's market.[29] Money continues to serve as the medium of exchange but it is no longer so desirable a store of value as it might otherwise be; we may therefore say that in a certain sense its liquidity has been reduced. (Of course, there is a sense in which the whole economy is "too liquid.") Yet it should be also noted that monetary ease is not ubiquitous; Soviet enterprises do get into financial difficul-

[27] Regarding controls over the liquid assets of enterprises, see Garvy, *op. cit., passim;* Donald R. Hodgman, "Soviet Monetary Controls through the Banking System," in Gregory Grossman (ed.), *Value and Plan,* University of California Press, Berkeley, pp. 105–124; and our chapter in Benjamin H. Beckhart, *Banking Systems,* Columbia University Press, New York, 1954, pp. 733–768. On magnitude of bank balances see Hodgman, *op cit.,* p. 120; on clearing by offset, which in 1959 accounted for some 45 per cent of all clearings under the aegis of the Gosbank, see *ibid.,* pp. 113ff. and Shenger, *op. cit.,* Ch. VI. A concise, up-to-date description of the structure and functions of Soviet banking will be found in Egon Neuberger, "Banking in the Soviet Union: An American View," *The Bankers Magazine,* 148, 1 (Winter 1965), 24–27.

[28] See Powell, *op. cit.,* Ch. 1.

[29] To the enterprise, bank balances above a certain level may even have zero value, since they are liable to seizure ("redistribution of working capital") by superordinate entities. See Robert W. Campbell, *Accounting in Soviet Planning and Management,* Harvard University Press, Cambridge, Mass., 1963, pp. 205–206. Excess inventories of goods may also be subject to seizure, but, paradoxically, they are less visible to the authorities than bank balances.

ties and even become insolvent. In the latter case they are taken into a kind of receivership on the part of the Bank. Lastly, we may observe that Soviet law has tended to recognize the limited desirability of money and is more likely to award relief to the injured party through specific performance or restoration of goods in kind than through monetary compensation of damages.[30]

The terms "active money" and "passive money" have been gaining acceptance, thanks largely to the writings of Peter Wiles[31] in the West and of Włodzimierz Brus[32] in Poland. For both, the distinction hinges on whether magnitudes expressed in monetary terms directly influence economic decisions or whether such magnitudes are employed for controlling compliance with directives only. The spheres of circulation of the two kinds of money correspond respectively to the domains of the market mechanism and the command principle; as with the latter dichotomy, the dividing line between monetary activity and passivity is not a sharp one. For example, as Wiles notes in passing,[33] monetary magnitudes may be a decision-making criterion for the planners but not for the enterprises. Further, although production targets may be expressed in value terms, nonetheless, money may remain passive; Wiles recognizes this as a new function of money—money as a "means of command."[34]

A closely related distinction is between money circulating in the household sector and that circulating in the state sector. (The collective farms may be usefully subjoined to the household sector for this purpose.) These are two physically distinct sets of means of payment: chiefly bank deposits in the state sector and primarily currency in the household sector. The flow from the latter to the former—that is, the conversion of currency into deposits held by state-owned entities—is encouraged, whereas the reverse flow is tightly controlled by Gosbank's near-monopoly

---

[30] A. K. R. Kiralfy, "Attempts to Formulate a Legal Theory of Public Ownership," *Soviet Studies*, VIII, 3 (January 1957), 338–342; Dietrich A. Loeber, "Plan and Contract Performance in Soviet Law," University of Illinois *Law Forum*, Spring 1964, pp. 142, 159–160.

[31] See both his "Rationality, the Market, Decentralization, and the Territorial Principle," in Grossman, (ed.), *Value and Plan,* p. 188, and *The Political Economy of Communism,* Harvard University Press, Cambridge, Mass., 1962, *passim.*

[32] *Ogólne problemy funkcjonowania gospodarki socjalistycznej,* Warsaw, 1961, pp. 126–142. A similar distinction (though without the epithets) will be found in Jean Marczewski, "La monnaie en économies socialistes," *Revue d'économie politique* (mars–avril 1958), 433–449.

[33] *Political Economy of Communism,* p. 107.

[34] *Ibid.,* p. 68. It should be noted also that whereas the operation of the market mechanism presupposes active money, the command principle may rely on no money at all so well as on passive money. An example is the erstwhile deliveries in kind to machine-tractor stations.

over the disbursement of currency for wage payment.[35] Different, too, are the main forms of monetary control in the two sectors. As we have just observed, the use of payment by state enterprises is—in theory at least—regulated with reference to every single transaction and each firm's bank deposit is subject to individual surveillance. To the Soviets this is part of that broad category, "control by the ruble"; we might designate it as "microfinancial" control. By contrast, monetary management with regard to the household sector concentrates on keeping the total supply of currency in that sector at an appropriate level; we might call it "macro-monetary" control. As Hodgman has pointed out,[36] since the first two of these control the same range of activities, one or the other would seem to be superfluous at first glance. The explanation that he offers emphasizes the imperfect effectiveness of either administrative or microfinancial controls, and the principle that the extension of varieties of control may be more effective than the intensification of a narrower range of them. One might add the consideration, so common in Soviet practice, that the multiplication of controlling agencies also helps to control the controllers.[37]

We now digress to inquire into a particular problem—the financing of fixed-capital investment by bank loans—which, it is hoped, will place in relief certain aspects of the role of money in the production sector of the Soviet economy and will prepare us for some general conclusions and comments in the last two sections of this essay.

V

If the essential politicoeconomic meaning of the Soviet command economy is, in Robert W. Campbell's apt phrase, "totalitarianism harnessed to the task of rapid industrialization and economic growth,"[38] then nothing should be of greater concern to the regime than the direction and tempo of the investment in fixed capital and its technological embodiment. The crucial decisions are made in physical terms, but their outcome is

[35] On the last, see Garvy, op. cit., p. 65. An early but still valid investigation is Joseph S. Berliner's, "Monetary Planning in the USSR," The American Slavic and East European Review, IX, 4 (December 1950). See also Franklyn D. Holzman, Soviet Taxation, Harvard University Press, Cambridge, Mass., 1955, passim.

[36] Op. cit., p. 107.

[37] The multiplicity of controllers must not be confused with the effectiveness of controls. Garvy writes that during a recent trip to Russia he was told that 30,000 Gosbank officials are engaged in inspecting the operations of individual enterprises. An article that has appeared since (Ekonomicheskaia gazeta, (hereafter EG, November 25, 1964, p. 10), coincidentally entitled "Thirty Thousand Auditors," suggests that most of the auditors dispatched from financial institutions to enterprises accomplish very little.

[38] Soviet Economic Power, Houghton Mifflin, Cambridge, Mass., 1960, p. 8.

not indifferent to the accompanying financial arrangements. The latter at once localize the supervision of investment as a "real" activity, shape the incentives for its effective and efficient execution, and to some extent unlock the constructive initiative resting at the various levels of the economic hierarchy.

Broadly speaking, there are three sources of finance for fixed capital within the state sector: the state budget (itself a hierarchy rather than a point in economic-administrative space); the banking system; and the retained profits and depreciation reserves of the enterprises themselves or their immediate superordinate entities. (The last-named source we shall call "own funds.") Control over the direction and speed of investment and the execution of the regime's so-called technological policy (*tekhnicheskaia politika*) in individual industries calls for maximum centralization of financing, that is, appropriation from the state budget, preferably at a relatively high governmental level. A second reason for central financing in this case is the need to coordinate planned financial flows with planned material flows in the investment-goods sector, the latter of course being also highly centralized—in part for similar reasons—in Soviet practice. On the other hand, extreme centralization of investment financing entails some major costs: long lines of communication, divorce between those who have an ultimate interest in economizing real investment resources and those who are in the position to do so, oversight of opportunities (individually minor, but in the aggregate, major) for advantageous investment, and (closely bearing on the last) the stifling of initiative at lower levels. As always, superimposed on these considerations are various political and particular interests. The consequent centralization-decentralization problem has persisted throughout the Soviet period.

The solution opted for in the course of the so-called Credit Reform in the early 1930's,[39] at the beginning of the command-economy era has been one of nearly maximal centralization. Most of the decentralized sources that appeared during the NEP were abolished. The vast bulk of funds for fixed-capital investment were henceforth to come from the state budget, in the form of nonrepayable grants. True, a certain fraction also comes from the retained profits of enterprises; but this is almost a financial fiction, a mere simplification of the accounting, as the control over this portion is tightly held by higher authorities. For more effective supervision of the investment activity a set of "special banks" was created; strictly speaking these were not banks at all but agencies for the disbursement of the Treasury's moneys and for continuous auditing and surveillance. The special banks also manage and disburse the depreciation reserves obligatorily turned over to them by the enterprises. And, logically, they serve as commercial banks for the construction industry because of the impossi-

---

[39] An extensive description of the Credit Reform will be found in Arnold, *op. cit.*

bility of drawing a line between the *working* capital of that industry and the *fixed* capital-to-be of the rest of the economy. (Since 1959 there has been a single special bank, the *Stroibank.*)

Some decentralized sources remained. The enterprises could use a small portion of their retained planned profits and a much larger part of their above-plan profits for fixed-capital investments more or less at their own discretion. They could—in fact, if not in theory—apply some of their so-called capital repair reserves to the same end. Finally, they could, and often did, unlawfully convert some of their working capital into fixed capital, later replenishing the former with funds from the Bank or the state budget. To utilize local initiative, in 1932 Gosbank was authorized to extend short-term loans for "small mechanization" with a payback period of under one year. These provisions, very slightly liberalized in 1938, 1951, and 1953—and supplemented in 1941 by provisions for short-term loans to expand the production of consumer goods—entailed so much red tape that they remained virtually unused.[40] Thus, in 1952, the aggregate value of the loans extended by the Gosbank under both these rubrics together was only 18 million (post-1960) rubles. (See Table 1.) The problem of utilizing dispersed initiative for modernization was still acutely present when the Soviet economy entered the post-Stalin era; at the same time its leaders became increasingly concerned with technical backwardness on the one hand and organizational improvement on the other.[41]

By decree of August 21, 1954, the role of the Gosbank in the economy was somewhat expanded in order to strengthen "control by the ruble." (The reader will recall that this was in the last semester of the "Malenkov era" and in the midst of the initial post-Stalin decentralizing of the old ministerial structure of economic administration.) For example, the Bank was given additional powers over enterprises in financial difficulty. Another part of the decree considerably liberalized—though still within narrow limits, as we shall see—the Bank's authority to extend loans for "mechanization and improvement of production technology." Still another part enlarged Gosbank's powers to extend loans for the expansion of consumer goods production, but the problems in this instance are quite similar to those raised by loans for technical modernization, and, for lack of space here, we shall not discuss it separately.[42]

[40] For a brief historical sketch, see V. Markov, *Kredit na novuiu tekhniku,* Moscow, 1960, p. 29.

[41] Mme Lavigne's *Le Capital dans l'économie soviétique,* pp. 276ff., contains a most valuable discussion of the twin problems of equipment modernization and financial decentralization from the NEP onward. Our brief treatment in this section owes much to her analysis.

[42] As of 1960, the only two other kinds of financing fixed-capital investment

At present—there have been several minor liberalizations of the terms since 1954; the principles that govern the extension of the modernization loans seem to be as follows.[43] They are available only for projects not included in (higher-level) capital investment plans and only for renovation or partial replacement of fixed capital, not for new construction or "complete reconstruction" of an enterprise. The loans must be repaid in no more than two to three years, the maximum duration depending on the branch of the economy with the longer term applying to some heavy industries, and the capital sum must be recoverable from the cost savings engendered by the projects themselves. That is to say, eligible projects must have recoupment (payback) periods no longer than two to three years, which of course eliminates all but the most attractive ones.[44]

A maximum value for such loans for the whole country is planned annually—for 1963 it was 450 million rubles—and "limits" apply to individual offices of the Gosbank. (It would be interesting to know how these limits are set.) The aggregate amount extended per year rose sharply after 1954 until it reached a plateau of around 400 million rubles in the late 1950's where it has remained since (Table 1).[45] Thus, its share in aggregate capital investment is small; for instance, the figure planned for 1963 was to finance only 4 per cent of the acquisition of new equipment[46] and corresponded to only somewhat more than 1 per cent of total gross fixed-capital investment in the state sector in that year. More significant are

---

in the state sector by the Gosbank were short-term (up to three years) loans for the construction of movie theaters and seasonal loans for "capital repair"; see E. Vainshtein and M. Iampol'skii, *Kreditovanie zatrat v osnovnye fondy,* Moscow, 1960.

[43] See Shenger, *op. cit.,* p. 364; Markov, *op. cit.,* pp. 38ff.

[44] Mme Lavigne stresses that this requirement was a major factor in the legitimation of the internal-rate-of-return (recoupment-period) approach in the U.S.S.R. We believe other needs—in engineering design ("project making") and for the rewarding of innovators—were as important. See our "Soviet Growth: Routine, Inertia, and Pressure" in *American Economic Review,* L, 2 (May 1960), 65ff.

Addendum. The situation as described in this paragraph in the text refers to late 1964. Since then, the credit terms have been somewhat liberalized. To wit, the longer loan maturity, three years, now applies to *all* industries, and may in some cases be extended to five years. Repayment may now be made also from additional profits stemming from above-plan output. See S. Egorov in *Den'gi i kredit,* 12 (1964), 3–8, and *Finansy SSSR,* 4 (1965), 91. I am grateful to Mr. Babitchev for drawing my attention to this development, as well as for pointing out (in reference to footnote 42, above) that beginning in 1960 the Gosbank has been extending credits, up to three years in duration, to state farms for the construction of productive facilities.

[45] More detailed numerical data may be found in Markov, *op. cit., passim.* Shenger, *op. cit.,* p. 367, *Den'gi i Kredit* [hereafter *DK*], 10 (1963), 6ff.

[46] *DK,* 10 (1963), 7.

TABLE 1. Loans for Technical Modernization Extended by Gosbank
and Stroibank (million post-1960 rubles)

	Aggregate Value of Loans Extended During the Year	Value of Loans Outstanding at End of Year
1952	18[a]	24[a]
1953	(not available)	11
1954	30	19
1955	136	100
1956	297	233
1957	344	310
1958	408	368
1959	359	346
1960	386	370
1961	401	398
1962	421	413
1963	453[b]	429

[a] Includes "loans for enlargement of consumer goods production."
[b] Plan for 1963 was 450 (*DK*, 10 (1963), 6.)
Sources: *VE*, 11 (1958), 59; Tsentral'noe statisticheskoe upravlenie, *Narodnoe Khoziaistvo SSSR v 1962g.*, Moscow, 1963, p. 640; *idem*, *Narodnoe Khoziaistvo SSSR v 1963g.*, Moscow, 1965, p. 659; Markov, *op. cit.*, p. 16; V. F. Popov (ed.), *Gosudarstvennyi bank SSSR*, Moscow, 1957, p. 85.

the modernization loans in relation to *noncentralized* investments, within which they accounted (in 1961) for as much as 11 per cent, and even for as much as 50–65 per cent for individual industries (textile, iron and steel, coal and shale, machine building).[47] The average duration of a loan has been steadily something under one year, as the collation of the two columns in Table 1 shows. In sum, the modernization loans clearly play a very small role in Soviet capital-formation or technological progress.

This is so despite great advantages frequently claimed for the system of financing investment *via* Gosbank loans. The repayable nature of the credit and the application of the recoupment-period criterion forces the enterprises to exercise prudence in the drawing up of projects and to good management in the course of their execution. (By contrast, this often is not the case with budget-financed projects.) The banker, being subject to his "limit," selects only the best projects and keeps a watchful eye on their progress. Moreover, the extension of a modernization loan gives the banker a reason to exercise tighter financial control over all of the enterprise's activities—too much so, some complain. The loan can be ap-

[47] *Ibid.*

plied for any time of the year, in contrast to the rigid annual rhythm and long lead-times of centralized planning. At the same time, management has an avenue for the realization of its initiative and aspirations—although some managers may prefer to have retained an excuse for inaction.[48]

Indeed, one of the moot questions is the extent to which management is at all interested in taking advantage of the opportunities presented by the availability of modernization loans. The obstacles and disadvantages seem to be many; the incentives, few. Budgetary financing is not repayable; a loan is, and in a very short period of time at that. To qualify for bank financing the project must have an internal payback period of as little as two to three years. Obtaining the loan is beset with much red tape, according to many sources. The Ministry of Finance has imposed in effect a penalty in the form of additional *planned* profit of up to 25 per cent of loan repayment in the given year.[49] Moreover, when the loan is repaid the new level of profitability is presumably incorporated into the enterprise's plan; that is to say, the added benefit flows almost entirely to the Treasury and not to the enterprise.

And yet, in 1963, the one year for which the planned value of such loans is available, the actual value of loans even slightly exceeded the—admittedly modest—planned figure. This suggests that a significant part of the demand for modernization loans may have remained unrequited in that year. The same impression is obtained from the fact that the *average* duration of a loan has steadily been under one year, less than one-half or even one-third of the maximum permissible duration. We shall presently see that spokesmen for industry have called for enlargement of the loan program, although on more liberal terms. At the same time a writer who frequently reflects the Gosbank's points of view has also argued, on the basis of a sample survey of enterprises, that there is considerable room for expansion of the loan program even under the present rapid payback terms and has proposed that all modernization projects with recoupment periods of up to two or three years be financed exclusively by bank loans, releasing budgetary and own funds for financing new capacity.[50]

After mustering the incentive and meeting the severe tests, having obtained a modernization loan, the enterprise still has to surmount a major (and at times insuperable) obstacle: the difficulty of obtaining the material inputs for the investment. Nearly all the important materials and types of equipment are centrally allocated, but the allocation plans do not provide for any needs arising from modernization financed by the Gosbank. As

---

[48] See Joseph S. Berliner, *Factory and Manager in the USSR,* Harvard University Press, Cambridge, Mass., 1957, p. 307, in regard to such loans.

[49] *DK.,* 8 (1963), 39; *EG,* December 18, 1963, p. 13, and September 19, 1964, p. 5.

[50] N. Barkovskii in *DK,* 10 (1960), 8–11.

a result, much scrounging for materials and equipment is necessary; some of the loans cannot be used; and often the enterprises are forced to rely on their own resources.[51] The last is a handicap from management's standpoint but a possible blessing for the economy in that the difficulty of obtaining materials forces enterprises to "mobilize their internal reserves." It may also serve as a handy excuse for inaction in the face of weak incentives. As though responding to such excuses, a writer in the Gosbank's journal has emphasized that the necessary materials would often be found if only the *sovnarkhozy* were to look in their own backyards.[52]

Nonetheless, all evidence tends to agree that the materials problem is a real and serious one in the case of the modernization loans, as it is in all other cases in which some decentralization of production decisions is undertaken. For instance, in a recent economic experiment aiming to relate consumer goods production more closely to final demand, the so-called *Bol'shevichka-Maiak* experiment, the limits of flexibility were largely imposed by this consideration.[53] Even more striking is the case of *Sel'khoztekhnika,* the organization established in 1961 to supply collective and state farms with agricultural equipment, fertilizer, and other industrial products in response to the farms' need and demand. The melancholy results are documented almost daily in the pages of the Soviet press. Rarely even in Soviet history have need and demand been more flagrantly disregarded and mocked for the sake of the producers' convenience and the distributor's (*Sel'khoztekhnika's*) "easy life" than in this instance. The materials problem in these cases is of course nothing less than the tangible manifestation of the persistent conflict between the two organizing principles operating in the Soviet-type economy—to anticipate the argument in the next section, namely, decentralized initiative and decision making on one hand, and the command principle on the other, the latter represented most starkly by centralized materials rationing. The contest is an unequal one, for the materials allocators hold the ultimate economic power in a taut economy, the power over the disposition of physical goods. Those—like the late Academician V. S. Nemchinov—who have advocated the abolition of materials distribution and its supersession by "normal" commercial distribution of producer goods have in effect proposed not only a fundamental systemic change but also a drastic redistribution of effective power in the economy.

[51] V. Markov in *VE,* 9 (1959), 43, 45; Shenger, *op. cit.,* p. 369; P. I. Verba, *Rol' kredita v razvitii promyshlennosti sovnarkhozov,* Kharkov, 1961, p. 108; V. Ganshtak and I. Ioffe in *Promyshlenno-ekonomicheskaia gazeta,* November 27, 1957; *EG,* September 19, 1964, p. 5. The tendency to rely on own resources of materials and labor was confirmed in our interviews with Soviet managers during a study trip in 1960. It should be also noted that regulations permit no more than 40 per cent of the loan amount to be spent on wages (Markov, *op. cit.,* p. 35).

[52] F. Dronov in *DK,* 8 (1963), 37–38. See also *EG,* September 19, 1964, p. 5.

[53] See *VE,* 11 (1964), 116.

But to return to our case study, spokesmen for industry have called both for longer loan maturities, higher maximum amounts, and formal allocation of the material counterparts to the more important projects and for permission to use enterprises' own working capital for projects with somewhat longer recoupment periods than the Gosbank will now finance[54] (which would legalize the hitherto proscribed conversion of working into fixed capital). Shenger, a strong advocate of this type of financing, though within "definite bounds," also favors longer term loans and would solve the materials problem by setting aside a special reserve of "building materials, metals, and standard equipment" at the republic level.[55] However, one wonders what would happen to the decentralized nature and the consequent advantages of this method of investment financing if it were placed at the mercy of the implacable force which is the Soviet system of materials allocation.

To be sure, bank loans are not the only conceivable financial means of carrying out noncentrally initiated investment projects in the Soviet system. Own funds of enterprises obviously are another. Even budgetary funds could be so administered as to give broad scope to dispersed initiative for investment on the lower, if not the lowest, levels of the economic hierarchy. In fact, something like the last was proposed in a little noticed but remarkable statement made by Khrushchev during the first, euphoric year following the liquidation of the "anti-Party group" and the formation of the *sovnarkhozy,* and only a few weeks after his assumption of the Premiership. It was not common in those days for the First Secretary's public utterances to remain unreported in the press. Yet the idea advanced by him on April 12, 1958, in a speech before a congress on construction, was evidently so jarring that it remained unpublished for nearly three months and was eventually carried only by a secondary trade newspaper. His words are worth repeating at length:

Something should be said about the method of distributing investment [funds]. It would seem that in the future we shall have to distribute investment [funds] among the *sovnarkhozy* without specification of particular projects (*tituly*). Let me explain how it could be done. For every economic region one could indicate its construction volume for the quinquennium without any breakdown by branches of industry. At the same time, every *sovnarkhoz* should be assigned the main kinds of output and volumes of production for each branch by individual years. This must be done in order that the development

[54] Cf. K. D. Petukhov, chairman of the Moscow city *sovnarkhoz,* speaking at a Central Committee Plenum (*Pravda,* June 25, 1959, p. 2), and A. Krylov, director of the Likhachev Automobile Plant in Moscow, in *Kommunist,* 6 (1957), 47. The latter's is one of the most candid published statements of a Soviet manager's problems and point of view.

[55] *Op. cit.,* p. 372. A similar view is expressed by S. Egorov in *EG,* September 19, 1964, p. 5.

of branches of the economy be coherent, that there be no disproportions. Knowing their assignments and taking into account local conditions, the economic regions [that is, *sovnarkhozy*] will then develop the various branches of industry in a more rational way and will properly untilize the capacities of construction organizations . . . Then we shall have no waste, which, unfortunately, now exists. [Here Khrushchev went on to relate a striking example of waste in the course of the construction of the Bratsk hydroelectric station.] . . . However, this question should be carefully studied and thought through before this method of planning investment can be adopted.[56]

The question clearly did not withstand additional study and thought. Less than a fortnight later, on April 25, 1958, the Presidium of the Supreme Soviet issued its famous decree aimed against "localism" among the *sovnarkhozy*, and thereafter the distribution of investment funds from the budget and the allocation of capital goods were progressively and pronouncedly recentralized. With all the wisdom of hindsight we can say that it hardly could have been otherwise.

Nevertheless, the issue of the proper dividing line between the Bank and the budget as sources of fixed-capital investment financing has continued to remain topical. Soviet writers tend to see it, as do Western students such as Mme. Lavigne,[57] as one of centralization-decentralization, of economic efficiency and central control. Under the banker's eye decentralized financing ensures better husbanding of resources, but it also raises the danger of their direction to lower priority uses. From the regime's standpoint the former is desirable but the latter is sinful. It is probably for this reason that bank loans have not been available for "reconstruction and expansion of enterprises," let alone the construction of new ones, although in the view of some observers they could be very effectively so employed.[58] The pleas of "many managers" and "recommendations by a series of special conferences and meetings" have been countered by the Board of the Gosbank with the opinion that such an extension of the scope of bank loans would lead to "disruption of the proportions in the [officially] confirmed investment plans, to indirect amendment of such plans, to the diversion of budget funds to the repayment of bank loans extended for the financing of construction that has not been provided for by capital-construction plans."[59] On a more general plane, it is said, in response to proposals that bank financing be greatly enlarged in scope, that financing investment from the budget "guarantees direction of the economy

[56] *Stroitel'naia gazeta,* July 2, 1958. I am grateful to Dr. Herbert Block for bringing this passage to my attention.

[57] *Op. cit.,* pp. 289–294; see also Shenger, *op. cit.,* pp. 91ff.

[58] Ganshtak and Ioffe, *loc. cit.*

[59] *Ibid.* The authors characterize this stand by the Board as "dogmatic." In point of fact, budget funds are already sometimes used to repay modernization loans, *VE,* 11 (1958), 62.

by the state and its growth at desired rates and proportions. If the financing of capital construction . . . were delegated to the Bank and to enterprises, then the control of the economy and of finances by the state would be weakened in some measure." "The existing system of financing [investments] from the budget relates to the objective conditions of socialist economic operation (*khoziaistvovanie*) and is determined above all by the necessity of having a centralized policy with regard to the bulk of accumulation and the regulation of economic proportions by the state."[60] Other Soviet economists carry principle even further, against any repayment of capital advances from the state by enterprises. After all, since the state owns the enterprises and whatever capital they possess, repayment has no theoretical basis; it would only complicate financial relations and lead to price increases.[61]

Yet, the impression we leave would be a distorted one if we did not stress that the drift in Soviet economics has been in the opposite direction in recent years. The view has been gaining that the enterprises must be subjected to more stringent financial discipline with regard to their fixed capital (where there has been almost none heretofore), that they should pay interest on the state's investment in them to ensure its more economical treatment, and that even the capital sums should be repayable under some circumstances.

The problem is complex—theoretically, practically, and politically. By now it is deeply entangled in the broad and many-faceted debate on the future of the Soviet economic system. It cannot be resolved on its own merits alone. This is perhaps why the highest level statement yet uttered in favor of substantial extension of the system of financing fixed-capital investment *via* bank loans has been more notable for its vagueness than for its promise. And yet, in view of its author—A. N. Kosygin, then first deputy Prime Minister, speaking at the XXIInd Party Congress in October 1961[62]—it may still carry some promise.[63]

[60] Both quotations are from Moskovskii finansovyi institut, *Problemy sovetskikh finansov*, Moscow, 1960, comprising the papers of a conference on financial matters held in 1959. The first quotation is from the paper by A. M. Aleksandrov (p. 53); the second, from the conference's resolution (p. 206).

[61] V. F. Kotov in A. V. Bachurin and D. D. Kondrashev (eds.), *Tovarno-denezhnye otnosheniia v period perekhoda k kommunizmu*, Moscow, 1963, p. 363.

[62] "It would be useful (*tselesoobrazno*) to shift by way of experiment, capital investment from budget financing to long-term loans. Gosbank's experience of extending long-term [sic?] loans for 2–3 years for the modernization and improvement of existing equipment has fully justified itself. This system could be also applied to the reconstruction and expansion of existing enterprises . . ." (*Pravda*, October 23, 1961, p. 6). *Addendum:* Mr. Kosygin's economic reform of September 1965 in fact incorporates such a measure.

[63] Since this essay was written, an "experiment" extending bank financing to new investment project was started. The following is quoted from *Radio Liberty*

VI

Our digression through some inner corridors of Soviet investment finance serves to bring to the fore one of the most fundamental issues of the Soviet-type economy: the antinomy between two organizing and coordinating systemic principles that are simultaneously at work in the allocation and distribution of scarce resources. One of them, the command principle with its inevitable centralist bias, has been dominant, though not triumphant, throughout the Plan Era. The other, the *khozraschet* principle, a very limited market mechanism in the production sector, has been repressed but not routed, and, in its own innumerable mundane ways, remains defiant. Admissible only insofar as it does not conflict with the will or undermine the values of the central authority, *khozraschet* is the manager's behavior rule for solvency and profits. Nevertheless, it is always the firm's plan, the carrier of the regime's will, that sets the limits and defines the conditions for profit making and contract enforcement, and its fulfillment has undisputed priority for the enterprise.[64] Symbolically, in the firm's annual operative directive, the *tekhpromfinplan,* "fin[ance]" comes after "technology" and "production." Nonetheless, an "absolute

---

Dispatches (New York) of April 30, 1965, referring to a TASS statement of April 8, 1965:

> "Entitled 'Economic Experiment,' the TASS report discloses that, commencing this year, eighteen large construction projects, ranging in value from one to 29 million rubles, will be financed through long-term credits from *Stroibank* instead of outright state grants, as is normally the case. 'By this means,' noted TASS, 'the specialized bank will try out credit as an effective and flexible means of speeding up construction, recovering investments and lowering the volume of unfinished construction.' The projects concerned are scheduled for completion within 2 to 4 years. The credits must be repaid within 1 to 4 years from the profits obtained from the completed plants. Normal interest charges of 0.5 per cent per annum will be levied on the loans; these will be increased to 1.5 per cent on overdue loans. If the project is completed ahead of schedule, the interest charge for that year will be cut by 25 per cent. Finally, although this sounds too generous to be feasible, if it exceeds the plan, the building organization will reportedly receive a bonus exceeding the loan for that year."

See *EG,* May 26, 1965, p. 30. See also *EG,* June 2, 1965, on granting of permission to Stroibank to extend loans of up to six years duration for the expansion—outside of capital investment plans—of old or establishment of new enterprises producing consumer goods or services.

[64] Two telling illustrations, if any are required. In 1959, the following proportions (in per cent) of enterprises under *sovnarkhoz* jurisdiction failed to meet the indicated targets (in parentheses, the same for 1962): gross output: 11; labor productivity:18 (20); cost reduction: 21 (23); profit: 27 (30). The relative priorities of the targets are hereby vividly illustrated. (Profit fares worse than cost, in part because certain outlays, such as fines, affect the former but not the latter under Soviet accounting rules.) Sources: *VE,* 11 (1960), p. 37; *Pravda,* April 6, 1963, pp. 2–3; *EG,* March 30, 1963, 13. The second illustration is a quotation from an article by G. Sakhanovskii, Ukrainian Minister of Trade, in *Pravda,* September 30, 1963,

command economy," the complete centralization of decisions in the production sector (let alone in the household sector), is an impossibility.
Something must be left to local initiative and dispersed decision making.
So *khozraschet* remains a logical necessity, an unfriendly bridgehead that
always threatens to seize ground wherever the planner fails or defaults.[65]

We have already suggested elsewhere[66] that the command economy
is the resultant of a union of a particular authoritarian ideology with the
logic of hasty industrialization; that the imperatives of scarcity under such
conditions press for the continuous extension of the command principle;
that the growing complexity of a rapidly modernizing economy—not to say
the logic of dictatorial rule[67]—accentuates this process; that the command
economy is necessarily driven to both planning and what the Germans
call *Bewirtschaftung* and the Russians *khoziaistvovanie* of the whole
economy [The very idea, no less than the alien words, "fall(s) like a
mournful thud on English ears," to quote Tawney.] *in natura;* and that the
market mechanism and its partner, active money, can perform their necessary but secondary work only with difficulty (except in the household sector). Very much the same propositions with like terminology have been
argued at length by P. J. D. Wiles in his stimulating *Political Economy of
Communism.*

Other Western writers have arrived at similar conclusions. David
Granick, for instance, has imaginatively developed with the help of organi-
zation-theoretic concepts a "fundamental model" of the Soviet system, to
which *khozraschet* "stands in flat contradiction."[68] What is now a distinct
West German school of writers on the *Zentralverwaltungswirtschaft* con-
ceives of it as a *Wirtschaftsordnung* that stands in opposition to such elements of the market economy that exist in its midst.[69]

---

p. 2: By virtue of a 1960 decree "consumer goods production plans must rest on
orders placed by trading organizations. . . . However, [such] orders are frequently
disregarded. In the event of a discrepancy between contract and plan, the arbitration court usually resolves the conflict in favor of the plan. In other words,
industry receives the right to produce goods for which there is no consumer demand."

[65] See Eugène Zaleski, *Planification de la croissance et fluctuations économiques
en U.R.S.S.,* SEDES, Paris, 1962, p. 291.

[66] Especially in "The Structure and Organization of the Soviet Economy," *Slavic
Review,* XXI, 2 (June 1962), 203–222 [reprinted in Donald W. Treadgold (ed.),
The Development of the USSR: An Exchange of Views, University of Washington
Press, Seattle, 1964, pp. 41–60] and in "Notes for a Theory of the Command
Economy," *Soviet Studies,* XV, 2 (October 1963), 101–123.

[67] Gerschenkron, "The Changeability of a Dictatorship." *World Politics* XIV,
4 (July 1962), p. 583.

[68] "An Organizational Model of Soviet Industrial Planning," *The Journal of
Political Economy,* LXVII, 2 (April 1959), 109–130, esp. p. 123.

[69] See, for example, K. Paul Hensel, *Einführung in die Theorie der Zentralverwaltungswirtschaft,* Gustav Fischer, Stuttgart, 1954; Hans Hirsch, *Mengenplanung*

Quite understandably, these lucubrations of "bourgeois economists" were received first with pointed silence and then with outspoken hostility in the Soviet economic literature.[70] The Soviet economist does himself a disservice if his suspicions of the "bourgeois economists' " motives and his distaste for "unscientific" terminology lead him to dismiss out of hand the problem itself. Those, like Ostrovitianov, who focus their sights rigidly on the nature of property relations and obtain therefrom their "juridical" explanations of the law of value and money in the Soviet economy—these members of the old guard are prone to see nothing but harmony between plan and *khozraschet*. Nevertheless, even so orthodox a writer as Kronrod is primarily interested in the autonomy of the enterprise, and autonomy—be its "contradictions" "antagonistic" or no—necessarily raises in principle the question of diversity of interests and rules of behavior among hierarchical levels. Economists of a more independent bent, like Malyshev and Sobol', probe even further to grasp the sense of the Soviet system from its functional characteristics with relative disregard to doctrinal dicta, as we have seen. The most undogmatic are perhaps those who attempt to bypass the "why money" (or "value") question altogether.

Indeed, one of the more engaging aspects of the Great Debate of the past decade has been the subtle emergence of the awareness of an antimony within the Soviet economic system among many Soviet writers. It is now commonplace in Soviet economics that the "objective economic laws" of socialism do not, as Stalin may have thought, constitute a fully consistent set of imperatives, but that they rather reflect different and partly conflicting forces at work in the real Soviet economy. The Law of Value was to be a faithful handmaiden of the Law of Planful, Proportionate Development; instead, it has gradually come to stand for its antithesis—for the primacy of rules and deference to inevitable regularities, in opposition to the voluntarism of which the latter "law" cannot quite cleanse itself. The concept of *khozraschet* has also been evolving from that of a narrow manager's manual which keeps the factory solvent and its accounts tidy, to that of an overarching principle for the coordination of economic activity on the basis of enterprise autonomy, active money,

---

und Preisplanung in der Sowjetunion, J. C. B. Mohr, Tübingen, 1957, translated as *Quantity Planning and Price Planning in the Soviet Union,* University of Pennsylvania Press, Philadelphia, 1961; R. Roland Oertel, *Das System der Sowjetwirtschaft,* Duncker & Humblot, Berlin, 1957; Peter D. Propp. *Zur Transformation einer Zentralverwaltungswirtschaft sowjetischen Typs in eine Marktwirtschaft,* Osteuropa Institut (Berlin), *Wirtschaftswissenschaftliche Veröffentlichungen,* Band 20, Duncker & Humblot, Berlin, 1964. Much of this literature is heavily influenced by the writings of the late Walter Eucken; e.g. his *Grundsätze der Wirschaftspolitik,* Tübingen, 1952; also Rowohlt, Hamburg, 1959.

[70] See S. Khavina, "Kritika burzhuaznoi teorii 'tsentral'no-upravliaemogo' khoziaistva", *VE,* 6 (1964), 87–99.

direct and voluntary contracts, flexible prices, the profit motive, and limited but presumably more effective central planning—a controlled market mechanism in fact if not in its second name.[71] But perhaps the most interesting displacement has been undergone by that Leninist workhorse, the concept of "democratic centralism." Whereas the emphasis has traditionally been on the noun, lately—in some of the economic literature at least—the stress has tended to shift to the adjective as a way of ideologically legitimizing schemes of significant decentralization of the economy with the aid of rational prices, the marginal calculus, mathematical techniques, and transformed central planning.[72] The content of the terminology tends to adapt itself to the issues at hand, in this instance to the problem of reconciling the simultaneous operation of the two organizing principles.

All this is hardly surprising. One speaks in the language one knows best, and, in the face of a demanding holistic ideology, terminological conservatism is a *sine qua non* of social innovation. Thus, we find the keynote speech at the meeting of the Central Committee of the Czechoslovak Communist Party which launched the consistent introduction of the market mechanism in that country characterize the reform as "the close union of the improved economic plan with the active utilization of the law of value and commodity-money relations," although "explicitly reject[ing] all attempts to see in the proposed measures a deviation from Marxism-Leninism or advances to bourgeois-liberalism."[73]

Lest the preceding discussion be misconstrued it should be observed at this point that the Soviet economic system is not alone in experiencing a conflict of two different organizing principles. No society worthy of the name is without its interplay of some form of central authority with decentralized, spontaneous forces, that is, some institutions through which these forces operate on the economic arena, and some conflict between them. The point rather is that in the Soviet case it is the institutions expressing the will of the central authority that have dominated the economic processes (outside of the household sector), and have been doing so to a degree and in a fashion that tend to limit severely the effectiveness of even very limited decentralized processes and dispersed initiative. Moreover, the nature of planning, prices, incentives, and political controls is such as to militate powerfully against any redressing of the balance.

[71] See V. S. Nemchinov, "Sotsialisticheskoe khoziaistvovanie i planirovanie proizvodstva," *Kommunist*, 5 (1964), 74–87.

[72] See especially V. V. Novozhilov, "Voprosy razvitiia demokraticheskogo tsentralizma v upravlenii sotsialisticheskim khoziaistvom," *Trudy Leningradskogo inzhenerno-ekonomicheskogo instituta: Kafedry obshchestvennykh nauk*, Vyp. 24, (1960?), 150–156 and his other recent works.

[73] J. Lennart in *Rudé Právo*, February 2, 1965; here quoted from an English version distributed by Pragopress, pp. 10, 15. For the use of the "law of value"

VII

We have already had occasion to describe and interpret elsewhere[74] the partial demonetization of the Soviet economy following the demise of the NEP and the establishment of the command economy, as well as the accompanying virtual elimination of the market mechanism and, for most of the Stalinist period, drastic restrictions on labor mobility. To be sure, money continued to perform its traditional functions, but with many important exceptions. Money remained most in its own in the relations between the state and the households and the household sector itself, but even here there has been a wide range of important exceptions, extending from the use of prison labor through the rationing of urban housing at nominal rents to the growth of free services. As a medium of exchange, money was removed, or almost so, from a considerable variety of transactions in the production sphere: from nearly all capital transactions in the state sector and, in agriculture, from a large proportion of the relations between the state and the collective farms (payments in kind for tractor services, quasiconfiscatory acquisition of so-called obligatory deliveries, and so forth). Lastly, the advent of physical planning and the absence of prices, or realistic prices, from most factors of production other than labor greatly constricted the role of the monetary unit as a unit of account, replacing it in part with various technological criteria and in part with nothing at all.

The contrast with the "classical" industrialization experience—in which monetization, "marketization," and resource mobility, and therefore the scope of choice, all unfold and advance—is neither accidental nor entirely suprising. "The institutional gradations of backwardness seem to find their counterpart in men's thinking about backwardness and the way in which it can be abolished."[75] The Imperial Russian state under Witte attempted to meet its industrializing aspirations by bribing or financially pressuring resources to move into the modern sectors. It took care to enhance the monetization of the economy, from exerting fiscal pressure on the lowliest peasant to adopting the gold standard and inviting foreign capital. The state under Stalin, by contrast, saw fit—"fitness" here is of course not independent of the ideological imperatives of the regime and the subjective compulsions of the dictator—to mobilize and deploy resources as if on the field of battle. In terms of our epigraphic image, the sword displaced gold. Partial demonetization—like the abolition of the market mechanism and the restrictions on labor mobility—may have been

in the Polish discussions of 1956 (and later), see Brus and J. Pajestka in *Oxford Economic Papers,* N.S., IX, 2 (June 1957), 190–224.

[74] "The Structure and Organization of the Soviet Economy," pp. 212ff.

[75] Gerschenkron, *Economic Backwardness in Historical Perspective,* p. 26.

ideologically grounded, but its functional purpose was to constrict the individual's range of choice in the face of the state's demands upon him.

It was therefore not incongruous that the partial relaxation of Stalinist methods on the political and administrative planes was paralleled by a shift in the official attitude toward the place of money and related categories in the economy. If, on the one hand, Stalin foresaw (in the *Economic Problems of Socialism*) both a gradual tapering off of the role of money on the way to full communism and a step-by-step transformation of "commodities" into "products," the new received doctrine maintains that "commodity-money relations" will continue to expand steadily during the current stage of "construction of communism." True, this raises the irksome problem of how money is to be abolished upon society's arrival at full communism, but most Soviet economists seem content to leave its solution to the happier future. If Stalin denied the status of "commodities" (in the Marxian sense) to producer goods, these are now so designated and are thereby delivered to the operation of the law of value—though there is the widest disagreement about what this actually means and entails. As we have seen, the principles of price formation for producer goods and the evaluation (if not always pricing) of some original factors of production, such as land and mineral resources, have been hotly debated since 1956, after almost three decades of nearly complete silence on the subject. An important step forward taken in the late 1950's was the legitimation of the recoupment-period method in the selection of technological alternatives—in effect, a limited application of the interest rate to planning. The *actual payment* of interest by enterprises on the *whole* capital entrusted to them by the state is under discussion and may soon become a reality in the Soviet Union as it is in several other Eastern European countries.

In the realm of actual transactions (distinguished from planners' calculations), the post-Stalin remonetization has been confined largely to agriculture where relations *in natura* had been (and to some extent continue to be) especially conspicuous.[76] Otherwise, the demonetized areas have remained largely unaffected.

Even only within the state sector the purchase and sale of natural resources and intangibles would have to overcome major doctrinal hurdles, but payments by enterprises for the use of natural resources, such as meaningful and not merely nominal land rents, mineral rents, stumpage fees,[77] may be introduced along with the just-mentioned interest charges in order to induce managers to economize in the use of resources within their reach.

[76] See Frank A. Durgin, Jr., "Monetization and Policy in Soviet Agriculture Since 1952," *Soviet Studies*, XV, 4 (April 1964), 375–407; and Jerzy F. Karcz and V. P. Timoshenko, "Soviet Agricultural Policy, 1953–1962," *Food Research Institute Studies*, IV, 2 (1964), 123–163.

[77] Even the previous nominal land rental payments by nonagricultural state enterprises were abolished in 1955 and 1959, and farms have never paid any. Appreciable but inadequate stumpage fees were reintroduced in 1949.

By contrast, in the household sector, in addition to the remonetization of substantial parts of peasants' incomes and other similar measures, the official tendency—as yet only mildly promoted—is toward increasing, in the form of free services, the share of personal income accruing to individuals. Whereas the collectivized enterprises must be induced to economize, the already economizing households are to have more of their consumption collectivized.

Withal, the "expansion of commodity-money relations on the way to communism," surely a sensible policy even within the limits of a command-economy structure, should not be confused with promoting passive money into active money. This cannot be emphasized too strongly. The difference between the two may be one of degree in the sense that even under the most rigorous centralization some scope is necessarily left to the operation of *khozraschet*. Nonetheless, this difference of degree, if carried far enough, is crucial, pertaining as it does to the range of choice accorded to the economic agent and to the form in which this choice is cast. Under present Soviet conditions the increasing monetization of the economy is a significant but not fundamentally revolutionary development, insofar as it merely expands the scope of operation of *passive* money. Thus, not only was the substitution of transactions in money for certain relations in kind in the collective-farm sector of Soviet agriculture not a very radical advance, but generally it coincided with a marked tightening of administrative controls over the farms. Passive money may be thought of as a means of controllership—to borrow a term from the American world of business—in that giant corporation that Alfred G. Meyer has aptly called "USSR, Inc." The greater the monetization of the economy, the more effective the controllership, but not necessarily the wider the range of effective choice on the part of the economic agent.[78]

By contrast, the "activization" of money in the production sector would indeed be revolutionary for it would imply decision making at the firm level with primary reference to pecuniary advantage, an overriding pecuniary goal such as monetary profit, a substantial degree of enterprise autonomy, and a market mechanism of sorts for at least short-term coordination. On the planners' level, active money implies the primacy of decision-making rules over voluntarism, retreat from various technological biases and much of the short-term physical planning, and the assignment of *some* (not necessarily rational) prices to all scarce factors. It need not mean the abandonment of centrally posited social goals or of planning in the broad sense, least of all of long-term planning and macroeconomic guidance. Nevertheless, in many ways, both obvious and subtle—the con-

[78] This may be the point at which to remind the reader that we are now considering the production sector. In the household sector, money is essentially as active in the U.S.S.R. as anywhere in the sense that there is substantial freedom of consumer choice. As anywhere else (if not more so), money in the U.S.S.R. is subject

comitant organizational decentralization, the inculcation of Weberian formal rationality, the emphasis on corporate if not individual acquisitiveness (the latter is already emphasized within legal bounds by the "principle of material incentives"), the tighter drawing of the "veil of money" around economic relations, the depoliticization of much economic life, above all, because of an inevitable shift of power on the lower and middle rungs of economic life—the activization of money would be of the greatest sociopolitical import in the Soviet system.

In fact, passive money accords well not only with the processes of the command economy but also with the realities of the larger sociopolitical system of which the command structure is an integral part. From the standpoint of the (Western) monetary theorist, the passive money in the production sector of the Soviet economy is perhaps the closest approximation to that abstract and pure phenomenon, neutral money, neutral because largely powerless as an active determinant of social behavior. But from the standpoint of the social scientist it is anything but neutral precisely because it is powerless; that is to say, it has been rendered passive in order not to challenge the regime's political authority. In the little space remaining at our disposal in this essay we shall briefly comment on the relationship between passive money (or its activization) and several key sociopolitical elements of the Soviet system.

Social Goals and Priorities

In the economic domain, these are now by and large communicated directly to the producers, primarily in the form of planned targets and input rationing. The objectives of the economic unit and those of society have the same dimensions; if the regime wants more corn it orders more corn to be planted and if it wants to economize on copper it rations copper more tightly. Pricing *is* used to expand production or reduce consumption in the state sector, but only in an ancillary fashion. In Tinbergen's terminology, the economy's instrument variables are essentially the same as its target variables. Monetary prices of the original factors and of other inputs do not reflect to a substantial degree the social goals and priorities; they do not perform what Hans Hirsch calls the "evidence function" of money.[79] It is the political and administrative channels that carry the evidence function in the Soviet instance. The purpose of course is to enforce the will and safeguard the values of the dictatorship; some of the major

---

to the perils of inflation, a central problem of the Soviet-type economy that we must here leave aside for lack of space. (But see Andrzej Brzeski, *Inflation in Poland, 1945–1960* (Ph.D. dissertation), University of California, Berkeley, 1964, for an exhaustive treatment.)

    [79] *Quantity Planning*, p. 46. We should exempt wages from this generalization. There being a large measure of freedom of job choice, the situation regarding labor is different from that regarding other factors.

consequences are the politicization and ideologization of everyday economic life, bureaucratization and a certain inescapable amount of willfulness in the exercise of economic power, and a good deal of goal ambiguity and conflicting performance standards for the enterprise.[80]

The less Soviet money performs the evidence function as a unit of account, the more its moneyness—its potential command over resources—carries with it the power to subvert the official goals and priorities. On the other hand, the more passive the money, that is, the more its use is subordinated to physical planning and checked by materials allocation, the less its subversive potential. Yet, ironically, the same conditions ensure the prevalence of innumerable particular disequilibria, thereby inviting illegal uses of liquid funds. As a result, the bank balances of enterprises are deliberately held down to a minimum; currency holdings by them are virtually forbidden; the liquidity of funds is impaired through earmarking and transaction controls by the Bank, and decentralized methods of financing locally initiated projects—such as the modernization loans of our case study—are given only the minimal scope. Khrushchev's abortive proposal to turn over to the *sovnarkhozy* large lump sums for investment purposes (see above, Section V) stands out in this light as one of his most unrealistic ideas.

The Party and Other Organs of Supervision and Control

These, at least in their lower and intermediate levels, are essential components of the *economic* system. They thrive on the continual local crises. They goad on the sluggish, seek to safeguard the official values and priorities, and coordinate and expedite things. In other words, they do precisely what active money and its corollaries—equilibrium prices, profit seeking, market relations, an orderly conduct of affairs—would do for the economy. Passive money equals active Party. The converse—active money, passive Party—need not quite follow, for the Party may and most likely would (compare Yugoslavia) retain a crucial and decisive overall economic role. However, active money would deprive many Party functionaries of their present functions, powers, and benefits.

More generally, rationalization of economic activity tends to carry secularization in its wake, as the late Robert A. Brady forcefully argued thirty years ago in regard to the German experience of the twenties.[81] In the U.S.S.R. such a development would affect both the power position of the Party *apparat*—that "priesthood with police powers" in T. H. Rigby's

---

[80] That the last two have a definite eufunctional effect in the Soviet system has been strongly argued by Andrew Gunder Frank in "Goal Ambiguity and Conflicting Standards: An Approach to the Study of Organization," *Human Organization,* XVII, 4, 8–13.

[81] Robert A. Brady, *The Rationalization Movement in German Industry,* Berkeley, University of California Press, 1933 pp. 401ff.

phrase[82]—and the very basis of the Party's rule, insofar as it rests on ideological grounds. The veil of money thus blurs the sharp outlines of a totalitarian ideology.

Management

Management would presumably fall heir to many of the Party's functions, powers, and benefits in the event of the activization of money. Whether it would also welcome the attendant responsibilities is not certain. In such an event, present management would also have to meet serious challenges from two directions: from another breed of manager, not the production engineer but the adept manipulator of active money, a kind of socialist businessman; and from the rank and file who may start pressing for Yugoslav-style "self-management" as soon as the enterprise has a meaningful measure of autonomy, thanks to active money. Passive money protects the present power structure *within* the enterprise as well.

Secularization, rationalization, depoliticization, greater choice and competition—should these tendencies encroach upon the Soviet command economy with its passive money, the effects on the society are not likely to be limited to the economic sphere, a thesis that has been recently eloquently argued by T. H. Rigby.[83] Yet, for a sobering thought, we might note with Max Weber that "where complete market freedom is given, the highest degree of formal rationality in capital accounting is absolutely indifferent to all the substantive considerations [by which he meant the ultimate social goals and ethical requirements] involved. But it is precisely the existence of these substantive factors underlying monetary calculations which determine a fundamental limitation on its rationality."[84] He was thinking of the distribution of *income*. Alexander Gerschenkron has expressed a similar idea in terms more consonant with the half-century that has elasped since Weber wrote: ". . . more important than economic efficiency is—to use Thomas Hardy's phrase—the economics of vitality, or, I should say, of viability of dictatorship. It is my belief that in dictatorships the delegation of power means its diminution. Decentralization of decision making must needs lead to the erosion of that power. And power is the resource that a dictatorship must husband above all other resources."[85]

[82] "Traditional, Market, and Organizational Societies and the USSR," *World Politics,* XVI, 4 (July 1964), 552. Rigby feels, however, that the phrase fails to do justice to the Party's administrative and economic functions.

[83] *Ibid.*

[84] *The Theory of Social and Economic Organization* (edited with an introduction by Talcott Parsons). Free Press, Glencoe, Ill., 1964 printing, p. 212; also, Parsons' comments, pp. 33ff.

[85] *The Stability of Dictatorships,* Harvard lecture. Yale University Press, New Haven, 1963, pp. 10–11.

FOREIGN TRADE BEHAVIOR OF CENTRALLY PLANNED ECONOMIES

Franklyn D. Holzman
Tufts University

The earliest comprehensive and still relevant analysis of foreign trade in a centrally planned economy (CPE) can be found in Alexander Gerschenkron's Economic Relations with the U.S.S.R.[1] In large part, the present paper constitutes an extension of his work.

Traditionally, the foreign trade behavior of centrally planned economies has been characterized by a notoriously high degree of autarky, currency inconvertibility, bilateralism and discrimination. Although these phenomena occur also in trade among capitalist nations, they do not constitute its "normal" features. Not only are the capitalist deviations from uncontrolled trade of lesser significance, but the issues they raise often differ from those raised by Eastern European trade controls. This is primarily because of the impress on the foreign trade mechanism of certain unique characteristics of the centrally planned economies.

An attempt will be made in this paper to show the effects of central planning on foreign trade practices. In Section I the special characteristics

● Many ideas for this paper developed while I was a consultant to the United Nations in 1963. My ideas were clarified in discussions there with Sidney Dell. Rudolph Nötel, Nita Watts, Stein Rossen, Juri Ryska, and Valery Naborov. I am also indebted to Joseph Berliner, Richard Caves, Herbert Levine, Charles Kindleberger, Egon Neuberger and Raymond Vernon for comments on an early draft. The views reflected in the paper are my own and should not necessarily be attributed to any of the above individuals or organizations with which they are connected. Finally, I am indebted for financial assistance to the American Council of Learned Societies.

[1] This brief monograph was published in New York in 1945 by the Committee on International Economic Policy in cooperation with the Carnegie Endowment for International Peace.

of centrally planned economies that influence their foreign trade will be briefly described. Next, in Section II, it will be shown how they, together with some other relevant factors, affect foreign trade behavior. Finally, a few suggestions, emerging from the analysis, for amelioration of trade within the basic framework of central planning will be outlined in Section III.

I

We outline below certain characteristics of centrally planned economies which affect their foreign trade behavior. Some of these characteristics (and the foreign trade behavior resulting), should not be viewed as absolutely necessary to central planning, nor are they present to the same degree in each of the centrally planned economies. They are included because they have been relevant in most Eastern European nations until the present time.

"Irrational" Internal Cost and Price Structures and Disequilibrium Exchange Rates

The prevalence of "irrational" costs and prices in the centrally planned economies is almost universally acknowledged and needs little elaboration. Basically, these are the result of: (a) extensive use of differential sales taxes and subsidies to implement certain internal policies;[2] (b) the Marxist failure fully to account in the cost structure for rent, interest, and depreciation; and (c) insensitivity of prices to supply-demand forces.

Another well-known feature of these economics is the prevalence of disequilibrium exchange rates. Those, of course, are of negligible practical importance anyway, because of the direct controls used to plan and implement foreign trade.[3]

Autarky

The desire for self-sufficiency in those commodities produced at a comparative disadvantage motivates all nations to some extent, thereby reducing the possible volume of world trade. The nations with centrally planned economies appear to be more strongly motivated in this direction than capitalist economies, for the following well-known reasons. First,

---

[2] Such as, for example, a high rate of investment and military expenditures (large sales tax), or encouragement of new types of capital equipment (subsidies).

[3] Whether exchange rates are in equilibrium is of little importance, of course, given the prevalence of irrational prices. Under the latter condition, unrestricted trade at the equilibrium exchange rate cannot be relied upon to benefit the domestic economy (see below).

because of the complicated input-output interrelationships among intermediate products, most of which are directly allocated, central planners try to avoid heavy dependence of the domestic economy on foreign supplies and, thus, to insulate it from the vagaries, both imaginary and real, of the world market.[4] Second, all nations endeavor to achieve a certain degree of self-sufficiency for reasons of military security—to diminish the risks of economic warfare. Owing to this universal desire, countries where all industry is nationalized are likely to reduce trade to a greater extent than those in which a large part of economic activity is in private hands.[5, 6] Under capitalism, competition exists naturally and protection requires an explicit act by the government; under central planning as it is presently practiced, protection is the rule unless the government makes an explicit decision to allow imports to replace domestic production. Third, the autarkic bias of centrally planned economies may possibly be enhanced by their irrational price systems; in fact, it is often very difficult for the planners to decide what they should trade. These are serious impediments to trade.[7]

State Trading

It has been said that " . . . economic planning of the type practiced in Russia is not feasible without the use of a foreign trade

---

[4] This view is not restricted, in the centrally planned economies, only to the international trade but has its counterparts in domestic trade. In the Soviet Union, for example, one of the major reasons for the 1957 reorganization was the fact that the ministries and enterprises developed autarkic policies which led to excessive cross-hauling (within ministries) and an inordinately low level of subcontracting by enterprises. Since the reorganization, regional autarky (*mestnichestvo*) has been adopted by individual *sovnarkhozy* and has created similar problems. The reasons for these local exhibitions of autarkic behavior are somewhat different from that at the international level. Lack of dependability in the former case is due primarily to difficulties with the internal direct-allocation supply system and to the managerial incentive system.

[5] This factor operates to curtail Eastern trade with the West much more than intra-bloc trade. Along these same lines might be mentioned the desire of many nations to industrialize at any cost rather than submit to comparative advantage even when long-run comparative advantage suggests less industrialization. Rumania is a case in point. (*New York Times,* January 19, 1964, p. 21.)

[6] The strategic controls imposed by Western nations on trade with the East also contribute somewhat to the low level of East-West trade, although much less so now than in the past decade.

[7] In the early 1930's, the Soviets increased foreign trade temporarily to meet urgent needs and to lessen the dependence on imports over the long run. The import:GNP ratio rose from less than 1 per cent to almost 4 per cent in 1932 and then declined to $\frac{1}{2}$ per cent by 1937. See this writer's "Foreign Trade" in *Economic Trends in the Soviet Union,* edited by A. Bergson and S. Kuznets, Cambridge, 1963,

monopoly . . ."[8] Whatever the reasons, foreign trade is nationalized in the centrally planned economies and is usually conducted by combines which function as agents of the state. This has at least three major consequences for foreign trade behavior.

First, among the Eastern nations, foreign trade is conducted primarily to obtain essential imports. Exports are considered not as an end in themselves but as a means to finance the necessary imports.[9] This view of the foreign trade process seems natural enough since the CPE nations, typically pursuing overfull employment policies (see below) can hardly be interested in mere employment effects of exports. If, notwithstanding this, some of the CPE nations have led intensive export promotion campaigns, it was because of the balance-of-payment pressures generated by rapid growth (see below), that is, ultimately, to pay for rising imports. In the West, the level of exports is just as (if not more) important a goal as the level of imports. Some individual traders export, others import, with gains to the economy, presumably reflected in private profits, in either case.

Second, the centrally planned economies take a barter-type approach to foreign trade and view exports and imports as interdependent. Profitability is assessed primarily with respect to overall "terms of trade" rather than on the basis of profit on each individual transaction. This is a consequence of the import orientation of trade (above) as well as of "irrational" internal prices, and of the predisposition, inherited from internal planning, to operate in categories of physical allocations.

Third, because foreign trade is run by a state monopoly, tariffs are basically redundant; trade is controlled by implicit import and export quotas. The decisions to trade are made directly by the government, often without the mediation of price comparisons. In the absence of such explicit decisions, trade will not take place, a reaction equivalent to that achieved by employing prohibitive quotas. By comparison, in capitalist nations profitable opportunities for trade may be pursued unless the government makes an explicit decision to the contrary. Such decisions may be implemented by tariffs, quotas, or exchange controls.

---

p. 290. Statistics on the degree of autarky in each Eastern nation are contained in F. Pryor, *The Communist Foreign Trade System*, Cambridge, 1963, p. 27.

[8] Gerschenkron, *op. cit.*, p. 18. It should be noted that the character of the state trading could be substantially changed if internal planning practices were "liberalized."

[9] "Russia exports solely in order to obtain the wherewithal for payments for imports. In this sense, she is likely to live up to the classical doctrine of foreign trade and to reject the tenets of mercantilism. This, no doubt, sounds paradoxical, but is undeniable. From the Russian point of view exports are a loss and not a gain." (*Ibid.*, p. 47.)

Overfull Employment Planning

An important aspect of the centrally planned economies has been their tendency, not unlike that of capitalist nations during wartime, to over-commitment of resources. The resulting excess demand by consumers for final products and by enterprises for factors and intermediate products expresses itself as either open or repressed inflation. Moreover, the strained plans lead to sellers' markets and to a relative lack of concern for the quality of output,[10] including goods for export. Although overfull employment planning is presently less pervasive than it was in earlier years, it still persists.

Quantity Targeting

Generally, enterprises have as their major goals output targets stated in physical or value terms rather than in other so-called success indicators such as profits, cost reduction, and so forth. This, together with the fact that most intermediate products are directly allocated, reinforces the tendency noted just above for management to be less concerned with "quality" than it otherwise might.

Rapid Economic Growth

Rapid economic growth is the overriding goal of the centrally planned economies, one in which they have achieved signal successes. The process of growth usually, though not always, generates import requirements more naturally and easily than exportable items.

Method of Balances

Supply and demand for most intermediate products are balanced quantitatively by direct controls—in the Eastern European nations. This procedure, known as the "method of balances," is used because central allocation rather than the market performs the task of distributing essential industrial supplies.

This concludes the brief survey of various characteristics of centrally planned economies which have an impact on foreign trade behavior. Some (the first three) are more important for our purposes than others, but they are all included for completeness.

II

We turn now to foreign trade behavior. The most important and interesting are the related problems of inconvertibility and bilateralism, which will be treated first. Others, discussed below, have to do with discrimination, most-favored-nation (MFN) clauses, monopoly power, and dumping.

[10] Quality here refers to all characteristics of a commodity including delivery.

INCONVERTIBILITY

Currency convertibility in its commonly used meaning refers to the right or possibility of the holder of a currency to exchange it for gold or for "hard" currencies. Limitations are placed on convertibility when a currency is in excess supply on foreign exchange markets or, what amounts to the same, when other currencies or gold are in excess demand by the holders of the currency in question. Among capitalist nations such limitations on convertibility are likely to be put in force if a currency is overvalued, owing to inflation or to more fundamental structural factors. With overvaluation, there is a tendency for imports to exceed exports. Usually, nonresidents are allowed to convert current earnings of the currency in question into their own currencies; balance is maintained by restricting imports, that is, by placing limits on convertibility for residents.[11]

Why are the currencies of the centrally planned economies, say, the ruble, inconvertible? Before the revaluations of 1961 most, if not all, Eastern European currencies were overvalued. Overvaluation, although a sufficient condition for inconvertibility under capitalism, is neither necessary nor relevant, given the foreign trade institutions and practices of the centrally planned economies. So long as internal prices are disorderly and world prices are used as the basis for trade, and the composition and volume of trade are determined by direct controls and administered by a foreign trade monopoly, the exchange rate remains merely an accounting device. Its changes have no effect on trade. Thus, for instance, the substantial devaluations of April 1936 and January 1961, both of which brought the ruble into rough equilibrium in a purchasing power parity sense,[12] had no discernible impact on either the volume, composition, or manner in which Soviet trade is conducted.

[11] Under extreme circumstances, nonresidents may be denied convertibility into their own currencies, particularly on capital account. Whether nonresidents are allowed to transfer the currency in question to residents of third countries depends on the degree of overvaluation with respect to all other currencies. Usually, conversion is allowed into "softer" but not into "harder" currencies or into gold. At present, any bloc currency is probably equally "soft," relative to the major Western currencies since general convertibility prevails in the West. On the other hand, my guess is that some bloc currencies are less desirable than others in intra-bloc trade although "which" and "by how much" are impossible to say under the present institutional arrangements.

[12] By this we mean that the foreign trade prices (that is, world prices) of goods exported and imported are, on the average, approximately equal to the domestic prices of the same goods at the given exchange rate. Given the controls which exist over Soviet trade, this appears to be the only operational definition of exchange rate equilibrium which is possible. Equilibrium, under this definition may deviate substantially from "true" equilibrium, of course. A more extended discussion of this point is contained in this writer's "Soviet Foreign Trade Pricing and Exchange Rate Policies," unpublished.

Currency inconvertibility in centrally planned economies is in part a reaction to balance-of-payment pressures and the lack of sufficient foreign exchange reserves. Yet, although these factors (related to rapid growth, overfull employment planning, inadaptability of exports, and repressed inflation) might partly justify the prohibition against converting domestic currency into foreign exchange by residents, they can hardly be adduced to explain the existing convertibility restrictions on nonresidents. Typically, the Soviet bloc laws do not permit nonresidents to convert domestic currencies into foreign exchange or gold, nor do they even allow them to accumulate such currencies.[13] These extreme legal restrictions on convertibility (to be explained below) obviously reduce the demand for bloc currencies. Their effect, additionally weakening the international financial standing of the bloc nations, has been superimposed on other factors discouraging the potential nonresident demand for bloc currencies. Clearly, even if foreigners were allowed to accumulate rubles, for example, their demand for Soviet currency would be blunted by circumstances always present under central planning.

First, there would be the considerable uncertainty on the part of nonresidents regarding the possibility of purchasing goods with bloc currencies. Nonresidents are quite limited in the scope of possible purchases from the Eastern European nations, not because the latter do not have a large fund of exportables but because most commodity flows are directly planned and it is difficult to buy items not earmarked for export (implicit trade controls). That is to say, within the existing system of allocation, foreign holders of, say, rubles, are not allowed much, if any, opportunity to compete for goods with Soviet enterprises and domestic consumers. Their difficulties might be additionally increased by the fact that trade negotiations are usually conducted with special foreign trade organizations subordinate to the foreign trade monopoly rather than directly with producing or distributing enterprises. This substantial limitation on purchases by nonresidents is aptly called by Oscar Altman, "commodity inconvertibility," in contrast with "currency inconvertibility."[14]

Second, uncertainty generated by inaccessibility of bloc exportables is compounded by the irrationality of internal pricing and the overvalued exchange rates which make it difficult to determine in advance of negoti-

[13] Exceptions to this rule occur in the use of temporary imbalances in bilaterally balanced trade relationships as well as according to provisions in some bilateral agreements for payment in gold or convertible currency if imbalances exceed prescribed limits for a period of time.

[14] Oscar Altman, "Russian Gold and The Ruble," *Staff Papers,* April 1960, pp. 430–431. Note that "commodity convertibility" essentially means absence of restrictions on exports. The term "free trade" on the other hand, is typically used to denote absence of restrictions on imports, though in theory it encompasses exports as well.

ations the prices at which goods may be bought or sold. The foreign trade prices, therefore, usually deviate considerably from domestic prices and are, as a "first approximation," based on "world prices." Although this practice largely eliminates the overvaluation problem and may, additionally, reduce somewhat the uncertainty (due to irrational internal prices) in the case of simple standardized commodities, the prices of complex products remain quite conjectural. Finally, uncertainty as to the "value" of a ruble is still further increased by factors mentioned above concerning the quality, delivery, and general unadaptability of exports to foreign makets.[15] To sum up, from the point of view of nonresidents, bloc currencies are not only inconvertible in the usual sense, but also undesirable because of the substantial uncertainties regarding their exchangeability for goods.

Owing to the significance and uniqueness of "commodity inconvertibility" of bloc currencies it is impossible to explain its existence and implementation without discussing the foreign trade monopolies of centrally planned economies.

First, and most important, since central planning is implemented primarily by direct allocation of resources, the planners deem it necessary to insulate the flows of products from external disruption. This is accomplished by the foreign trade monopoly by prohibition of foreign-held ruble balances and by inconvertibility of rubles into other currencies as well as commodities.

Second, when internal prices are not "rational" as indicators of the relative values of goods to the planners or in terms of some measure of "real costs" (for reasons discussed earlier), free trade (commodity convertibility) cannot be allowed (nor can the foreign trade monopoly be dispensed with) because it would lead to a pattern of trade disadvantageous to the centrally planned economies and productive large gains for their Western trading partners.[16]

This is easily demonstrated in Chart 1. Let A represent the desired position on the production possibilities curve of the planned economy.[17] Let P_i be the actual internal price ratio set by the planners, putting a high price (sales tax) on consumers' goods relative to that for producers' goods

---

[15] One might also mention here that Western governmental controls and consumers' resistance to imports from the bloc countries have similar effects on the "value" of their currencies.

[16] Gains and losses would probably be erratically distributed in intra-bloc trade. Note: the next three paragraphs assume an "equilibrium" exchange rate but irrational internal prices. These constitute the more serious and intractable problem.

[17] Whether a planned economy with characteristics as described above would be likely to reach its production possibilities curve is a problem that cannot be discussed here.

CHART 1

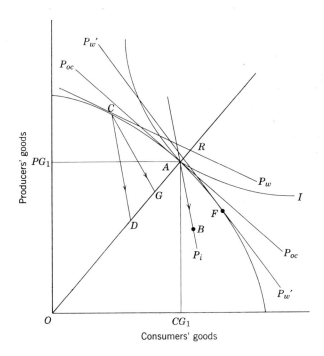

Consumers' goods

(in comparison with a real cost ratio of P_{oc}). Assume a world price ratio, P_w. Clearly, foreigners will be happy to import producers' goods and export consumers' goods to the planned economy. If output remains at A, trade at internal prices will take place along P_i in a southeasterly direction to, say, B where the planned economy is clearly worse off, not only being on a lower indifference curve, but also not having the desired mix of goods, OA. If production is shifted to C (to take advantage of what appears to be comparative advantage) and trade then leads to the desired mix of goods, the new after-trade position will be a "low" OD.[18] Even if trade were transacted at P_w, there would be a tendency to trade at a point beyond the optimum because of the exaggerated spread between P_i and P_w.

Still another possibility would be the case if the internal price ratio, P_i, were steeper than the ratio of world prices, P'_w, whereas the latter in turn would exceed the real cost ratio P_{oc}. If this were the case, the comparative advantage would lie in consumers' goods, yet the tendency would be to export producers' goods.[19] Here the losses are due not only to accep-

[18] One can similarly show that the gains to the Western nation would be exceptionally large.

[19] Production would be somewhat above A (say C) and exporting would be along a line parallel to P_i (for example, CD).

tance of poorer terms of trade than necessary (as in the previous case), but also to specializing in the wrong goods. It is interesting to note that in this case not only trade at internal prices, but trade at world prices, leads to losses owing to incorrect specialization. Thus if production is at point C, trade will lead to G.

Let us sum up these conclusions in another way. Given the irrationality of internal prices, resident convertibility (free imports) cannot be allowed because it will lead to large-scale importation of commodities which have relatively high prices but which, in fact, may be more cheaply produced at home (for example, many consumers' goods). On the other hand, strict controls over exports,[20] discouraging potential ruble holdings by foreigners, must be maintained lest nonresidents compete in domestic markets for goods which, owing to subsidies or some other costing quirk, have a low price but, in fact, are expensive to produce. Nonresident "free" expenditure within the bloc countries cannot be allowed, because it may involve losses to their domestic economies. As noted earlier, the bloc nations do not grant convertibility rights to nonresidents except in the special instance when the swing credit limits of a bilateral agreement are exceeded. Moreover, foreigners are usually prohibited from accumulating bloc currencies, whether within or outside the centrally planned economies. The only exception to this prohibition is that made for temporary imbalances within the rigid framework of bilateral trade agreements. Presumably, this is because the availability of bloc currencies to outsiders might lead to large discounts in world currency markets, something the Eastern European planners undoubtedly wish to avoid.[21]

[20] Which exist, as we saw above, partly because of the direct-control method of balances approach to supply planning.

[21] It might be argued that the bloc nations could avoid the pricing-uncertainty problem by pricing net of sales taxes and subsidies *or* that they could circumvent the internal price problem by simply agreeing to buy or sell freely at world prices. Although it is true that the pricing predicament is somewhat overstated by the consumer-producer goods dichotomy in the text, it is also true that sales taxes and subsidies are not the only reasons for irrational prices in the bloc countries (see section I). If it were, the bloc countries would undoubtedly have solved by this time the intra-bloc pricing problem and would no longer have to rely on the embarrassing solution of using world prices in their trade. The many articles which have been published in the Eastern European journals on how to choose commodities for foreign trade are a tribute to the intractability of the problem (see Pryor, *op. cit.*, Ch. 4 for a sample of the East German literature). A recent Soviet source makes the following commentary: "Wholesale prices, as is known, do not reflect with adequate completeness and precision the socially-necessary labor outlays for the manufacture of goods. Prices of means of production are mainly below value while the prices of many consumer goods are above value. Moreover, the prices of goods within each of these departments also diverge from their value. Thus, numerically-equal outlays of social labor are expressed in different prices. The use of such wholesale prices in internal trade leads to a certain violation of the equivalence of exchange. *That is why, in our opinion, the internal wholesale prices now*

In the case of Western nations with inconvertible currencies, nonresidents are encouraged to hold, or spend, the "inconvertible" currency—the problem is that they don't want to. The centrally planned economies are in the peculiar position of being unable to try to boost their exports, thereby improving the position of their currency, by allowing nonresidents freely to import from them.[22, 23]

BILATERALISM[24]

The percentage of bilaterally conducted trade is higher in the centrally planned economies than in either the Western industrial or the developing

---

in force cannot be utilized for forming a new system of prices in trade between the socialist countries (italics in original). Otherwise the prices of the world socialist market would have the same shortcomings as the internal wholesale prices and would not reflect the outlays of socially necessary labor. In view of the fact that the composition of exports and imports of countries is not the same, trade at such prices would bring about an unjustified redistribution of the national income. States in which the share of goods with prices below value is higher for exports than for imports would turn over part of their national income to countries with a bigger share of exports at prices above value." (A. Alekseev and A. Borisenko, "A Price Basis of its Own," *Problems of Economics,* April 1964, p. 47, translated from *Ekonomicheskaia gazeta,* March 9, 1963.)

As for world prices, they are at present clearly an uneasy expedient. For one thing, there are few, if any, homogeneous commodities. In addition, even in those instances in which commodities appear to be virtually homogeneous, it turns out that different prices are quoted from place to place and from month to month. The concept "world price" is largely an abstraction for the purpose at hand. Finally, even if there were "world prices," they would not always be relevant for pricing bloc products because of the differing comparative advantage (supply-demand) conditions within and without the bloc.

[22] The problem of freeing trade and establishing convertibility with disequilibrium prices is the foreign trade counterpart of the internal problem of decentralizing and using the profit motive without rationalizing the price structure.

[23] From another point of view, one can demonstrate that commodity convertibility (free trade) is an impossibility under the assumptions underlying Chart 1. Suppose that convertibility is decreed and the planners shift to production point C in order to engage in trade. The planners would try to trade at world prices, P_w, and in so doing they would actually reach a higher welfare point, $OR;$ the West, on the other hand, would want to trade at P_i (along CD). One could not have two entirely different sets of relative prices existing side by side for long. Since the planners would be unwilling to trade without limit at P_i, whereas the West would trade at either P_i or P_w, albeit preferring the former, the planners (presumably unwilling to allow their prices to "adjust" to changing trade relationships [the counterpart of free choice rather than sovereignty in consumers' goods markets] and world prices) would soon retreat to inconvertibility and trade controls.

[24] A valuable study dealing with this problem is that of R. F. Mikesell and J. N. Behrman, *Financing Free World Trade with the Sino-Soviet Bloc,* Princeton Study in International Finance No. 8, Princeton, 1958.

nations. Moreover, it is higher now than it used to be in the same economies during the 1930's when they were still in the capitalist orbit.[25] Intra-bloc trade is more bilateral than East-West trade.[26] Institutionally, the high degree of bilateralism is accomplished by means of annual and long-term trade and payment agreements which attempt, within limits and after taking account of credits, to keep trade between the two participating countries in balance over the period in question. These agreements are implemented, of course, by direct governmental controls over the level and composition of imports and exports.

The centrally planned economies recognize the advantages of multilateralism and have even taken some tentative steps toward increasing its scope in intra-bloc transactions. Why, despite that very recognition, bilateralism is still so strongly adhered to can be attributed to currency inconvertibility and the factors behind it discussed above. Since no nation is willing to hold balances in rubles, *levs*, and so forth, payments of the centrally planned economies must be balanced insofar as they are unable to produce gold or develop export surpluses with convertible currency nations.

A second factor leading to bilateralism is the tendency among bloc countries to strive for overall payments balance (especially among themselves), and therefore, erroneously, for bilateral balance (see below). The main reason for the attempt to achieve overall balance has to do with the already discussed view that exports are not an end in themselves but simply a means of financing imports. To the extent that trade policy is guided by such considerations, there is a tendency to strive for an overall payments balance, in the first place, there is no strong incentive to develop an overall export surplus. Next, imports are confined by controls to the amount which can be financed currently through exports, previous policies of not developing export surpluses having produced no large foreign exchange reserves. Consequently, like all nations under balance of payments

---

[25] Michael Michaely's ("Multilateral Balancing in International Trade," *American Economic Review,* September 1962), calculations show the following. The share of trade conducted multilaterally in 1958 averaged (unweighted) 29.2 per cent for all non-Soviet nations. In comparison, the share of multilateral trade for five Soviet bloc nations in 1958 was 9.6 per cent. The same nations averaged 23.8 per cent in 1938.

[26] My own calculations for 1958, using Michaely's method (*op. cit.*), give the following percentages of multilateral trade in intra-bloc, as opposed to East-West, transactions:

	Intra-Bloc	*East-West*
U.S.S.R.	8.7	26.1
Bulgaria	4.5	16.3
Poland	8.6	18.8

pressures (owing to rapid growth, difficulties in adapting to export markets, and so forth), centrally planned economies resort to the ultimate adjustment of payments by limiting imports to the level of possible exports.

Now, the necessity or desire to achieve overall balance does not logically require bilateral balancing by nation. Among capitalist nations, however, it has been observed that nations with export marketing problems sometimes resort to bilateral balancing agreements to absorb each other's second-line exportables. The propensity to do so is much stronger among the planned economies. In fact, it is difficult to see how a substantial degree of multilateralism could be achieved by these economies, simultaneously with the desired overall balance. The twin objectives are accomplished imperfectly under capitalism via the automatic operation of price, income, and capital flow adjustment mechanisms that do not function under central planning. The easiest way to achieve overall balance in the latter case is undoubtedly by planning for a high degree of bilateral balance.[27]

Envision the difficulty of planned multilateralism with overall balance. Suppose country A trades with B, C, and D. Overall balance can be achieved by relatively simple balancing with each nation. This is not to say that bilateral balancing is easy, for it undoubtedly requires considerable negotiation and, on the part of one or both partners, either some uneconomic trading or the foregoing of some profitable trading. On the other hand, suppose A runs a surplus with B. This means that A (B) goes into negotiations with C and D requiring a net deficit (surplus) equal to the surplus (deficit) with B (A). But there may be no particular reason why C and D should want to run surpluses with A exactly to offset deficits with B. Under planning, where prices are misleading and only the relatively few goods specifically earmarked for export or import can be traded, nations may be loathe to accept a surplus (deficit) with another nation because of the subsequent difficulty of buying (selling) more than can be sold to (bought from) third countries. This, in effect, is equivalent to a situation in which the various inconvertible currencies have different values to different holders. If interest conflicts occur along these lines, there is no economic adjustment mechanism to resolve them. An administrative reconciliation, if any, would undoubtedly involve a substantial reduction of profitable trade and/or addition of unprofitable trade. The problems are likely multiplied as the number of nations in the system increases. (In a system with economic adjustment mechanisms, the problems would probably be lessened as the number of nations increased.)

A third factor encouraging bilateralism is the opportunity that bilateral agreements offer the economically stronger nations (often, in this context, the nation least dependent on the trade in question) to improve

[27] Further discussion of this point will be found on p. 262.

the terms of trade. This possibility may motivate the Soviet Union, at least, to trade bilaterally with its smaller partners.

Fourth, the tendency toward bilateral balancing in foreign trade may be strengthened by carryover from the general use of an analogous technique, the "method of balances," in internal commodity planning.

Finally, some of the non-bloc nations with which the centrally planned economies trade prefer bilateral arrangements because of balance of payments problems. Even if a centrally planned economy were prepared to trade on a multilateral basis, it would be forced into bilateral trade by such trading partners.[28]

FOREIGN TRADE DISCRIMINATION

A basic objective of the Western trading community has been to achieve trade without discrimination. In the foreign trade usage discrimination means that one not buy in the lowest—or sell in the highest—price markets.[29] To the extent that restrictions (tariffs, quotas) are applied to trade, the objective is to have them applied equally to all nations, that is, in a nondiscriminatory manner. Foreign trade discrimination may be motivated by either economic or political factors; discussion will proceed from the former to the latter.

Inconvertibility and bilateralism have almost inevitably involved the introduction of apparently discriminatory controls by capitalist nations; the situation is similar in the case of the centrally planned economies. Western nations discriminate against their trade partners *via* exchange controls and explicit commodity and/or country import quotas. The centrally planned economies achieve the same results by implicit controls which are the outcome of implementing planning decisions regarding the volume, content, and direction of trade.

Among Western nations, where inconvertibility has often been due to overvaluation, serious questions have been raised whether those apparently discriminatory practices observed have in fact really constituted true discrimination.[30] Suppose, as was the case after World War II, that the British pound was overvalued with respect to the U.S. dollar, but not with respect to the Greek drachma. Suppose also that, at going exchange rates,

---

[28] For continuity, the reader is referred to the discussion in section III of possible reforms relating to the inconvertibility-bilateralism problems.

[29] The term price is taken here to include all commercial considerations. In contrast with foreign trade discrimination, monopolistic price discrimination means using market power to buy cheaper and sell dearer than the competitive price. See this writer's "Discrimination in International Trade," *American Economic Review*, December 1949, pp. 1234–1244.

[30] That is, not buying in the cheapest and selling in the dearest markets.

Greek tobacco was more expensive than American tobacco. If the British bought Greek rather than American tobacco, they could be accused, under current conventions, of not buying in the cheapest market, hence of discriminating. It could be argued, however, that if one takes into account the overvaluation of pound and drachma vis-à-vis dollar, Greek tobacco is actually cheaper to the British than American tobacco, and that the apparent discrimination is an illusion resulting from the maintenance of unrealistic pegged exchange rates.[31] It could also be argued that adherence to the ideal of nondiscriminatory application of quotas and exchange controls under these circumstances would unduly and unfairly reduce the volume of trade.

Can discrimination by the centrally planned economies be rationalized on similar grounds? The answer is a hesitant yes, hesitant because the reason is somewhat different. As we have seen, inconvertibility of bloc currencies cannot substantively be attributed to overvaluation in a "purchasing power parity" sense. In fact, by adopting world prices as a first approximation in their foreign trade negotiations, the CPE's are in effect adopting implicit exchange rates which are, in the purchasing power parity sense, "equilibrium" rates.

On the other hand, however, one could interpret the various uncertainties, mentioned earlier, which are responsible for inconvertibility, as indications of a discounted value of currency. Presumably, there is some discount rate at which foreigners would be willing to hold rubles, *levs*, and so forth, if allowed to.[32] Or, more realistically, one might say there is a price (interest rate, terms of trade) at which foreigners could be prevailed upon to adapt themselves to large-scale, bilaterally balanced trade with bloc nations. The extensive trade of the centrally planned economies with each other at the expense of trade with non-bloc nations, then, may be attributed in part at least, not to discrimination but to the unwillingness of non-bloc nations to adapt themselves, without a charge, to large-scale trade with the centrally planned economies, under the CPE ground rules. To the extent that there is trade between West and East, it is conducted largely according to the former's ground rules—multilaterally, with imbalances settled in convertible currencies or gold.[33]

The extraordinarily large amount of foreign trade discrimination

---

[31] See Holzman, *op. cit.*

[32] There may not be an exchange rate which would eliminate the currency discounts—that is, reduce the interest rate in question to zero—since the discount is not entirely due to overvaluation.

[33] If bloc exchange rates were operational, rather than merely accounting devices, then because of the discount on bloc currencies, prices in intra-bloc trade would tend to be higher than prices in East-West or West-West trade. In fact, as we have seen, bloc trade is conducted at world prices regardless of the exchange rate

which does exist between East and West[34] is ascribable not primarily to the economic factors just discussed but to politically strategic factors. Both the centrally planned and the Western nations are guilty of politically motivated trade discrimination. Important special instruments of such discrimination are: (a) the controls by the United States and COCOM nations over so-called strategic exports to the centrally planned economies as well as (b) the strong preferences[35] for direct intra-bloc trade among the centrally planned economies. The chances for growth of political discrimination are greater in the centrally planned economies than in the Western nations because of nationalization of trade resulting in closer interconnection between political and economic decisions. The interconnection is inevitably less intimate where the conduct of trade is largely in the hands of private enterprise. Finally, it is worth noting that if discrimination results from the formation of preferential trade areas and customs unions in the West, it usually takes the form of differential tariffs. The CPE's, on the other hand, implement their "customs union" by implicit quotas. Whereas it is possible for outsiders, if they can surmount tariff barriers, to buy or sell within a Western customs union, it is much more difficult for the outsider, regardless of cost-advantage or need, to break into the planned intra-bloc trade.

MFN CLAUSE TARIFF PROBLEMS[36]

The nations of Eastern Europe customarily request MFN treatment on tariffs in their trade with the West. In return, they purport to reciprocate in ways described in section III below. The usefulness of such reciprocal guarantees has been questioned in the West ever since the late 1920's when the U.S.S.R. revived its trade with Europe. The question is of considerable importance today because so much of the increase in world trade

---

and under these circumstances, the potential discount on bloc currencies cannot easily be isolated statistically. The actual statistical picture shows bloc exports to the West at lower prices and imports from the West at higher prices than those prevailing in intra-bloc trade. This is believed the result largely of Western discrimination against and controls over trade with the East. (See this writer's articles in the *Review of Economics and Statistics,* May and November, 1962; and in *Soviet Studies,* July, 1965.)

[34] The evidence for this is that today's intra-bloc trade amounts to almost three-fourths of the trade of these nations (Eastern Europe), whereas their mutual trade amounted to only about one-fourth of the total before World War II.

[35] These have substantially weakened in thet past few years.

[36] The effect of the most-favored-nation clause is to place on the conceding State the obligation to grant to the nationals and goods of the beneficiary State, either in general or in certain specified respects, the treatment accorded or in future to be accorded to the nationals and goods of the State receiving most favorable treatment in the territory of the conceding State.

and reduction in trade discrimination comes about through the mutual lowering of tariff barriers in which the MFN clause plays an obvious role.

The basic difficulty faced by the CPE nations in adapting to the MFN clause on tariffs is quite obvious. Whereas in the West the mutual cutting of tariffs provides a free market price criterion of the appropriate change in volume and distribution of trade, in the centrally planned economies the decisions (a) to import or not to import and (b) from whom to import,[37] are made quantitatively by quotas that are implicit in the planning process. It is well known that sensitivity to price is in this case much lower than in capitalist countries. It is also worth noting that regardless of the level of tariff, in a centrally planned economy,[38] imported commodities are ordinarily sold at the same price as comparable domestically produced goods. Differences between the "import price plus cost of distribution plus tariff" and the price of the comparable domestically produced goods are equalized by offsetting taxes or subsidies. When the planners have finally decided to import a commodity, tariffs have no impact on final domestic price—nor is the domestic price necessarily affected (in the short run, at least) by the decision to increase through imports the availability of a commodity. Last, but not least, import decisions continue to be largely "quantitative"; tariffs cannot be allowed to assume their usual market functions so long as exchange rates are in disequilibrium and the relationship between internal prices and costs of production is distorted.

During the past few years, the Soviet Union and Hungary have introduced new double-column tariffs with the clear purpose of providing bargaining weapons against discriminatory treatment by EEC and EFTA.[39] Those nations which do not grant the Soviet Union and Hungary MFN treatment will pay duties according to the higher of the two tariff schedules, all others according to the lower. The foreign trade combines presumably will have an incentive to shift their purchases to countries which receive the lower schedule of duties, because both their profits and the premia based on these profits are reduced by imports from the higher tariff countries.[40] It may appear that granting MFN status under these double-column

[37] The decision "from whom to import" is probably less centralized than the one dealing with "what and how much to import" in bloc trade with the West. The Foreign trade combines are often told to buy or sell such and such commodities but are left to themselves to seek the best market.

[38] Not all of the centrally planned economies have, or have had, tariffs.

[39] For discussion, see United Nations, *Economic Bulletin for Europe,* Vol. 14, No. 1, 52–58. The original Soviet announcement appeared in *Vneshniaia torgoviia,* No. 10 (1961).

[40] That is to say, ". . . profits are calculated on the basis of the value of their deliveries of imported goods to domestic distributing, etc., enterprises at the uniform domestic price of those goods *minus* the foreign exchange cost of their imports together with any duty payable on them . . ." (*Economic Bulletin,* p. 53).

tariffs is equivalent to granting MFN status under free market conditions, but in fact it is not. First, it is unlikely that the extensive planned bilateral intra-bloc trade would be disrupted or altered for small price differentials, which may develop in favor of Western nations as a result of granting the latter MFN status. Second, for reasons already mentioned, the lowering of a tariff would have no effect on the decisions "how much" and "what" to import—that is, competition with domestic suppliers would not be allowed. The only possible effect of the new system, then, would be to redistribute trade among a nation's Western trading partners.[41]

MONOPOLY POWER

The conduct of trade by state organizations inevitably introduces elements of monopoly power into foreign trade. Monopolistic market power is, of course, often exercized by capitalist trade concerns, for example, those connected with petroleum and aluminum. The major objection to monopoly power in international trade is that it may lead to an unequal distribution of the gains from trade. This consequence of monopoly power has usually been accepted by the market economies as an undesirable, but natural and inevitable concomitant of trade conducted by private enterprise.[42] Objections raised with respect to state trading reflect the conviction that state traders have much more power to drive a hard bargain than private monopolists. This, however, is not necessarily true. As in the case of private traders, the power of the state trader is determined by his share in the world market, the importance of the commodity in his domestic market, etc.—that is, it depends on the assorted relevant "elasticities." In the case of wheat, for instance, the state trader may have relatively little power, in the case of aluminum, relatively much—and in either commodity, possibly neither more nor less power than a private trader.

In bilateral agreements between East and West, the bargaining power of the East is strengthened by another institutional factor already mentioned. The CPE's are more interested in imports than exports—the latter are viewed as a necessary evil. On the other hand, Western nations are just as interested in maintaining the level of exports. This has led to temporary and unplanned surpluses of West with East during the course of bilateral agreements. Under these circumstances, the burden of achieving balance largely falls on the Western nation which does not want to extend

[41] For continuity, the reader is referred to the discussion of possible reforms in section III.

[42] However, the recent United Nations World Conference on Trade and Development provided strong evidence that the underdeveloped nations consider their poor terms of trade a result of their weak bargaining power and something which should be changed.

credit.[43] This may involve accepting in payment goods which are of lower priority and higher price than are available elsewhere in the world market.

DUMPING: DEFINITION AND IDENTIFICATION

Dumping is usually defined as selling abroad at a lower price than at home. When the commodity is not sold domestically and therefore has no home price, "domestic cost of production" or "export price in third markets" are sometimes substituted. The Soviet Union has been accused of dumping in Western markets a number of times, first in the early 1930's, particularly in regard to grain, and again more recently, aluminum, tin, glass and so forth.[44] That the Soviet Union and other state traders have the power to dump[45] is unquestioned. Whether the above criteria of dumping are proper for a centrally planned economy (of the sort described above) is a more difficult question.[46]

First, to the extent that the currencies of the centrally planned economies have been or are substantially overvalued by official exchange rates, comparison of domestic and export prices is a misleading criterion of dumping. Under these circumstances, exports must be nominally subsidized. The nominal losses on exports are matched, of course, by larger nominal profits on imports.

Second, as noted above, relative domestic prices in the centrally planned economies reflect subsidies and sales taxes introduced to satisfy domestic fiscal and other requirements. Here again, comparison of domestic and export prices is a misleading criterion of dumping even when exchange rates are not overvalued.

Third, the centrally planned economies, following the labor theory of value, have a different concept of "cost of production" from that of the West. This makes the use of "cost" an imperfect substitute for "price" in assessing dumping. The problem can be exemplified by commodities like petroleum whose "cost" does not include the quantitatively important categories of rent and interest. Yet, a fairly strong case can be made,

[43] The provision in many of these bilateral agreements for payment in gold or convertible currency in case the imbalance persists or exceeds certain limits prevents this factor from assuming larger proportions than it otherwise would.

[44] The Eastern European nations have been forced to sell fairly systematically below world prices in Western markets in the postwar period because of real or imagined inferiority of Eastern goods, for political reasons, and so forth. See this writer's papers in the *Review of Economics and Statistics,* May and November, 1962.

[45] That is to say, they have sufficient monopoly power to separate the various markets in which they sell as well as to prevent the reimport of goods. They can also easily subsidize losses on dumping out of the general treasury.

[46] For an excellent discussion of dumping, see Gerschenkron, *op. cit.,* pp. 45ff.

in connection with dumping, for accepting the labor theory view of "cost" prevalent in the East. To begin with, when all commodities are so valued, the resulting generally lower price level is accounted for by the commensurately higher value of the equilibrium exchange rate. Next, the configuration of relative prices that emerges from this kind of cost accounting may be treated in the same category as the differences in relative prices which exist between nations as a consequence of different preference structures. Like differences in consumers' tastes, the permanent and basic differences in ways of evaluating "cost" may be accepted as parameters of the world trading system.

Fourth, and in many ways most difficult to deal with, is the fact that export and import decisions are not independent of each other as in capitalist economies; instead, state monopolies view exports as payment for imports.[47] The connection is especially close in bilateral agreements.[48] Thus, for example, a state trader who sold a commodity at one-half of domestic cost could hardly be accused of "true" dumping, if the foreign exchange earned were used to import goods purchased at one-third of domestic cost. A nominal financial loss on exports would be in this case more than offset by the financial gain on imports[49]

Although this approach may seem fair from the point of view of the CPE's, it fails to take account of the rationale behind antidumping legislation.[50] A major purpose of antidumping legislation is to prevent the disruption of domestic markets and loss of domestic production facilities as a result of what might be termed unfair competition. If one's markets and production facilities are lost in (fair) competition with a truly lower cost producer, one can expect, in return, assured imports at lower prices. If, however, a foreign supplier sells below domestic price because of temporary surplus or in an attempt to break into a market, the low price is not likely to be maintained and the disruptive effect is without compensating benefits. CPE exports offered at a loss in order to reap a large profit on imports would seem to fall into the second category; they would not necessarily reflect a stable comparative advantage position. They are, therefore, potentially "disruptive" and should not be allowed.

[47] On this point Gerschenkron (*op. cit.,* p. 46) writes: ". . . What on the face of it looked like a case of dumping reveals itself on closer scrutiny as a normal application of the principles of international specialization. . . ."

[48] However, in my view, it would probably not be possible to link specific exports and imports.

[49] It is this view of the trade process which has enabled the centrally planned economies to maintain overvalued exchange rates and still engage in a reasonable volume of trade.

[50] The centrally planned economies would, of course, welcome Western dumping. Their major foreign trade objective is to get as good terms of trade as possible and they have no fear of market disruption.

Finally, systematic data on the prices, taxes, and subsidies to commodities exported by the centrally planned economies are not easily available. Consequently, an evaluation of dumping charges is difficult, if not impossible, regardless of the criterion used.

III

We have concluded our survey of the impact of central planning, as it is practiced in Eastern Europe, on foreign trade behavior.[51] Clearly, national economic planning has some inconvenient and costly consequences for the bloc nations in the foreign trade area. We will now consider briefly what, if anything, might be done *without* fundamental change in the central planning system to alleviate some of the difficulties relating to inconvertibility and MFN clauses.

INCONVERTIBILITY AND BILATERALISM

Inconvertibility and bilateralism are probably the knottiest problems facing the Eastern nations. They, themselves, have been actively concerned for many years over the disadvantages of their rigidly bilateral trading system. The most recent evidence of this concern is the establishment of the International Bank for Economic Cooperation, which at present devotes its efforts to setting in motion a type of payments union for multilateral clearings (to be discussed below).[52]

Can the planned economies eliminate inconvertibility without substantially changing their planning system? If the analysis presented above is correct, they cannot. Until their price systems are rationalized and especially until central allocation of resources is less rigidly adhered to, commodity inconvertibility will remain a fact. Furthermore, their currencies will remain essentially inconvertible into foreign exchange. This is in striking contrast to the situation of capitalist nations. There pure overvaluations (due to differential inflation) may be simply eliminated by devaluation, and deeper seated disequilibria (due to shifts in international supply or demand, wartime destruction, etc.) can usually be either "worked-off" or

[51] The survey was by no means complete, however. Another problem, for example, is that of arbitration of disputes with and suing of trading partners which are, in effect, national governments. On this, see Harold Berman, "The Legal Framework of Trade between Planned and Market Economies: The Soviet-American Example," *Law and Contemporary Problems*, Summer 1959, pp. 482–528.

[52] The original statute was published in a *Bulletin of the Supreme Soviet*, No. 7 (February 1964), 135–150. See also reports in the *New York Times*, November 12, 1963, p. 57; December 9, 1963, p. 57; March 30, 1964, pp. 43, 47.

adapted to overtime, given the application of a proper assortment of policies including devaluation.[53]

Yet, although full convertibility, particularly "commodity" convertibility, may be infeasible, it may still be possible to achieve partial "currency" convertibility or transferability as well as to reduce the rigidity of bilateral clearings. Three proposals are considered, the last of which is currently being tried by Comecon.

1. Partial "currency" convertibility[54] might be achieved if the centrally planned economies were willing: (a) to let nonresidents hold their currencies in the event of deficits; (b) to guarantee the value of these holdings against devaluation vis-à-vis convertible currencies or gold; and (c) to pay interest on such funds at a rate which would overcome the reluctance to hold them generated by the uncertainties mentioned earlier.[55] The advantage of establishing "currency" convertibility along these lines would be that it permits a considerable multilateralization of trade. Deficits and surpluses not only become possible but can be offset against each other through trading of currencies. Even if deficits and surpluses are not "cleared," extension of short-term credit automatically takes place, of course, though presumably at a relatively high cost.

The clear disadvantages of this system, if it is to operate in both intra-bloc and East-West trade, are twofold. First, and possibly of overwhelming importance, is the fact that bloc currencies would undoubtedly sell at a substantial discount relative to Western currencies and gold. For prestige reasons, this might seem unacceptable to some of the bloc nations. Secondly, the need to pay high interest rates on currency balances held by Westerners would reduce if not eliminate the profitability of East-West trade. Under these circumstances, the bloc nations might feel impelled to retreat to the present system of running import surpluses only when these can be financed out of stocks of convertible currency, gold, or formal loans.[56]

---

[53] See, for example, Charles Kindleberger, *International Economics,* 3rd Edition, Homewood, Ill., 1963, Chs. 26–30.

[54] This proposal is an elaboration of a suggestion made by Altman, *op. cit.,* pp. 430–431.

[55] Presumably the high discount rate will not only encourage nonresidents to hold bloc currencies per se, but will discourage them from converting to hard currencies or gold. The possibility of converting to hard currencies or gold would lower the discount rate at which nonresidents would be willing to hold the bloc currencies. Whether or not it would be possible to get nonresidents to hold bloc currencies without convertibility rights is problematical. The required discount rate would certainly be very high.

[56] For psychological and institutional as well as economic reasons, formal loans repayable in convertible currency would undoubtedly be made at lower nominal rates of interest than would be required to get nonresidents to hold one's currency on an informal basis.

In intra-bloc trade, where bilateralism creates great difficulties, the first objection noted above would become immaterial,[57] and the second would be of much lesser importance. The greatest difficulty would appear to be the problem of getting a group of nations committed to Marxist economic doctrines to agree to such a program and to allow it to operate with a sufficient degree of flexibility. Clearly, without such flexibility the discounts and premia on the various currencies in question could not properly reflect their changing values in intra-bloc trade. However, if some flexibility were achieved, the way would be opened to multilateral clearings. Furthermore, the system would have a built-in mechanism to discourage nations from running deficits to obtain from others involuntary credits—the greater the deficit, the higher the discount rate since other nations become less eager to hold one's currency.[58]

There is some similarity between this system and the swing-credit bilateral clearing presently in use in intra-bloc trade. At present, a nation running a deficit (unplanned) that exceeds prescribed limits is required to pay the excess in gold or convertible currency. Since gold and convertible currency are at a premium, this is equivalent to paying a charge or interest rate for running a deficit with another nation. The important advantages of the above proposal over the existing system are two: For one thing, the various bloc currencies could be exchanged for each other, thereby multilateralizing clearings and facilitating the development of a short-term credit mechanism. In contrast, at present, incentives are designed to ensure bilateral balancing. Moreover, the value of each nation's currency (the interest one must pay on balances outstanding) would depend not on its various *bilateral* balances outstanding but on its *overall* surplus or deficit.[59]

2. If currency convertibility cannot be achieved along the line suggested above, it might still be possible to sidestep the inconvertibility problem but nevertheless achieve an increase in multilateral clearings. This could be done if the planned economies were in the position to build up substan-

---

[57] Undoubtedly, exchange relationships to Western convertible currencies would develop or be established; but since they would operate only within the bloc, they could be limited to reasonable amounts.

[58] It might be argued that if interest rates became high enough, the creditors would have an incentive not to import from the debtors because the return on the debt was higher than could be obtained in alternative uses. The present scheme envisages free negotiability of debts. Thus, if the interest rate on a nation's balances became inordinately high, other nations in the bloc would want to purchase such balances, thereby driving the interest down to reasonable levels.

[59] In this respect, the solution envisaged above is similar to that of the old European Payments Union. Another similarity is that under the EPU, the percentage of gold and dollars required in settlement of deficits increased as the deficit increased. Under our proposal, presumably the interest rate on outstanding balances would increase as the overall deficit increased.

tial reserves of convertible currencies, reserves large enough to finance any normal deficits which might result from trading multilaterally with all nations in a position to do so.[60] Admittedly, in practice this may be quite difficult. The addition to reserves needed for extension of multilateral transactions is probably small in comparison with bloc nations' national product and trade volume, perhaps in the scale of two to three billion dollars.[61] Yet, even this relatively minor increase may well prove infeasible in the immediate future. The Eastern nations have recently been soliciting credits from the West—this is hardly the climate in which to expect them to develop export surpluses. It may be especially difficult, if not impossible, to develop the necessary surpluses in Western markets where gold and hard currencies would be obtained.

Furthermore, the system could work for any length of time only if the centrally planned economies, having accumulated the appropriate amount of reserves, would succeed in maintaining them. This means that an overall balance of payments must be achieved with all nations by each bloc member or, given a convertible currency pool within the bloc, by the bloc as a whole with the West. Such a discipline may be difficult to achieve in view of the factors mentioned at the beginning of this paper. Historical experience gives support to doubt since there probably has been

[60] Even now the CPE nations trade fairly multilaterally with many Western nations on the basis of convertible currencies and gold. See footnote 26 of this chapter.

[61] It is not a simple matter to determine the amount of reserves required to finance unconstrained multilateral trade. Crude orders of magnitude are suggested by the relationships of reserves to the total trade and to multilateral trade in the non-bloc world. Reserves of gold and foreign exchange amounted, in 1958, to about $55 billion (Robert Triffin, *Gold and the Dollar Crisis,* New Haven, 1961, p. 73). In the same year, total imports (or exports) were about $100 billion (*ibid.*), and multilateral trade about $25 billion (Michaely, *op. cit.,* p. 691). The total trade of the bloc was about $11 billion in 1958. If the non-bloc ratio were to hold in the bloc, reserves of $5–6 billion would be in order. If the same percentage of the $11 billion were multilateralized as is the case in the West, about $3 billion of multilateral trade would be implied. Apply the non-block ratio of reserves: multilateral trade suggests reserves of $5.5 billion, the same figure as in the preceding estimate. If the bloc has, say, $3 billion in reserves, it would need to accumulate another $2–3 billion to have multilateral trade by the reasoning developed above. There are some caveats to the above. Much depends not on aggregates, but on the distribution of both trade and reserves. (For example, it is probable that the U.S.S.R. has a disproportionate share of bloc reserves.) Second, there is nothing sacred about the 55:100 ratio of reserves to total trade for 1958. This ratio was .37 in 1913 and .45 in 1928, and it may be that a lower ratio than .55 might be satisfactory today. Third, bloc trade has risen since 1958, whereas our reserve figure is probably more nearly accurate for 1964. Finally, the extent to which nations are willing to multilateralize trade on the basis of reserves is partly a psychological matter—and the liquidity preferences of bloc members may be higher or lower than those of Western nations.

a substantial net outflow of (decline in) reserves from the bloc, particularly from the U.S.S.R., over the past decade.

Last, one may question whether the Eastern nations would be willing to develop deficits with each other if these were to be paid in convertible currencies and gold. Why not use the funds to buy in the West? Again, to keep hard currency reserves in the bloc would require the sort of discipline noted under the previous point. The real difficulty here lies in the lack of incentive in bilateral transactions for bloc nations freely to incur deficits with each other that would be financed with highly valued convertible currency.[62]

3. The new bloc clearing arrangement[63] mentioned above is somewhat less ambitious financially than either of the two preceding proposals. In effect, it provides that all intra-bloc transactions take place through the Bank and be accounted for (paid for) in so-called transferable (*perevodnye*) rubles. Payment in transferable rubles means that a surplus with one nation can be used to pay off a deficit with another. To ensure that no nation will take advantage of the system to obtain involuntary short-term credits, the agreement specifies that each participant must balance its account in transferable rubles over the calendar year. According to a newspaper report,[64] this is to be accomplished by following up the original bilateral trade negotiations with multilateral negotiations in which the net surpluses and deficits would be offset against each other by additional commodity exchanges.

The system appears simple; will it work? It seems obvious that if it does work, that is, if multilateral clearing takes place and all accounts are balanced at the end of each year, success should be attributed not to the clearing arrangement per se, but to the negotiations which prearrange the balance. It may well be argued that, given the negotiating mechanism, the transferable rubles are totally unnecessary, except perhaps as a psychological fillip to the proceedings. The new value and usefulness of nonresident holdings of national currencies will arise from multilateral negotiations; the transferable ruble system simply accounts ex post for what has already been determined.[65]

---

[62] It might be argued that if the convertible currency could not be used in the West, it might lose its value. However, so long as it is potentially expendable in the West, it will continue to command a premium.

[63] Eventually the Bank established to implement the clearing arrangement will, in addition to performing clearing operations, provide short-term credits for trade among the contracting parties and perhaps finance longer term projects in which two or more nations are interested.

[64] *New York Times*, March 30, 1964, pp. 43, 47.

[65] If the transferable rubles have any functions at all, they would seem to be connected with credit creation and with the possibilities that the prearranged balances will not be realized. In either instance, it would seem more useful to use transferable rubles than national currencies.

If one grants the peripheral significance of transferable rubles, the real workability of the system will be seen to depend on the success of the bilateral-multilateral negotiation in achieving balance and improving the volume and distribution of trade. The achievement of overall balance may be no simple matter in the absence of economic adjusting mechanisms or incentive devices,[66] and in view of the fact that the position of a net debtor tends to strengthen a nation's ability to force undesirable goods on others. The effect of the system on the volume and distribution of trade is difficult to assess. On a priori grounds, one would think that there must be many latent trilateral and multilateral trading possibilities to be revealed under the new system, possibilities which, if realized, could improve the distribution of trade. However, we know little about the bases upon which foreign trade decisions are made; improvements, if any, may be small. Much will depend, for example, on the degree to which intra-bloc surpluses and deficits form "closed" or "open" circuits after initial negotiations.[67]

If a large percentage of the aggregate surplus-deficit forms an "open" circuit, then aggregate balance will only be achievable at the price of further trade (bilateral balancing) between the net creditors and net debtors; this may be considerably less advantageous to either or both than bilateral balancing was to individual bloc nations under the old system, and certainly less advantageous than a hard currency settlement.

Much will also depend on the fashion in which nations, no longer committed to bilateral balance, determine their bilateral export-import cutoffs. If bloc nations, freed from the necessity of bilateral balancing, evaluate their cutoffs not only in terms of domestic opportunity costs but vis-à-vis Western markets as well, a reduction in intra-bloc trade could result.

It seems highly probable in view of the difficulties in achieving overall balance that, in fact, the bloc nations will be largely unwilling to run surpluses or deficits with each other in the initial bilateral negotiations. In other words, not much multilateralization of trade will take place, for the reasons discussed under the second heading in section II, above.

To sum up, the prospect of *substantial* gains arising out of the new

[66] Such as having to: pay a net overall debt in convertible currency or gold; or pay a high interest rate on debts in transferrable currency; or change prices of goods imported and exported (devaluation). The EPU increased the percentage of gold and convertible currency required in payment of overall debt as the size of the debt increased, to discourage persistent deficits.

[67] A closed circuit is that circumstance when A owes B, B owes C, and C owes A. If the amounts owed are equal, deficits cancel out. In an open circuit A owes B, B owes C, and C owes D. Here B and C achieve balance but A ends up owing D. The open circuit exists when other currencies in question are not equally "soft" or "inconvertible," a likely possibility under the circumstances.

clearing mechanism appears slim in the absence of better bases for making foreign trade decisions and in the absence of an economic, as opposed to administrative, balancing or equilibrating device. Therefore, it is not surprising that the Poles reportedly have already asked for a replacement of transferable rubles by convertible currencies.[68] This suggests that at least one of the contractual parties to the new agreement is opting for a system outlined in the previous proposal (B).

The problem of "commodity inconvertibility" deserves a few final remarks too. There seem to be at least two ways in which its seriousness might eventually be reduced. First, it is apparent, particularly in the case of the U.S.S.R., that the pace of overfull employment planning has slowed down and that persistent shortages, sellers' markets, and so forth are now somewhat less of a problem than in the past. If this trend continues and if inventories gradually become larger relative to flows of goods, it may eventually become possible to relax the restrictions on export. Nonresidents may eventually be allowed to buy commodities more freely without fear of disrupting planning. Second, the usual reasons adduced for autarky do not hold strongly in the case of consumer's goods. Extensive and relatively unrestricted trade in consumers' goods would not threaten the integrity of planning because consumers' goods are final outputs, not inputs. Furthermore, since most consumers' goods are highly substitutable (in comparison with inputs, especially in the short run), interruptions in supplies of particular items need cause little loss in household satisfaction. Moreover, the military importance of most types of consumers' goods is low and there is no need on these grounds to seek self-sufficiency.

MFN RECIPROCITY

Before World War II, the Soviet Union (presumably) reciprocated MFN status by agreeing to increase its imports (and exports).[69] Although this expedient satisfied a number of the Soviet trading partners, it deviates in several respects from the ideal. First, the bilateral guaranteed expansion of trade and pricing arrangements are almost certainly not equivalent to what they would be under a mutual reduction in tariffs.[70] Second, in theory a mutual bilateral lowering of tariffs should increase trade between the

---

[68] *New York Times*, March 31, 1964, pp. 43, 47.

[69] M. Domke and J. N. Hazard, "State Trading and the Most-Favored-Nation Clause," *The American Journal of International Law*, January 1958, pp. 55–68.

[70] Precise equivalence is unknowable. There are at least two respects in which equivalence would not be achieved. First, the centrally planned economies have a much wider range of choice in buying and selling a given quantum of goods than have the free market economies. Second, as is well known, there is not equal access to technical know-how for East and West; the Eastern nations incur a large, implicit import surplus along these lines, for which they make no proper payment.

participants as a result of both trade creation (competition with domestic suppliers) and trade diversion. In fact, there is nothing in these agreements to ensure such results, and it may be that a preponderance of the bilateral increase of trade is at the expense of other nations. This fosters bilateralism and is contrary to the "equal treatment" and antidiscriminatory spirit of MFN clauses.[71] The third point is related to the above, that is, once MFN is in effect, the Western partner has no way of knowing whether the Eastern partner has actually increased access to its markets to third nations, an access which should be extended equally to the Western nation in question, as a privilege of MFN status.

These objections can largely be met, in practice, if not in theory. In answer to the first objection it can be argued simply that if the guaranteed expansion of trade and pricing arrangements are not satisfactory to the Western trading partners, it need not grant MFN status. Presumably this is a negotiable matter.[72]

The third objection could be met by including in the bilateral MFN agreement a stipulation that the Eastern nation's imports from its Western trading partner are to increase as rapidly as the Eastern nation's trade as a whole.[73] The Eastern nation would only be allowed to deviate from this formula if it could show that: (a) its increased trade resulted from granting MFN status to third nations or (b) that it had shifted its trade to third countries on strictly commercial grounds.

The second objection is more difficult to handle under traditional bilateral MFN negotiating procedures. It is important to note, however, that to the extent that trade expansion develops on "strictly commercial grounds," as noted above, the seriousness of the second objection will gradually be reduced. A more complicated, but also more substantive approach to our second objection was originally proposed by Alexander Gerschenkron for U.S.S.R.-West trade[74] and has since been expanded by a number of writers to include all East-West trade. According to this, to reduce the discrimination and bilateralism automatically involved in bilateral MFN treaties, the latter should be multilateralized and concluded by the U.S.S.R. (or all Comecon nations simultaneously) with, perhaps,

[71] "When we recognize that the most-favored-nation clause does not serve its purpose in trade relations with a foreign trade monopoly, and have introduced quantitative stipulations into trade agreements, we have still not established equality of trading opportunity. We have merely provided for a certain volume of trade . . . there is no reason to assume that quantitative regulations embodied in agreements concluded between pairs of countries would provide for equality of trading opportunity," Gerschenkron, *op. cit.*, p. 29.

[72] What satisfies a trading partner may not be "true" MFN, of course.

[73] If bloc preferential treatment is to be taken into account, the last eight words should read: "as the Eastern nation's trade with the West."

[74] Gerschenkron, *op. cit.*, pp. 37ff.

the NATO nations or the EEC. Under such an arrangement the Eastern commitments to expand trade would be in terms of a global quota for all nations entitled to MFN status. At the same time, the distribution of trade would be determined by commercial considerations. The implementation of such a proposal might be cumbersome, but probably no more cumbersome than the tariff-reducing negotiations which now regularly take place under GATT.

PRESSURE AND PLANNING
IN THE SOVIET ECONOMY

Herbert S. Levine

University of Pennsylvania

I

This paper is about the Soviet experience with centralized planning and the significance of this experience for our general understanding of the functioning of economic systems. Building on a well-known Gerschenkronian hypothesis about Russian economic history, the paper argues that because Soviet centralized planning is so enmeshed with the exertion of pressure on the internal economy by the Russian State, it is difficult clearly to ascribe causes to observed effects. Therefore, the Soviet experience should be used with care by economists in discussions of the characteristics and consequences of centralized economic planning. The argument is to some extent modified toward the end of the paper owing to the possibility that there may exist a somewhat general joint-productness about pressure and centralized planning. But more about that in awhile.

Among the "hypotheses" of Professor Gerschenkron—those broad, insightful generalizations so cautiously wrung from masses of carefully collected empirical evidence—there is one describing a pattern of Russian economic development which is observable on a number of occasions in the course of Russian history.[1] The history of Russia, for the past five hundred years, is dominated by the theme of territorial expansion: from the small principality of Muscovy just emerging from Mongol rule, Russia grew to its present great size. During this process of expansion, the Russian State frequently came into contact and conflict with Western nations more advanced and more powerful than she. Such confrontations forced upon

---

[1] See Alexander Gerschenkron, *Economic Backwardness in Historical Prospective,* Harvard University Press, Cambridge, Mass., 1962, pp. 17–18.

the leaders of Russia the painful realization that they would not be able to attain what they wanted to attain because of the extreme backwardness of the Russian economy. In such situations, Gerschenkron asserts, the Russion State would take on the role of initiator of economic development. The State would apply pressure to the internal economy to get it to grow rapidly and thus be able to support the foreign policy aims of the State in as short a period as possible. This relationship between military affairs and economic growth was the cause of the fitful nature of economic development observed in Russian economic history. When the military needs of the State were pressing, the economy was pressured into rapid growth. When a degree of power parity was reached, the need for further rapid growth subsided and the State removed its pressure for growth. Because so much growth was compressed into such short periods, the burden of sacrifice borne by the people living in Russia during those periods was great. To exact this sacrifice, extremely oppressive means and institutions were employed. The increase of pressure and the exaction of sacrifice were often so intense that they led to the exhaustion of the internal population; consequently, a period of rapid growth was very likely to be followed by a long period of little or no growth.

This was the pattern of Russian economic development described by Gerschenkron. It should be added, that he was careful to point out that the pattern was intended as a framework for understanding the forces at work in Russian economic growth and was not meant to describe "some iron law of evolution" through which Russian development had to proceed:

> What is implied is that the actual development seems to conform to a certain pattern and that such conformities and uniformities as can be observed do help us understand the course of events . . . That the development followed a certain course does not preclude the possibility of alternative routes, but it does suggest that the forces which propelled the Russian economy along its actual course must have been strong indeed.[2]

The pattern is most clearly and fully seen in the period of Peter the Great. It is also observable in the period of rapid growth of the 1890's, although this spurt of development is not followed by a long period of relative stagnation.[3] Finally, it is seen in the massive industrialization drive launched under the Soviets.

This last period is still in progress, and, whereas it remains to be seen whether future events will conform to the pattern, it is evident that the course of past events, since the end of the 1920's, does clearly conform.[4] The key role played in the pattern by the conflict between military

---

[2] *Ibid.,* p. 157.

[3] For discussion, see *ibid.,* pp. 130–142.

[4] See *ibid.,* pp. 147–151.

needs and economic backwardness is graphically illustrated in a famous speech delivered by Stalin, at the beginning of the industrialization drive, in which he said:

> One feature of the history of old Russia was the continual beatings she suffered for falling behind, for her backwardness. She was beaten by the Mongol Khans . . . the Turkish beys . . . the Swedish feudal lords . . . the Polish and Lithuanian gentry . . . the British and French capitalists . . . the Japanese barons. All beat her . . . for her backwardness: for military backwardness, for cultural backwardness, for political backwardness, for industrial backwardness, for agricultural backwardness . . . . Do you want our socialist fatherland to be beaten and to lose its independence? If you do not want this you must put an end to its backwardness in the shortest possible time . . . We are fifty or a hundred years behind the advanced countries. We must make good this distance in ten years. Either we do it, or they crush us.[5]

In the Soviet industrialization drive, the State has been the initiator and controller of economic growth. To force the speed of this growth, it has applied pervasive pressure on the entire internal economy. Cruelly oppressive means have been used to exact severe sacrifice from the Russian people.

Soviet economic development and Soviet economic institutions can best be understood against the background of this pattern in Russian economic history. Stalin's use of collectivization is in many ways a functional analogue of Peter the Great's use of serfdom. Centralized planning is the means by which the State exerts its control over the economy and through which it transmits pressure for rapid growth.[6] To see Soviet collectivization merely as a device to increase production is to miss its vital function in exaction of sacrifice from the peasantry. Further, to see Soviet centralized planning merely as a Marxian device to eradicate the disproportions resulting from the anarchy of market systems is to miss its role both in giving the political leaders control over the course of Soviet development and in giving them a means of forcing rapid structural change on the economy, in order to modernize it and so bring it up to parity with the West.

The Soviet economy in the Plan Era is often taken as *the* case study

[5] J. Stalin, *Selected Writings,* International Publishers, 1942, p. 200.

[6] This is not the place for a full discussion of the definition of the term *centralized planning.* Briefly speaking, what is meant is a system wherein the major economic decisions are made by central authorities and are communicated to the periphery by means of directives; the units at the periphery act in response to these directives, or "commands," rather than in response to parameters such as prices. See J. Zielinski, "Centralization and Decentralization in Decision Making," *Economics of Planning,* December 1963, pp. 196–208; G. Grossman, "Notes for a Theory of Command Economy," *Soviet Studies,* October 1963, pp. 101–123.

of centralized planning, and the operating characteristics of the Soviet economy (as described in the works of Berliner, Granick, Nove and others)[7] are often taken as *the* necessary consequences of centralized planning. It is the argument of this paper that such views of the economic significance of the Soviet experience with centralized planning ignore the background of the Soviet use of centralized planning. They ignore, specifically, the role played by pressure, that pressure exerted on the economy by the political leaders through the means of centralized planning. It will be argued that the observed operating characteristics of the Soviet economy can be said to be as much if not more a result of the pressure in the system than they are of the mechanism of centralized planning itself.

II

When the Russian economy, at the end of the 1920's, had reattained its pre-World War I levels, the Soviet leaders turned away from the loose policies of the NEP period and toward the highly centralized means of economic planning and control which have marked the Plan Era. Undoubtedly, centralized planning had certain political and ideological attractions for the Soviet leaders,[8] but it also had important economic attractions. Having made the decision to embark upon forced draft industrialization—to close the "fifty to one hundred year-gap" between Russia and the advanced nations of the West in ten years—the regime needed economic organization methods appropriate to the task. In a situation wherein the aim of the State is to make a rapid and massive structural change in the economy, when this aim is clearly the dominant aim and when the priorities, the things that have to be done to accomplish the aim (the concentration on basic industrial commodities and machinery), are also clear, then direct centralized planning commends itself.[9] In such situations, indirect, decentralized methods of economic organization and control, relying on the price mechanism and marginalist calculations, can be said to work too slowly, moreover, not very effectively. When concentration is on new products, new industries and new regional complexes,

[7] J. Berliner, *Factory and Manager in the USSR,* Harvard University Press, Cambridge, Mass., 1957; D. Granick, *Management of the Industrial Firm in the USSR,* Columbia University Press, New York, 1954, and "An Organizational Model of Soviet Industrial Planning," *Journal of Political Economy,* April 1959, pp. 109–130. A. Nove, *The Soviet Economy,* Praeger, New York, 1961, Ch. 6 and *passim.*

[8] See A. Gerschenkron, *The Stability of Dictatorships,* Harvard Lecture, Yale University, April 3, 1963; A. Bergson, *The Economics of Soviet Planning,* Yale University Press, New Haven, 1964, pp. 173–174.

[9] Compare the United States and United Kingdom's uses of centralized planning techniques during World War II.

the constants needed to make close marginal decisions are themselves variables. Uncertainty runs rampant, and externalities, which cannot easily be internalized by individual decision makers, become of major importance.[10] Under such circumstances, centralized planning offers the state in some ways a more promising means of effectuating its control over the economy, for it is both a means of directly concentrating economic efforts on high priority sectors and diverting the impact of mistakes onto low priority sectors and a means of transmitting pressure and urgency to the economy.

The pressure transmitted by the Bolshevik regime to the Soviet economy was essentially of two different types. One was the pressure on the living standards of the Russian people, which was manifested in the rising rate of investment out of G.N.P., falling rate of consumption, and, for long parts of the Plan Era, falling levels of per capita consumption.[11] The second was the pressure exerted on the producing units in the economy to increase output. This pressure for more output per unit of input, this search for reserves of productivity was ubiquitous, and it was supported by a multitude of economic, social and political incentives: the monetary rewards for surpassing production targets, the red banners for victory in interplant competitions, the political promotions (or demotions) for production successes (or failures). It imparted to all the producing units in the economy a constant and omnipresent condition of excess effective demand.

Although it is the first type of pressure, the pressure on the living standards of the people, which is of major interest to Gerschenkron in his pattern of Russian economic development, it is the second type of pressure, the pressure on the productive capacity of the basic enterprises, which is of major interest in this paper.

The pressure on producing units was a result not only of the conscious policy on the part of the regime; it was also intensified, consciously and unconsciously, in the process of plan construction and implementation. A Soviet plan is not intended as a tool to achieve harmonious operation of the economy, but as a tool to mobilize resources for the attainment of a rapid rate of growth.

State plans established for the enterprises must mobilize all workers, manual and professional, in the struggle for the plan, in the movement forward toward the conquering of difficulties and the attaining of new growth in the national economy.[12]

[10] See T. Scitovsky, "Two Concepts of External Economies," *Journal of Political Economy*, April 1954, pp. 143–151.

[11] See J. Chapman, "Consumption," in A. Bergson and S. Kuznets (eds.), *Economic Trends in the Soviet Union*, Cambridge, Mass., 1963, pp. 236–244.

[12] *Pravda*, March 1, 1947, p. 1.

Therefore, at the very beginning as a matter of policy, the intention is to give the enterprise a "taut" plan.[13] There is to be little slack between the full productive capacity of the enterprise and the output demanded of it. In fact, the intention is to set the target somewhat beyond the "full capacity" so as to force the enterprise to seek out reserves of increased output.

In the process of plan construction—speaking now of the annual plan, and primarily of the industrial plan—the conscious policy of putting pressure on all producing units is embodied in the control figures, the preliminary aggregate targets constructed by the state planning committee (*Gosplan*)[14] after consultation with the political leaders, and communicated by *Gosplan* down through the planning-control hierarchy to the producing units.[15] The input norms used in the construction of the control figures are highly optimistic ones, in this way imparting a significant degree of tautness to the plan at its inception.[16] This pressure is undoubtedly relieved somewhat in the counterplanning and bargaining as the plan comes back up the planning-control hierarchy. The enterprises seek to implant protective fat in the plan; although the superior organs do cut out some of the fat, they are restrained somewhat by the "family relationship" which exists between the superior body and the enterprises subordinate to it.[17] A considerable amount of pressure is reinstated in the plan when it comes back into *Gosplan,* for the central planners are not part of the same family

[13] See H. Hunter, "Optimum Tautness in Developmental Planning," *Economic Development and Cultural Change,* July 1961 (Part I).

[14] We will use the term *Gosplan* to refer to the central planning body responsible for the construction of the annual plan even though at various times a different organization had this responsibility.

[15] For a description of the process and chronology of plan construction, see A. Bergson, *The Economics of Soviet Planning;* H. Levine, "The Centralized Planning of Supply in Soviet Industry," in Joint Economic Committee, *Comparisons of United States and Soviet Economies,* Washington, D. C., 1959, pp. 151–176; H. Levine, *A Study in Economic Planning,* Unpublished Doctoral Dissertation, Harvard University, 1961.

[16] In actuality, the conscious policy of pressure appears even earlier than the control figures in the chronology of plan construction. In the first stage, that of preparing the statistical base, done in the first part of the planning year, the planners have to project available data to the end of the planning year, that is, to the eve of the planned year. To assure the discipline of the plan, this projection should be done on the basis of all the growth rates planned for the (planning) year, but by the time these projections are undertaken, some knowledge is available on how the plan for the planning year is going. Thus, to the extent that current failures are ignored in the statistical projections, the plans for some sectors and some enterprises are extra taut.

[17] The aspect of the "family relationship" important here is that the performance of the superior organ is a sum of the performances of the subordinate enterprises.

as are those directly responsible for production, and therefore they are free to bargain for the degree of tautness in the now much more detailed plan that they had originally put in the aggregate plan when it first began its journey down the administrative hierarchy. We would probably be safe to assume that when the plan is accepted back into *Gosplan,* it is in general less taut than when it began but not substantially so.

At this point, it is the task of *Gosplan* to work out the internal consistency of the plan. The method used is that of the material balances, in which an accounting balance, listing planned sources and uses of a product, is constructed for each of a large number of major products. The consistency of the plan is achieved by forging a balance between planned sources and uses in each and every material balance.[18] The material balances are often said to resemble aspects of input-output tables. This is true, although it should be noted that a material balance is similar to a row, not a column, of an input-output table and thus does not explicitly reflect the production technology of the economic plan.

The material balance method and Soviet planning practice do have a spiritual kinship with the input-output approach insofar as the assumption of fixed input coefficients is concerned (or, in the Soviet case, at least temporarily fixed coefficients). The production function used in the construction of a Soviet plan is of the following nature:

$$X_k = \min\left(\frac{x_{1k}}{a_{1k}}, \frac{x_{2k}}{a_{2k}}, \ldots, \frac{x_{ik}}{a_{ik}}, \ldots, \frac{x_{nk}}{a_{nk}}\right),$$

where, X_k = the planned output of the kth good,

x_{ik} = the planned flow of the ith good to the kth sector,

a_{ik} = the planned input of the ith good per unit of output of the kth good.

This function states that the output of any good is equal to the smallest ratio of an input flow divided by that input coefficient.[19] Aside from questions of inventory planning, it is the aim of planners to get all the relevant ratios equal to each other and equal to the desired level of output.

If the planned level of output of, say, the kth good turns out, on first inspection of the kth good's material balance, to be less than the planned uses of the kth good $\left(\sum_{i=1}^{n} x_{ki}\right)$, as is generally the case, how do

---

[18] This process is discussed in the sources in footnote 15 above. The number of material balances has varied in the postwar period from approximately 760 to 1600.

[19] For example, if, $x_{1j} = 10$, $a_{1j} = 2$, $x_{2j} = 28$, $a_{2j} = 4$; then, $X_j = \min(10/2, 28/4) = 5$. (This means that 8 units of x_{2j} are in "excess" supply.)

Soviet planners achieve the required balance? That is, how do they increase the planned output of k and/or decrease the planned uses of k? One possible approach is to increase X_k by increasing each x_{ik} (in proportion to each fixed a_{ik}) and/or to decrease Σx_{ki} by decreasing all or some of the x_{ki}s. This approach, however, requires that a multitude of subsequent changes be made. As each input flow into $k(x_{ik})$ is increased, each input into each input (x_{vi}) has to be increased, and this has to be done a number of times before each material balance in the set will be sufficiently balanced (and similarly, *mutatis mutandis*, on the down side). I have argued in detail elsewhere that, although Soviet planners do go back a few levels when the output of a key product is increased, this iterative approach is not the sole nor probably even the primary method they use to attain a consistent set of material balances.[20] Briefly put, the computational requirements of the iterative approach, given the form of the material balances and the computational technology in use (desk calculators at best), make it clear that this is an infeasible approach, and it is confirmed by the Russians' own statements.

How, then, are the output levels of deficit products increased and/or demand requirements decreased?[21] It appears that much reliance is put on methods which avoid the necessity of making secondary changes, thus avoiding reverberation of a change through the entire set of material balances. Output levels are increased, without increase in inputs; planned distributions to users are decreased, without decreasing the output levels of the user sectors. The approach is not to change the x_{ik}'s and the x_{ki}'s, but to change the input coefficients, the a_{ik}'s and the a_{ki}'s. This adds to the tightness of the plan, to the pressure on the producing enterprise. This increased pressure may at times be applied where protective fat still exists, and thus it may not be undesirable or unrealistic pressure. However, since buildup of pressure at this stage is not a result of conscious effort to remove fat but, rather, a by-product of a primitive planning technique used by harried planners to hammer out consistency in the plan, it must be assumed that in many instances it will be applied where there is not an ample layer of fat. That this is so is attested to by the statements of many Soviet authorities, including an official statement of the Communist Party to the effect that planned input relationships are often unrealistic, leading to "excess tension in the fulfillment of plans."[22] Furthermore, it

[20] See H. Levine, in "Centralized Planning of Supply . . . . ," pp. 163–167. For a somewhat divergent view, see J. Montias, "Planning With Material Balances," *American Economic Review,* December 1959.

[21] The phrase "deficit product" is used here to mean a product for which demand is greater than planned supply during the process of plan construction.

[22] *Direktivy KPSS i sovetskogo pravitel'stva po khoziaistvennym voprosam,* Vol. IV, Moscow, 1958, p. 670.

should not be thought that perhaps the excess pressure on some enterprises is 'balanced off' by the excess fat of others. The pressure on an enterprise is not easily relieved by the presence of fat at another enterprise because in an atmosphere of heavy pressure an enterprise jealously guards whatever surplus resources it might have in anticipation of needing them itself someday (soon).

There are several other nonsecondary effect steps taken to reduce imbalances in the material balances and which are worth discussing. Planned levels of input stocks are often cut down excessively in an effort either to increase the output of a deficit product into which the stock in question is an input or to reduce the demands on a deficit input. In practice, stocks actually held are usually significantly greater than planned levels. The proclivity of Soviet enterprise managers to hoard inventories is well known, and we will discuss this further on. However, here we wish to point out that one reason Soviet managers hold above-norm stocks is simply that the planned levels of these stocks are set too low. At times when inventories of input materials are even twice as high as planned levels, these inventories prove to be insufficient to prevent production stoppages.[23] Actually, Soviet inventory levels (related to flow of output) should be higher than those in say the United States. This is so because to a certain extent inventories and unused productive capacity are substitutes for each other and because under Soviet conditions of general plan tightness there is a relative unavailability of excess productive capacity in the Soviet economy. Another balancing technique which avoids secondary effects is to accelerate the introduction of new productive capacity and include its planned output flow in the material balance of a deficit product. Under the best of conditions, the precise scheduling of the introduction of new capacity is difficult to accomplish; but under Soviet conditions, it is well nigh impossible, for with the tightness of plans, the consequent unreliability of supply, and the general deficiencies of excessive centralization (see below), the introduction of new capacity is almost always held up for want of one or another needed material or piece of equipment. Under such conditions, the reliance on output from new capacity to be introduced during the planned year, a fortiori when the introduction schedule is artificially speeded up, constitutes an element of "paper consistency" and thus adds to the pressure built up in the plan.

Further pressure is put on the enterprise by certain indirect ways of reducing input coefficients. For example, the planned flow of materials to be used in maintenance work is often reduced below required levels. Thus, when the need for maintenance becomes pressing, the enterprise

[23] See, e.g., N. Ivanov et al., *Material'no-tekhnicheskoe snabzhenie v mashinostroenii*, Moscow, 1956, p. 144.

must shift materials from direct production work to maintenance, in this way increasing the pressure in its production plan.[24]

The buildup of pressure in the process of plan construction does not end with the working out of the internal consistency of the plan but continues into and through the stage at which the plan is officially reviewed and confirmed and also in the stage wherein the confirmed plan is brought down through the administrative hierarchy to the producing unit.

When the draft of the plan has been reviewed and altered by the political leaders it is not clear whether the changes made are mostly increases or decreases in outputs whether they are intended to increase or relieve pressure on the specific sectors involved. Perhaps the approach varies both at a given time and over time. What is clear, however, is that when the political leaders make changes in outputs, it is hardly possible for the planners, in the short time they have at this stage (normally about two weeks), to work out the indirect consequences of these changes. Therefore, even if they were able to forge a consistent draft of the plan to present to the political leaders, it comes back unbalanced and remains unbalanced. To the extent, then, that the plan is more inconsistent than it was, the pressure in it is further increased.

The confirmed plan contains output, input, and other types of commands addressed primarily to the high-level administrative bodies. Before 1957 these were the ministries; at this writing they are mainly the administrative-planning bodies at the republic level (also the remaining and recreated ministries and the state committees). In the pre-1957 period, for which the picture is clearer than now, the relevant parts of the plan were sent to the ministry involved, and the ministry and its intermediary organs were supposed to subdivide the ministerial output targets and input allotments among the subordinate enterprises. In order to give themselves more maneuverability and thus more protection, the ministries practiced what the Russians call reinsurance planning and reserving.[25] Reinsurance planning describes the ministerial practice of assigning output targets to subordinate enterprise so that the total assignments totaled more than the ministerial output assignment. By increasing targets in this way, the ministries put pressure on all enterprises to produce at higher levels (with lower targets, they might have stopped producing at lower levels), thus giving themselves more of a protective cushion against the possibility that some of their enterprises would not fulfill even the lower targets. This practice

---

[24] A. Savkin, "Zadachi uluchsheniia material'no-tekhnicheskogo snabzheniia promyshlennosti," *Planovoe Khoziaistvo*, 1, (1956), 61–62.

[25] Reinsurance planning is what Berliner refers to as clearance planning. See Berliner, *op. cit.,* pp. 83–85, 257–259. It is to be assumed that these practices were continued by the relevant administrative bodies after the 1957 reorganization.

was officially recognized by the government, which set a limit of 10 per cent on the amount by which the sum of assignments to enterprises could exceed the ministerial output assignment.[26]

Reserving was another form of ministerial self-protection. This refers to the practice whereby a ministry did not distribute to its subordinate enterprise all the input allotments it received. The ministry reserved to itself a part of the allotments which it could then dispatch to trouble spots as they appeared during the course of the planned year. This practice too was officially recognized by the government, which permitted the ministry the right to reserve no more than 5 per cent of the total ministerial allotment.

Although these practices added to the maneuverability of the ministry and in this way may have reduced the pressure on it, they added substantially to the pressure on the enterprise. They may be viewed as a means of redistributing some of the slack the ministry previously permitted enterprises to retain (in the bargaining process when the plan was coming up the hierarchy). By these methods such slack was transferred from the individual enterprises to the ministry as a whole, leaving the enterprise in a more highly pressured condition.

III

The question now to be faced is how all this pressure built up in the system leads to the observed characteristics of the Soviet economy? In this discussion, we do not intend to deny the role played by centralized planning itself and its many deficiencies. However, many of the characteristics, although related to the deficiencies of centralized planning, have been brought to their observed intensity by the presence of pressure in the system, and in addition there is a set of observed characteristics which are more directly related to pressure than they are to the presence of centralized planning.[27] We will examine the impact of pressure on Soviet economic activity under three major headings: the incentive system, the empty economy and the seller's market. These are not three separate, airtight compartments, nor do they all operate at the same analytical level. They are at best loose classifications, and their effects are in many ways interrelated. But they are, nevertheless, useful categories with which to develop the argument.

Before proceeding to an analysis of the impact of pressure, let us look first at the impact of the direct deficiencies of centralized planning. The Soviet economy suffers from many ills of overcentralization, of which the major cause is that the planners at the center do not know and indeed

---

[26] *Direktivy* . . . . , III, p. 90.

[27] Somewhat similar ideas are discussed in Granick, "An Organizational Model . . ."

cannot be expected to know all the details of the real situations at the basic producing units.[28] The information required by central planners in the Soviet system of centralized planning is monumental.[29] Moreover, because the information which the enterprise supplies has an important effect on the tasks and resources given to the enterprise, the enterprise will distort the information; for example, it will "pad" its requests for materials (this is of course a generally observed characteristic of bureaucracies which operate under analogous conditions). It appears that Soviet central planners at times try to avoid confrontation of masses of information, of doubtful reliability at that, and try to conduct their business without being burdened by too much information from the enterprises. Under such conditions plans are constructed with even less knowledge of real conditions at the periphery. As a result of the limited knowledge at the center, enterprises often receive detailed plans which do not take into account either the actual production capabilities and specialities of producing-enterprises or the specific input needs of consuming-enterprises. There is a frequent lack of coordination among the different plans (outputs, inputs, deliveries, finances, etc.) given to the enterprise by different superior planning organs. It is commonplace to see complaints in Soviet economic literature about enterprises' being given delivery assignments which are greater than their output targets, or allocations of input materials without sufficient allocation of financial means to purchase them. Moreover, this problem is aggravated by the great number of changes in the plans for enterprises made by superior organs during the course of the planned year (see below), for it often happens that changes are made in one set of plans without compensating changes being made in the others. All this creates a general condition of unreality in plan assignments and unreliability of planned inter-enterprise relationships.[30]

[28] See, A. Bergson, *Economics of Soviet Planning,* pp. 331–332; and L. Smolinski, "What Next in Soviet Planning," *Foreign Affairs,* July 1964, pp. 602–613.

[29] As an extreme example, to supply the information requested by its supply administration for the central construction of input norms, the Ural Machine Building Factory submitted a document 17,000 pages long (*Voprosy Ekonomiki,* 7 [1958], p. 46).

[30] The following blistering attack is by a prominent Yugoslav economist, quoted in B. Balassa, *The Hungarian Experience in Economic Planning,* Yale University Press, New Haven, 1959, p. 79:

> The balancing of supply and demand in a centrally planned economy occurs in offices where a few people unaware of the real effects of their authoritarian plan become the supreme judges of the destinies of all producers and consumers through their bureaucratic machine. From this source of authority, plans lead further down to smaller bodies, splitting unrealistic averages into still smaller averages, according to norms born in offices which, when they reach the enterprise level, have little resemblance to the conditions of actual life.

(Perhaps centralized planning in the Soviet Union was not quite so bad as it apparently was in Yugoslavia—HSL)

In addition to the above, centralized planning visits upon the Soviet economy the multitude of maladies flowing from the overgrowth of bureaucratic administration: red tape, delays in reaching decisions and getting things done, multiplicity of paper work, conflicting and overlapping lines of authority, and so forth.

There are other disadvantages directly attributable to centralized planning, but these are the most important ones. Keeping them in mind, let us go on to our argument that it is the pressure imposed on and built up within the economic system rather than centralized planning per se that to a significant extent accounts for many of the observed characteristics of the Soviet economy.

The pressure in the plan is communicated to the directors of enterprises through the application of the system of rewards and penalties. The Soviet incentive mechanism, with its high rewards for successful fulfillment and overfulfillment of plan assignments and its monetary and position penalties for failure, is clearly geared to transmit the pressure in the plan. And since bonus rewards for plan fulfillment are not an insignificant part of managerial income, accounting for about 40 per cent of that income, the incentive system transmits the pressure in an intensified way.[31] Its impact is pervasive, but closely interwoven with the operation of the other categories we will consider, and thus often difficult to distinguish. Nevertheless, many of the things discussed by Berliner and Granick are clearly related to the pressure transmitted by the incentive system.[32]

First of all, there is the search for safety. Since success is a function of performance relative to expected (or commanded) performance, rewards can be acquired not only by performing on a high level, but also by being assigned low expectations. Therefore, the pressure on the enterprise in the plan, magnified by the incentive mechanism, greatly intensifies the general bureaucratic tendency to seek out ways of increasing security by understating productive capacity, by overstating input requirements, and by hoarding hidden inputs. Furthermore, the pressure transmitted by the reward and penalty system leads also to a group search for safety, the protective family circle.

Another aspect of the search for safety in the face of pressure from the incentive system is the operation of the "ratchet principle":[33] the enterprise manager tempers his rate of plan overfulfillment in order not to get too high a plan the following year, and he resists innovation (which always entails some risks) because the penalty for failure is great, and the reward for success short-lived.

Many familiar operating characteristics of the Soviet economy are pri-

---

[31] See especially Berliner and Nove in footnote 7 of this chapter.

[32] See footnote 7 of this chapter.

[33] Berliner, *op. cit.,* pp. 78–79.

marily responses to the pressures communicated by the incentive system. The pressure to fulfill the dominant physical output plans is so great that enterprises ignore costs, "storm" at the end of the accounting period, falsify output data, skimp on quality, distort the planned output mix by emphasizing those outputs where the bonus per unit of available resources is highest.[34]

The second of our categories is the "empty economy." The heavy pressure leads to a situation of general tautness in the Soviet economy. There is an absence of slack, and reserve stocks of resources are not easily available. This condition is what Hicks referred to as the "empty economy" when describing the post-World War II English economy. In such a situation, he said, the economy becomes accident prone, and minor mishaps become major crises.[35] This is just what happens in the Soviet economy; since there are insufficient protective reserves, even a minor shortage of an important material often becomes a major bottleneck.[36] This not only calls for the pursuit of bottlenecks in the construction of Soviet plans, but also leads to the great number of changes which are made in the operating plans during the course of the planned year in an effort to attack bottlenecks as they appear.[37] The unavailability of reserves coupled with frequent unrealistically tight plans, leads to the unreliability of the Soviet materials supply system and its consequences: work stoppages, use of inferior but available substitute inputs, and the enterprise's network of expediters searching for needed inputs in all parts of the country. It also intensifies the tendency toward the hoarding of input materials, and it encourages producing units to integrate vertically, to produce as many of its needed inputs as possible; thus the economy loses the potential economies of specialization.

The pressure in the system and the way rewards are established in relation to the physical output plan have led to a chronic condition of sellers' market in the Soviet economy. This term means simply the situation wherein demand, under the given "rates of exchange," is consistently greater than supply.

This sellers' market has had a marked effect on the operation of the

---

[34] This distortion of the product-mix is associated with the absence of a meaningful price system in the centralized economy. However, the enterprise's need to engage in such activity is greatly intensified by the pressure in the system.

[35] J. Hicks, "The Empty Economy," *Lloyds Bank Review,* July 1947, pp. 1–13. I am indebted to Prof. F. Holzman for calling my attention to this article. See also H. Charlesworth, *The Economics of Repressed Inflation,* London, 1956.

[36] Shortages may arise because enterprises failed to operate properly or because the plans themselves were unrealizable.

[37] See, e.g. *Pravda,* February 19, 1957, p. 3.

Soviet economy. Moreover, its impact was intensified during the pre-1957 period (and to some extent afterward) by the strategic role of producers' organizations in the construction of the central plan. It was the sales administration of the producing ministry which, in the final stages of plan construction, was responsible for setting the highly detailed production plans for enterprises within its ministry and for establishing detailed product flows from producing-enterprises to consuming-enterprises, all within the bounds set by the official annual plan. (After the 1957 reorganization these tasks were performed by *Gosplan* organs, entitled main administrations of interrepublican deliveries and based upon the former ministerial sales administrations.) This arrangement intensified the influence of the sellers' market because the ministerial sales organs were concerned with interests of the producers, the group with strong market power, rather than with the interests of the purchasers, the group with weak market power, thus in many situations adding a contributing force to the sellers' market rather than a countervailing one.

Given the sellers' market and the dominance of the physical output targets, the Soviet enterprise does not have to worry at all about being able to sell its output; it can concentrate its efforts on getting its needed inputs and making sure it is able to meet its output targets. Among other things, this accounts for the Soviet enterprise's greater aversion to innovation in products than to innovation in processes. Under the conditions stipulated, the producing-enterprise has no incentive to improve its product in order to make it more useful to the consuming-enterprise (as we saw before, it has little incentive to improve its production processes because of the operation of the "ratchet principle"). Furthermore, it is not pressed to do so by the sales administration of its ministry because the sales administration is more concerned with the production problems of its own ministry than with the needs of consumers.

The producer's one-sided concern with its own production needs and lack of concern for the needs of consuming enterprises lead also to a lowering of the quality of output and to a failure to produce the output assortment most needed by the users, the producer concentrating on the output mix most easy to produce and yielding the highest bonus. In addition, the sellers' market affects the timing of output and deliveries. Soviet steel-rolling mills, for example, tend toward long, uninterrupted runs of individual items of their output mix, which is fine for meeting their output targets but is highly detrimental to the interests of, say, a machine plant customer who needs a number of different types of rolled steel to produce a machine. Finally, because of the lack of attention paid by the sales administration of the producing-ministries to the needs of individual consumers, a consuming-enterprise is often assigned an irrational array of suppliers; its orders are spread out among a large number of them rather than concentrated in a few, and it also is often assigned different suppliers from year to year.[38] This contributes further to the unreliability of inter-enterprise relations in the Soviet economy.

Before leaving this question, let us look briefly at some of the methods which are used to counteract the deleterious effects of the sellers' market. One important method is vertical integration but here with a slightly different focus from the one we discussed in relation to the "empty economy." Here the aim is to make sure that the quality and mix of inputs are in accord with the needs of the consumer. Furthermore, it is sometimes used to foster product innovation as was done when the coal ministry produced its own coal cutting machinery.[39]

Another method is the fairly frequent use of wholesale prices established F.O.B. point of destination, that is, one price for all consumers or for all consumers in a given region.[40] By including transportation charges in the price, an incentive for achieving a rational geographic distribution of orders is given the producers rather than the consumers. This is wise, both because it is the sales administrations of the producers that play the dominant role in fixing producer-consumer ties and because under conditions of a sellers' market, purchasers may be willing to buy from any producer no matter what the extra transportation cost, whereas sellers if they have to cover transportation costs might be more apt to try to minimize these costs.

The most formal effort to counteract the uneven market power of sellers and buyers is the attempt to gain legal protection of the rights of buyers through the use of legal contracts enforced by the system of arbitration courts. However, its effects are somewhat reduced by the reluctance of buyers to apply contractual sanctions against suppliers violating these contrasts, because of the fear of antagonizing suppliers they may be dependent upon in the future.[41]

IV

The hypothesis put forth in this paper has concerned the role and impact of pressure in the Soviet economy. It has been argued that the pressure on the basic producing units exerted by the political leaders and built up in the process of plan construction is manifested through and intensified by the incentive system, the "empty economy," and the sellers' market,

[38] See A. Vorob'eva, *Voprosy ekonomii syr'ia i materialov v promyshlennosti,* Moscow, 1958, p. 259.

[39] See *Ugol'naia promyshlennost' USSR,* Moscow, 1957, pp. 503–522.

[40] See M. Bernstein, "The Soviet Price System," *American Economic Review,* March 1962, p. 77 and the sources listed there.

[41] See, e.g., A. Savkin, *op. cit.,* p. 65.

and is responsible to a great extent for many of the observed characteristics of the Soviet economy frequently attributed to the mechanism of centralized planning itself.

The hypothesis has been argued; what is needed to test it are some observations on the operation in the Soviet economy of a system of centralized planning without pressure. Is such a situation possible? More practically, is it to be expected?

Theoretically it appears feasible, although some problems of incentives would need discussion. In the realm of Marxian theory, it fits well with what Marx and Engels seemed to have had in mind on the rare occasions when they spoke of planning in a socialist society. To Marx, the aim of having a central plan was the eradication of anarchy and the gearing of the economy to the wants of society.[42] There was no thought of using it to apply pressure to the economy.

After the death of Stalin and especially after his removal from the ranks of the deities in 1956, Soviet leaders began to talk about the reduction of pressure on producing units. In discussing the draft of the Seven Year Plan, Khrushchev said that "the Seven Year Plan is being drawn up in such a way that it can be implemented without overstrain," and he went on to describe some of the negative features of overly tight plans.[43] Others have also spoken about the dangers of overstrain and complained of its presence, but at the same time, complaints are also heard about excessive looseness in the plans. The debate continues and it is not clear yet to what extent there has been a change in the amount of pressure in the plan.

By extending the Gerschenkron pattern of Russian economic development, with which this paper began, to the present period, it might be argued that the time is ripe for the removal of pressure. Russia has built up its economic base. It has achieved a state of military parity with the West. There is no longer the gnawing tension between what the State wants to do and what it can do because of a relatively backward economy, for the economy is no longer so relatively backward. Furthermore, the leader associated with the economic development drive is dead, and his political influence removed. In the past workings of the pattern, it was after the death of Peter the Great and after the removal of Count Witte, that the State withdrew its pressure from the economy. Perhaps such political events are important for changing the atmosphere. The period of pressure has been long, and it has included a terribly destructive war, certainly

---

[42] "(Labor's) apportionment in accordance with a definite social plan maintains the proper proportion between the different kinds of work to be done and the various wants of the community." K. Marx, *Capital*, Vol. I, Moscow, 1954, p. 79.

[43] *XXI S'ezd KPSS*, Vol. I, Moscow, 1959, p. 46.

the people must be exhausted. There are signs now that the pressure on
the standard of living of the Russian people has been reduced. For example,
consumption levels have grown significantly in the decade of the 1950's,[44]
and now many notable Russian political figures and economists are calling
for a relative increase in the growth of consumption. Perhaps one of the
strongest statements and most pertinent for our purpose was made recently
by a leading Soviet economic official:

> In the period of the construction of the material and technical base of
> socialism the industrialization of the country entailed sacrifices; it was necessary
> to economize on everything, including personal consumption. Today our econ-
> omy is so healthy and industry is so well developed that we have every possi-
> bility of successfully solving the problem of creating the material and technical
> base for communism and, on this basis, strengthening defenses and simultane-
> ously stepping up the personal consumption of the Soviet people.[45]

It must be noted that Professor Gerschenkron has never, to our
knowledge, extended his pattern of Russian economic development to the
point of using it to indicate the strong possibility of the Soviet political
leaders' withdrawal of pressure from the economy. The extension is the
author's. Gerschenkron has in fact put forth an hypothesis on dictatorships
which to a significant extent runs counter to this. In his 1963 Harvard
Lecture at Yale University, he argues that modern dictatorships must con-
tinuously legitimatize themselves in order to remain in power. They do
this by (among other things) the "maintenance of a permanent condition
of stress and strain," and by the "incessant exercise of dictatorial power."[46]
He does not go so far as to deny that the Soviet leaders have not or
may not reduce stress and strain but to the extent that they do, he argues,
their power will erode.[47]

Do the recent signs of the reduction of pressure indicate that nonpressure centralized planning in the Soviet economy is just around the corner?
We do not think so. At the same time the degree of pressure may be
changing, the forms of planning and control are also changing. This is
so not only because the Soviet economy today is larger and more complex
and thus more difficult to plan, but also because there has been change
in economic focus. Centralized planning has accomplished what its use
was intended to accomplish: the radical and rapid structural transformation of the Soviet economy. On almost all counts (with the exception of
proportion of labor force in agriculture and also perhaps, the overall level

[44] J. Chapman, *op. cit.*

[45] Academician A. Arzumanian in *Pravda,* February 24, 1964, as translated in
the *Current Digest of the Soviet Press,* XVI, 8, (March 18, 1964) p. 4.

[46] A. Gerschenkron, *Stability of Dictatorship,* p. 5.

[47] *Ibid.,* pp. 34–36.

of technology), Russia is today a highly industrialized nation. The aim now is to improve the efficiency of the economy, to get more output per unit of input, and to change the product mix in a slower and not altogether predetermined way. This is not a situation in which the brute force methods of centralized planning recommend themselves. When the task is to improve economic efficiency, decision making must be moved to the level of the producing units, and useful choice parameters (prices) must be provided so that relative benefits and costs can be compared and economically meaningful choices made.

That this situation calls for an increase in decentralized methods of planning and control is apparent, and it is also apparent from the current discussions (Libermanism, and so forth) and from some current actions that this is the direction the Soviets are taking. However, since the Soviet leaders undoubtedly want to maintain control over the general path and pace of development (including avoidance of glaring disproportions, maintenance of full employment, and so forth), reform will undoubtedly stop far short of complete decentralization. At a minimum, the political leaders will retain control over the amount and direction of investment. Also, they will most likely retain some power to assure aggregate sectoral balancing and the production and inculcation of major elements of technical change.[48] The development of computers and computer techniques for data collection, processing, and use will help the centralized aspects of such a mixed system operate more effectively than would be the case in the absence of these computational devices.

What is in store, then, is a Soviet economy with perhaps less pressure but also with less centralized planning. It appears that we may never get to observe real nonpressure centralized planning in the Soviet economy. For that matter (and for similar reasons), the entire subspace of economies with nonpressure centralized planning may be empty. Thus we are left with an hypothesis about the separate effects of the separate components, pressure and centralized planning, when in reality the two components may be a joint product. They appear together, both in relation to dynamic, determinate structural change, and they fade together when the economic focus switches to the channels of slower growth, less determinate and more moderate structural change. The analysis presented here is, hopefully, of analytical interest, but to the extent that pressure and centralized planning do operate as a joint product, the value of treating them separately may, we regret to say, be somewhat limited.

Before closing, a word on non-joint responsibility. We have in this paper used—or misused—some of the hypotheses of Professor Gerschen-

[48] The power to assure aggregate sectoral balancing and sectoral technical change may require the reintroduction of branch line ministries. This may appear to be a contradiction of decentralization, but it is not necessarily so.

kron. It should be clear, however, that all responsibility for what has been said here lies with the author. It is the task of the apprentice to learn the master's methods, but the master should never be held responsible for the foolishness of the apprentice. A wrathful God once spoke of *poked awon avoth al banim,* but even he did not countenance, *poked awon banim al avoth.*[49]

[49] For those who, unlike Alexander Gerschenkron, cannot handle a multitude of foreign languages: A wrathful God once spoke of "visiting the sins of the fathers upon the sons," but even he did not countenance "visiting the sins of the sons upon the fathers."

INDEX